Grandjean **Ergonomics of the Home**

Etienne Grandjean

Ergonomics of the Home

Taylor & Francis Ltd, London

Monotype set by the Lancashire Typesetting Co. Ltd., Bolton, Lancs.
Printed and bound in Great Britain by Taylor & Francis (Printers) Ltd.,
Rankine Road, Basingstoke, Hampshire.

Distributed in the United States of America and its territories by
Halsted Press (a division of John Wiley & Sons Inc.),
605, Third Avenue, New York, N.Y. 10016.

Ergonomics of the home is here presented as an interdisciplinary field of study, which investigates the habits and reactions of people in their domestic life. Its objective is to work out a scientific basis by which buildings and rooms and their fitments can be matched to human requirements. The main purpose of the book is to make scientifically based recommendations for the design and erection of houses and flats.

People's domestic needs can be classified into physiological, psychological and social, and if this book seems to lay most stress on the physiological, it also takes account of psychological and social needs as far as possible. This is essential because man is an integrated whole, and to define his needs from the one-sided viewpoint of any single scientific discipline would be to give an incomplete picture.

Another focal point of the book is housework, which plays a decisive part in the well-being of the housewife, and hence indirectly in that of the rest of the family. The problem of household duties is further complicated by the ever-increasing number of housewives who go out to work, and it is one of the ironies of our time that the prestige of the housewife should stand so low. Consideration of ergonomic principles and recommendations can be critical for the health, well-being and even vitality of people in their home circle. This is the contribution that we hope this book will make to the building of houses and flats – a contribution that could fittingly form a link between the commercial thinking of landlords and the wishes and dreams of architects.

Zürich, May 1972 Etienne Grandjean

Acknowledgements

This book was made possible only by the specialist assistance of many colleagues. I am particularly grateful to:
- Fräulein Nelly Escher for her secretarial assistance and for numerous corrections
- Herr Wilhelm Hunting for drawing the figures
- Frau Dr Silvia Huser, Herr Dr Alfred Gilgen and Frau Michaela Suchantke for their help in assembling and abstracting the literature
- and finally, the authorities of the Eidgenössische Technische Hochschule in Zürich for granting me a term's leave of absence, during which the greater part of the work on this book was carried out.

Etienne Grandjean

Home is a word having many connotations: for most people it at least denotes security, comfort, companionship and leisure. There is a tendency to forget that domestic work is one of the world's major occupations, and that there are more accidents within the home than outside. Modern house-work involves the use of much sophisticated machinery.

The modern science of ergonomics is concerned with relationships between Man and the machines he has created, with the objective of creating environments in which the man-machine system becomes efficient and the injurious effects of machinery on Man are avoided. Up to the present, most ergonomists have been concerned more with industrial situations than with the home, and the wide application of ergonomic principles to domestic situations is overdue.

In this volume Professor Grandjean, Director of the Institute of Industrial Hygiene and Work Physiology in Zurich, has done much to remedy this situation. He has collated the information presently available from his own researches with that of others in many countries and has applied this knowledge to the home environment. This translation will be welcomed by all concerned with domestic design and arrangement in the English-speaking world; the extensive presentation of European research results will be particularly welcome to the British at a time when they are entering the European Economic Community.

While the various recommendations apply to any home, in certain instances local byelaws and national building regulations may need to be taken into account in their application: armed with the information given here, the designer will find no difficulty in achieving a safe and efficient compromise where the legal and ergonomic requirements are in conflict.

The information will be of benefit to ergonomists and architects, and to all concerned with design of domestic furniture and appliances. It is clear that this work will do much to establish a more human approach by those who plan homes, and that the human environments resulting from the application of these principles should be happier, safer and more comfortable than ever before.

Guildford, Surrey,   P. R. Davis.
June, 1973.

1 Housework

Contents of Chapter 1

Summary   Domestic work-loads can be assessed under the following headings:

Energy consumption.
Heart rate.
Static muscular effort.
Time and motion.

In an average day the overall consumption of energy by a housewife fluctuates between 2,600 and 2,700 kilocalories, and on wash-days or during spring cleaning it rises to 2,800–3,000 kilocalories. Domestic energy consumption is thus comparable with a moderately hard occupation outside the home, particularly heavy calls upon energy being made when making beds, scrubbing and washing floors, cleaning windows, ironing and going up and down stairs. During house work, the heart rate increases by 20–30 beats per minute, and striking increases occur when beating carpets, cleaning carpets by hand on the floor, and scrubbing floors. Domestic work-load is more easily assessed by observing the pulse rate than from measurements of energy consumption, presumably because housework requires much static activity and this is reflected more in heart rate changes than in energy consumption.
Static muscular efforts, which are both heavy and tiring, occur commonly in household activities, many of the jobs requiring unnatural postures such as a stooped back, and many having to be done in one fixed position. A common problem is backache, often caused by some damage to the intervertebral discs; much backache could be prevented by avoiding stooped positions as much as possible, and by not pushing or pulling clumsily at heavy loads.
The basic working week of a housewife who does not go out to work is about 50–55 hours. A housewife who also has a job spends much less time working in the home, but her total working hours for the week may be very high. In spite of the introduction of many time-saving household appliances in the last few decades, no reduction in the total of working hours can be seen compared with earlier surveys. It is puzzling why the length of a housewife's working day does not decrease at a time when a shorter working week is gradually creeping into all other forms of employment.

The fundamentals of work physiology

Muscular effort and muscle power

Bodily movements and physical efforts are made possible in the first place by the operation of muscles. The most important characteristic of a muscle is its ability to contract: it can shorten itself by up to half its normal length. Contraction is the means by which an internal expenditure of energy produces externally visible and measurable work.

Muscle power

The absolute limit of power in human muscle is about 4 kg per square cm of cross-section.(1). This means that a muscle of one square centimetre cross-sectional area can exert an effort of 4 kg. The maximum possible effort increases linearly with the cross-sectional area. Training increases the cross-sectional area, and with it the power of the muscle.

The maximum power that can be developed during a movement depends on the following factors:

a. The cross-sectional area of the muscles involved. The greater the number of muscles that can be brought into play in a movement, the greater is the maximum effort that can be deployed.

b. A muscle develops its maximum power when it is at its resting length, and muscle power diminishes progressively as it contracts. Thus the greatest power output is obtained by making movements with the muscles initially relaxed as much as possible.

c. The mechanics of the bones as levers. The relationship of the muscle attachment on the bones to the position of the joint determines the joint angle at which the greatest effort can be exerted.

Optimum postures for manual operations

The following working positions provide maximum power during manual activities.

a. To turn a knob inwards the hand is most powerful if it starts off in a position of supination, i.e. turned outwards. Conversely to turn the knob ontwards, the hand should start off in a position of pronation, i.e. turned inwards,

b. The greatest power in elbow flexion with the hand open and the palm facing upwards occurs at an angle of about 90°. In this position the elbow muscles exert the greatest leverage.
In a sitting position there is less power in a steady pull than in a sudden tug. It is essential at the same time to have rests for the feet and the back. Jerk power is greatest if the elbow joint is straight, and if the hand grips at shoulder height about 70 cm in front of the back-rest. A steady pull is at its maximum when the angle of the elbow is 150°–180° and the hand grips at a height of 20–25 cm above the level of the seat.

d. The maximum power for lifting a burden is obtained when the point of grip is about 40 cm above ground-level, and this factor should be given special consideration in the design of loading ramps and surfaces from which heavy objects have to be lifted

e. When manual controls are being planned it is necessary to consider when strength is going to be needed for the work involved. The more strength is needed, the more muscles, (i.e. the more limbs), must be employed. The fingers alone are sufficient for operations needing little force, but when more strength is needed the muscles of the arms and back must be brought into play.

The following guides are recommended for manual controls:

Force required	Appropriate manual controls
Small (operating force 50–300 g)	Push-button. Tumbler switch. Small control knob.
Medium (operating force 300–2,500 g)	Large control knob for the whole hand (35–75 mm diameter); Horizontal lever.
Large (operating force 2–10 kg)	Vertical lever. Hand-wheel. Pedal.

Static and dynamic muscular effort

Work physiology distinguishes between work when in motion (dynamic muscular activity) and work while stationary (static muscular activity).

During dynamic activity the muscles contract and relax rhythmically. During static activity a muscle remains in a particular state of contraction for a long period, and so gives little external sign of doing useful work. Work of this sort can be compared with the performance of an electromagnet, which supports a given weight without movement but with a steady consumption of energy. There are many intermediate types of work in which a combination of the two forms of muscular effort is needed; movements that take place very slowly, and exert a great deal of force can be classed as either static or dynamic.

Examples

Examples of dynamic effort are: walking, climbing stairs, turning a handle, most manual cleaning operations, knitting, or stirring things in a pan.

Typical static efforts include holding objects, or holding the arms away from the body. Standing upright, keeping feet, knees and hips in a fixed position, is possible only through the static effort of the muscles concerned. A sustained bending of the spine either forwards or sideways calls for static holding forces from several spinal muscles.

Typical examples of combined effort, static + dynamic, arise when we hold an object in one hand and operate on it with the other. This happens during housework, when a pan is held in the left hand while the right hand is cleaning it, or when the left hand holds a potato and the right hand peels it. Other examples of combined muscular effort include times during bed-making or floor scrubbing when the back is held in a bent posture while the arms are performing dynamic work: or during carrying, when the muscles of the back and shoulders are performing static work in holding a heavy object, and the legs are performing dynamically.

Blood circulation

The two kinds of muscular effort need to be considered separately, since the demands that they make on the muscles, and the fatigue they each produce are very different. This is linked to differences in blood-flow. During dynamic muscular effort blood is squeezed out of the muscle during contraction, but flows back easily during the subsequent relaxation. As a result, the blood flow through the muscle is accentuated, promoting a plentiful supply of oxygen and of energy-producing substances such as glucose; at the same time the waste products produced in the muscle by the breakdown of the nutrients are rapidly eliminated. During dynamic effort the muscle functions like a mechanical pump, which not only supplies blood to the muscle more efficiently, but also increases the flow of blood between the heart and the active musculature. For this reason, dynamic effort can be carried on with an appropriate rhythm for many hours at a stretch without any sign of fatigue. The best example of this is the heart muscle, which carries on a continuous muscular effort for a whole lifetime. During static muscular effort, the situation is very different. Prolonged muscular contraction stops the flow of blood into the muscle, leading to a diminished supply of oxygen and a build-up of waste products.

Pain and fatigue

The build-up of waste products, particularly carbon dioxide and lactic acid, brings about a painful state of fatigue. This can easily be demonstrated by holding a chair in the air at arm's length, when after only a short time pain will start in the shoulder muscles, and will increase until it is unbearable and the chair will be dropped.

Sustained static effort

The extent to which the flow of blood is restricted in a muscle that is making a static effort depends on how much effort is being demanded of it. The greater the effort, the greater the restriction of blood-supply, and the sooner the fatigue pains begin to appear. Static effort can be sustained for one minute if the force being exerted is 50% of maximum, but for four minutes if the effort is only 30%. A decisive turning-point is reached if the effort being expended falls to only 20% of maximum, because then the static effort can be sustained for several hours. Physiological experiments have shown that such a low output of static effort does not lead to any restriction in blood supply to the muscle in question. *Figure 1* shows the maximum duration of static muscular effort for given levels of muscle activity.

For these reasons *work must be so planned, and work-places and domestic equipment must be so designed that static muscular effort is either eliminated or reduced to a point at which less than 20% of maximum effort is required. This is the most practical way of lightening the housewife's work load.*

Energy consumption

Conversion of energy producing substances

The chemical energy that is taken into the body in the form of food is converted into heat by all body tissues; in the muscles it is also converted into mechanical energy. The energy-rich carbohydrates, proteins and fats go through a series

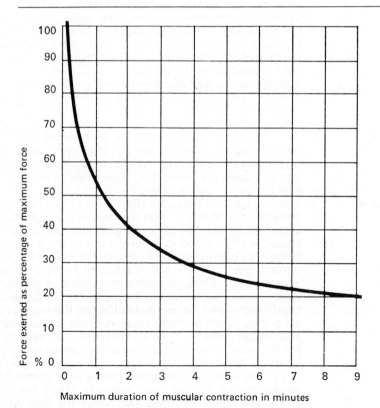

Maximum duration of muscular contraction in minutes

Figure 1   Maximum duration of a static muscular effort in relation to the force exerted   After Monod (7) and Rohmert (8)

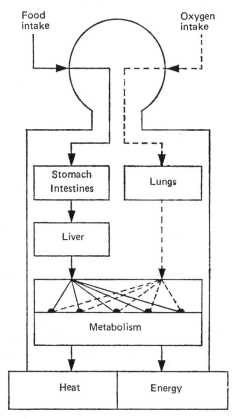

Figure 2   Diagrammatic representation of the transformation of food into energy   The energy containing elements of the food are absorbed by the digestive organs, and pass to the liver where they are partly broken down. Subsequently all tissues of the body convert this chemical energy into heat and mechanical energy

of chemical changes and are progressively broken down into water, carbon dioxide and urea. The complete process of change from the original nutrients is called metabolism.

This process can be compared with a smouldering fire, and the comparison is all the more apt because metabolism, like a fire, uses oxygen, which is absorbed into the blood from the air breathed into the lungs. *Figure 2* sets out the complete process of metabolism diagrammatically.

Within limits, the consumption of energy increases linearly with work done, and can be used as an indicator of the work-load during manual activities.

Measurement of energy consumption

The energy consumed in metabolism is expressed in kilocalories (kcal). The measurement of energy consumption is achieved indirectly through the determination of oxygen consumption, the burning of one litre of oxygen being equivalent to an energy consumption of about 4.8 kcal.

Oxygen consumption during a particular piece of work can be measured with the aid of a breathing apparatus, and if the measured consumption of oxygen is multiplied by the factor of 4.8, the energy consumption can be expressed in kilocalories.

Energy consumption and efficiency

From the point of view of energetics, human bodily activity is comparable to that of a machine. A machine converts the chemical energy of petrol or coal into mechanical performance, but wastes some of this energy as heat.

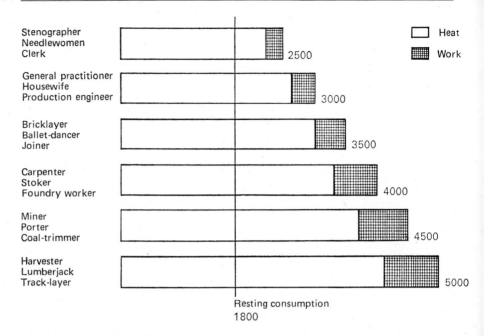

Figure 3   The distribution of energy consumption between physical work and heat in various occupations   As the energy requirement for physical effort increases, so does the amount of energy converted into heat. After Lehmann (9)

Similarly, the human body loses a large part of the energy expended as heat, and only a small part is turned into useful mechanical energy. *Figure 3* shows graphically the relationship between these components for different occupations.

For both the machine and the body it is possible to speak of an 'efficiency', which expresses the relationship between the externally measurable useful performance and the total energy consumption. Under the most favourable conditions human activity can reach an efficiency of 30%, in which case 70% of the energy is converted into heat.

As soon as an activity involves static effort the efficiency falls off, since static effort does not result in any measurable performance of useful work. This is particularly true if work has to be done with a stooped back.

Table 1 compares the efficiency of a few human activities.

Table 1   Efficiency of various human activities

Activity	Percentage efficiency
Shovelling, cleaning floors, or making beds when stooping	3–5
Shovelling, cleaning floors or making beds in upright attitude	6–10
Lifting loads	9
Manual work, and work with heavy tools	15–20
Dragging loads	17–20
Ascending and descending stairs	23
Cycling	25
Walking on level ground	27
Hill climbing with a 5° gradient	30

Energy consumption
and work-load

Thus *the less static work in a given activity, the greater is the efficiency of bodily effort.*

As already stated, the consumption of energy increases in proportion to the bodily effort and this additional consumption may be expressed alternatively as so many *calories of work*. The value of these calories of work can be obtained by working out the difference between the consumption of energy while work is being performed and that under resting conditions.

Table 2 brings together the values of the calories of work during a few different kinds of human activity, while *Figure 4* gives the effect of body posture on energy-consumption.

The energy consumption is measured for different occupations, and calculated for a 24-hour period. During the Second World War these values were taken into consideration in food rationing. *Table 3* sets out some of the values obtained by *Lehmann* and his colleagues (9), and it must be noted that they were dealing with an average value; considerable reductions of these values may occur with smaller body weights, and by special conditions arising both during working and leisure periods.

Table 2   Energy consumption in some basic human activities   The number of work calories = total energy consumption minus resting consumption. After Lehmann (9) and Müller (10)

Activity	Conditions			Work calories
	slope	load	velocity	kcal/min
Sitting				0.3
Kneeling				0.5
Squatting				0.5
Standing				0.6
Stooping				0.8
Walking unladen	level		3 km/h	1.7
	level		4 km/h	2.1
	rough ground		3 km/h	5.2
Walking with load	level	10 kg	4 km/h	3.6
		30 kg	4 km/h	5.3
Climbing	14°		11.5 m/min	8.3
Climbing stairs	30°		17.2 m/min	13.7
Climbs stairs with load	30°	20 kg	17.2 m/min	18.4
Cycling			16 km/h	5.2

Sitting   Standing   Stooping   Kneeling
3–5%   8–10%   50–60%   30–40%

Figure 4   Percentage increase in energy consumption produced by various body postures   Taking the energy consumption when lying down as 100%

Table 3   Energy consumption in various occupations   After Lehmann (9)

Occupation	Energy consumption in kilocalories per 24 hr	
	Men	Women
Bookkeeper, stenographer, clockmaker	2400–2700	2000–2250
Weaver, bus driver, doctor	3000	2500
Shoemaker, mechanic, postman, housewife	3300	2750
Stone breaker, production line worker, housewife on heavy day, chimney sweep	3600	3000
Ballerina, carpenter on building site	3900	3250
Miner, farm labourer, lumberjack, transport worker	4200–4800	

It should be noted that energy consumption is increased only by bodily activity; *mental* activity has no measurable effect. Energy consumption can be used only to assess physical activity.

Heart rate (pulse rate) as a measure of bodily stress

Heart rate has been more and more used in recent years to measure the extent of human stresses. This is valid because within certain limits the heart rate rises in direct proportion to energy consumption. It has also become evident that heart rate is a good way of measuring heat stress as well as being particularly applicable to static conditions. For the research and conclusions in this field we are indebted to *Müller* (11, 12).
During light work the pulse rate rises quickly to the appropriate height and remains there as long as the work continues, but during heavy work the pulse

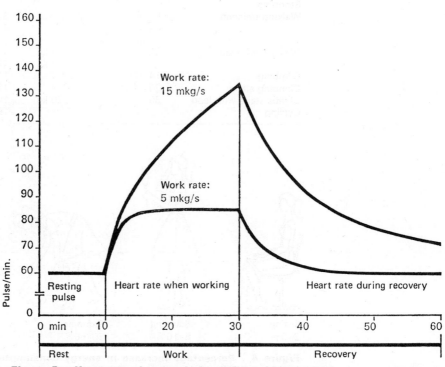

Figure 5   Heart rate changes during light and heavy work

rate continues to rise up to its maximum of about 180 beats per minute. At this point the work must be interrupted either because of overstrain or the threat of exhaustion. *Figure 5* shows changes in pulse rate under standardised conditions of stress.

Limits of sustained effort

Karrasch and Müller (12) have defined the upper limit of tolerance as that point at which the heart rate neither continues to rise as the work continues nor requires more than 15 minutes to fall back to the resting value after the work is completed. This limit seems to correspond to a work load for which the consumption of energy exactly balances the demands of the muscles concerned. The greatest possible work load that fulfils these conditions is nowadays accepted as the limit of sustained effort for an eight-hour working day. In practice, and where healthy men and women are concerned, *this limit is not exceeded as long as the pulse rate does not exceed the resting value by more than 30 beats per minute.* In other words: the limit of sustained effort is 30 'working-pulses', if 'working-pulses' are defined as the difference between the resting rate and the mean value while the work is going on. Since the resting heart rate under normal conditions ranges from 60–80 beats per minute, the limit of sustained effort for most people lies between 90 and 110 beats per minute.

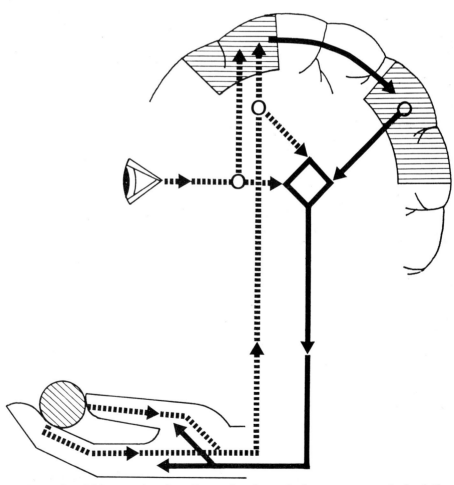

Figure 6   Diagram showing the main elements in nervous control of the fingers during skilled movements

Assessment of the resulting measurements	To assess the work-load by means of the pulse rate, subjects can be checked over in advance with a bicycle ergometer: the pulse rate is measured at increasing levels of work output, and simultaneously compared with other circulatory components, such as oxygen intake and rate of ventilation of the lungs. Research of this kind gives an insight into the working capacity of the subjects under study, and may subsequently give physiological significance to measurements of heart rate taken during working conditions. *Astrand* (13, 14) used this kind of approach to study domestic tasks.

Skilled work

Nervous control	During skilled work the nervous activities directing the necessary movements are decisively important. *Figure 6* demonstrates the most important factors involved in a grasping movement, and indicates the complexity of nervous activity involved in skilled operations.

Visual information reaching the eyes is relayed to the brain, and informs it continuously of the relative positions of the object and the fingers. In the brain this information is 'processed' and new nerve impulses are initiated, which travel along the motor nerves to the musculature of the hand and fingers to produce the grasping movements required by the brain. Sensory stimuli are now added to the visual information, and tell the brain the texture of the object being gripped, as well as the grasping force that is being exerted. Using all this information, thousands of stimuli per second, the brain directs the entire sequence of operations.

Facilitation	The learning of a skilled operation depends essentially on bringing into play new directive mechanisms which with increasing skill make progressively fewer demands on conscious direction. These new paths are shown by thick arrows in *Figure 6*. If conscious control can be entirely excluded, and nervous control in the physiological sense becomes entirely automatic, then skill reaches its zenith.

Table 4 brings together three basic factors in a skilled operation, and the steps needed to make them easier. Yet another elementary principle is featured here: *Because the elbows are hinged and can bend at right angles, man can exert both his highest skill and the greatest force with his hands in front of the body (33).*

Table 4   Improving the efficiency of skilled work

Operation	Provision
1. Observation	Information presented clearly Visual control of movements Tools and materials visible and available Good illumination, of the correct colour value
2. Concentration Processing of information Thought; decision	Prevention of distractions Exclusion of noise Logical sequence of operations
3. Sequence of movements	Rhythmical sequence of movements Hands free to move No muscular effort at the same time Accessories logically arranged Tools well designed

Domestic work-load

Energy Consumption in Household

Total daily consumption
of energy

Past studies (9) have shown that the housewife has an average daily consumption of 3,000 kcal. *Kraut, Schneiderhöhn and Wildemann* (15) verified these conclusions in 1956, when they found in five representative households that the total energy consumption of the housewife on a year's average varied between 2,400 and 2,800 kcal per 24-hours.

Table 5 summarises the energy consumption of a housewife who runs a household for five people. The table shows that for about 100 days in the year this housewife does a job which is as hard as that of a postman, a stone-mason or a production-line operative. On the remaining working days of the year her energy consumption is equivalent to the light to moderate work of a bus-driver, a mechanic or a meter-reader.

Household activity and
energy consumption

Lehmann (9) studied the energy consumption output of a series of typical housewives from time to time during the day. His results are set out in *Figure 7*. Numerous studies of energy consumption during household activities were carried out by *Bratton* (16) and by *Passmore and Durnin* (17). The most important of their results are summarised in *Tables 6* and *7*.

By and large the values of these two tables are in overall agreement with those of *Figure 7*. The only exceptions are the sharp divergences for ironing: possibly the cause of these differences lies in the different kinds of iron used as well as the varying states of fitness and body-weights of the research subjects. *Passmore and Durnin* (17) quote the body-weight of their subjects every time, and this is sensible, since heavy people have a higher energy consumption than lighter ones.

Interpretation of the
results

How are these values for energy consumption during household tasks to be interpreted? On the one hand they show which tasks require a particularly high energy consumption, and hence which activities should be made easier by further improvements in working techniques, in equipment and installations. The activities concerned in the first instance are:

Making beds.
Scrubbing and washing floors.
Cleaning windows.
Ironing.

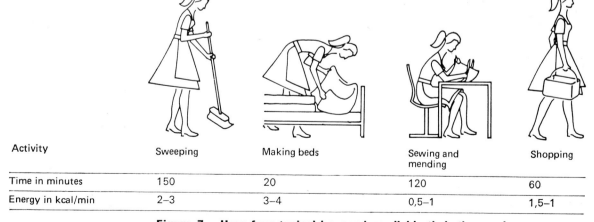

Activity	Sweeping	Making beds	Sewing and mending	Shopping
Time in minutes	150	20	120	60
Energy in kcal/min	2–3	3–4	0,5–1	1,5–1

Figure 7   How four typical housewives divide their time and energy
After Lehmann (9)

Table 5   Energy consumption of a housewife in a household of 5 persons
Averaged over the year. After Kraut and colleagues (15)

Activity	Energy consumption kcal/24 hr	Number of days per year
Normal day	2660	213
Housework day	3030	40
Washday (including preparation and ironing)	2820	60
Sunday	2130	52
Average for the year	2650	

Table 6   Energy consumption (resting and work calories) during different activities in the household   After Steidl and Bratton (18)

1. Rate : 1 kcal/min	Resting
2. Rate : 1–2 kcal/min	Light work sitting down − sewing − knitting − peeling potatoes Work standing up − ironing − washing-up − reaching for objects 56–183 cm above floor-level
3. Rate : 2–3 kcal/min	Walking Sweeping Dusting Cleaning floors with long-handled equipment Hanging out clothes Playing the piano
4. Rate : 3–4 kcal/min	Washing floors Polishing floors Making beds Holding objects 10 cm above the floor Cleaning staircarpets
5. Rate : more than 4 kcal/min	Climbing stairs Lifting loads from the floor Dancing Gardening

Table 7   Energy consumption (resting and work calories) during various household activities   After Passmore and Durnin (17)

Activity	Body weight (kg)	Energy consumption (kcal/min)
Light work when seated	84	1.7
Writing when seated	64	1.9
Gardening	65	5.6
Cleaning windows	61	3.7
Scrubbing floors, kneeling	48	3.4
Cleaning floors, kneeling and stooping	84	5.9
Ironing	84	4.2

On the other hand it must be considered that occasional bursts of physical effort have some value in training, increasing the level of fitness, so that subsequently moderately hard tasks (such as for example dusting, cooking and shopping) can be carried out more easily. Climbing stairs, gardening, and playing games in one's spare time are all particularly good for such training purposes. On the other hand activities which require much static muscular effort are undesirable, since they are fatiguing and may cause pain, and steps should be taken to reduce these to a minimum.

Since those activities which call for more than 3 kcal/min take up only a minor part of the working day, it is not surprising that the normal daily demand for calories is only between 2,600 and 2,700 kcal/24 hr. Such a work-load must—as already stated—be rated as light to moderate, but allowing for the heavy expenditure of energy on scrubbing days and washing days, it is clear that *from the point of view of energy consumption housework is a moderately heavy occupation.*

Criticism of the use of energetics as a standard

In recent years many authors (18, 19) have doubted whether energy consumption is a good criterion of the housewife's burden. Energy consumption is in poor overall agreement with the physical difficulty of the job, as far as this can be estimated from the unbalanced static strain on individual groups of muscles. Further, energy consumption tells us nothing about whether the subject is feeling tired. If an individual muscle group is heavily involved, for example, in the left arm when it is holding a heavy object while all the other muscles are doing little or no work, there will be only a slight increase in total energy consumption, but the housewife will rate such an activity as very arduous.

It is for reasons such as these that recently several workers have abandoned the use of energy consumption, and have used heart rate in the analysis of tasks facing the housewife.

Heart rate during housework

Astrand's studies

Astrand (13) and *Kilbom and Astrand* (14) studied the pulse rates of female research subjects during the performance of various household tasks. Three healthy subjects were available for study. Each subject was examined carefully beforehand on a bicycle ergometer, so that their pulse rates, oxygen intakes and lung ventilation rates for standard physical tasks were known. Their pulse rates during household tasks could then be used as a measure of the physiological difficulty of the tasks. The most important results can be summarised as follows:

Cooking

During cooking the heart rate ranges between 82 and 116 beats per min. compared with 69 to 79 when at rest. Values above 100 beats per minute were registered during baking; this was the most fatiguing work. The heart rate was somewhat higher when cooking with raw ingredients than when cooking prepared foods. The latter called for a much shorter working time. The authors calculated the product of pulse rate per minute multiplied by working time, and this, too, was considerably lower when working with prepared foods.

Washing-up

During washing-up by hand the pulse rate ranged from 84-120 beats per minute; when stacking the dishes in a dishwasher, 93–111. While the pulse rates show no significant difference, the time required is very different: 11–23 minutes are needed for washing-up by hand, as against 6–17 minutes with the dishwasher. The authors think that it is the effort of grasping the crockery while filling the dishwasher that accounts for the relatively high pulse rate. Using a dishwasher means a saving of time, but not of effort.

Astrand (14) further compared the effects of four different types of dishwashers with one another, and with all four types the pulse rate varied between 100 and 102 beats per minute.

Cleaning windows and floors

The author (14) also studied the operations of cleaning windows and floors. Window-cleaning gave rise to pulse rates between 97 and 136, and a comparison between three different methods showed no difference. When scrubbing floors in a kneeling position with brush and floorcloth, the pulse rate varied between 98 and 117; when cleaning in a standing position using a long-handled scrubber and cloth, the pulse rate reached 109–137. There is evidence that the pulse rate tends to be higher when cleaning in a standing position, and this is consistent with the calories of work shown in *Table 2*.

Cleaning carpets by hand, and with a vacuum-cleaner

Wiggert (19) studied the pulse rate and the time needed when cleaning carpets and a bare floor. In addition the use of a vacuum-cleaner was compared with hand cleaning under standardised conditions. The results are set out in *Figure 8*. They demonstrate clearly the efficiency of using an electric vacuum-cleaner: time expenditure is much less, and the physical strain (as measured by heart rate) is also much less than when cleaning by hand. In an

Heart rate throughout the day

earlier study *Astrand* studied the heart rate of three subjects continuously occupied with housework throughout the day. The values obtained are summarised in *Table 8*.

The determination of the output expressed as a percentage of the maximum possible stress on the circulation showed that the three housewives had reached about 45% of their maximum values. This level of activity is in general agreement with the increases shown in other occupations. *Stübler* (20) has recently recorded the pulse rate continuously during housework, and his results are similar to those of *Astrand* (13). This author found that a healthy

Table 8   Cardio-vascular load in three female research subjects performing housework for a whole day   After Astrand (13)

Subject	Mean heart rate	Standard deviation	Percentage of maximum heart rate
1	125	16	47
2	102	22	43
3	99	17	46

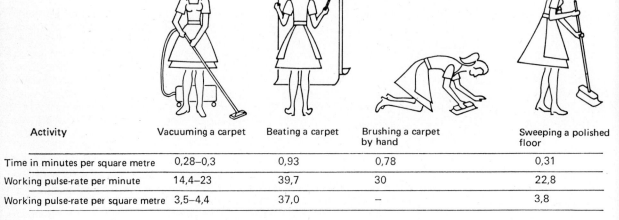

Activity	Vacuuming a carpet	Beating a carpet	Brushing a carpet by hand	Sweeping a polished floor
Time in minutes per square metre	0,28–0,3	0,93	0,78	0,31
Working pulse-rate per minute	14,4–23	39,7	30	22,8
Working pulse-rate per square metre	3,5–4,4	37,0	–	3,8

Figure 8   Time expended, and working pulse-rate while sweeping carpets and a polished floor   After Wiggert (19)

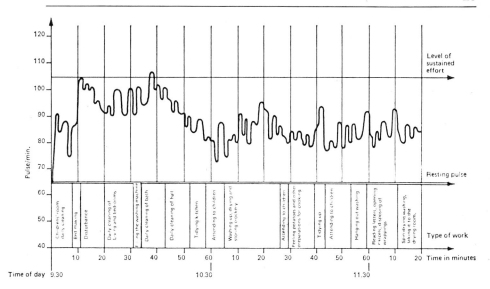

Figure 9   Pulse rates of an efficient housewife during the course of a morning
After Stübler (20)

subject had an average heart rate of about 90 per minute, and another, considerably less fit subject, had an average of 110, close to her limit for sustained activity.

The pulse rates of the two subjects are given in *Figures 9* and *10*.

Interpretation of the results

The results of Astrand (13) and of *Stübler* (20) show that the average heart rate during housework is quite high. A precise comparison with energy consumption is not possible. Nevertheless these pulse rate levels seem higher than would be expected from a housewife's energy consumption. While

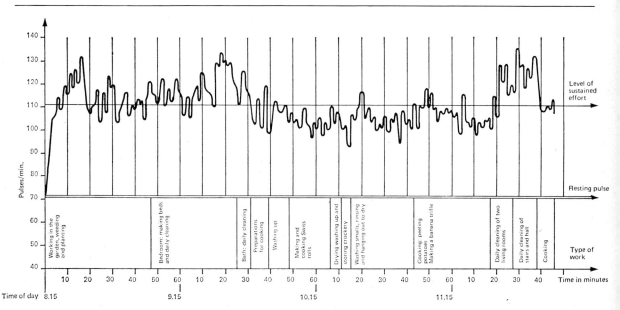

Figure 10   Pulse rates of an inefficient housewife during the course of a morning   After Stübler (20)

2,700 kcal/24 hrs is consistent with light to moderate work, the average pulse-rate of 100–125 is higher than that for moderate to heavy work, and leads to the conclusion that this value lies not far from the limit for sustained activity as defined by *Müller* (11).

One must conclude that there are many household tasks in which static effort has a far greater effect on heart rate than it does on energy consumption.

Strains set up by static muscular effort in domestic situations

As explained on page 17, static muscular strain arises in manual work through holding the body in unnatural positions, and through having to hold objects. Unnatural positions may be defined as attitudes which cause any part of the body to exert a continuous force of more than 15% of its maximum possible effort. The commonest strains of this kind are produced by stooping, in which position the back muscles have to support a comparatively heavy weight.

Figure 11 gives some examples of static effort.

Estimation of static strain

Even today there is no quantitative way of measuring the degree of static muscular effort in practical situations in domestic work. For this reason, we have to refer to observations made on subjects in other occupations, the

Bed making   Lifting a heavy pan   Doing the washing-up   Reaching for badly stored objects   Ironing

Cleaning   Stooping to reach equipment   Tending a child   Carrying   Hanging out washing

Figure 11   Forms of static effort common in house work

results of which can be used in comparison with domestic situations. An idea of the frequency with which static effort occurs can be obtained by time-and-motion studies, but to the author's knowledge no studies of this kind have been carried out for household tasks.

Static effort of a saleswoman

As an example let us take a work analysis carried out on saleswomen in a store, whose movements are similar to some of those performed by a house-wife. By the use of a multimoment analysis on 24 saleswomen taken on 24 days (5280 observations) many observations were possible, among them being the frequency with which they held the body in a position of static strain. Part of the findings are set out in *Table 9.*

The total times in which static muscular effort was needed varied with the number of customers, and the observed values were:

Back and legs	4 hr 30 min to 5 hr 12 min
Back and arms	1 hr 42 min to 1 hr 54 min

These times include 1 hr. 45 min. to 2 hr. for 'holding and lifting goods' as well as 'handling objects under the counter'. These results show that static strain in saleswomen occurs particularly in the muscles of the legs and back. This was confirmed by data for aches and pains obtained from 200 saleswomen in the same store. These results are given in *Table 10.*

Static effort and health

An exceptional feature of this survey was the large number of complaints concerning the legs and feet, whereas in studies of other groups of women such complaints were seldom or never made. It seems certain that there is a causal relationship between the static muscular strain affecting the legs and the frequency of complaints.

Static activity in the home

In their book 'Work in the home' *Steidl and Bratton* (18) cited ten authors who described the static effort involved in cooking, tidying, baking, cleaning utensils, laying and clearing tables, and making beds, and they made a number of observations on the angle of inclination of the back, and the frequency with which the body assumed an unnatural attitude. In a similar way the authors (18) made a number of observations on the holding and lifting of objects, and

Table 9   Static muscular strain experienced by saleswomen during a working day of 8¼ hours Multimoment analysis on 24 saleswomen over 24 hours (5280 observations).

Activity	Time spent per day
Standing still without support	3 hr 55 min
Standing still with some support	1 hr 30 min
Stooping	62 min
Walking	58 min
Absent	55 min

Table 10   Complaints of painful discomfort by saleswomen 200 Saleswomen were asked an open question on this point, and 79 of them (39.5%) gave the information set out below (multiple answers)

Complaints	Number of times made	Percentage
Legs and feet	17	20
Back	16	18.8
Headache	16	18.8
Digestive organs and liver	8	9.4
Rheumatism, arthritis, neuralgia	6	7.1
Nerves	5	5.9
Heart	4	4.7
Kidneys	4	4.7
Other (including menstruation)	9	10.6

gave quantitative data about handling such things as water, washing, children, utensils, provisions and many kinds of household equipment, the weights involved, and the frequency with which they occurred.

Body posture during ironing

With the help of cine film *Knowles* (22) studied bodily stance during ironing, and from this estimated the degree of bending of the spine. This increased as the working height was lowered; for a very low working height the subject remained in a stooping attitude throughout the period of observation, but with the working level at moderate height she straightened up after each period of ironing.

Body posture when folding material

With the aid of photographs, and under varying conditions, *Bratton* (23) observed the angular changes in the upper limbs when folding pieces of cloth. At a working height of 91.4 cm the 10 subjects raised their upper arms to a given angle three times more often when sitting than when standing. According to *Bratton*, the frequency with which the upper arm is lifted away from the body is a practical indication of the strain in the shoulder caused by static effort.

Bodily attitude at a drawing-board

An analysis of attitudes at the drawing-board made by *Grandjean, Kahlcke and Wotzka* (24) may be cited as a model of a study of bodily attitudes. They photographed the position of the spine and head for a large, a medium and a small male subject, each working at three sections of the same drawing-board. *Figure 12* shows the bodily attitudes taken up at the 10 drawing-boards studied, and *Figure 13* the angles at which the back and head were held, as shown by the photographic record.

When working in the middle sector of the drawing-board, the back was inclined at angles from 8–56°, according to the board in question, and angles of 20–34° between head and back were observed. On the basis of their observations the authors made the following recommendations concerning the design of drawing-boards: the height and slope must be adjustable;

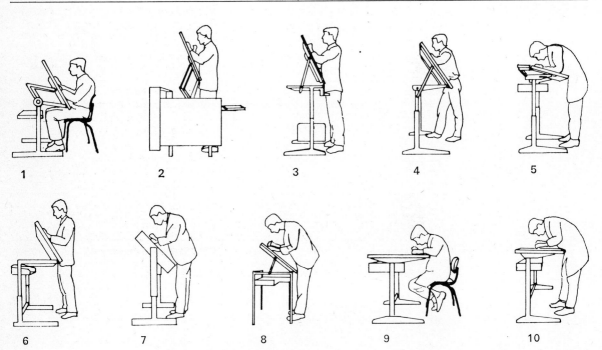

1   2   3   4   5

6   7   8   9   10

Figure 12   Ten different drawing-boards and the postures adopted for their use.   All have insufficient height adjustment

Figure 13 Bodily attitudes when working at a drawing-board, as determined from a photographic record a = angle between the axes of head and back. b = slope of back away from vertical 1, 2, 3 = Zones of drawing-board in which work is performed

the minimum height should be 65 cm for men and 61 cm for women, and the maximum height 130 cm. The slope of the surface must be adjustable over the range of 0–75°

Electromyography in relation to static effort

Another method of studying static muscular effort is electromyography, in which the electrical activity of the muscle is recorded from suitable electrodes. The application of this method to housework is difficult. *Lundervold* (25) and more recently *Floyd and Ward* (26) have used the method under standard conditions, with the subjects sitting still.

The Back Problem

Many medical studies agree that more than 50% of adults suffer from backache during at least one period of their lives. Since housewives are likely to suffer in this way as often as other people, and several household activities involve unnatural attitudes of the spine and may cause acute pain, any consideration of domestic work loads must include a section devoted to backache.

The spine

The spine is shaped like an elongated S ; at the level of the breast-bone the spine is gently curved with a posterior convexity, to which the name *kyphosis* is given. In contrast, in the lumbar region, the spine has a slight anterior convexity known as the *lordosis*. The shape of the spine allows the body to cushion the shocks of running and jumping.

Between the bony vertebrae lie the intervertebral discs, formed of an internal pad of elastic viscous material surrounded by a tough, resistant fibrous layer. The discs act as cushions between the vertebrae and give the spinal column its flexibility.

Disc troubles

For reasons that are still not understood the fibrous layer of the intervertebral discs frequently becomes diseased and loses its firmness and resistance. It becomes brittle and fragile. As a result there is a breakdown of the disc mechanism, leading to a reduction of movement between the vertebrae, and to pain.

This process becomes more serious if the viscous material in the centre of the disc escapes through the ruptured fibrous layer. The disc is then said to have herniated. The viscous fluid may then press either on the spinal cord or on a nerve root, causing acute pain along the sciatic nerve, and sensory disturbance and paralysis in the legs.

The narrowing of the intervertebral discs, the consequent pinching and grinding of the adjacent tissues, and, in advanced cases, the extruded discal fluid are the causes of the common aches, muscular cramps and numbness that afflict sufferers from disc trouble. These painful sequelae are called sciatica, lumbago or spinal arthritis depending on the location of the main symptoms.

People who are physically active suffer more from these complaints, and are more heavily handicapped in their occupation than are those who have a sedentary job.

Adverse factors

Lifting and carrying, and occupations requiring frequent stooping, all impose hazards on the intervertebral discs.

These activities impose excessive strains which hasten the wearing out of intervertebral discs. They all occur frequently during housework.

Forces on the vertebral column

The forces on the vertebral column increase from above downwards, partly because of the weight of the body, so that a pressure of 40–45 kg can easily fall on the lowest vertebrae. This strain increases even more if the person bends forwards at the hips and trunk. Then, according to *Münchinger* (27), a force of 300 kg may be imposed on the lowest vertebrae because of the leverage.

Moreover, bending the back produces an unequal distribution of force on the intervertebral discs, as is shown diagrammatically in *Figure 14*.

The avoidance of stooping and of lifting and carrying loads in a bad posture is the most important medical consideration in planning housework

Lifting loads

Since severe backache is often directly caused by load lifting, the housewife should adhere to the following five rules:

1. Before lifting a load, remove any obstacle that may be in the way.
2. The optimum height for a load to be lifted is 40 cm above ground level. All loads should be rested on a convenient platform from which they can be picked up again.
3. When lifting, keep the load as close to the body as possible.
4. Keep the back straight at all times.
5. Start with the knees bent and the trunk held as upright as possible, as shown in *Figure 14*.

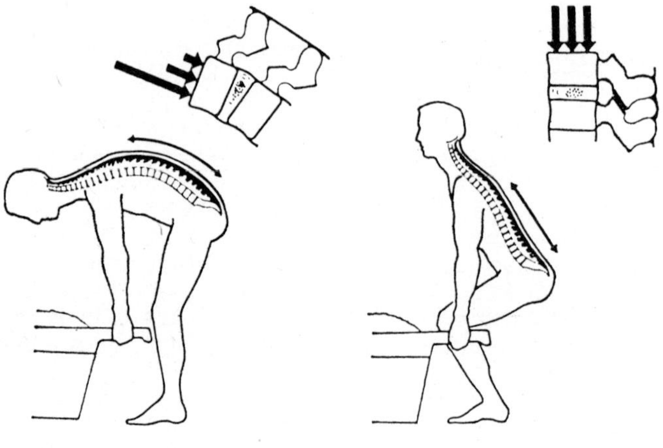

Figure 14   The effect on the lumbar vertebrae of lifting a heavy load with a bent back   With a bent back (left figure) the force on the intervertebral discs is unequally distributed, the greatest force being on the front edge of the disc, which is squeezed backwards. This posture increases wear and tear on the spine, with an increased risk of back trouble. With a straight back (right figure) the force on the disc is distributed equally, and there is less risk of disc trouble. After Münchinger (27)

A bent back is to be avoided, not only because of painful static muscular strains, but also of the danger to the vertebral column.

There are two decisive steps in the prevention of spinal curvature

Guides for housewives and domestic designers

1. *The housewife must take care to avoid bending the back by bending the knees whenever possible, if necessary by stretching out one leg.*
2. *Architects, builders, interior designers, furniture-makers and installation firms must, whenever possible, create conditions in which the housewife can keep her back in a natural, upright attitude.*
   Particularly important are correct working heights, adequate handles with room to grasp them, and the provision of furniture and fittings matched to the human body.

Figure 15 demonstrates a few ways of avoiding bad body postures, and *Figure 16* gives an example of how it should not be done.

Working time

Scientific recommendations

In industry the 5-day week and a working day of between 8 and 9 hours have been generally adopted, giving a total working week of 40–45 hours. There is a tendency towards further shortening of working hours, partly by the taking of longer holidays. With increasing prosperity and productivity workers will not only gain increased wages but will also have more leisure time. Specialists forecast that during the next few decades the working week will be reduced to 30 hours, and holidays will extend to 5 or 6 weeks per year. Studies by work scientists have shown that the reduction in working hours and the interpolation of rest periods in the working day have automatically tended to raise the tempo of work and to increase hourly output. Usually a rest period of 10–15 minutes is given in the middle of the morning and again

bad posture

good posture

Figure 15   How good posture can avoid an unnecessarily bent back

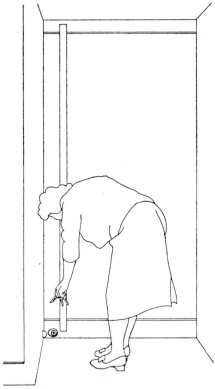

Figure 16   A bolt placed at the bottom corner of a door   for the sake of appearance, forces the housewife to stoop down about one thousand times in the course of a year

in the afternoon: in particularly strenuous work regular 5-minute rest periods have been provided.

In contrast to a continuous working day with a midday pause of 45 minutes, it has been shown that a shorter midday mealtime with breaks midway through the morning and the afternoon improve the well-being of the employees and increases their readiness for work.

Pauses

Time-and-motion studies have shown that a working man always takes breaks during his work. Four kinds of pause can be distinguished:

a. Arbitrary pauses.
b. Disguised pauses (pseudo-activity).
c. Work dependent pauses.
d. Prescribed pauses.

Arbitrary pauses occur when the worker clearly stops working, has a rest, and then starts again. Disguised pauses involve the worker in activities not necessary for carrying out his proper work: with such pseudo-activity the operative tries to conceal an interruption in his work that he will need to make up. Many disguised pauses pass unrecognised as such and conceal the fact that the man is being idle for some reason. At most work places there are many opportunities for disguised pauses; unnecessary cleaning of the work space; exchange of meaningless information; changing the bodily stance; ordering materials before it is necessary, and so on.

Work dependent pauses are stoppages necessitated by the operator having to wait because of the organisation of the work, the supply of materials, the running of the machine, or the reaction-time in chemical plants.

Work-study has shown that net working time is often only 70–80% of the attendance time, and that disguised pauses commonly occupy 10–20% of attendance time. Furthermore several studies have shown that the introduction of prescribed pauses decreases the number of arbitrary and disguised pauses. *Graf* (28) described examples of this kind.

These observations lead to the conclusion that men cannot work without rest times, and that they will always take the necessary breaks themselves if they are not provided by the nature of their work, or by the management

Time-and-motion studies in the household

Kraut, Schneiderhöhn and Wildemann (15) have measured the energy consumption of housewives together with the time spent at work. In a small household, a working year consisted of 2323 hours, and in a large household

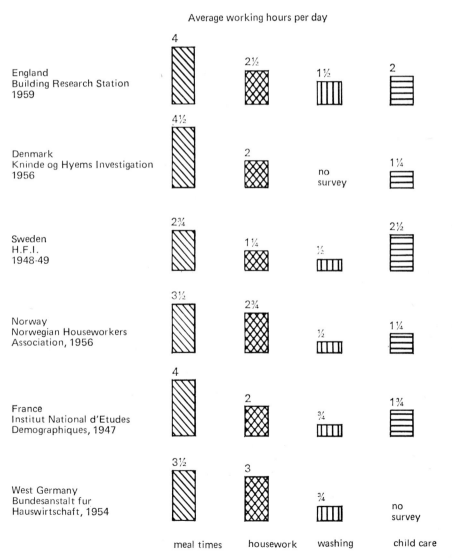

Average working hours per day

England
Building Research Station
1959

Denmark
Kninde og Hyems Investigation
1956

Sweden
H.F.I.
1948-49

Norway
Norwegian Houseworkers
Association, 1956

France
Institut National d'Etudes
Demographiques, 1947

West Germany
Bundesanstalt fur
Hauswirtschaft, 1954

meal times   housework   washing   child care

Figure 17   Average time spent by housewives on four activities in six European countries   After Hole and Attenburrow (30)

Table 11   Average working week for housewives in Switzerland From a survey of the Schweizerischen Institutes für Hauswirtschaft (29)

Activity	Working time, hours per week
Cooking, washing up, tidying kitchen	16
General housework	11
Washing and ironing	7
Mending, sewing, knitting	4
Caring for children	6
Shopping	4
Other household tasks	5

3896 hours. If these hours are spread evenly they amount to a working week of between 44 and 74 hours, depending on the size of the house. According to a study made by the *Schweizerische Institut für Hauswirtschaft* (29) the average working week of a housewife in Switzerland averages 53 hours. The sub-division of this working week is given in *Table 11*.

Figure 17 summarises the average working times of the housewife in 6 European countries, the data being taken from a paper by *Hole and Attenburrow* (30). Although the six surveys are not strictly comparable (different definitions, different selection procedures for the groups to be questioned, different survey techniques) by and large they reveal similar tendencies. They show that the time spent in various tasks can be summarised as:

mealtimes	$2\frac{3}{4}$–$4\frac{1}{2}$ hours
housework	$1\frac{1}{4}$–3 hours
washing	$\frac{1}{2}$–$1\frac{1}{2}$ hours
looking after children	$1\frac{1}{4}$–2 hours

In each of the surveys work in the kitchen occupied the most time; housework took next place, whereas washing and looking after children took the least time.

Effects of gainful employment

Two more recent studies may be quoted. *Zander* (31) in 1966 analysed a total of 204 preliminary questionnaires in a casual survey among former pupils of a domestic science college in Hesse, Germany. The results for housewives who were not gainfully employed and for those who were are compared in *Table 12*. *Table 13* gives an interesting comparison with an earlier survey.

Another comparison with an earlier survey was carried out by *Walker* (32) in 1296 households in Syracuse (New York). In addition to an interview each

Table 12   Distribution of working hours of urban housewives with and without other occupations according to size of household Housework is distributed over 7 days, the other occupation over 5; this is also evident in the total weekly working hours. After Zander (31)

Size of household	Hours per day Housework	Other occupation	Total
1 or 2 people			
– no other occupation	6.7		6.7
– with other occupation	5.8	6.9	10.8
3 people			
– no other occupation	8.8		8.8
– with other occupation	9.6	4.7	13.0
4 people			
– no other occupation	10.3		10.3
– with other occupation	10.0	3.4	12.4
5 people			
– no other occupation	10.6		10.6
– with other occupation	10.5	5.8	14.6

Table 13   Comparison between surveys made in 1953 and 1966 for a household of 4–6 persons   After Zander (31)

| Occupation | | Hours per day | | | | |
		Meals	Housework	Shopping	Other work	Total
Housewives	1953	2.4	2.8	0.9	4.7	10.8
without other occupation	1966	2.2	3.3	0.7	4.5	10.7

Table 14   Daily time required for all household tasks in 1296 American urban families   After Walker (32)

Number of children	Hours per day
0	4.8
1	6.8
2	7.8
3	7.7
4	8.2
5 or 6	8.5
Average for all families	7.3

family filled up a form giving details about the expenditure of time on two set days. The results were compared with two similar surveys in the years 1926/27 and 1952. The most significant results are collated in *Tables 14* and *15*.

In the German survey carried out by *Zander* (31) those housewives who had gainful employment spent the same time on household tasks as those who did not. In contrast to this the American survey of *Walker* (32) showed that those housewives who went out to work spent considerably less time on housework.

Have technical advances no importance?

Comparison of the earlier and later surveys gives an overall impression that the housewife's working hours have hardly changed, but this observation is hard to interpret. Have all the technical advances only made housework easier, but not speeded it up? This can hardly be possible, since many time-saving domestic appliances have been introduced in the last twenty years. Or have women a tendency always to spend the same length of time on their housework, even if technical improvements have reduced the time needed for some operations? This must remain an open question, because too little evidence is available to provide the answers.

Table 15   Daily time needed for various household tasks in urban areas in the USA

| Task | Housewives without other occupation Hours per day | | | Housewives with other occupation Hours per day | |
	1926/27	1952	1967/68	1952	1967/68
Preparation of meals	2.8	2.6	2.3	1.9	1.6
General housework	1.3	1.6	1.6	0.8	1.2
Care of clothes	1.6	1.6	1.3	0.8	0.9
Looking after the family	1.2	1.1	1.8	0.3	0.8
Shopping and accounts	0.4	0.5	1.0	0.3	0.8
Total housework	7.3	7.4	8.0	4.1	5.3

General conclusions

Most authors are agreed on the following points:

The housewife has a very long working day, beginning around 7 a.m. and ending towards 9 p.m. Of the 14 hours, 7 to 10 are needed for the actual housework (the net working time) and during the rest of the time she shops, visits friends, collects the children, tends the garden, sews, reads and rests. The housewife can never relax completely, even on Saturdays or Sundays.

For that reason, the working week of 50–55 hours, as calculated by most authors, is a relatively high one
It is remarkable that the housewife's working week has not changed in the last few decades, whereas occupations in general have shown a tendency towards shorter hours

2 Domestic Habits

Contents of Chapter 2

Summary

Research into domestic behaviour uses sociological methods combined with detailed surveys of houses to study the effects of particular types and layouts on the behaviour and habits of the occupants. Over the past twenty years a series of large scale surveys has been carried out in various European countries. One outcome of these surveys is the discovery that many families prefer to eat in the kitchen, the frequency with which they take meals there increasing with the kitchen area. The living room is the main centre of communal activities; it is hardly used during the daytime, but in the evening it becomes the centre for leisure pursuits, among which television plays a dominant role. Although there are signs that the erstwhile 'best room' may be changing into a general purpose room, a high proportion of older people still cling to the traditional function of the living room.

Among the adverse comments recorded, the most important were insufficient space and inadequate sound insulation for noises originating inside the building. A high proportion of those questioned agreed that they would like to live in a larger dwelling. Among changes suggested, the most important items were additional kitchen equipment, more room for hanging clothes, more rooms with sunshine, better sound insulation, better arrangements for sleeping, washing and personal hygiene, and better shopping facilities.

Finally the research methods used in these studies are critically analysed.

Research methods

The main objective of research into domestic behaviour is the analysis of the habits and reactions of people in relation to particular housing conditions and social factors. 'Domestic habits' comprise all the customary behaviour of the people who use the dwelling, and include the usage of individual rooms. Since the duties of the housewife have already been dealt with in a special chapter they will be omitted from what follows.

After the end of the Second World War many countries carried out extensive programmes of sociological research into domestic habits in relation to social factors and architectural data. The main purpose was to establish people's requirements in the way of housing, how it should best be planned, and how equipped. This research was particularly intensive in countries where there were big social programmes of subsidised house building. A selection of these research results will be assembled for comparison in the following chapters.

Domestic research in Sweden

Holm's investigations

Holm (34) carried out a long investigation from 1951–54 in several Swedish towns, in the course of which 600 persons who lived in newly built two- or three-roomed homes were questioned. Factors considered in the choice of a new home were placed in order by two different groups as follows:

	Groups	
	A	B
Working arrangements in the kitchen	1	3
Clothes storage	4	1
Washing facilities	2	5
Bedroom layout	3	6
Lavatory accommodation	7	4
Freedom from disturbance by neighbours	6	7
Sunny rooms	–	2
Convenience for shopping	5	–

From a time-study, carried out partly by experts and partly by the housewives themselves, a picture emerged of the time each member of the family spent at home, in which room, what activities he carried on there, and by what means. *Table 16* sets out these data for men and for women, from Monday round to Sunday. *Table 17* gives the activities of the housewife on each day of the week. The two tables reveal the following regular pattern:

Women work for 11 hours every day, and have 4 hours of free time, kitchen work and the care of clothing claiming a great deal of this. Sewing and mending are mostly done in the first half of the week; washing has its peak-day on Monday, ironing on Tuesday, and house-work on Friday. Baking takes place mostly on Fridays and Saturdays.

Table 18 summarises the uses of individual rooms. It is particularly noticeable how much the kitchen is used, and how little the living room.

Holm (34) also analysed comings and goings in the household, his results being given in *Table 19*

A further analysis studied the habits of children at home, and *Table 20* compares the duration of different activities of the children with that of their elders.

Table 16   Time spent in minutes on various forms of activity on each day of the week   After Holm (34)

Activity	Day of week							Average	
	Mon	Tues	Wed	Thurs	Fri	Sat	Sun	min	hr
Females									
Personal hygiene	35	57	36	43	40	41	39	42	$\frac{3}{4}$
Care of children	79	54	79	79	91	75	65	76	$1\frac{1}{4}$
Cooking and mealtimes	220	226	247	234	262	253	212	236	4
Cleaning	85	93	98	106	151	105	59	100	$1\frac{3}{4}$
Care of clothes	244	200	189	160	132	101	55	154	$2\frac{1}{2}$
Shopping	44	48	40	43	54	82	0	44	$\frac{3}{4}$
Free time	193	222	211	235	170	303	410	248	4
Total	900	900	900	900	900	960	840	900	15
Males									
Personal hygiene	38	35	37	43	40	57	43	42	$\frac{3}{4}$
Care of children	18	25	15	21	21	29	44	25	$\frac{1}{2}$
Housework	19	20	25	28	18	34	53	28	$\frac{1}{2}$
Mealtimes	80	79	74	83	78	86	86	81	$1\frac{1}{4}$
Occupations outside the house	583	587	604	566	605	418	80	491	$8\frac{1}{4}$
Free time	162	154	145	159	138	336	534	233	$3\frac{3}{4}$
Total	900	900	900	900	900	960	840	900	15

Table 17   Occasional activities of the housewife   Percentage of those questioned. After Holm (34)

Activity	Days of week						
	Mon %	Tues %	Wed %	Thurs %	Fri %	Sat %	Sun %
Sewing, mending	82	71	75	69	55	48	27
Going out, recreation	36	42	41	44	44	62	49
Washing	60	46	41	41	35	35	3
Ironing	30	40	34	31	25	27	6
Visiting	18	34	20	27	26	20	32
Baking	13	20	21	18	45	41	9
Shopping in town	13	6	6	13	8	22	–
Beating carpets	11	11	13	13	28	8	1
Cinema, theatre	6	2	4	2	–	5	15

Table 18   Time spent in various rooms between 0700 and 1900 hrs   After Holm (34)

Room	Time spent in minutes	
	Women	Men
Kitchen	378	68
Living room	65	31
Bedroom	63	24
Bathroom	39	8
Remaining rooms	88	26
Outside the home	87	563
Total	720	720

Table 19   Number of entries into individual rooms.   In-and-out counts as one entry. After Holm (34)

Room	Number of entries
Bathroom	20
Living-room	20–25
Bedroom (2-roomed flat)	20
1st bedroom (3-roomed flat)	20
2nd bedroom (3-roomed flat)	15–20
Kitchen	60–70
Entrance to block of flats	90–115
Out of the building	5–10

Table 20   Time (in minutes) spent on various activities by children of different ages   After Holm (34)

Activity	Age in years less than 2	2–3	4–6	7–9	more than 9
Studied over a week					
Eating	79	81	88	82	75
In the house	314	265	217	161	169
Out of doors	82	276	382	466	465
Sleeping	965	818	753	731	731
Total	1440	1440	1440	1440	1440
Studied by the day					
Eating	19	58	64	49	38
In the house	340	406	244	135	181
Out of doors	81	167	379	517	484
Sleeping	1000	809	753	739	737
Total	1440	1440	1440	1440	1440

According to this Swedish enquiry, children at all stages of their lives spent little time in the living room; 2–6 year-olds were very often in the kitchen for up to 3½ hours per day, whereas they spent only about one hour awake in the bedroom. From 4 years on they were increasingly out of doors (6–8 hours).

The living room was used for meals when there were guests, and about half the women questioned used it in the daytime for mending, but it was overwhelmingly a room to be used in the evening. On the other hand, the sewing machine was stored in the bedroom or in the kitchen, but only rarely in the living room.

Children in small houses usually played in the kitchen or the bedroom, and in bigger dwellings preferably in the bedroom. They rarely played in the living room. Similarly, childrens' playthings were visible in the kitchen in two-roomed flats, and otherwise usually in the bedroom. More than half of the children were not allowed to use the living room, though 30 per cent of children did their homework there. The great majority of them were satisfied to play on the balcony, provided that it was big enough – 3–5 square metres – and for that reason there was a distinct preference for private balconies.

As a result of his work *Holm* (34) reached the conclusion that two-roomed flats are unsuitable for families with children. He said that, as a first priority the poor facilities for storing clothes, for washing, drying and ironing must be brought to a higher standard: the area of the kitchen ought to be not less than ten square metres, and that of the living room not less than 18 square metres.

Sound insulation should be improved, and the door to the staircase ought to be a double one.

The work of Boalt

Between 1960 and 1965 *Boalt* (35) carried out a much bigger investigation, studying more than 2500 households with the aid of questionnaires, surveys and interviews. The investigations took place in five neighbourhoods (labelled A–E) in the vicinity of Stockholm, from which comparisons could be drawn between detached houses and terraced houses, and between dwellings in 1950 and in 1960.

Out of 2893 households
56.3% had a car
85.8% had a television set
33.6% had a washing machine

About half of those questioned wanted somewhere new to live, the most pressing reasons being either 'this place is too small' or 'not a nice neighbourhood'.

On average the *kitchen* was thought more of than the rest of the house. The standard of kitchen equipment in the houses was just about the same in 1960 as it had been in 1950, but the newer houses had bigger working surfaces and bigger refrigerators. The big kitchens were rated very highly, the best being those with 17 square metres of floor area, whereas kitchens of 9 square metres and built-in seating were less popular. Deep kitchens, with the eating place at the window and an adjacent working surface parallel to it were rated lower than kitchens with working spaces under the window.

The kitchen was used for many other activities besides cooking. Meals were always eaten in the kitchen on weekdays, and often also on Sundays, and when there were guests. The kitchen was also used for ironing, and for using the sewing machine, and the children played there and did their homework. The *living* room was used mostly in the evenings, but very rarely for eating, for the childrens' play or homework, or as a bedroom. On the whole people were dissatisfied with their living rooms, and few gave them a favourable report. Size and shape were less important than their being well arranged with doors in convenient positions. Living rooms in neighbourhood B were rated the lowest, having only 18 square metres of floor space and two windows, with doors opening into the kitchen, the bedroom and the hall. Living rooms in neighbourhood A rated highest: they had 19–20 square metres, with two windows in the short wall, and one door each to the bedroom and the entrance hall.

Toilets with bath and WC in the same room, and without any windows, were rated considerably lower than other variants.

In the course of the same investigation *Boalt* (36) analysed particularly the habits of children. She reported on 140 children, 118 of whom were of school age.

In 28% of the two-roomed flats more than two persons slept in the bedroom and both living room and kitchen not infrequently served as bedrooms for the children. Only 23% of all children had their own bedroom. One third of all the mothers questioned were dissatisfied with their children's sleeping arrangements. It is obvious that children sleeping in the same room will disturb one another, even if the radio and television have not already disturbed them. Two thirds did their school homework in the bedroom, the others in the kitchen. Children seldom brought their friends into the living room, but often brought them into the kitchen. The mothers questioned found the play-space for small children more satisfactory than the leisure space for the older ones.

Architecture and domestic behaviour

An interesting experiment was carried out by *Krantz* (37) from 1954 to 1962 in a new residential quarter of Göteborg. The first survey of 1956 covered 139 experimental dwellings and 143 normal ones, and a second survey was made in 1962.

All the normal dwellings had a kitchen-cum-dining room with a total floor-area of 51 to 72 square metres. The experimental dwellings had larger living rooms designed as general purpose rooms to contain activities transferred from the kitchen, such as ironing and sewing. The area of the kitchen was reduced, allowing either one or two small additional bedrooms to be provided. The total floor area amounted to between 58 and 89 square metres.

There was little difference between the first and second surveys. The 1962 survey showed less satisfaction than that in 1956, the author considering this to be due to the rise of living standards over the period in question.

In the normal households practically all meals were taken in the kitchen: in the experimental households 50–90% of those questioned ate in the kitchen in spite of the reduced room there. In 1962 both types of household spent their evenings in the living room, a fact that was attributed to television. A tendency for a few activities to move out of the kitchen into other rooms was evident in the experimental households: whereas in normal households ironing and sewing were always done in the kitchen, the kitchen was used for these purposes in only two-thirds of the experimental households.

In the normal households there was often a bed in the living room, and occasionally even in the kitchen, but such things were only rarely seen in the experimental households.

In 50% of normal households the furniture of the living room included a dining suite as well as a lounge suite, although meals were always taken in the kitchen. The experimental households more frequently had a dining table in the living room: in 1956 30% had a dining suite; in 1962 all of them had a dining suite, as well as additional furniture, particularly furniture used when watching television.

In 1956 30% and in 1962 58% of those questioned wanted a larger home, the most important reasons being shortage of space, and dissatisfaction with the house or with its location.

The study showed that it is doubtful whether domestic habits can be altered by architectural means.

Domestic research in Switzerland

The investigations of Bächtold

In Switzerland *Bächtold* (38) studied 160 households in 1961. The survey covered dwellings in Bern that were built between the years 1955 and 1959. The great majority were two- to four-bedroomed dwellings; only 12 of them had five or more rooms. Those participating had incomes as follows:

Fr. 550–950 per month   33
Fr. 950–1500 per month   87
Fr. 1500 and more per month   40

Tables 21, 22, 23 give particulars of the 160 who were questioned

Table 21   Use of the kitchen by 160 people in Switzerland: given as percentages of those participating in the survey. After Bächtold (38)

Activity	%
Cooking	100
Breakfast	68
Midday meal	55
Evening meal	57
Washing and ironing	64
Children playing and working	15
Reading, knitting, playing	18

Table 22   Use made of the kitchen in relation to its area: given as percentages of those participating in the survey. After Bächtold (38)

Activity	Kitchen area in square metres		
	Up to 6m²	7m²	8m² and more
Breakfast	49	66	85
Midday meal	42	48	71
Evening meal	40	53	74
Washing, ironing	42	74	78
Children playing and working	2	8	25
Spending leisure time	11	15	26

Table 23   Percentage of people taking meals in the kitchen, in relation to income levels. After Bächtold (38)

	Income groups in Swiss francs		
	550–950	950–1500	1500 and more
	(n = 31)	(n = 87)	(n = 40)
Breakfast	76	80	66
Midday Meal	76	63	18
Evening meal	73	67	25

From these Tables the following conclusions may be drawn:

- The kitchen was being used increasingly for additional purposes.
- The taking of meals in the kitchen appeared to be related to its area: with an area of eight square metres three quarters of those questioned ate in the kitchen, but in smaller kitchens only 40–50%.
- Eating in the kitchen is related to income level. At the lower and middle levels about 70% of those questioned took all their meals in the kitchen, while in families with higher incomes only breakfast was commonly taken in the kitchen, and the two other meals only rarely.
- Washing and ironing were carried out in the kitchen as far as possible, the area of the kitchen being the deciding factor.
- Only a minority used the kitchen as a play-space for the children, and as somewhere to carry on leisure pursuits. Here, too, the area of the kitchen was important.

81% of those questioned used the living room as the principal room of their home, and 129 people questioned listed their usage as follows:

Resting, reading, listening to radio, watching television	98%
Receiving visitors	89%
Sitting together as a family	90%
Sewing, mending, knitting	72%
Childrens' play and homework	31%

87% used their bedroom exclusively as a bedroom; 12% gave the following further uses:

As a workroom for the housewife	6%
As an office for the husband	4%
As a playroom for the children	2%

155 of those questioned had balconies, which they used for the following purposes:

Reading, mending, knitting	85%
Brushing clothes and cleaning shoes	82%
Hanging washing	68%

As play-space for the children   48%
For meals   36%
Balcony not used   5%

Table 24 gives details of where the children played, in 96 families with children of 'playing age', that is, below 16 years of age.

Table 24   Rooms in which children are allowed to play   Given as percentages of those participating in the survey. After Bächtold (38)

Room	%
Childrens room	93
Balcony	48
Corridor, anteroom	39
Living-room	31
Kitchen	15
Parents' bedroom	2
Elsewhere in the flat	9

The work of Henz and Vogt

In 1966 *Henz und Vogt* (42) used 494 interviews in urban and semiurban areas of central Switzerland to make a study of multiperson households, in which the head of the household was gainfully employed, but not self-employed. To obtain an insight into the ideal situation, as imagined by the people questioned, the authors developed a technique of showing them a table of dwellings of different sizes, with the corresponding rents.

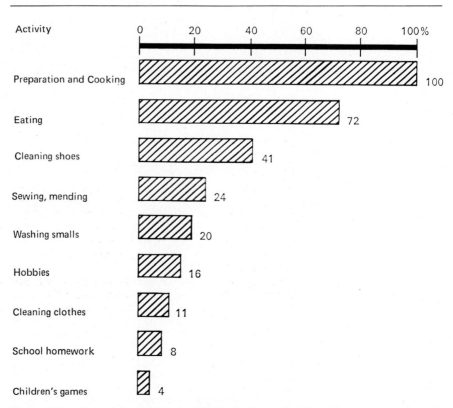

Figure 18   Use of the kitchen in 494 Swiss households   The percentage in each case relates to the number of people questioned. After Henz and Vogt (42)

Analysis of disturbance from noise showed that 80% of those questioned were disturbed by external noise in the daytime, and 60% at night. Daytime sources of noise included buses and trams (35.6%), cars (21.2%), and the noise of children (18.9%). The same sources of noise also predominated at night time. About two-thirds of those questioned were disturbed by noises from other houses, the commonest being water, music, doors banging, and the sound of footsteps.

Figure 18 gives information about the use of the kitchen.

Even though the kitchen was not really big enough, or was not designed for the purpose, 72% of those questioned took one or more meals there each day. The allocation of kitchen space in the estates that were studied and the net kitchen space that seemed desirable, are shown in *Table 25*.

Table 25   Distribution by size of the kitchens in 494 households, the third column shows the size preferences of those questioned   After Henz and Vogt (42)

Kitchen area m²	Percentage of households	Percentage of those questioned who would like this size
less than 4	4.5	6.2
4.1–6	21.0	41.4
6.1–8	30.3	–
8.1–10	25.1	–
10.1–12	10.8	52.4
12.1–14	4.5	–
more than 14	3.8	–

The commonest kitchen sizes lay between 4 and 10 square metres (76%) whereas more than half of those questioned about their ideal home gave priority to having a kitchen area of from 10 to 12 square metres.

The bathroom, which usually had an area of between 2 and 6 square metres was used for other purposes besides personal toilet

For washing small quantities of clothes	70%
For care of infants	20%
For sponging and cleaning clothes	5%

Since only a small fraction of the housewives questioned had babies, the 20% figure means that practically all the women used the bathroom for changing their babies. For their ideal home 79% wanted a bathroom with an area of 4–6 square metres, and 21% gave priority to having a bathroom of 6–8 square metres. These figures therefore show clearly that more household tasks are carried on in the bathroom, and more facilities need to be provided there, than the planners are aware of.

In 1969 *Barrier and Gilgen* (43) carried out 355 interviews in the city of Zürich, as part of an investigation into the natural and artificial lighting of dwellings. The majority of those concerned were dwellings of two to four and a half rooms. In this survey the tenants were asked whether there was one outstanding alteration – apart from the rent – to which they attached special importance. Those questioned were shown 9 cards set out with different criteria, which they had to arrange in order of desirability, and their replies are shown in *Figure 19*.

From this it emerged that 'space indoors' and 'enough sunshine' were ranked as 1, 2 or 3 by 59% of those questioned. The results were similar to those of *Holm* (34) in whose investigation sunshine and enough space came equal first in the rating.

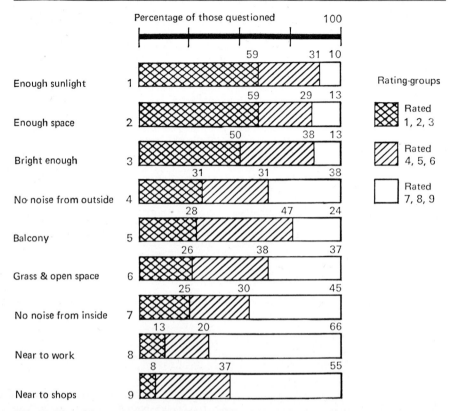

Figure 19   Nine criteria placed in order of importance when a change of flat was under consideration   335 people questioned in the city of Zürich. After Barrier and Gilgen (43)

Table 26   Number of rooms, excluding kitchen, bathroom and WC, in 332 dwellings in relation to occupation.   After Huser *et al.* (124)

Occupational category	Size of dwelling (rooms)		
	3 and 3½	4 and 4½	5 and 5½
Number of people questioned	117	120	95
	Percentages		
Skilled workers	20	11	6
Employees who have served an apprenticeship; technical occupations	55	47	45
Higher staff, and self-employed without a High School certificate	10	24	24
Occupations requiring a High School leaving certificate	15	18	25

Table 27   Reasons for last move of house   329 persons questioned. After Huser *et al.* (124)

Reason for move	Percentage.
First home	19.0
Better situation	10.0
Previous home too small	32.5
Place of work changed	28.5
More favourable rent	2.0
Other reasons	8.0

In 1970 *Huser, Grandjean, Gilgen, Ries and Suchantke* (124) carried out a survey into 332 dwellings built during the years 1966–70, on the outskirts of Zürich. 203 of these were buildings of unit construction, and 129 were conventionally built. *Table 26* gives a summary of the tenants and the sizes of their dwellings.

The families living in both types of dwelling were sociologically comparable, and in each household it was the housewife who was questioned. About half of these were exclusively occupied with household affairs, while more than a third of the total had gainful employment as well.

The reasons they gave for their last move are summarised in *Table 27*.

The commonest reasons for moving were the desire for a bigger place to live, and improvements in working space.

Table 28 gives information about housing density. About three-quarters of the households resulted in a housing density of 0.5–1 person per room. 303 of the dwellings were open plan, the living room being open to the hall. About three-quarters of those questioned preferred this type of dwelling, whereas the rest objected to it on the following grounds:

Disturbance by or to the children	45%
Lack of privacy	41%
Not sufficiently cut off from the front door	14%

The survey of the use of different rooms in the dwellings showed results similar to those of *Bächtold* (38) and other authors (34, 39, 40). Thus the living room was little used during the day, though 40% of those questioned used it occasionally as play space for the children. The childrens' room served in 12.5% of cases as a working space, in 6.5% of cases as a guest room, in 7.5% as a combined guest room and work room, and in only 57% exclusively as a childrens' room.

The survey of eating habits showed that here, too, meals were most frequently taken in the kitchen. The relevant results are set out in *Table 29*.

Of the numerous opinions expressed concerning the design of individual rooms, the following may be noted:

Opinions concerning kitchens were related to the dimensions as well as to the total area. Kitchens with a breadth of less than 1.8 m were rated considerably lower than wider kitchens with the same floor area. Kitchens with 9.3 or

Table 28 Density of occupation of dwellings (persons per room) Numbers given as a percentage of the number of households questioned. After Huser *et al.* (124)

Size of dwelling	Number of households n	Density of occupation in persons per room: percentage of households in this category			
		up to 0.5	0.51–1.00	1.01–1.50	1.51–2.00
3–3½ rooms	120	2.5	84.0	12.5	1.0
4–4½ rooms	121	13.0	67.0	20.0	–
5–5½ rooms	90	8.0	81.0	11.0	–

Table 29 Frequency of meals in the kitchen Percentages relate to the 332 households questioned. After Huser *et al.* (124)

Mealtime	Percentages	
	On weekdays	At weekends
Breakfast	76	41
Midday meal	55	30
Evening meal	45.5	31
With guests	–	8

13.7 square metres and a breadth of 2.4 or 3.7 m were assessed as 'just right' by 77% of the people questioned, or 89%.

Childrens' rooms were rated as big enough by a majority if the floor area lay between 11 and 14 square metres.

A balcony area of 7.5 square metres was rated best; an area of 4.5 square metres was judged too small by 38% of those questioned.

Domestic research in France

Investigations by
Cornuau and Rétel

In 1965 *Cornau and Rétel* (39) carried out investigations in the immediate out-skirts of Paris and in four other large towns in France, studying 1070 house-holds, each with 1–4 children. All the dwellings had been built since 1950, and the average income of those questioned amounted to FFr 1676 per month ($\pm$ FFr 650). On the average their time was divided as follows:

Sleep:	
— men	8 hrs
— women	$8\frac{1}{2}$ hrs
Occupational work	8 hrs. 45 mins
Travelling to and from work	1 hr
Time spent together on working day:	
— the whole family	1 hr 53 mins
— father and mother	3 hrs 20 mins

The evening meal, the time when the family were most often gathered all together, was taken:

In the kitchen	52%
In the living room	38%
In a room designated as dining room	7%
In the kitchen and one other room	4%

The larger the kitchen, the more often were meals taken there.

Less than 5.3 square metres	30%
More than 12.3 square metres	79%

20% of those questioned had some professional work to do at home, which they carried on in whichever room was most convenient. The children played mostly in the children's room, but usually they did their homework in the living room.

85% of those questioned who lived in a dwelling with a balcony used it:

for raising plants and flowers	73%
for resting	64%
for keeping an eye on the children when they were out of doors	53%
for drying washing	51%
as a play space for children	41%
to put their babies in the fresh air	33%
for taking meals	13%

76% of the households questioned had a television set, which in the great majority of cases was watched until transmissions closed down. 57% of the grown-ups switched the television on every evening. The set almost always stood in the living room.

In the better months of the year 60% of those questioned went out every Sunday, and 30% went out on Sunday once or twice a month. Almost none went away for weekends; 4% possessed a weekend cottage.

42% of those questioned wished that they could move to a new place because they wanted more space, and on average their requirement was the equivalent of an extra half-room. In addition to shortage of space, the standard of sound-insulation was criticised as inadequate. The noise level was designated as:

unbearable	6%
very disturbing	18%
moderately disturbing	28%
slightly or not at all disturbing	48%

The survey was also interesting on the subject of ideal homes. Of those questioned who wished to move somewhere else, 70% hoped to find a one-family house, and for 90% it was an essential feature of their ideal home that it should be a one-family dwelling.

Chombart de Lauwe (80) concerned himself especially with the habits of children. In 1957 in France he studied three concepts for building houses and housing estates, among them the well-known "Maison radieuse" of le Corbusier, with its residential block providing two-storied apartments. The results are summarised in *Tables 30, 31* and *32*.

Table 30   Where children are permitted to play in the house   Given as percentages of those questioned in each type of housing. After Chombart de Lauwe (80)

Type of housing	Percentages for each type of housing			
	Allowed to play anywhere	In living room	In childrens' room	In other rooms
La Plaine	17	10	58	15
La Benauge	11	18	47	24
Maison radieuse (flats on two stories)	7	23	50	20

Table 31   Where children play in flats of various sizes   After Chombart de Lauwe (80)

Size of flat number of rooms	Anywhere	Living room	Bedroom/ childrens' room	Other rooms	No reply
1	50	–	–	50	–
2	22	22	28	22	6
3	9	12	67	9	3
4–5	11	18	46	19	6

Table 32   Where children play, according to size of family   After Chombart de Lauwe (80)

Number of children in family	Anywhere	Living room	Bedroom/ Childrens' room	Other rooms	No reply
1	25	19	37	13	6
2 & 3	8	15	51	20	6
4 and more	17	15	49	17	2

Childrens' rooms are predominantly used as places for play. In the two-storied apartments of the 'Maison radieuse' the living room was used for play rather more often, allegedly because this makes it easier for the mother to keep an eye on them.

In general, whenever it is possible for the children to have a room of their own this room is heavily used, though it is interesting to note that there are occasional children who stay beside their mother and follow her from room to room.

Domestic research in West Germany

Investigations by Meyer-Ehlers

From 1964–67, in 235 newly built dwellings in Berlin, *Meyer-Ehlers* (40) carried out investigations into room usage, and into the opinions of their homes that were held by 952 people. Housewives used the living room only occasionally during the day: the children used it between 17.00–22.00 hrs, and the fathers between 18.00–23.00 hrs. *Meyer-Ehlers* also found an increased use of the living room if it contained the television set. *Figures 20, 21, 22* give full details of these findings.

92 of the dwellings had either a dining room or a dining alcove, and these were used most frequently around 08.00 and 13.00 hours, and in the evening between 18.00–19.00 hrs. An interesting point was the length of time that some children lingered over the dining table at midday, some until 15.00 hours when they should have been back at school.

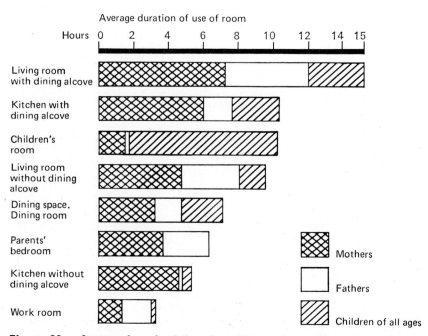

Figure 20   Average length of time for which various rooms are used between 05.30 and 24.00 hrs   After a survey by Meyer-Ehlers (40) in 235 newly-built apartments in Berlin

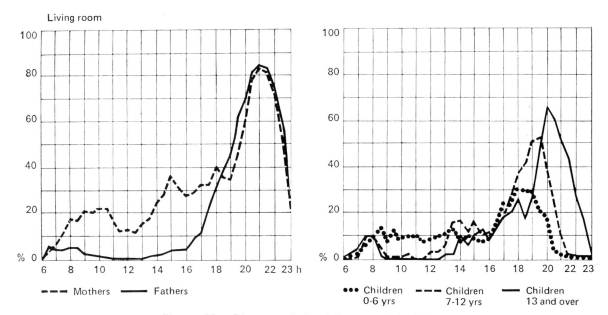

Figure 21   Diagram of the daily use of the living room by parents (left) and children (right)   After Meyer-Ehlers (40)

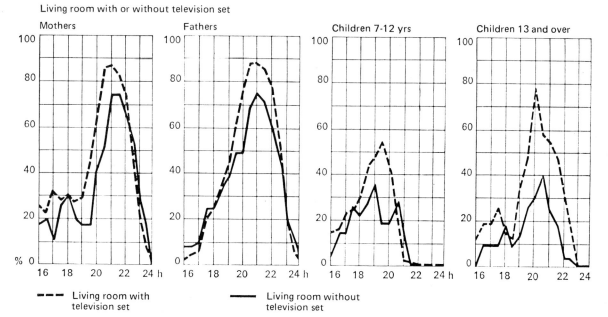

Figure 22   Diagram of the daily use of the living room, with and without a television set   After Meyer-Ehlers (40)

The adults' bedroom was practically unused during the daytime, but the childrens' room was used intensively. Children up to the age of six spent 30–60% of their time there, while older children were present there mostly in the afternoon. Interesting, too, were the findings about the most frequent social contacts between children. Children visited each other most frequently

1. Order of precedence according to the housewife's experience

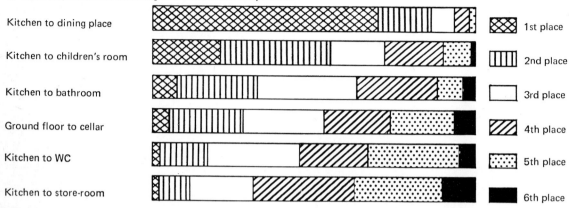

2. Effect of the ages of children on the frequency of journeys between kitchen and children's room
Housewives with children in age-groups:

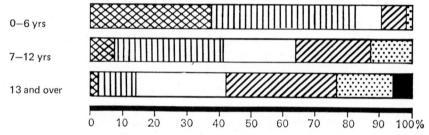

3 Order of precedence as measured by the number of steps taken (average values)

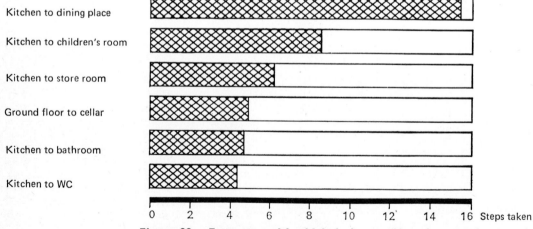

Figure 23 Frequency with which the housewife makes certain return journeys every day within the flat   After Meyer-Ehlers (40)

between the ages of 7 and 12 years, when 95% of them received visits 'sometimes' or 'often'. In all age-groups the childrens' room rated highest for getting together with friends.

Figure 23 gives information about the housewife's movements around the house during the day, from which the housewife's own estimate of the number of steps she takes can be compared with actual counts.

Table 33 Use of the living room Percentages are of the number who replied.
*this investigator did not ask about this. ** not classified into boys and girls.

Activity	Percentages: According to Meyer-Ehlers (40)		According to Silbermann (41)		
	Men	Women	Men	Women	Total
Listening to music or radio	83	90	76	70	73
Reading newspaper or book	82	78	84	78	81
Watching television	66	66	40	36	38
Writing letters	47	60	*	*	*
Communal family activities	39	39	41	34	37
Sewing, mending, tinkering	3	38	26	39	33
Resting in the daytime	30	35	74	71	72
Childrens play or hobbies	17**	–	–	–	–
Childrens homework	13**	–	*	*	*
Mother's outside occupation	–	5	*	*	*
Receiving visitors	*	*	84	86	85

Comparison with Silbermann's results

In Germany *Silbermann* (41) also undertook extensive studies of domestic habits. His surveys took place in 1961–62 and covered more than 2000 West German housewives. *Table 33* compares the results of *Meyer-Ehlers* (40) with those of *Silbermann* (41), as far as they relate to activities in the living room.

There is a striking difference between their results for 'watching television' and 'resting in the daytime'. Possibly there were fewer television sets in the housing estates studied by *Silbermann* in 1961–62 than there were in Berlin three years later, but no explanation can be offered for the discrepancy in the numbers of those who replied 'resting in the daytime'.

If there was a dining room as well as a living room, or a dining alcove was available, then according to *Meyer-Ehlers* (40) other activities were transferred to these, notably school homework, childrens' play, and certain communal activities of the family as a whole. *Silbermann* (41) grouped activities carried on in the living room as follows:

Communal relaxation and entertainment
Recreational activities
Meeting people
Work, and activities related to work

Both authors concluded that the living room has undergone *a complete change of function, from the 'best room' in the traditional sense to that of 'general purpose room'*.

Recently *Pfeiffer, Kirschenmann, Knorr, Kraus and Kramer* (81) concerned themselves with the special problems of children at home. The basic needs of children show little relationship to social stratification. The authors questioned 13 specialists, the majority considering a communal playroom to be desirable or essential for the whole play period of childhood. Up to the age of six either the mother or some other member of the family must be able to keep an eye on them. Children play with others from the age of one-and-a-half onwards. Up to the age of six the child needs a helping hand, and up to eight years old needs to touch others during play. Whereas babies up to the age of eighteen months live in a world of their own, from then up to $3\frac{1}{2}$ years of age they feel themselves to be part of the family circle, and particularly close to their mother. Up to the age of six it is desirable that they should be within call of their mother when they are sleeping.

Up to the age of fifteen months children should preferably play within a playpen of four square metres, and after that they should have a play space ranging from four to ten square metres. The survey shows a preference for moveable play-spaces for children up to the age of 3.6 years, and after that preference is equally divided between mobile and fixed play spaces.

On the basis of this survey the authors have made recommendations regarding the number and size of articles of furniture for work, for play and hobbies, and for sleeping.

Domestic research in England

Research by Hole and Attenburrow

In England in 1947, and again in 1961, *Hole and Attenburrow* (30) questioned 5300 and 2300 persons respectively about their behaviour in their own homes. On a weekday evening it was the children up to nine years old, and the men and women over 59 who were most often at home. Those of either sex between the ages of 15 and 59 spent only 8–34% of their weekday evenings at home. Foremost among activities at home on a weekday evening were mealtimes and housework, and in 1961, television. Before the introduction of television more than 50% of those questioned listed reading, writing, knitting and sewing, or a hobby among their activities, but in 1961 only 27% still mentioned any of these. The English survey showed that the whole family was almost never gathered together at mealtimes, and this was the main reason why the kitchen was so often used for meals. In fact, in dwellings with a separate living room, meals were taken as follows:

always in the kitchen	44%
always in the living room	30%
in either room	26%

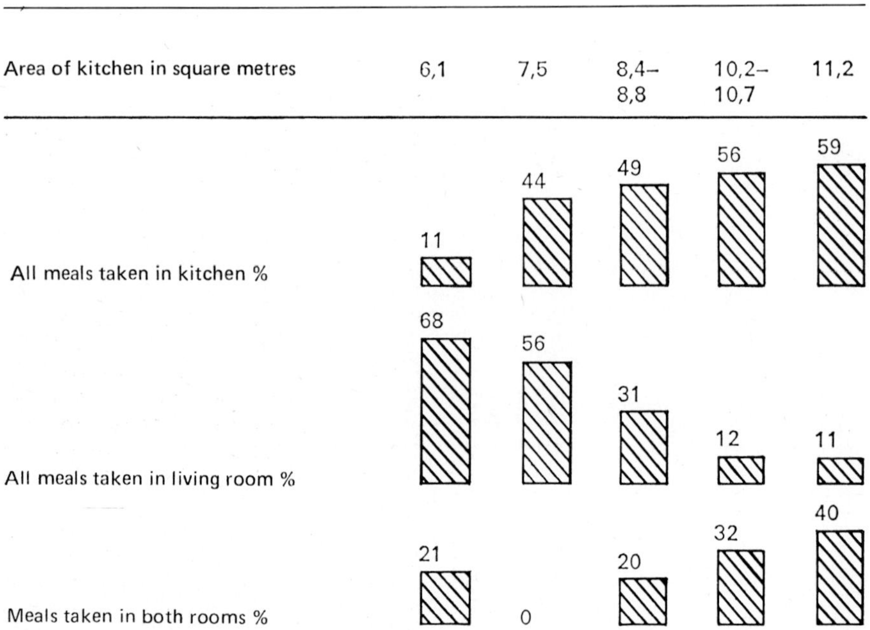

Area of kitchen in square metres	6,1	7,5	8,4–8,8	10,2–10,7	11,2
All meals taken in kitchen %	11	44	49	56	59
All meals taken in living room %	68	56	31	12	11
Meals taken in both rooms %	21	0	20	32	40

Figure 24   Effect of size of kitchen on where meals are taken   After Hole and Attenburrow (30)

In homes with a dining room, meals were taken as follows:

always in the kitchen	19%
always in the dining room	43%
in either room	38%

Figure 24 shows the influence of the size of the kitchen on the site for meals in houses with a dining room.
In England those questioned often wished that they had a second day-room; i.e. a dining room as well as a living room: among families of more than three people more than half mentioned it.

What does research teach us about domestic habits?

General considerations

While the foregoing investigations reveal some differences, there is an astonishing degree of overall agreement. The differences will not be discussed here: they may represent variation between one country and another, but they may also have been produced by different methods of investigation, and since it is impossible to say which is which, discussion seems fruitless. So in the following sections an attempt will be made to create a picture of domestic habits in these homes, and of some the more important opinions expressed, using not only the overall results, but also some individual items which seem particularly significant.
In every home the following forms of activity were included:

sleeping
eating and drinking
leisure-time activities
housework
personal toilet
care of children

Individual and communal fields of activity

Most of the activities arise naturally in one particular room of the house, and only housework and child-care take place in several or all rooms. Furthermore, the rooms may be categorised as those which exist primarily for individual activities, and those which cater for the joint activities of several persons (family rooms). Sleeping and personal toilet are essentially individual activities, and so bedrooms and bathrooms and lavatories might be put into the first group. Eating and drinking, and many leisure-time activities, are preferably carried on in the company of several other persons, or communally *en famille*: these activities are provided for by the living room, and the dining room when appropriate. Most of the housework finds its natural place in the kitchen, which used to be the housewife's own domain, but which nowadays is becoming more and more a communal room, with all the family eating in the kitchen and helping with the washing-up.

Taking meals

Of special interest is the location of the family dining area. Taking meals in the kitchen seems to be a widespread habit. The observations show how closely the frequency of meals in the kitchen is correlated with its area, even in families with a separate dining room, and this must be taken as an indication that considerably more families would eat in the kitchen if it were big enough. This is confirmed by the Swedish observation that kitchens are generally bigger there, and meals are commonly taken in the kitchen.

These results show that kitchens of less than eight square metres are not suited to modern family habits

Is the modern living room taking on new functions?

The living room, the principal room of the family circle, is little used during the daytime, but in the evening, it becomes the centre for leisure activities, foremost among which is watching television. In earlier periods the 'salon' was typical of the solid bourgeois class, and was used only on special occasions. In smaller dwellings this function of 'show room' was taken over by the living room, which was turned into a status symbol by the purchase of 'fine' furniture, pictures and carpets, and was usually referred to as the 'best room'. It appears from this research that, while it is true that significant changes have taken place converting the best room into a general purpose room, it still stubbornly preserves its traditional function as status symbol. This is evident from the little use that is made of it during the day, when the living room is seldom used by the housewife for her jobs, or by the children for either play or homework. It is striking how often not only the housewife but also the children stay in the kitchen. Obviously the housewife does go into the living room every day, if only to tidy it and put it into good order so that it will be ready for the whole family in the evening.

Disappointing, and somewhat discouraging were the results obtained by *Krantz* (37) who found that, notwithstanding the reduction in size of kitchens, and the growth in size of living rooms, the conversion of living rooms into general purpose rooms was taking place only to a very limited extent. Must we then conclude from these findings that the possession of a spotless, tidy living room is still a major consideration with many of the older generation? I think we must.

What is important to the occupants?

A striking feature is the unanimity of critical views on the deficiencies in dwellings. The commonest complaints are shortage of space and inadequate insulation against noisy neighbours. Wanting more room is the commonest reason given for wanting to move, and there is also a clear consensus of opinion about what particular features those questioned would like to have, if they did move to another place. First priority goes to kitchen equipment, a room for the clothes, more sunny rooms, better sound insulation, washing machines, better arrangements for sleeping, and for personal hygiene, and better facilities for shopping.

Critical opinions about these research methods

Finally, a few criticisms may be made about this type of enquiry into domestic habits. From the sociological point of view it is often pointed out that the opinions expressed by those questioned tell us little about their real needs, because they are based only on those features that the respondents happen to know about. A person cannot be a judge of something quite outside his experience. Furthermore it is doubtful whether, on the whole, the occupants questioned are giving a mature and unprejudiced opinion: their views are coloured by the habits of years. Sociologists also criticise the undesirable effects of the environment, of trend-setters, and of conformity to the group-norm, as well as of other social factors.

It cannot be denied that some criticism of parts of the research are justified It is also undeniable that interpretation of the surveys is very difficult, and open to many reservations.

Relationship between the opinions expressed and the physical facts

If it is correct that approval of a domestic feature has only limited value as evidence, because the person questioned may have no standards of comparison, conversely *an adverse opinion has considerably more value*. This is especially true if a correlation can be obtained between the frequency of a complaint and the incidence of this feature as objectively recorded.

Two examples may illustrate this. If the frequency of complaints about noise is statistically correlated with the actual values of the decibels recorded, then a causal relationship between noise and complaint is most probable, particularly if those questioned have been chosen at random. As a second example, the findings of *Bächtold* (38) as well as those of *Hole and Attenburrow* (30) may be cited. These authors, independently of one another, found that the frequency with which meals were taken in the kitchen was related to the area of the kitchen. One can hardly doubt that there is a causal relationship between floor-area and eating habits, as far as a random selection provides a fair comparison between the different groups. Since this result was also found in dwellings which had a dining room (30) it seems to be valid for contemporary housing conditions. Nevertheless the objection must be accepted in principle that this statement is valid only for those types of dwelling on which the study was based. It tells us nothing about the widely-coveted dining-space in homes with a different room arrangement, for example with a kitchen opening into a dining alcove.

It is important, at the time the occupants are questioned, to make a quantitative assessment of the domestic details, from which a valid correlation may be sought. Giving oneself such a target often promotes interdisciplinary cooperation, a thing which is becoming increasingly important in research.

Domestic research as a feedback system

In conclusion, a powerful argument in favour of sociological surveys in domestic research may be put forward. Many fields of research seek the reassurance of a 'feedback mechanism', to maintain control by providing a way of monitoring the success or failure of the measurements or arrangements that are being carried out. By feedback is meant the principle that information about the state of a process being directed is fed back to the control centres, so that the controlling agency can match the results to the programme. In the field of dwelling construction the study of domestic habits, and of the views of the occupants constitutes such a feed-back system. Domestic research allows to see whether or not domestic habits arise in conformity to the design of the dwelling, and hence the results of domestic research could provide a basis for planning. *Domestic research should always analyse reciprocal influences between domestic details and human reactions, and should seek to ascertain how the building reacts upon its occupants.*

If it is remembered how often the form of the building reflects either the dream-fulfilment of the architect, or the rentability as visualised by the owners, it will become clear how important domestic research can be for the anonymous occupant, for whom buildings are planned and erected without prior consultation.

3 Elbow Room

Contents of Chapter 3

Summary

The space that people require depends upon the elbow room needed for their job, and that for their psychological satisfaction. The physical need for space is determined by the size of person, the space needed to move round the equipment and the space necessary for passage to and fro.

The principal dimensions of people when standing and sitting are collated in *Tables 34* to *38*. To avoid unnatural bodily attitudes which are tiring and damaging to health, any furniture or equipment must be suited to the vertical and horizontal reach of the operative. The principal data concerning length of reach are presented in *Figures 26* and *27*.

Rules for correct working heights when sitting and standing, and for the space necessary for trunk movements, can be derived from current knowledge of anthropometry and work physiology. There have been many analyses of required dimensions for kitchen installations such as sinks, stoves and ironing-boards. In general, stoves should be 80–85 cm high, sinks 90–95 cm at the rim, and ironing boards should be adjustable between 78 and 90 cm.

Thiberg (44) studied the relationship between the preferred height for equipment and the standing height or elbow height of the user over a large range of activities. The calculated regression coefficients are given in 8 diagrams in this section.

Adequate space is especially important where a woman is dealing with cupboards, shelves, and other storage, and recommendations must take into account not only the length of the subject's arms, but also whether the back of the shelf can be reached. The main rules of thumb are:

- maximum upwards reach = 1.24 × height.
- convenient heights to reach lie between 65 and 150 cm.
- a cupboard depth of 60 cm can only be reached with ease at or below shoulder height (120 cm).
- all kitchen shelves should be adjustable.

Studies of housewives' movements in the kitchen have indicated the best arrangement for equipment: from left to right the sequence should be: sink, main working surface, cooker, and somewhere to put things down.

Experimental studies carried out by *Robins* (70) on freedom of movement in relation to breadth of passage-way and size of subject provide a model for further investigations, since the space usually provided in rooms for handling objects and for working with them is often unsatisfactory. Working space will not be dealt with further in this chapter, but will be discussed later in relation to the design of individual rooms.

A problematic question is that concerning the psychological needs for space. Since no precise quantitative knowledge exists in this field, we are restricted to reflections of a general nature and to theoretical considerations. This ignorance is the more regrettable since houses and flats have been becoming progressively smaller in recent times. Enquiries into the space necessary for psychological well-being should be an important part of building research. The beginnings of such enquiry can be seen in the work of *Acking* (75, 76) and *Jeanpierre* (77, 78, 79).

General features of spatial needs

Spatial requirements

People's spatial requirements consist of:

- elbow-room for the person, i.e. on anatomical and functional grounds.
- work space, that is the floor space needed to use built-in features as well as free standing equipment.
- psychological needs.

Thiberg (44) has published a short bibliography concerned with this group of problems, comprising 928 references.

Classification of spatial needs

The space that people need for their activities indoors can be classified as follows:

a. *Space for the limbs when either standing or sitting.* This is a direct anatomical and functional requirement of the human body, and includes the radius of action of the arms, the back and the legs. Examples can be found in papers (3), (6) and (46).
b. *Space required by the human body when operating equipment.* Examples include the use of such installations as cookers, baths and toilets, using control knobs and push buttons, and putting things into and taking them out of storage in cupboards and elsewhere. *Work space*, that is the floor space that must be kept free for standing, while using a particular piece of furniture or equipment is also included under this heading. Examples of the last are seen in the floor space needed for sitting down and standing up, for using a cooker, the clear space round a bed, for opening and shutting a cupboard, or for using a wash basin or other sanitary equipment.
c. *Circulation space in rooms and corridors.* This is based on studies of transit movements and from analysis of the use made of corridors and passages.
d. *Movements of people around the dwelling.* Studies of the demands that arise in each room as well as time-and-motion studies throughout the house are the methods used here.

The principles of this classification will be applied in the next section, but two problems must be excluded at this point. Firstly *work space* comes into the section that deals with the design of individual rooms, since this requirement is especially important in their lay-out. Secondly, movements indoors are a part of domestic habits, and so must be seen in relation to room usage. Hence the present chapter must give some brief consideration to psychological needs for space.

Space needed for sitting or standing

Anatomical dimensions when at rest

Methods

It is customary nowadays not only to quote the average measurements but also to indicate the limits of size for groups of people. It is usual to indicate the 95% confidence limits (the 95 percentile) and use them as a measure of variation from the mean measurement. This confidence zone indicates that, for the measurement in question, 95% of the population sampled fall inside the given limits.

Table 34 Height of women in different countries N = number of women measured. T = limit of confidence for 95% of normal distribution (2.5–97.5%)

Country	N	Average height cm	T = 95% cm	Reference to literature
Germany	133	164.8	153 –176	(46)
Germany	16,700	161	148 –174	(47)
Germany	1,166	163.4	149.6–177.2	(55)
USA	10,042	160.5	149 –174	(48)
USA	230	162.6	–	(49)
France	319	160	–	(50)
France	100	157.8	149.9–167	(51)
France	140	160	148.6–171.4	(52)
England	56	162.5	149.1–175.9	(53)
England	–	160.6	145.4–175.8	(56)
England	–	165.1	153.7–175.3	(3)
Holland	–	163	–	(54)
Switzerland	508	158.8	137.8–179.8	(45)
Switzerland	–	160	148 –172	(57)

Since it is expensive to survey a large population, one starts nowadays with small samples to establish the relationship between the mass of the population and its different sections, and one can then draw conclusions about the sections from values already available for the big population.

Figure 25 sets out the procedures commonly used in sampling and the values that they gave in certain investigations (45). The distances between particular parts of the body that are mentioned in what follows refer as a rule to the parts of the body shown in this diagram.

Standing height

Table 34 gives a synopsis of heights of women from different countries.

The literature contains many studies of standing height in men, and a few are summarised in *Table 35*.

The two tables show that average stature varies slightly from one country to another. However, the average values obtained from different samples in a given country can vary almost as much as this, so that we need not attach much importance to either international or inter-sample variation. One would not be far wrong if one used the following values for all the countries concerned:

adult females ..   ..   *161 cm*
adult males   ..   ..   *172 cm*

These are also values reached by *Kroemer* (47) on the basis of 17,700 measurements of women and 15,700 measurements of men, and calculated as the averages for people aged 20–65 in Germany.

Table 35 Height of men in different countries A small selection from the surveys. * Large, random samples, representative of the adult population. N = number of men measured. T = 95% confidence limit for normal distribution (2.5–97.5%)

Country	N	Average height cm	T = 95% cm	Reference to literature
USA				
– recruits	4,062	175.5	163 –188	(58)
– car-drivers	306	174.1	–	(59)
France				
– car drivers	296	170.2	158.6–181.8	(60)
Germany	15,800	172	158 –186	(47)
England*	–	170.7	157.3–184.1	(61)
Switzerland				
– recruits	35,000	172.0	158 –186	(57)
– staff-list	500	169	150 –188	(45)

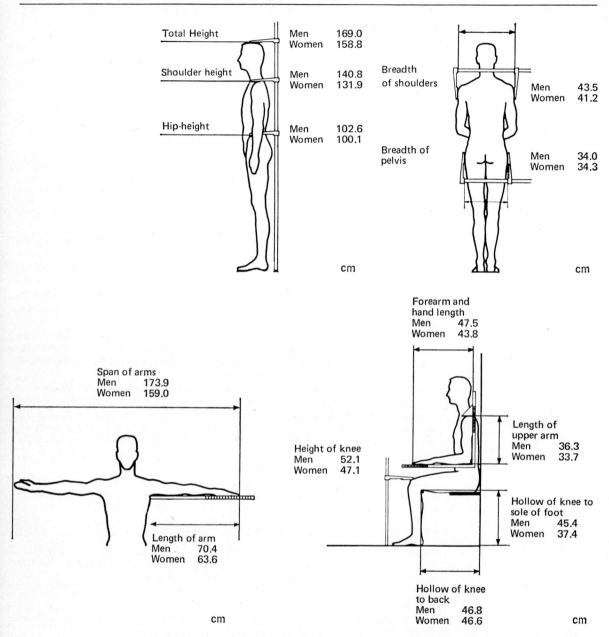

Figure 25   Diagram showing procedure for measuring bodily dimensions
Distances measured, and average values found for men and women in a group of 500 men and 508 women in Switzerland (45)

Body measurements of Swiss employees

In one particular study (45) we measured 500 men and 508 women aged between 15 and 69, chosen at random from the staff list of a Swiss machine factory. The firm also included 180 Italian workers, whose body length averaged 2.5–3 cm less than that of the German–Swiss. In contrast both male and female apprentices had a standing height of 2–4 cm more than those of the adults. This relatively heterogeneous group produced a scatter in the measurements bigger than in other anthropometric surveys. The results of these measurements are shown in *Table 36*; the parts of the body measured correspond with those shown in *Figure 25*.

Measurements of parts of the body

Tables 37 and *38* give bodily measurements important in the design of domestic equipment and furniture for men and women respectively.

For further examples see *Murrell* (3), *Scherrer* (6), *Steidl and Bratton*(18), *Thiberg* (44), *Kroemer* (47) and *Peters* (55).

Space needs in terms of vertical and horizontal reach.

The vertical and horizontal distances that people can reach are of considerable importance.

Vertical reach

A woman's vertical reach is of critical significance for the lay-out of cupboard-space and shelving, as well as for the placement of fitments, such as the cooker switch, water taps, or electric sockets. Vertical reach can be defined as the radius of action of the upper limb with the hand able to grasp objects. *Figure 26* sets out the values, which take into account the author's measurements of the distance from the axis of the shoulder-joint to the middle of the palm of the hand (45). These are in overall agreement with similar information obtained by *Hertzberg, Daniels and Churchill* (58).

Kroemer (71) used the distance from the back to the tips of the fingers as the forward reach, and his average values were 87 cm for men and 75 cm for women.

Horizontal reach

For all manual operations horizontal reach must be determined at the height of the working surface, which for most purposes lies 3–10 cm below the elbow *Figure 27* gives the relevant measurements for being able to grasp things at this level, and for optimum working conditions. The operational field of each arm extends from the lowered elbow to the thumb, and the reach from the shoulder-joint to the middle of the palm.

Table 36   Anatomical measurements in a resting posture   A random sample of the personnel of a Swiss factory (45). N = size of sample. $\bar{x}$ = average measurement. r = extremes for this measurement. s = standard deviation. T = 95% confidence limit for normal distribution. (2.5–97.5%) M = men   F = women

Bodily dimension		N	$\bar{x}$	R	s	$T = 95\%$
Body length	M	500	169.0	140–191	9.5	150.0–188.0
	F	508	158.8	136–179	10.5	137.8–179.8
Shoulder height	M	500	140.8	120–163	9.4	122.0–159.6
	F	508	131.9	112–163	11.8	108.3–155.5
Height of hips	M	500	102.6	85–118	11.5	79.6–125.6
	F	508	100.1	85–114	8.9	82.3–117.9
Length of upper arm	M	500	36.3	29– 50	2.8	30.7– 41.9
	F	508	33.7	28– 50	2.5	28.7– 38.7
Knee height, sitting	M	500	52.2	42– 60	2.7	46.8– 57.6
	F	508	47.1	37– 57	2.5	42.1– 52.1
Hollow of knee to sole of foot	M	500	45.4	35– 50	2.2	36.6– 54.6
	F	508	37.4	32– 48	2.2	28.6– 46.6
Hollow of knee to back	M	500	46.8	33– 57	3.3	40.2– 53.4
	F	508	46.6	33– 57	3.0	40.6– 52.6
Span of arms	M	500	173.9	145–204	10.0	153.9–193.9
	F	508	159.0	135–189	9.8	139.4–178.6
Breadth of shoulder	M	500	43.5	32– 55	2.5	38.5– 48.5
	F	508	41.2	31– 49	2.7	35.8– 46.6
Breadth of pelvis	M	500	34.0	28– 46	3.0	28.0– 40.0
	F	508	34.3	28– 46	2.7	28.9– 39.7
Arm length	M	500	70.4	50– 85	4.7	61.0– 79.8
	F	508	63.6	50– 77	4.5	54.6– 72.6
Forearm and hand	M	500	47.5	35– 55	2.2	43.1– 51.9
	F	508	43.8	32– 55	2.5	38.8– 48.8

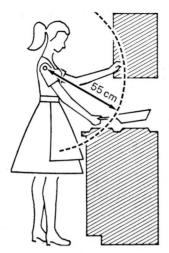

From shoulder joint to middle of the palm

Women:
$\bar{x}$ = 55 cm
T 95% = 47–63 cm

Men:
$\bar{x}$ = 62 cm
T 95% = 54–70 cm

Figure 26 Vertical reach The values given are taken from the studies made by Grandjean and Burandt (45)

Table 37 Bodily measurements of men when standing and sitting The values from (3) are in part estimated. $\bar{x}$ = average value. T = 95% confidence limit for normal distribution (2.5–97.5%)

Measurement	Country	$\bar{x}$ (cm)	T = 95% (cm)	Reference to literature
Height of eyes when standing	Germany	161	147 –175	(47)
	England	163.8	154 –174	(3)
	France	160.5	147.9–173.1	(62)
Height of shoulders, standing	Germany	142	129 –155	(47)
	England	142.2	133 –150	(3)
	France	137.5	126.1–148.9	(63)
	Switzerland	140.8	122 –159.6	(45)
Breadth of shoulder	Germany	45	40 – 50	(47)
	England	45.7	41.5– 49.8	(3)
	Switzerland	43.5	38.5– 48.5	(45)
Span of arms	Germany	175	155 –195	(47)
	Switzerland	173.9	153.9–193.9	(45)
Elbow-ground, standing	Germany	106	96 –116	(47)
	England	106.7	99 –115	(3)
	Switzerland	104.5	94 –115	(45)
Height above seat when sitting	Germany (upright)	90	83 – 97	(47)
	France	89	82.6– 95.4	(60)
	England	91.5	85 – 97	(3)
Thigh height above knee, seated (see fig. 28)	Germany	55	50 – 60	(47)
	France	53.7	48.7– 58.7	(62)
	Switzerland	52.2	46.8– 57.6	(45)
Back of knee to floor, when seated	Germany	45	41 – 49	(47)
	France	41.9	37.7– 46.1	(62)
	England	42	39 – 45	(3)
	Switzerland	45.4	36.6– 54.6	(45)
Front edge of knee-back (seated length to knee)	Germany	59	53 – 65	(47)
	France	59.6	53.6– 65.6	(60)
	England	59.7	54 – 64	(3)
Elbow height above seat	Germany (upright)	24	19 – 29	(47)
	France	23.5	18.9– 28.1	(62)
	England	24.1	19 – 29.4	(3)

Table 38   Bodily measurements of women when standing and sitting $\bar{x} =$ average. $T = 95\%$ confidence limit for normal distribution (2.5–07.5%)

Measurement	Country	$\bar{x}$ (cm)	$T = 95\%$ (cm)	Reference to literature
Height of eyes,	Germany	150	136 –164	(47)
standing	USA	151	–	(49)
	England	154.9	143 –164	(3)
Shoulder height,	Germany	131	118 –144	(47)
standing	France	130.3	119.9–140.7	(52)
	USA	133	–	(49)
	England	133.4	124 –143.5	(3)
	Switzerland	131.9	108.3–155.5	(45)
Breadth of shoulders	Germany	41	36 – 46	(47)
	USA	36	–	(49)
	England	40.6	38 – 45	(3)
	Switzerland	41.2	35.8– 46.6	(45)
Span of arms	Germany	155	135 –175	(47)
	Switzerland	159	139.4–178.6	(45)
Elbows above floor,	Germany	97	87 –170	(47)
standing	USA	100	–	(49)
	England	100.3	92 –109	(3)
	Switzerland	98	87 –109	(45)
Height above seat	Germany	85	78 – 92	(47)
when sitting	England	85.1	–	(3)
	USA	84.7	–	(49)
Thigh height above	Germany	50	45 – 55	(47)
knee, seated	England	49.5	43 – 54.7	(3)
(see fig 28)	France	48.8	44.6– 53.0	(51)
	Switzerland	47.1	42.1– 52.1	(45)
Back of knee to floor,	Germany	43	39 – 47	(47)
when sitting	USA	37.8	–	(49)
	England	39.4	36.6– 42	(3)
	France	38.5	34.3– 42.7	(51)
	Switzerland	37.4	28.6– 46.6	(45)
Front edge of knee-back	Germany	57	51 – 63	(47)
(Seated length to knee)	USA	59.4	–	(49)
	England	55.9	51 – 61	(3)
	France	55.5	50.5– 60.5	(51)
Elbow height	Germany	24	19 – 29	(47)
above seat	USA	22.9	–	(49)
	France	23.5	18.3– 28.7	(51)
	England	23.7	20.5– 26.9	(53)
	England	22.9	21.2– 25.4	(3)

Space needs in relation to furniture and fitments

First let us deal with the relationship of the human body to working surfaces particularly to table tops.

Working heights when seated

When seated as much as when standing, the rule of thumb set out on page 24 must be observed: that the hands are at their best in both power and precision when the elbows are at the sides and bent at right angles (33). When the height of the seat is 40–42 cm the elbow height above the floor of a woman is about 63–65 cm and of a man, 64–66 cm. If we allow for a necessary 2 cm clearance between the arms and the table top, a table height of 61–63 cm is ideal for women and 62–64 cm for men. On the other hand, women require knee room of 63 cm beneath the table, that for men being 66 cm. With a table

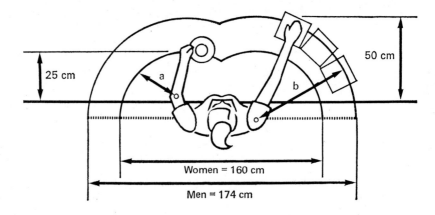

		Men cm	Women cm
Working field a with the elbows lowered	$\bar{x}$ $T\,95$	40 36–44	36 32–40
Grasping-circle b from shoulder joint	$\bar{x}$ $T\,95$	55 47–63	50 42–58

Figure 27   Horizontal reach for grasping and for working on a surface 3–5 cm below the level of the elbows   The values are calculated from French (62), Swiss (45) and American (58) records

top 2 cm thick, the lowest possible height for the table therefore becomes 65–68 cm, a little higher than the ideal height.

Table-heights such as this are suitable for manual work requiring a limited amount of strength. Similar heights are needed for using a typewriter, since the keyboard stands 10–15 cm above the table top. Higher tables are desirable for very fine skilled work, as well as for writing, drawing and reading, because at these occupations it is more comfortable to rest on one's elbows. Under these conditions most authors recommend table heights of between 70 and

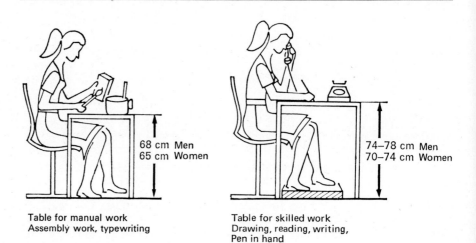

Table for manual work
Assembly work, typewriting

Table for skilled work
Drawing, reading, writing,
Pen in hand

Figure 28   Heights recommended for tables for work when seated

78 cm, and this is the preferred height for a dining table. Since these heights are suited to the needs of a taller person, a smaller person may need a foot rest; this is strongly recommended for a work table. All the recommendations for working heights when seated are set out in *Figure 28*.

Working heights when standing

General principles

Most authors recommend that the working-height for standing activities should be suited both to the height of the elbows above the floor and to the requirements of the manual operations being carried out. Furthermore it is occasionally necessary to work out a special height to suit the nature of the work, or the tools or working habits of the operator. If the work calls for the application of considerable force with contributions from the muscles of the back and shoulders then the bench top must be distinctly lower than the level of the elbows. Higher levels are suitable for manual operations which do not require much strength: for such jobs the bench top should generally be 10–15 cm below elbow height, depending on the amount of handling of boxes and other containers, working tools and materials which takes place there.

To relieve the muscles of the back during very delicate work the elbows may be rested on the bench, as in seated work, and this requires a bench top above elbow level. *Figure 29* illustrates working heights for standing work.

Preferred working-heights according to Ward and Kirk

Ward and Kirk (53) with the help of 56 female subjects, studied the most convenient working heights for activities equivalent to ordinary kitchen work. The average size of the participants was 162.5 cm in height, 99.7 cm for elbow height when standing, and 61.2 cm for elbow height when seated. The average value for the preferred working heights and the corresponding distances from elbow to work surface are collated in *Table 39*.

These results are in good overall agreement with the guiding principles given above. They suggest that working heights that are considered right by the operator are also physiologically correct.

Bench tops cannot be as low as those found by *Ward and Kirk* (53) to be desirable, because of the need to leave knee room for people to sit at their

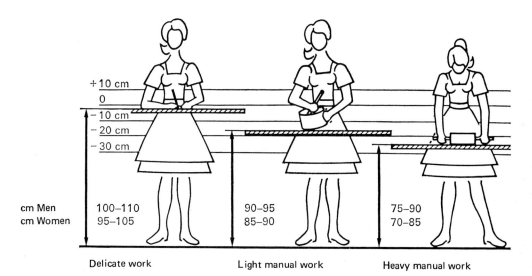

	+10 cm		
	0		
	−10 cm		
	−20 cm		
	−30 cm		
cm Men	100–110	90–95	75–90
cm Women	95–105	85–90	70–85
	Delicate work	Light manual work	Heavy manual work

Figure 29   Heights recommended for tables for standing work   The horizontal zero line is that of elbow height which on average is 104 cm for men and 98 cm for women

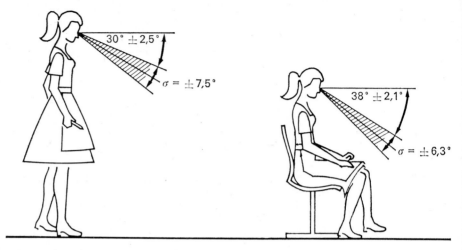

Figure 30   Preferred inclinations of the head when working standing up and sitting down   After Lehmann and Stier (46)

work. For this reason these authors suggested adjustable working surfaces in kitchens, so that the surfaces can be lowered to suit persons with relatively short legs.

Attitude of the head

For both standing and sitting the angle of the head depends upon the place of origin of visual information. The head is held in position by the static effort of the neck muscles, and the visual information ought to be so arranged that the direction in which the gaze is most frequently directed causes the least static strain in these muscles and the least possible spinal curvature in the neck and chest. For this reason *Lehmann and Stier* (46) investigated the most desirable angles of the head and direction of the gaze. Their findings are set out in *Figure 30*.

The most suitable angle of the head with the least static neck strain is obtained under the following conditions:

The angle between the main direction of gaze and the horizontal must lie between 32° and 44° when seated and between 23° and 37° when standing

The best location for the most important sources of visual information thus lies within these limits.

Table 39   Preferred heights for working surfaces   Details of 56 research subjects, female. After Ward and Kirk (53)

Attitude	Activity	Working surface above floor (cm)	Elbow-height to working surface (cm)
Standing	above working surface	88	+ 11.9
Standing	on working surface	91	+ 8.8
Standing	using force on surface	87.5	+ 12.2
Sitting	above working surface	60	+ 1.2
Sitting	on working surface	64	− 2.8
Sitting	using force on surface	61.5	− 0.15

Elbow-room when stooping or bending the body

Many household activities call for the body to be held in an unnatural position. Examples are a kneeling position when holding an object 30–60 cm from the floor or bending the back while making beds.

Bent attitudes like these are undesirable, but nowadays are often unavoidable. It is important, however, that even unnatural bodily attitudes should be impeded as little as possible, since in a restricted space the 'unnaturalness' of the attitude can be aggravated by cramped conditions.

We have found no systematic investigations concerning space requirements in flexed positions of the body. The norms and recommendations that are put forward in the literature must be estimates only, based on anthropometric data.

When leaning forwards the measurement needed is that from head to buttocks. This measurement never appears in the literature, but it must be roughly the same as the length of the body above the seat. Hence the following approximate values can be extracted from *Tables 37, 38.*

Distance head–seat
medium-sized men (average)   90 cm
big men (97.5%)   97 cm
medium-sized women (average)   85 cm
big women (97.5%)   92 cm

To this anatomical minimum must be added a certain amount of space above the head and behind the seat to allow for movement. We reckon that the tolerance must be comparatively large because when a person stoops he has a poor idea of how much room there is behind him, and is also afraid of banging his head. *Robins* (70) found that when walking upright down a corridor there must be 7 cm of free space on either side if locomotion is not to be impeded. In the same way we estimate that when the back is bent there needs to be 10 cm both ahead and behind. This is necessary to avoid the risk of bumping into fixtures or furniture. Our recommendations are given in *Figure 31.*

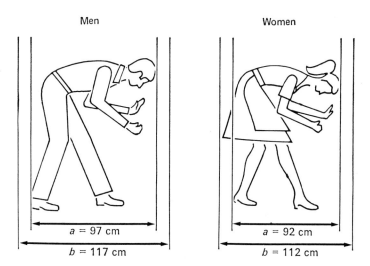

Men   Women

a = 97 cm   a = 92 cm
b = 117 cm   b = 112 cm

Figure 31   The space required for stooping if the body is likely to bump against furniture or walls, either in front or behind   Figure *a* gives the dimensions of large men and women, and covers 97.5% of people. Figure *b* shows the space necessary for stooping

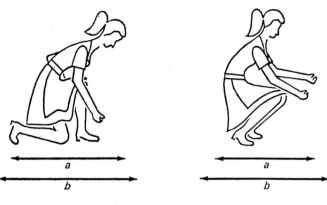

Resting on one knee   Squatting

Large men: Large women: Large men: Large women:
a = 102 cm   a = 97 cm   a = 90 cm   a = 85 cm
b = 117 cm   b = 112 cm   b = 110 cm   b = 105 cm

Figure 32   Space required for squatting on the haunches, or kneeling on one knee   All values are our own estimates, and apply to large men and women. a = anatomical measurement. b = space necessary

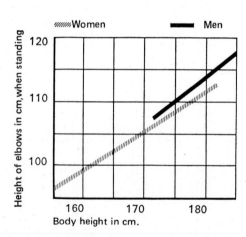

Figure 33   Relation of elbow height to total height   Drawn from data given by Thiberg (44)

Table 40   Preferred working heights for various activities in the kitchen
After Steidl and Bratton (18) where the original references can be traced.

Authors	Year	Washing-up	Whipping cream	Rolling and kneading	Cutting (chopping)	Ironing
Wilson, Roberts & Thayer	1937	82	80	86	90	83
Bratton	1959	84	81	88	92	87

If the hands have to grasp or manipulate anything close to the floor, a person can either kneel or squat. Our estimates of the room needed in these two attitudes are set out in *Figure 32*. Since no direct measurements are available in this context the basic anatomical measurements must be taken from anthropometric data.

The figures that we have recommended for consideration are considerably higher than the ones that are occasionally found in the literature. The latter usually correspond only to average values for the basic anatomical requirements, which is definitely insufficient.

Space needs and working heights for kitchen fitments

Preferred heights according to Steidl and Bratton

Steidl and Bratton (18), collated the results of a series of American studies. *Table 40* shows the average preferred height for working in the kitchen, and *Table 41* the preferred elbow height above the working surfaces.

Working with containers or receptacles necessitates a lower working height. Another interesting finding is that *the preferred distance from elbow height to working surface is linked with the height of the elbow from the ground. In taller people with ground–elbow heights 10 cm greater than average, the preferred distance to working surface increases by 6–7 cm.* This must mean that with increasing elbow heights the back becomes increasingly bent, and one might ask whether this is a matter of habit with taller people. In 1951

Sink and cooker

Bloch and Gfeller (64) studied working heights for sinks and gas cookers preferred by 12 female research subjects. They found that variations of $\pm 3\%$ from the optimum were acceptable. In general their studies established that a working level 10 cm below the elbows was most convenient when standing. They established the most favourable height for the sink rim at between 90–95 cm and for the cooker at 80–85 cm. The authors recommend a height of 93 cm for the sink and 83 cm for the cooker. Moreover they are of the opinion that whenever a compromise is necessary the cooker should be matched to the sink because more working time in the kitchen is spent at the sink than at the cooker.

Body dimensions and working heights according to Thiberg

Thiberg (44) recently analysed the relationship of preferred working heights to stature and elbow height, and calculated the regression coefficient and correlation coefficients in each case.

Figure 33 indicates the relationship between stature and elbow height for women and for men. As a first approximation we can say that if standing height increases by about 10 cm, elbow height increases by about 8 cm. The relationship between these two measurements is very similar in men and women, but not quite identical: the increase in elbow height is rather less in women.

Table 41 **Preferred height of elbow above the working surface in the kitchen**
Details from 500 female research subjects. After Steidl and Bratton (18)

Elbow height above floor	Preferred distance from elbows to working surface (cm)				
	Washing-up	Whipping cream	Rolling and kneading	Cutting (chopping)	Ironing
91.4	12.7	15.2	8.9	3.8	8.9
94	14	15.2	8.9	5.1	10.2
96.5	15.2	17.8	11.4	6.4	12.7
99	16.5	20.3	12.7	8.9	14
101.6	17.8	21.6	14	10.2	15.8
104.1	20.3	22.9	16.5	11.4	17.8
106.7	21.6	24.1	16.5	12.7	19
109.2	22.9	26.7	19	15.2	20.3
Average	17.8	21.6	14	10.2	15.2

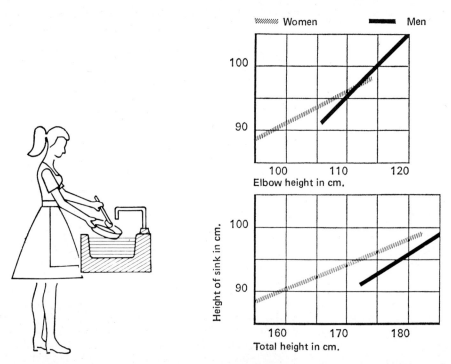

Figure 34   Relationship of the preferred height for a sink to elbow height and total height   Drawn from data taken from Thiberg (44)

Sink-height according to Thiberg

Figure 34 illustrates the preferred height for the sink (upper edge) in relation to elbow height and stature. In these experiments the preferred height of the sink for males increased at the same rate as elbow height, whereas for women the rate of increase was rather less than those of elbow height or stature. Again, this can only mean that tall women bend down to their work at the sink more than short women, and that this effect is more marked than in males. If the average size of a Swiss woman is taken as an example, it can be seen from the diagram that *a woman with a body-length of 160 cm or with an elbow height of 95 cm would prefer a sink height of 90 cm.*

The results of *Thiberg* (44) are in good general agreement with those of *Bloch and Gfeller* (64). In contrast, *Steidl and Bratton* (18), found a preference for considerably lower sink heights; the reasons for this difference remain obscure.

The ironing table

As already mentioned above, *Knowles* (22) and other American authors (18) studied preferred working heights while ironing. On average these lay between 83 and 87 cm, for which heights, according to *Bratton* (18), the preferred distance from elbow to working surface ranged between 8 and 20 cm (mean 15 cm).

In Switzerland, *Bloch and Müller* (65) studied the preferred working height and the working technique of 16 female research subjects when ironing at a hydraulically adjustable table. Standing heights ranged from 150 to 171.5 cm, irons of 1.4 kg and 2.4 kg weights being used. The results are given in *Table 42*.

Stature had a considerable effect on preferred height, the weight of the iron having little effect. *As a rough approximation it can be said that women of medium height (153–169 cm) preferred working heights between 80 and 85 cm.*

Table 42   Preferred height of working surface when ironing standing up, with a light iron (1.4 kg) and a comparatively heavy one (2.4 kg) After Bloch and Müller (65)

Height of person ironing	Preferred working height (cms)	
	light iron	heavy iron
150	77	71.4
151	77	75.9
152	78.5	–
152.7	75.8	–
153	80.1	80
159	83.4	83
164	82.6	81.1
164	83.5	–
165	89	–
168	82.1	–
168	82.4	–
168.8	85.3	84.1
169.5	91.5	88
171.5	90.1	–
171.5	94.4	93.1
171.5	94.5	92.5

Bloch and Müller (65) found a good approximation for the optimum working-height to be : half the stature + the shoe-heel height of the person doing the ironing. For working heights suited to individual requirements, the authors recommend an ironing-board adjustable between 78 and 90 cm, and they further recommend irons with a weight of 1.4–1.9 kg, and a loading of 1,000 W, controlled by regulator and thermostat. The ironing-surface should be not smaller than 120 × 60 cm, an area of 150 × 80 cm being most convenient. *Thiberg* (44) also concerned himself with work at the ironing-table. His results are set out in *Figure 35.*

The results indicate that women with statures of 155–165 cm (the commonest heights) need a working height for ironing of between 80–83 cm.

In this field the results of *Thiberg* (44) are in good general agreement with those obtained in the U.S.A. (18) and Switzerland (65).

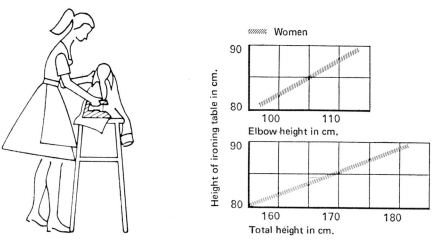

Figure 35   Relationship of the preferred height for an ironing table to elbow height and total height   Drawn from data taken from Thiberg (44)

Table 43   Comfortable and maximum heights of reach for women
Summarised from various sources.

| Country | Source | Heights of reach above floor-level | | |
		Comfortable	Maximum with lower cupboard	Maximum without lower cupboard
Germany	Wenke (66)	65–140	195	–
USA	McCullough (49)	66–137	168	193
England	Ministry of Housing (67)	170	195	200
Holland	Woningbouw Houses (54)	up to 170	185	–

For very tall people (over 170 cm) the preferred working heights obtained by *Thiberg* were somewhat lower than those obtained by *Bloch and Müller* (65). The American (18) and the Swedish (44) studies are also in general agreement that during ironing, comparatively long distances of 15–20 cm from elbow height to table top were preferred.

Space in relation to cupboards and shelves

The following factors should be taken into consideration in the design of cupboards, shelves and all kinds of storage-surfaces:

– the vertical reach as determined anatomically (page 71)
– the most comfortable, and the maximum height that can be reached when standing free or hindered.
– access in relation to the depth of the storage surfaces and their height above ground.

Table 43 collates a few of the most comfortable and the maximum heights that could be reached as revealed by earlier studies. The wide variations are to be attributed in the first instance to different assumptions. Certainly the necessity for access was viewed differently by the authors and by the authorities.

Accessibility

Hemelrijk and Sittig (68) made a detailed analysis of access to storage surfaces, using the armpit as their anatomical reference-point. Three degrees of accessibility were noted:

– easily accessible spaces, without the need either to stoop or to stand on tip-toe.
– spaces which could be looked into only by stooping or kneeling down.
– spaces which could be reached only by standing on tip-toe or on a stool.

Among other things these authors investigated the relation of maximum reach upwards to body-length, and arrived at the following formula:

maximum upward reach = 1.24 × body-length

On the basis of their analysis the authors calculated curves of accessibility for cupboard spaces. From these it can be read off that a woman of average body-length (162 cm) can reach with her hand into a cupboard at the following heights and depths:

Height of shelf	Depth of shelf
200 cm	15 cm
160 cm	50 cm
120 cm	60 cm
80 cm	53 cm
40 cm	45 cm

Table 44   Height of reach for various body lengths and under different circumstances

A = Height of a shelf 30 cm deep, on which the flat of one hand can be laid, without standing on tiptoe, when there is a lower cupboard 60 cm deep and 90 cm high

B = Height of a shelf 30 cm deep, on which both hands can be laid flat, under the same conditions as in A.

C = Height of a shelf 30 cm deep where the back wall can be touched with the tips of the fingers of one hand, under the same conditions as in A

D = as in A, but without the lower cupboard

E = as in B, but without the lower cupboard

F = as in C, but without the lower cupboard

After Berg, Boalt, Holm and Leander (69)

Body-length	A	B	C	D	E	F
155	171	170	157	177	175	164
160	178	177	164	183	181	170
165	185	184	172	190	187	176
170	193	191	179	194	194	183
175	200	198	186	202	199	189

Upward reach under different conditions

Berg, Boalt, Holm and Leander (69) investigated the height of reach of 45 female subjects (155–182 cm in height) in relation to their stature and under various conditions of study. The results are set out in *Table 44.*

Thiberg (44) calculated for men and for women the coefficients of regression and correlation for the relationships between stature and height of reach. These are set out in *Figures 36, 37, 38.*

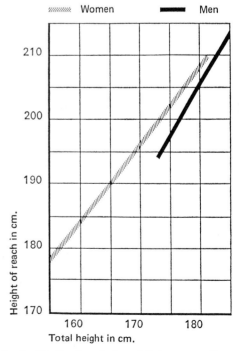

Figure 36   Height that can be reached with the hand placed flat on a surface, while standing, in relation to body size   Drawn from data taken from Thiberg (44)

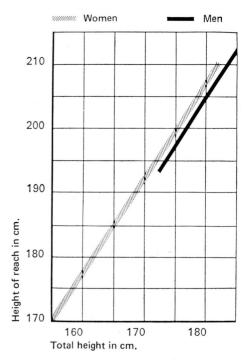

Figure 37   Height that can be reached with the hand placed flat on a surface, while the person is hampered by having to reach over a low obstacle   Drawn from data taken from Thiberg (44)

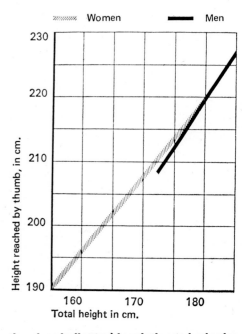

Figure 38   Vertical reach (using the thumb as indicator) in relation to body size
This measurement is critical when assessing fittings which are intended for hanging clothes or other objects. Drawn from data taken from Thiberg (44)

If we take as an example a woman of an average height of 160 cm we arrive at the following heights of reach:

Free space below cupboard, using one hand   186 cm
Cupboard on floor, using one hand   178 cm
Vertical upward reach to tip of thumb   202 cm

Interpretation of results

Investigations in Holland (68) and Sweden (69) have shown that heights of reach are dependent upon body size, the depth of the compartment and obstacles beneath the cupboard.

Heights of reach between 65 and 150 are rated as convenient, depending upon accessibility, and consequently a shelf depth of 60 cm can only be reached without difficulty if the shelf is not higher than 120 cm from the floor. According to the formula 1.24 × body-length, the following maximum heights of reach can be estimated:

Women	Height to tip of finger cm	Grasping height cm
Large	217	206
Medium	199	188
Small	182	171

Since stature plays a decisive part in determining *height of reach, we are of the opinion that shelves in both top and bottom cupboards should always have the maximum possible adjustment, so that they can be adjusted to individual needs.*
Recommendations for heights of reach in kitchens are summarised again on page 148.

Space at washbasins

The space needed when attending to one's toilet in front of various items of sanitary equipment has mostly been worked out from known anatomical data. These data, which have often found their way into 'norms' and other recommendations, will be presented on page 150. In the present section we shall

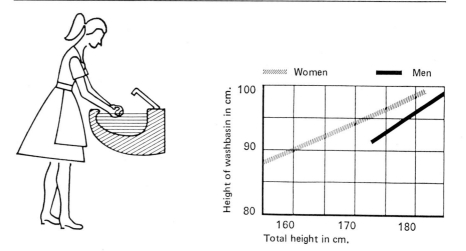

Figure 39   Preferred height for a wash basin in relation to total height   Height of wash basin = distance from floor to upper edge of basin. Drawn from data taken from Thiberg (44)

mention only the research of *Thiberg* (44) on washbasin height in relation to stature. The results of this survey are shown in *Figure 39.*

Finally from the averages and from the 95% confidence limits of the normal distribution of body heights one can derive values that are summarised in *Table 45.*

'Norms' for washbasin heights lie between 80 and 85 cm. These figures are too low for adults, but at the same time it is to be expected that children with much smaller heights will often need to use washbasins. Considering this, it seems that a norm of 80–85 cm is an acceptable compromise.

Table 45   Preferred heights for washbasins   Extracted from the regression curve of Thiberg (44), values marked* being extrapolated. Small and large persons are within the 95% confidence limits according to reference (47)

Persons	Height in cm	Height of basin in cm
Men		
– small	158	83*
– medium	172	92
– large	186	98
Women		
– small	147	85*
– medium	161	90
– large	175	96

Space in rooms and passages

Systematic analyses of the needs of passage have so far been carried out only for kitchens, and so only these can be discussed here.

Transit studies in the kitchen

These studies were based upon the idea that with a suitable kitchen lay-out the amount of walking could be reduced and working time shortened. At the same time transit studies would form a basis on which to plan the arrangement of work places to suit natural movements during kitchen work.

Study of the objectives of kitchen work shows that for a right-handed person, the focus of work shifts from left to right in the following sequence:

Sink – main working surface – cooker – storage area.

Most studies show that the most frequent movements are those between sink, working surface and cooker. Movements to the refrigerator and the larder are equally common. Particularly thorough studies were made by *Steidl* (71) in the U.S.A. and *Stübler* (72) in Germany.

The rational arrangement of working centres can be checked by means of the work-triangle, a device used in America as a means of assessment. It is based on the distances apart of refrigerator, sink and cooker. *The sum of these distances should not exceed 7 m in small to medium-sized kitchens, nor 8 m in big kitchens.*

In Germany, the so-called 'Fadenstudie' (line-studies) method has often been used, in which all the paths followed in the course of a particular job are recorded and drawn as lines in a ground plan of the kitchen. The more often a path is marked by a line, the more prominent it becomes on the ground-plan. When assessing the results of a 'fadenstudie' the following criteria must be established:

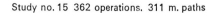

Study no. 19 471 operations. 329 m. paths   Study no. 15 362 operations. 311 m. paths

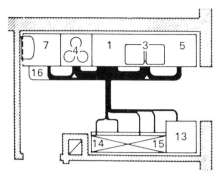

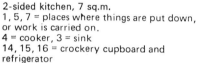

2-sided kitchen, 7 sq.m.
1, 5, 7 = places where things are put down,
or work is carried on.
4 = cooker, 3 = sink
14, 15, 16 = crockery cupboard and
refrigerator

U-shaped kitchen, 6.2 sq.m.
1, 2, 5, 6, = places where things are
put down, or work is carried on.
4 = cooker, 3 = sink
13, 14, 15, 19 = cupboards and
refrigerator

**Figure 40   Comparative line-study (Fadenstudie) of a working kitchen,
2-sided and U-shaped**   Thick lines lead to cooker, sink and major working places.
The superiority of the first arrangement is shown by the smaller number of crossing paths,
and the relaxed progress of the work. After Uhland, Deist and Stübler (73)

— few paths crossing each other.
— few long paths.
— high density of paths to a few working-places.
— closely adjacent starting-points – but nevertheless not closer than 60 cm
  to each other – with dense bundles of lines radiating from them, so as to
  allow ample freedom of movement.

Figure 40 demonstrates two examples of line-studies by *Uhland, Deist and
Stübler* (73).

Space in passages and corridors (*Communication spaces*)

In the literature there are a great many norms and recommendations for the
measurement of communication spaces in homes. These norms are derived
from basic anatomical measurements, to which have been added a loosely
defined allowance for freedom of movement.
The problem of mobility in communications areas was analysed a short time
ago by *Robins* (70). He used cine-photography to record the movements of
research subjects along various passages. The subjects were 11 men of above
average stature (164–193 cm, mean 180 cm) and of 59–97 kg body weight
(the commonest weights lying between 76 and 80 kg). One side of the passage
varied by changing moveable wall-panels. The other side was formed by
people sitting on chairs with their backs to the passage-way. The research
subjects were required to go along the passage repeatedly, so that their
behaviour in relation to the width of the passage could be recorded and
analysed. Assessment of the minimum breadth of passage was based upon
two criteria:

— passage with unrestricted mobility.
— passage not requiring twisting or turning.

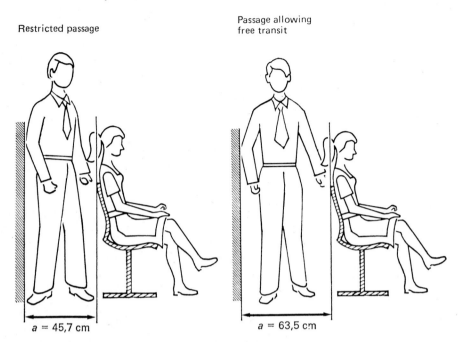

Restricted passage

Passage allowing
free transit

a = 45,7 cm

a = 63,5 cm

**Figure 41   Posture during transit though an unrestricted passage way (right)
and one that is restricted (left)**   a = narrowest point of passage. After Robins (70)

The minimum passage-way was defined as that in which the subject did not
need to make any compensatory movements. During a further series of experiments, behaviour while sitting down and getting up from a dining-table was
analysed using a similar technique. Two typical kinds of behaviour while
passing along a corridor are represented in *Figure 41*, while *Figure 42* gives the
values obtained by *Robins* (70) for passage between the wall and the row of
chairs.

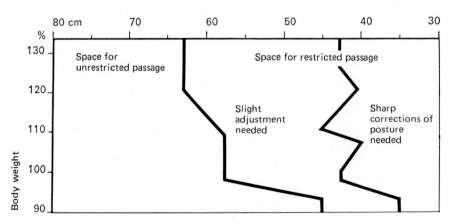

**Figure 42   Width of passage ways for unrestricted and for restricted transit,
in relation to weight of body**   100% = average body weight (i.e. 72.5 kg) (corrected
for age and height). Average height 180 cm in shoes. After Robins (70)

The borderline between free and restricted passage varied from 46 cm for the lightest to 63.5 cm for the heaviest of the research subjects

Robins (70) deduced that the following were the correct values for the passage between the wall and the chairs in his experiment.

Minimum width of passage
- *for restricted mobility*   *46cm*
- *for unrestricted mobility*   *63.5 cm*

The following norms are given in the literature for a similar situation:

England, Ministry of Housing (67)	60 cm
Sweden, recommendation by *Berglund* (74)	55 cm
U.S.A., recommendation by *McCullough* (49)	66 cm
Dutch recommendation (54)	60 cm

The results obtained by *Robins* (70) allow an estimation of the space necessary between the body and the walls to assure complete freedom of movement. According to *Kroemer* (47) and *Murrell* (3) the following distances should be allowed for the breadth of the hips:

Men:	Mean, 35 cm	97.5% value: 40 cm
Women:	Mean, 37 cm	97.5% value: 42 cm

Robins (70) did not measure the hips of his 11 men, but from their height we can deduce that their hips must have been about 40 cm across. It follows from this that *the free space between the hips and the walls of the passage must have at least 12 cm on either side.*

The experiments of *Robins* (70) on getting up from a dining-table showed that for a big man to get up without hindrance it was necessary to have a distance of 76.2 cm between the edge of the table and the wall. This is somewhat more than the recommendations made in the literature.

Robins' (70) work is presented here in such detail because in our opinion more experimental techniques for determining the minimum width of passages is needed in building research.

Moreover, even if the theoretical minima have been arrived at from a common-sense point of view, there still remains an uncertainty undesirable where minimum requirements are concerned.

The numerous recommendations and norms for corridors and communications areas in dwellings will be mentioned later when dealing with individual rooms.

Psychological needs for space

The volume of rooms and mental well-being

Human space requirements from the standpoint of anatomy and physical needs are well understood. Even if many of the measurements are based on data that have not been fully verified, common-sense usually allows the creation of useful recommendations and norms for the use of household fitments and furniture, and for passages, stairs and other building details. All these measurements, however, are partial measurements; that is, they concern only bits of the room.

There are no practical criteria for assessing the total volume of a room, or its proportions, but in spite of this, minimum heights, areas and often volumes as well figure in the building regulations of many authorities. These minimum measurements are usually a compromise between the economical viewpoint and a very vague concept of what space people need.

Open questions

What do we know about people's experience in relation to living-space? What do they recommend for small rooms and for big ones? Do they prefer the security of a small room to the liberty of a big one? What part do experience, education, imagination, the aesthetic picture, and social factors play in building up the image which determines what size of room is chosen? The list of questions could be extended still further, but there are no answers to them that have been verified, or even quantified. Only vague reflections and theories can be formulated. With the undoubted tendency of recent years for homes to become smaller, the question of what space is necessary for psychological well-being has become very real.

Arising out of considerations such as these, the 'Centre scientifique et technique du bâtiment' in Paris, and the University in Lund (Sweden) have set up interdisciplinary working-parties, composed of architects and psychologists, who have begun research into experience in spatial requirements. Since these studies are still in progress we cannot give any conclusive results here.

Swedish work

With the aid of model rooms of 100×100×50 cm and variable size, *Acking and Küller* (75) studied the reactions of 10 research subjects in different room volumes. In a second experiment the subjects had to vary the depth of the model room until the volume seemed to them to be the same as that of an adjacent standard model. The result showed that the proportions of a room significantly affected people's impression of its size. Walls in the proportion of 1.5 : 1 gave the impression of the room being smallest; longer and more nearly square rooms were effectively bigger.

In the second experiment walls in the proportion of 2.4 : 1 gave the smallest impression.

The authors would not generalise from this result, because the experimental situation with a model one fifth natural size cannot be rated as equivalent to a room of natural size. For this reason the experiments were continued with a full-sized room. Prefabricated units were used to construct four rooms, of which two were square and two had walls in the proportion of 2 : 1. One room of each type had a window, and in one series of experiments, the rooms were furnished. The results can be summarised as follows:

A room with walls in the proportion of 2 : 1 always seems smaller than a square room, and a furnished room smaller than an empty one. A room with a black floor seemed smaller than a room with a floor in pale colours (reflection coefficient 50%). If the lighting was at the same intensity in the two rooms the presence or absence of a window made no difference to the apparent volume. The same authors (76) have studied recently the effects of wall colour on the impression of size.

French research

Under the direction of *Coblentz, Jeanpierre* (77, 78, 79) carried out studies of the impression of space in an experimental room of variable dimensions. In a first series of experiments with 36 and 48 persons, the depth of the room was varied between 2.5 and 4 m. It appeared that 66% of the research subjects could detect a change in depth of the room of even 12 cm., while 95% were aware of an alteration of 24 cm.

In a second series of experiments, *Jeanpierre* used a room that could be varied in breadth between 150 and 400 cm, in length between 100 and 550 cm, and in height between 200 and 300 cm. The three variable units could be moved either together or independently. The experimental arrangement made it possible to determine the size and proportions that were preferred by the subjects.

In a preliminary experiment with only 8 subjects, the height of the room was varied between 200 and 300 cm. The following provisional results were obtained:

For a room with a floor area of 12 square metres, the following average heights were preferred:

– people standing	2.54 m
– people sitting	2.47 m

For a room with a floor-space of 30 square metres, the following heights were preferred:

– people standing	2.70 m
– people sitting	2.64 m

No connection could be detected between the size of the person and the size of room he or she preferred. Although these results do not provide a sufficient basis for generalisations, they nevertheless give one reason to think that the research subjects expressed a preference for the same height of room as they were used to in their own homes. At any rate this suspicion shows that research into psychological space preferences is full of problems.

4 The Physiological Design of Household Furniture

Summary

The stress of work must be offset by sufficient rest and sleep. Alertness, tiredness and sleep are all under the direction of the brain. The furniture of a home must be suited to the physiological needs of rest and sleep as well as to those of certain forms of work and leisure activities.

Sitting is a natural attitude for the body which reduces the static muscular effort of the legs, hips and back.

From an orthopaedic point of view seats should promote a seated attitude that reduces bending strain on the back and prevents the development of curvature of the spine. For young people they should permit alternation between a forward and a backward sitting position on the one hand and active straightening of the spine, with slight lordosis of the lower spine on the other. When sitting normally the pelvis is pushed back and the sacrum held in a position almost at right angles to the ground. Orthopaedic considerations require that backwards rotation of the pelvis should be minimised by suitable supports for the loins and the lower back to counteract curvature of the spine. In this way strain on the back musculature is minimised.

Ergonomists have analysed sitting attitudes in relation to habits, comfort and anthropometric data. Research into appropriate forms of seating, and orthopaedic measurements of bending forces in the spine have produced similar results: sitting attitudes that are comfortable also meet orthopaedic requirements.

Recommendations for the design of seating can be summarised as follows:

Armchairs for leisure

- should permit complete relaxation of the muscles of the back, while holding the spine in a natural attitude.
- the back-rest should consist of a convex support for the loins at the height where the sacrum joins the lumbar vertebrae, and have a slightly concave shape at the height of the thoracic vertebrae.
- the seat should slope at 20° to 26° and the angle between the back-rest and the seat should be 105°–110°.
- the seat should be 39–41 cm high and 47–48 cm deep.
- arm-chairs should be well padded. As a rule, the buttocks should sink into the cushions by 6–10 cm.

Seats for working

- working seats should be suitable for a forward and an upright attitude, with occasional periods of leaning back on the backrest or lumbar support.
- the height of the seat should be 27–30 cm less than that of the table-top.
- the height of seat and lumbar support should be adjustable as far as possible.
- to allow very small subjects to adjust themselves to a given working height (that of the table), foot rests should be provided with a height range of 0–18 cm.
- working seats should be lightly padded on both seat and back-rest.
- the ideal working seat should have a mechanism for altering the slope of both seat and backrest.

Multipurpose seats

- multipurpose seats should be suitable both for sitting forward and for reclining.

- the back rest should have slight padding at the small of the back and a slight concavity at chest height: it must extend at least 85 cm above the floor, as long as the seat is not higher than 43 cm.
- when compressed, the seat cushions should be not less than 43 cm from the floor.
- the height of the seat should be 43–46 cm.
- a pad of 2–4 cm of foam rubber over the whole seat is recommended.

The bed

- The bedstead and mattress must provide:
  good retention of warmth.
  comfort when lying down.
  sufficient absorption and permeability to allow ventilation.

Bed dimensions given in the literature should be taken as minima. We recommend the following measurements:

Length	210 cm
Breadth (single bed)	100–120 cm
Breadth (double bed)	180 cm
Height above floor	60–70 cm
Space for movement round bed	66–100 cm

- bed springs and mattress must conform to every change in sleeping attitude so that the spine keeps its natural shape while all the musculature is relaxed.
- suggestions concerning harder underlays are problematical and need further investigation.

Physiological aspects of sleep and relaxation

It is clear that provision for sleep and relaxation is one of the most important requirements in the home, so we will start with these two functions.

The sleep – work – leisure cycle

All living creatures exhibit a rhythm of energy consumption and recuperation, or in simple terms, of work and rest. This rhythm is a 'sine qua non' of human life. The cycle is necessary because, while the internal organs are self-regenerative, proper regeneration can only occur when the organs are in a resting state. While the sleeping and waking rhythm predominates in restorative activities in the body, there are other cycles which contribute. For example, people interpolate rest pauses in the course of their work, and regular mealtimes are similarly times of relaxation. A large part of leisure time serves for relaxation and is the counterpart of the work periods.

A review of human habits during the present century demonstrates a general practice of dividing the 24-hour cycle into three parts: 8 hours sleep, 8 hours work, 8 hours leisure. This three-part cycle is universally regarded as sensible and desirable, though there are many departures from it, for example housewives and many women who go out to work. It is likely to persist in principle even if the working day became shorter. Part of the extended leisure time is likely to be given over to work of another sort, such as further education.

Physiological control

The sleep – work – relaxation cycle is controlled by chemical and nervous processes. At the head of the control system lie two central nervous mechanisms which work in opposition, one stimulating and the other inhibiting activity.

The activating system

The activating system keeps the organism awake. Impulses which originate in the brain spread by way of the autonomic nervous system throughout the body to ensure physical and mental readiness for action. The activating system maintains this state of readiness and, in a crisis, alerts all parts of the body. The system responds to the hormone adrenalin, which is thus able to raise the sensitivity and capacity for action of the organism. The activating system is also responsive to all kinds of sensory stimuli, including noise, pain and light. Impressions from the outside world stimulate – and in extreme cases, alarm – the organism through its activating system and cause it to react to external conditions in appropriate ways. Thus the activating system has a key position in the links between the environment and the human body.

The inhibitory system

The inhibitory system works in opposition, reducing alertness and readiness for action. Its output creates in the brain the sensation of weariness, and it lulls the internal organs into a state of relaxation, assimilation and recuperation. Increased activity of the inhibitory system brings about sleep. The repressor system primarily reflects internal conditions in the body. It is probable that chemical transmitters act as intermediaries between the internal organs and the repressor system.

When the activating system is dominant in the brain, a person feels fresh and ready for action. When the inhibitory system predominates, the subject feels tired, and wants to stop work and relax. These processes are shown diagrammatically in *Figure 43*.

The conflicting effects of the two systems may be compared with a balance. This picture demonstrates what we also know instinctively, that our state of readiness may lie anywhere between the extremes of 'Sleep' or 'Panic'. The sensation of tiredness is a signal for an increased need of rest, which occurs naturally each evening and leads to sleep.

Sleep

We know from experience we need sleep. Repeated nights of reduced or disturbed sleep make themselves felt in great weariness, nervousness and irritability. Physiologists have repeatedly shown that prolonged shortage of sleep results in psychic disturbances including hallucinations and other psychotic symptoms.

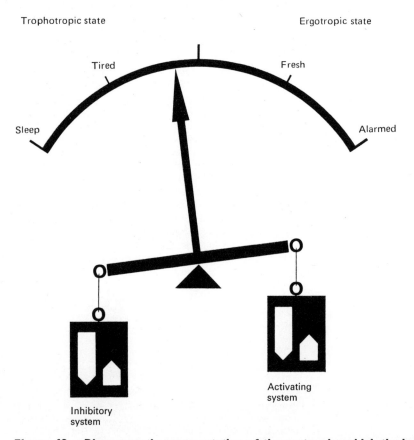

Figure 43   Diagrammatic representation of the system by which the brain is influenced in the direction either of being ready for work (ergotropic state) or for relaxation and recuperation (trophotropic state) This system can be compared with a balance, where more weight on one side or the other will tilt it over towards weariness and sleep, or freshness and alertness

Normal and disordered sleep

With the introduction of electroencephalography – recording and analysing the electrical activity of the brain – a new insight into the phenomenon of sleep has become possible. Two different states of sleep can be distinguished: normal and disordered sleep. Normal sleep is recognisable by the synchronisation of electrical activity in the periphery of the brain: the majority of nerve-cells discharge simultaneously to produce a picture in the electroencephalograph of a high-amplitude wave which decays slowly. Normal sleep occupies about two-thirds of the sleeping period. Disordered sleep, which occupies about a third of our sleeping time, is recognisable by a desynchronisation of electrical activity, visible on the electroencephalograph as a wave of low amplitude and abrupt decay. This form of electroencephalogram is similar to that observed during a state of active concentration. For this reason disordered sleep is also called 'paradoxical' sleep, during which rapid eye-movements may be observed, combined with a complete relaxation of muscles over the rest of the body. It is during these periods of sleep that dreams mostly occur.

Normal sleep can be further subdivided into light, medium and deep sleep. In man and domestic animals the last stage can be reached only when no external disturbances intrude. Deep sleep is rare among wild animals, as these must keep alert for possible dangers in the world outside.

No one knows the meaning of these electrical phenomena, nor what significance the periods of sleep have for the process of recuperation.

On the other hand we do know that during sleep certain recuperative processes occur, in which the restitution of enzymes in the interior of the cells is of particular importance. Moreover, physiologists assume that all the general processes of assimilation take place to a large extent during sleep.

General conclusions

To give people the conditions necessary for sleep and relaxation in their homes, one must reduce as far as possible all stimuli that will excite the activating system. Only then can the repressor system create the mood for relaxation and sleep. Appropriate measures include:

– exclusion of external noise, including the neighbours.
– exclusion of bright light.
– provision of furniture which ensures that the muscles relax as much as possible, by holding the body in a natural posture.

The problems of excluding noise and bright light will be dealt with in the relevant chapter. Here the physiological design of furniture will be discussed.

Seating

Physiological and orthopaedic aspects of sitting posture

Why do people sit down?

Sitting down is a natural human posture. People sit down because they feel that sitting is less fatiguing than standing. That this feeling is correct is corroborated by the following facts: when standing up the joints of the foot, knee and hips are held in position by static muscular activity. When sitting, this muscular effort ceases, and energy consumption is reduced. When standing the blood and tissue fluids tend to accumulate in the legs, a tendency reduced when seated since the relaxed musculature and the lowered hydrostatic pressure in the veins of the legs offer less resistance to the return of blood to the heart. To this extent sitting is better for the circulation than standing. The interference with circulation when standing is also the source of the painful fatigue in the legs that accompanies prolonged standing.

Disadvantages of sitting

Sitting also has certain disadvantages. A sitting posture causes the abdominal muscles to slacken and curves the spine, as well as impairing the functions of some internal organs, especially those of digestion and respiration. Sitting still also imposes a strain on the principal support areas of the body, and in the buttocks, the effects of heavy tissue pressure can progress from discomfort to intolerable pain.

Orthopaedics of sitting

Orthopaedic surgeons have given particular attention to posture and the shape of the spine when seated at school or at work. Postural disorders and spinal complaints, including Scheuermann's disease,* have increased greatly in recent years.

In 1967 *Wespi* (82) observed that 60% of 1740 middle-school pupils examined showed signs of spinal abnormality. In the same year, in Switzerland, 12.5% of 41,674 youths called up for the army were rejected for military service because of spinal defects.

---

*Scheuermann's disease is a disorder of the process of bone formation in the vertebrae. Commonly it also affects the intervertebral discs, leading to stiffness in those parts of the spine that are affected. In extreme cases the vertebrae may be partly fused together.

Causes of postural
disorders

School doctors and orthopaedic specialists are agreed that the causes of postural disorders include the accelerated growth rate and lack of exercise found in young people in modern times. Postural faults and the defective stance that results from these are thought by doctors to be remediable during the growing period, the most important preventive measures being physical training, more physical exercise, and proper seating arrangements. *Scheier* (83) is of the opinion that the final shape of the spinal column depends on the aggregate of all the postures during its growth. *Gschwend* (84) and *Schoberth* (85) consider that sitting for long periods deprives the body of the alternation of stress and relaxation, and as a result the correcting forces remain undeveloped. These authors suggest that it is not so much the postures themselves as the lack of corrective movements that leads to chronic defects. Arising out of this idea *Gschwend* (84) called for a seat for adolescents that would allow the posture to be changed from leaning forward to leaning back, so that uncomfortable positions could be avoided.

Certain studies (86) of office-workers have shown that bent backs and necks, and hunching the shoulders when sitting at a high desk caused fatigue and pain in the shoulders and neck, which, according to *Schoberth* (85) could lead to degeneration in the neck vertebrae.

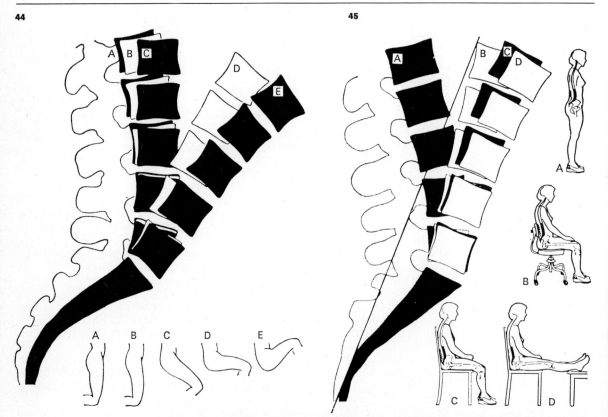

44   **45**

Figure 44   The form assumed by the spine during different attitudes when lying down   Drawn from radiograms of a young and healthy research subject. A–E show the different stages in the bending the hip joint. According to Keegan (96), position D results in a 'normal' posture of the spine

Figure 45   The posture of the spine when standing and sitting   Drawn from radiograms of a healthy young person. A–D show the four bodily postures. Sitting with the hip-joints at 90° brings about a reduction in the amount of lordosis, with a straightening of the lumbar vertebrae. After Keegan (96)

Sitting postures

As explained above, three sitting postures can be distinguished: a forward, an upright. and a backward reclining posture. Forward or backward postures mean the back slopes forward or backward respectively. A forward posture is essentially a working posture, while a backward posture is one of rest and relaxation.

Keegan (92, 96) used X-rays to study the shape of the spine during 34 different attitudes when standing, lying down and sitting. Orthopaedists are of the opinion that when lying down on one's side, with the lower limb held at an angle of about 45° at hip and knee, the spinal column preserves a 'normal' shape, in which the muscles of the back are at their optimum state of relaxation.

Spinal column when lying, sitting and standing

Figure 44 shows the spine when lying down and *Figure 45* when sitting and standing.

A comfortable, normal spinal attitude, with no strain on the vertebrae (lying down) is achieved by having the lumbar vertebrae nearly straight, with a slight lordosis and preferably a flat back. Sitting down with a 90° angle at the hip-joint results in a similar spinal posture. *Keegan* (96) nevertheless thinks that in this seated posture the compressive weight of the upper part of the body is harmful to the lower lumbar vertebrae. On these grounds he recommends for car seats that the backrest should slope well backwards at the level of the shoulder blades and should project forwards in the lumbar region.

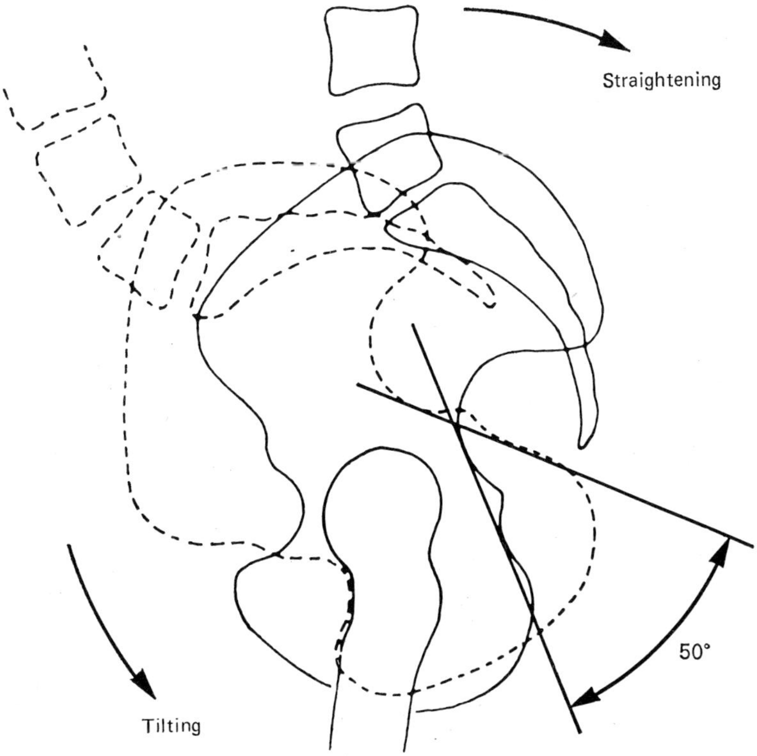

Figure 46   Tilting and straightening of the pelvis   The tilted position is shown in dotted lines. 'Tilting' means rotation of the pelvis forwards, with the sacrum assuming a horizontal position, and with tendency towards lordosis in the lumbar vertebrae. 'Straightening' means rotation of the pelvis backwards, bringing the sacrum into the vertical, and with the lumbar vertebrae becoming steeply upright again. (The sacrum is attached to the end of the vertebrae column, following the last free vertebra.) After Schoberth (85)

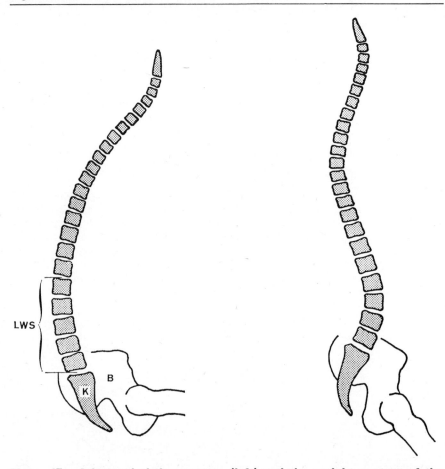

Figure 47   A forward sitting-posture (left) and the upright posture of the spine that results from sitting in the middle or back on the chair (right). K = sacrum. LWS = lumbar spine. B = pelvis   The forward sitting posture is accompanied by a backwards rotation of pelvis and sacrum, and causes a kyphosis of the spine above the lumbar region. ('round back'). Sitting upright is accompanied by a tilting of the pelvis, with the sacrum brought into the horizontal position, and a lordosis of the spinal column

The pelvis and vertebral column when seated

Recently *Schoberth* (85) analysed anew the effects of different sitting postures on the pelvis, distinguishing between a tilted and an upright pelvis. During tilting the whole pelvis rotates forwards around the hip joints, as a result of which the sacrum – the lowest part of the spinal column – makes a corresponding movement and approaches the horizontal. When stooping down from a standing position the pelvis is similarly tilted forwards. On straightening up, the pelvis rotates backwards and the sacrum assumes a more vertical position. Tilting of the pelvis produces lordosis* of the lumbar vertebrae, whereas straightening up flattens this region. The two positions of the pelvis and sacrum can be seen in *Figure 46*.

When a person is sitting in either an upright or a reclining posture and actively straightens up, the pelvis is rotated forwards and a lordosis is produced in the

Lordosis means a curvature of the spine that is convex forwards, in *kyphosis* the convexity is towards the back.

lumbar vertebrae. In contrast, a forward sitting posture is usually accompanied by backward rotation of the pelvis with flattening of the sacrum and lumbar vertebrae: the spine above this level is curved into a well-marked kyphosis (complete kyphosis), which is visible externally as a hunched back. These two seated postures are illustrated in *Figure 47*.

All orthopaedists agree that complete kyphosis – a hunchback – is an undesirable posture to hold for very long. The increased load on the musculature supporting the head produces muscular pain in the neck and the small of the back. They also agree that in many cases a bent back encourages disc trouble. For these reasons seats should be so designed that both in the forward and the backward sitting posture they provide support to the upper edge of the pelvis and the posterior face of the sacrum. The majority of orthopaedists do not advocate a true lordosis of the lumbar region, but wish to avoid excessive kyphosis by means of pelvic supports.

This 'moderate' aim is sensible, since prolonged maintenance of an upright seated posture with a lordosis of the lumbar spine, results in strain on the extensor muscles of the back.

Static activity of the back muscles

Åkerblom (88), *Lundervold* (281), and more recently *Schoberth* (87) and *Floyd and Ward* (26) have measured the electrical activity of the muscles of the back as an indication of static activity. These studies show that there is increased electrical activity when sitting in an exaggeratedly erect posture, and that it falls markedly when a forward sitting posture is assumed. Their subjects preferred the latter posture because the body weight is then balanced on the spinal column, and no static muscular activity is required. *Akerblom* (88) and *Floyd and Ward* (26) also established that, with the use of a back-rest, an erect posture may be assumed without electrical activity in the muscles of the back. *Figure 48* gives the results obtained by *Floyd and Ward* (26). *They proved that a suitable back rest is essential to avoid strain in the back muscles.*

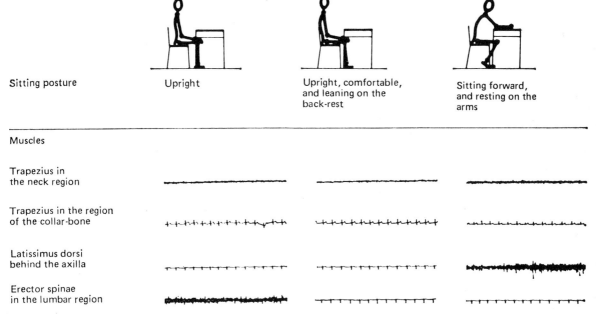

Sitting posture	Upright	Upright, comfortable, and leaning on the back-rest	Sitting forward, and resting on the arms
Muscles			
Trapezius in the neck region			
Trapezius in the region of the collar-bone			
Latissimus dorsi behind the axilla			
Erector spinae in the lumbar region			

Figure 48   Electromyography of the muscles of the back in three sitting postures   Leads taken from the left side. The thickness and height of the trace is a measure of the static effort being made by the back muscles. The small blips occurring regularly result from the activity of the heart. After Floyd and Ward (26)

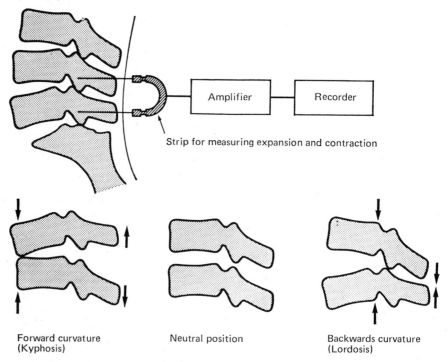

Figure 49   Method of Yamaguchi (89) **for measuring the tension between vertebrae, when the spinal column bends**

Åkerblom (88) concluded from his electromyographic measurements that the forward sitting posture is a distinctly restful attitude. The back muscles are relaxed and the weight of the upper body is borne by the bones, intervertebral discs and ligaments.

Sitting attitudes and intervertebral discs

As discussed on page 34, a curvature of the spine results in an unequal distribution of pressure on the intervertebral discs, one factor in the development of disc troubles. Hence the back has to be kept straight and upright if strains are to be avoided. This is also true of sitting postures, even if the relative forces are apparently smaller than when lifting heavy objects with a bent back. The studies of the Japanese orthopaedist *Yamaguchi* (89) are interesting in this context. In his research subjects, he investigated the forces acting between intervertebral discs and their dynamic responses in seated postures.

Measurement of spinal curvature by Yamaguchi

To measure vertebral compression, *Yamaguchi* inserted needles into the dorsal processes of two lumbar vertebrae. The change in the tension between the two dorsal processes during various sitting postures was recorded electrically. As a standard of reference he measured the tension when the subject was lying on his side with 45° angles at the hips and knees. In this position the intervertebral discs were subjected to minimal compression forces and the position could be taken as neutral.

Measurements were made on 122 persons with backache but without any displacement of the discs that could be seen by X-rays. The technique is shown diagrammatically in *Figure 49*.

In ten subjects the changes in pressure in the discs between the fourth and fifth lumbar vertebrae were measured, using fine needles.

The research subjects sat on a device in which the angle of the seat could be varied in steps of 5° between 0 and 20°. At each step the angle of inclination of the backrest to the seat was increased by 5° at a time from 90–135°. A summary of the results is given in *Figure 50*.

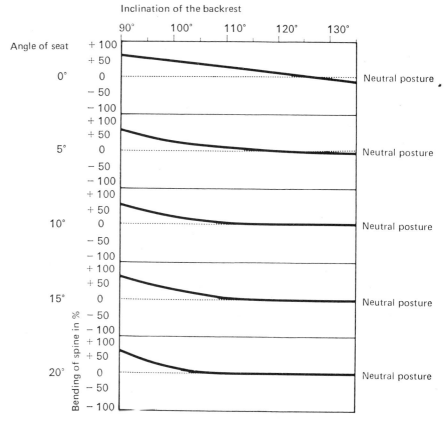

Figure 50   The angle between lumbar vertebrae 4 and 5 in relation to the angle of the seat and the inclination of the backrest   Average values for 122 people studied. The curvatures are expressed as relative percentages. Maximum kyphosis is +100%. Maximum lordosis is − 100%. Neutral posture is designated by 0. After Yamaguchi (89)

Optimal slopes for seat and back-rest

The results show that the neutral attitude (compression force = 0) cannot be achieved if the angle between the seat and the backrest is less than 105°, however large the slope of the seat. A relationship exists between change in the slopes of the seat and the backrest: the smaller the inclination of the seat, the greater must be the angle between seat and back-rest to achieve a neutral attitude. In other words, the more the seat is tilted back, the smaller must be the angle between seat and back-rest. If the slope of the seat is raised from 0° to 20° the angle between the back and the horizontal increases by 5°. To make this relationship easier to understand *Table 46* collates those

Table 46   Angle between the seat of a chair and its back rest, for varying angles of slope of the seat, to maintain the 4th and 5th lumbar vertebrae in a neutral attitude, with zero curvature   After Yamaguchi (89)

Angle between seat and horizontal °	Angle between seat and backrest °
0	125
5	123
10	120
15	115
20	110

angles of slope of seat and back-rest which result in a neutral attitude of the vertebrae, with a compression force of nil.

Measurement of the pressures inside the discs leads to similar results, the lowest values being reached when the slope of the seat lies between 15° and 20° and the back-rest between 120° and 125°. From these results *Yamaguchi* (89) draws the conclusion that *the forward sitting posture is associated with high compression forces in the intervertebral discs, and that sitting still for a long time in this position encourages degenerative processes in the intervertebral discs.*

The author therefore recommends work seats that can be altered from time to time between forward and backward sitting postures.

All these physiological and orthopaedic studies suggest the following requirements in the design of furniture for sitting:

Conclusion – deductions from an orthopaedic point of view

- *the seat should be so designed that the sitting posture can be changed frequently. It should have enough free movement for forward and upright postures to be changed periodically to a reclining posture supported by a back rest.*
- *to avoid complete kyphosis and strain on the back, working seats should be provided with back-rests for the lower part of the back which will effectively support the spinal column (including pelvis and sacrum) and relieve the back muscles of the strain of static effort.*
- *too upright a posture with lordosis of the spinal column will quickly lead to muscular fatigue, and must be avoided as a posture for prolonged sitting.*
- *the intermediate sitting posture with a straight lumbar region and slight forwards curvature of the upper body is a restful posture* in which the back muscles are relaxed and the weight of the upper body is borne solely by the vertebrae, the intervertebral discs and the ligaments. This posture should be adopted from time to time during work.
- *the optimal distribution of force in the discs can be achieved if both seat and back-rest are inclined backwards. This optimal angle should be considered particularly in the design of leisure seating (i.e. armchairs etc.).*

Techniques for ergonomic* research

In the last ten years ergonomics has been concerned to an increasing extent with designing seats to match the physiological, psychological and anthropometric requirements of their use. The principal techniques used up to now have been the analysis of sitting habits and of bodily sensations when seated. Sitting habits were studied by *Branton* (101) in railway trains, by *Floyd and Ward* (26) in schools, and by *Grandjean* and his collaborators (86, 102) in offices and auditoriums. Methods used included cinephotographs and multimoment techniques, but since these results are not applicable to household furniture no more will be said about them here.

Comfort while seated has been analysed by many research workers, and their results have often led to the formulation of principles and guides for seat design. The use of comfort as the criterion in the design of seating can be justified by arguing that orthopaedically unsatisfactory postures are uncomfortable. Certainly, excessive muscular strain brings on fatigue whereas a greater degree of comfort in a restful posture with relaxed muscles must accompany a natural attitude of the spine. Finally seats that are intended for rest and recuperation must provide a high level of comfort, with corresponding muscular relaxation.

Ergonomic methods

When making a comparative study of various types of aircraft seat, *Wachsler and Learner* (97) used the following criteria for recording degrees of comfort:

---

*Ergonomics is an interdisciplinary science which studies the relationships between people and their environments.

- the length of time that a person is prepared to occupy the seat.
- a survey of subjective impressions of comfort, by means of a scale of points running from -4 to $+4$ after 5 minutes, 4 hours and 7 hours of sitting.
- the time needed to produce a sensation of discomfort.
- the localisation of discomfort in the neck, shoulders, back, buttocks or legs.

Assessments of the seats in terms of comfort were the same after 5 minutes' sitting as they were after 4 or 7 hours. The authors find the most reliable measure to be those of 'discomfort in back and buttocks', and the time that it took for symptoms of discomfort to appear.

Jones's studies

Jones (98) studied posture and feelings of comfort in a highly adjustable car driving seat in optimal and all tolerable positions. As a rule it was possible to find *one* position of the seat that lay within toleration limits for all research subjects. Since the research subjects were typical English people, it was possible for Jones to develop a seat, and driving controls, adequate for 98% of English drivers.

Jones (98) values for car-seats are as follows:

Height of seat	30.5 cm
Depth of seat	43 cm
Slope of seat	7°
Angle of inclination of back-rest (between back and vertical when seated)	18°

In a further study *Jones* (98) observed changes in sensation in relation to length of time of sitting. The research subjects scored sensations in five steps from 'no sensation' up to 'painful sensation'. The sensation of 'discomfort' arose in different parts of the body after the following time in the car-seat:

	Hours
shoulders	None after 5 hours
ribs	4
lumbar region	$3\frac{3}{4}$
small of the back	$3\frac{1}{4}$
ischial tuberosities	$2\frac{3}{4}$
buttocks	$2\frac{3}{4}$
upper thighs	3
mid thighs	4
lower thighs	$4\frac{1}{4}$

This finding confirms the opinion of numerous authors *that the pelvis, sacrum and buttocks are the most sensitive parts of the body when seated, and play a decisive part in the comfort of sitting postures.*

Studies of Shackel

Shackel, Chidsey and Shipley (99) divided the degrees of seating comfort into 11 different steps from 'completely relaxed' to 'unbearably painful'. The research subjects had in front of them a questionnaire and opposite each of these verdicts there was a drawing of a column 10 cm high, which had to be marked with a line to indicate the measure of agreement with this description. In a similar way, the research subjects had to give their impression of each seat as it affected 15 different parts of the body, and of the dimensions of different parts of the seat. Finally they had to arrange the test seats into an order of comfort.

Using this technique each of 20 research subjects tested 10 multi-purpose seats in a protracted investigation lasting $3\frac{1}{2}$ hours, each seat being tested at a work-table and at a dining-table. The results showed practically no difference between male and female. The comfort level declined throughout the lengthy test.

The relevant results are given in *Figure 51*.

A few of the seats differed from the rest right from the beginning, whereas others began to seem different only after $1-1\frac{1}{2}$ hours of testing. After the test,

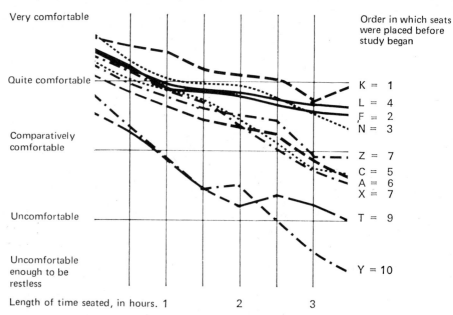

Figure 51   **How comfort diminishes with the passage of time**   K, L, F etc =
10 types of multi-purpose seats. After Shackel, Chidsey and Shipley (99)

the authors could divide the seats into four groups each of approximately
equal comfort. They concluded that different forms of seat were optimal for
the three conditions of the experiment, but that nevertheless it should be
possible to develop a 'compromise chair' that would be acceptable for several
uses. They particularly urged that a multi-purpose seat should be designed
that would permit the assumption of several comfortable postures.
In a second experiment *Shackel* and his colleagues (99) tested whether professional people were the right people to assess the comfort of chairs. It appeared
that they could not give a useful assessment either of the dimensions of the
seat, or of their own impressions of it. Only experimental techniques gave
useful practical results.

Oshima's experiments   A basic study of comfort in relation to seat dimensions has recently been
carried out by *Oshima* (100). On an experimental seat he varied the angle of
the seat between 4° and 10°; the angle of the straight back-rest between 12°
and 20° from the vertical; the height of the seat between 36 and 42 cm, and
the depth of the seat between 37.5 and 43.5 cm. Eight healthy research
subjects had to fill up a questionnaire giving their verdicts on the following
points, whether

— they slid forwards on the seat
— the seat was too shallow.
— they were restless.
— it was tiring.
— they felt areas of pressure.
— they had any feelings of pain.
— the surface was too hard.

The experiment lasted for 30 minutes, and objections and complaints increased
as time went on. The most frequent complaints were about back and buttocks.
The author added up all the objections and complaints and the results are
given in *Table 47*.

Table 47   Totals of all the negative verdicts on different combinations of seat angle and angle of back rest The angles given in brackets are those between seat and back rest. After Oshima (100)

Angle of back rest to vertical °	Angle of seat to the horizontal			
	4°	6°	8°	10°
12	258 (98°)	242 (96°)	257 (94°)	185 (92°)
14	215 (100°)	236 (98°)	283 (96°)	182 (94°)
16	198 (102°)	218 (100°)	256 (98°)	175 (96°)
18	189 (104°)	208 (102°)	192 (100°)	230 (98°)
20	158 106°)	211 (104°)	217 (102°)	176 (100°)

From the table the following tendencies can be deduced:

- angles of 98° between seat and back are always unsatisfactory, and lead to many adverse criticisms.
- seat-angles of 10° – apart from one example – call for few adverse comments.
- back-rests at angles of 18° and 20° give better results in general than smaller angles, except when they are combined with the high seat-angle of 10°.

Oshima (100) made a differential analysis of the relationship between the combination of angles and complaints relating to particular parts of the body. He found among other things that the angle of 98° between seat and back-rest quoted above was especially bad for the neck, arms and buttocks.
Furthermore, the author concerned himself with the effect of depth and height of seat on the frequency of complaints. Attention is drawn positively to the following:

- reducing the depth of the seat from 43.5 to 37.5 cm calls for a reduction of the angle of the back-rest.
- reducing the seat height from 42 to 36 cm requires an increased angle for the seat.
- increasing the angle of the back-rest calls for a reduction in seat height.
- *the best combination is as follows:*

angle of back rest	*20°*
angle of seat	*6°*
depth of seat	*43.5 cm*
height of seat	*42 cm*

Seats for resting

Domestic seating can be divided into three categories: seats for rest and relaxation, seats for working, and multi-purpose seats. Let us begin with the physiological design of seats for resting.

Orthopaedic aspects   The first important work in the field of design of seating takes us back to *Åkerblom* (90), and his pioneering monograph 'Standing and Sitting Posture' (1948). A few years later, the American orthopaedic surgeon *Keegan* (91) published his first paper.
Both authors started in the first place from orthopaedic considerations, and sought solutions on empirical grounds that would cater for the needs of the human spine. They demanded a backwards slope for the back-rest, which should have a profile similar to that of the vertebral column. A lumbar support

Table 48   Recommendations for the design of easy-chairs, after Keegan (29) and Åkerblom (90) These recommendations are empirical estimates, based on orthopaedic considerations.

Detail of chair	Recommendations: Keegan	Åkerblom
Lumbar pad	behind lumbar spine	17–21 cm above seat
Angle between seat and backrest	105°	100–110°
Depth of seat	41 cm	44 cm
Seat-height below knee	41 cm	40–43 cm
Seat tilted backwards	5°	5–7°

Figure 52   A 'sitting-machine' designed for studying comfort in relation to the profile of a chair.   After Grandjean and Burandt (93)

that was convex towards the front, and at the height of the lowest lumbar vertebrae was also recommended. A few of their recommendations for rest seats are summarised in *Table 48*.

In a few of our own studies (93, 94) we have analysed seating comfort in relation to the different profiles of rest seats for healthy research subjects and out-patients suffering from back troubles. For this purpose we built a sitting machine, shown in *Figure 52*.

Sitting machine

With this machine, we can vary at will, and infinitely, the shape of the seat and of the back-rest, the height of the seat and of the arm-rests. The seat and the back-rest consist of three frame-sections for holding removable sheets of plywood, from which the seat and back-rest can be built up into a profile. The entire seating surface is covered with a piece of foam-rubber 6 cm thick.

Techniques for recording of seating comfort

Each research subject has to fill up a questionnaire both before and after the tests. First of all seven bodily postures have to be assessed, giving the answers 'uncomfortable', 'indifferent', 'comfortable'. This provides one scale of comfort. Then individual components must be assessed, for example: 'Is the seat depth "too great", "good", or "too little"?' The questions posed can be seen in *Tables 49 and 50*.

If certain profiles are judged to be particularly bad or particularly good, the technique permits new profiles to be developed using information already gained

Example. If Profile A receives better reports than all the others in respect of lumbar support, then the characteristics of profile A at the lower end of the back-rest will be taken account of in the further development of a new profile. Unsatisfactory components can gradually be eliminated, while the good ones are retained.

Indirect measurement of comfort

It may further be mentioned here that, in the first experiment, besides systematic questioning, we also recorded bodily movements and the variation they produced in the pressures of the body on the seat and on the back-rest. These measurements told us nothing about the comfort of the subject, so we ignored this in the results. Observation showed us that direct questioning is a more suitable way of assessing comfort in the design of seats than are physiological measurements, since the latter can at best give us only indirect information. The studies of *Rieck* (95) on car seats and those of *Shackel, Chidsey and Shipley* (99) on multi-purpose seats may be mentioned in this context. They also found no correlation between the results of questioning and the extent to which people moved about when they had been sitting for a long time.

Seat profiles for healthy people

In a first series of experiments, five well-known seat profiles, including that recommended by *Åkerblom* were set up on the sitting machine and tested by 10 men, each for 150 minutes. In the second series 52 persons (36 men and 16 women), in periods of 8 minutes each, tested new profiles which had been developed from the findings of the first series of tests. Finally, taking the seat profile that was judged best, the angles of seat and back and the height of the seat were varied until each person had arrived at the optimum for him or her. All the experiments were carried out in duplicate, once while reading and once while resting. The ages of the 52 subjects ranged from 18 to 63; the females ranged between 152 and 171 cm in height, the males betwen 163 and 187 cm.

From the results of the first series of experiments, a new profile was obtained for an easy-chair (Profile VI), a development of that shown in *Figure 54*. Comparisons between this Profile VI and Profile 1 obtained from the first series are summarised in *Tables 49* and *50*.

It can be seen from the Tables that in several respects the new Profile VI earns high praise. Of particular note are the increased number of 'comfortable' assessments for head and neck, back and loins though only the first of these assessments were significant. On the other hand, the armrests were lowered to 23 cm, and were unequivocally voted inferior to those of Profile 1. This also emerged from the voting as 'uncomfortable' for the arms.

Table 49   Comfort of two easy chairs Statements from 52 research subjects Profile 1 was the best of an experimental series. Profile VI was a new design developed from experience of the first series. After Grandjean and Burandt (93). U = uncomfortable N = neutral C = comfortable

Part of the body	Verdict	Profile 1 % of answers	Profile VI % of answers
Head and neck	U	71	35
	N	19	28
	C	10	37
Shoulders	U	8	0
	N	29	24
	C	63	76
Back	U	10	4
	N	21	7
	C	69	89
Lumbar region	U	16	6
	N	29	17
	C	55	77
Buttocks	U	4	0
	N	25	20
	C	71	80
Thighs	U	24	12
	N	33	35
	C	43	53
Arms	U	21	39
	N	18	20
	C	61	41

Table 50   Assessment of the constructional details of two easy chairs Statements from 52 research subjects. Profile 1 was the best of the first series of experimental profiles. Profile VI was developed from the results of the experiments. * armrest height = its height above seat level. Slope of back = angle between back rest and seat. Slope of head = angle between back rest and head rest. For further details see Grandjean and Burandt (93)

Constructional detail	Assessment	Profile 1 Measurement	% of answers	Profile VI Measurement	% of answers
Height of seat	too great	44 cm	25	42.5 cm	23
	good		67		69
	too little		8		8
Armrest height*	too great	27 cm	18	23 cm	3
	good		59		39
	too little		23		58
Depth of seat	too great	48.5 cm	12	46 cm	6
	good		69		77
	too little		19		17
Slope of seat	too great	17°	8	20°	11
	good		75		78
	too little		17		11
Slope of back*	too great	95°	1	108°	4
	good		61		89
	too little		38		7
Slope of head*	too great	165°	14	156°	8
	good		25		45
	too little		61		47

Table 51   Analysis of the measurements of easy chairs judged as best by 52 research subjects   Seat angle = angle between the chord of the seat cushion and the horizontal; angle of back = angle between seat cushion and the tangent to the curved back cushion. After Grandjean and Burandt (93)

Seat angle in °	21 and 22	23 and 24	25 and 26	27 and 28	29 and 30	31 and 32
Chosen for resting by	0	3	29	14	6	0
Chosen for reading by	14	30	7	0	1	0

Angle of back in °	99 and 100	101 and 102	103 and 104	105 and 106	107 and 108	109 and 110
Chosen for resting by	0	0	2	15	28	7
Chosen for reading by	2	21	24	4	1	0

Seat height in cm	< 37	37 and 38	39 and 40	41 and 42	43 and 44	44+
Chosen for resting by	7	20	15	8	1	1
Chosen for reading by	0	6	31	8	5	2

Most comfortable dimensions

Table 51 gives the results of the last series of experiments, in which each subject recorded his preference for the best angle between seat and back, and the optimum height for the seat. The following were the measurements that were most often voted as most comfortable:

When reading:
- slope of seat   23–24°
- angle between seat and back   101–104°
- height of seat   39–40 cm

In a relaxed position when resting:
- slope of seat   25–26°
- angle between seat and back   105–108°
- height of seat   37–38 cm

All seating experiments with healthy subjects agreed that the participants gave preference to a profile for the back rest that gave them good lumbar support. This led to a profile for the back rest that is recognisable by its forwardly convex bulge, the lumbar pad, with its maximum projection coming at a height of 11–14 cm, vertically above the effective seat, i.e. the lowest point below the ischial process. This profile conforms in outline to the recommendations of *Åkerblom* (90), though he set the lumbar pad higher, 17–21 cm above the seat. It is further obvious from the results that a very sloping seat, with an angle of 20–28° is preferred. We accept the fact that a pronounced backward slope of the seat prevents forwards sliding and therefore makes better use of the back rest profile.

Seat profiles for back sufferers

For a study of people with back trouble we had initially at our disposal 17 men and 21 women who happened to be receiving treatment for back complaints at the Institut für physikalische Therapie des Kantonsspitals, Zürich. All had disc trouble between the fifth lumbar vertebra and the sacrum, diagnosed clinically and by radiology. At the time of the seating experiment, they had passed the acute stage, but all still complained of back trouble. Their ages ranged between 30 and 75 (average 59) for the women and between 33 and 82 (average 55) for the men.

Table 52   Effect of length of sitting time on chair comfort   Assessed by 38 subjects. After Grandjean, Böni and Kretzschmar (94)

Feelings	After sitting for 5 minutes			After sitting for 60 minutes		
	Uncomfortable	Average	Comfortable	Uncomfortable	Average	Comfortable
in the back above the lumbar region	1	3	34	1	6	31
in the lumbar region	4	4	30	2	4	32

H

Table 53   Assessment of the Profile VI easy chair by persons suffering from back ailments, as well as by healthy people   Length of test was 5 and 8 minutes respectively. n = number of testers. *p less than 0.025 **p less than 0.01. The significance was submitted to the χ^2 test. After Grandjean, Böni and Kretzschmar (94)

Subject of question	Persons with back ailments $n = 38 = 100\%$			Healthy persons $n = 52 = 100\%$		
	Uncomfortable	Moderately so	Comfortable	Uncomfortable	Moderately so	Comfortable
Head and neck	21	52	27	35	29	36
Shoulders	3	8	89	0	25	75
Back	3	8	89	6	8	86
Loins	11	11	78	8	17	75
Buttocks	0	3	97*	0	21	79*
Thighs	13	32	55	13	35	52
Arms	8	50	42	38	21	41
	too large	good	too small	too large	good	too small
Seat height (42 cm)	13	52	35**	23	67	10**
Height of arms (25 cm)	11	34	55	4	38	58
Depth of seat (48 cm)	11	50	39*	8	75	17*
Slope of seat (20°)	11	78	11	12	77	11
Slope of back (108°)	11	76	13	6	86	8
Slope of head-rest (156°)	11	26	63	10	44	46

The research subjects were divided into 'hyperlordosis' (back strongly rounded) and 'alordosis' (back flat). It is well known that women more commonly suffer from hyperlordosis and men more commonly from alordosis, and this was true of our subjects:

- hyperlordosis   13 women, 7 men
- alordorsis   4 women, 14 men

The seating experiment lasted for one hour at a time in a resting position using Profile VI, the profile developed after experiments with healthy persons. The questionnaire had to be completed twice in each experiment after 5 minutes and after 60 minutes.

Effect of duration of sitting on bodily sensations
Comparison with healthy persons

Table 52 summarises the verdicts on how the back and the loins felt after the two periods of 5 and 60 minutes. It shows that there was no significant difference between them.

Table 53 compares the results from the 38 subjects with back complaints with those from the 52 healthy persons. The former generally rated the easy chair higher than did the latter, but the distribution of symptoms for the different parts of the body – shoulders, back, loins – was the same in the two groups.

Statistical analysis showed that those with back complaints more often reported that the buttocks were comfortable, but that they complained more frequently that the seat was too low and too narrow.

A further point of interest was the finding that the assessments for back and loins showed no significant difference between the groups 'hyperlordosis' and 'alordosis'.

A profile suitable for people with back complaints

In a second series of experiments we tested on the one hand five different back profiles, to see if one particular profile would be acceptable to all back sufferers; and on the other hand we allowed each member of the group to work out the best profile for individual comfort. 68 persons (33 women and 35 men) were at our disposal for this second series of experiments, grouped as follows according to their clinical diagnosis:

- hyperlordosis   29 subjects
- alordosis   30 subjects
- normal lordosis   9 subjects

Frequency of preferences

The five profiles under test	Hyperlordosis $n = 29$	Alordosis $n = 30$	Normal lordosis $n = 9$	Total $n = 68 = 100\%$	
Profile I 	0	0	1	1	1%
Profile II 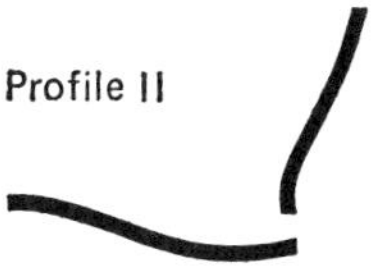	4	4	1	9	13%
Profile III 	1	2	1	4	6%
Profile IV 	9	13	3	25	37%
Profile V 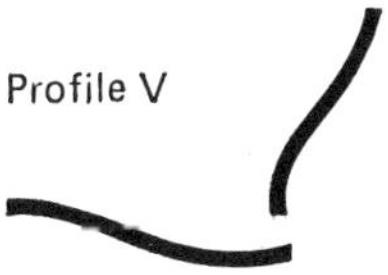	15	11	3	29	43%

Figure 53   Frequency with which 68 people who suffered from back ailments preferred various chair profiles   After Grandjean, Böni and Kretzschmar (94)

The average age was 52 (extremes 27 and 82) and the average height 166 cm (extremes 147 and 186 cm). All had completed their treatment in the clinic, but all still had occasional pain in the back. The results of tests on the five profiles are given in *Figure 53*.

The great majority (81%) of the research subjects preferred profiles IV and V, leading to the conclusion that *people with back complaints prefer a back-profile decidedly convex forwards at the height of the lumbar region and slightly concave forwards above this level*. A straight back rest (Profiles I and III) were rejected by virtually all research subjects (63 out of 68).

Application of the χ^2 test shows no significant difference between the groups 'hyperlordosis' and 'alordosis', and consequently the preferences shown in Figure 53 of the alordosis group for Profile IV and the hyperlordosis group for Profile V are not statistically significant. In spite of this the tendency is an interesting one: it could mean that persons with a hyperlordosis prefer a somewhat greater inclination of the back with a somewhat more pronounced lumbar pad.

Taking the 54 subjects who had expressed a preference for Profiles IV and V, all the adjustable components of the sitting-machine were varied until the optimum setting, free from any kind of complaint, was reached for each individual. Next, the research subjects remained at rest on the seat for 45 minutes, after which they stood up and then sat down again, and a second optimum position was obtained. Finally, each subject expressed an opinion concerning the ease of rising from the seat.

The results showed firstly that there was no noticeable difference between the first opinion and the one given after sitting for 45 minutes. Rising was inconvenient for 8 persons, but was convenient for everyone if the seat was tilted to 16°.

The average values of the most convenient individual settings can be seen in *Table 54*.

The zone of preference was much the same for the two profiles: only the angle of inclination of the back was apparently 3–5° greater for Profile V than for the other, and this might be attributed to the more pronounced lumbar pad of Profile V. With both Profiles, those with alordosis had a tendency to prefer a somewhat higher and deeper seat and a somewhat more sloping back. The difference was not significant, however, and so need not be taken into consideration.

Height of the lumbar support

The outstanding result of these individual adjustments is certainly the preferred height of the main lumbar support, which is 8–10 cm above the point of contact with the seat, with little individual variation

This finding contradicts the opinion of *Åkerblom* (90) and *Keegan* (92), who recommended a considerably higher lumbar pad (see *Table 48*). On the other hand, our observations are in good overall agreement with the views of

Table 54   Most comfortable individual setting for Profiles IV and V, by 48 subjects suffering from back ailments   After each average value the standard deviation(s) is given to indicate the extent of the scatter. The diagram shows the angles and lengths quoted in the Table. Lumbar height = distant between lowest point of surface of seat when it is sat on and highest point of support on the lumbar pad. After Grandjean, Böni and Kretzschmar (94)

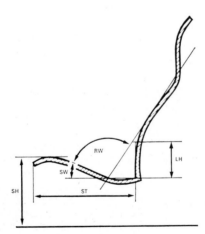

	SH (cm) Seat ht	ST (cm) Seat dpth	SW (°) Angle of seat	RW (°) Angle of back	LH (cm) Lumbar ht
Profile IV					
Hyperlordosis	40 ± 3.1	47 ± 3.2	21 ± 1.4	103 ± 1.2	10 ± 1.1
Alordosis	41 ± 2.5	49 ± 2.7	19 ± 1.1	105 ± 1.4	8 ± 1.6
Profile V					
Hyperlordosis	40 ± 2.0	47 ± 2.2	19 ± 1.1	108 ± 1.9	10 ± 1.4
Alordosis	44 ± 2.9	48 ± 2.0	20 ± 1.6	110 ± 1.6	8 ± 1.4

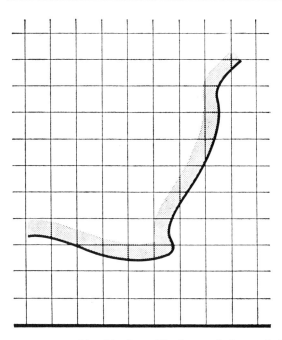

Figure 54   The ideal profile for a chair, as indicated by research, for both healthy people and those suffering from back ailments   The graticule consists of squares 10 × 10 cm. The heavy line indicates the hard body of the chair, and the stippled area is upholstery covering this to a thickness of 6 cm: latex, quality 'hard'. This design ensures that the chair will assume the correct profile when it is sat on. After Grandjean, Böni and Kretzschmar (94)

Schoberth (87) who proposed a back rest primarily to support the sacrum and the upper edge of the pelvis, in order to limit backward rotation of the pelvis, and to avoid the development of a hunched back.

Sitting comfort and orthopaedic measurements

If our results are compared with the pressure measurements of *Yamaguchi* (89) (p. 104 fig. 49) a very interesting point of agreement can be seen. *The seat angle of 19–21° and back rest inclination of 103–110° preferred by our back sufferers nearly all lie in the zone in which Yamaguchi recorded a neutral balance of forces between the vertebrae: i.e. compression force resulting from curvature of the spine = zero.*
Moreover this is also apparent in the settings chosen as most comfortable by the healthy subjects.

This agreement between the subjective impressions of comfort or discomfort and the relevant orthopaedic measurements shows that the original ergonomic hypothesis is correct; comfortable postures are also orthopaedically correct

Development of a profile for an easy chair

Starting from the two Profiles IV and V, which are very similar and differ little from Profile VI, chosen as best by the healthy research subjects, we derived a Profile for an easy chair which is illustrated in *Figure 54*.
In this compromise proposal the angle of slope of the seat and of the back rest caused more trouble than the other dimensions. *Figure 55* shows the angles and other dimensions in the form of a sketch, while *Table 55* summarises the average values of the settings preferred by fit people and those suffering from back-troubles, as well as a compromise proposal.

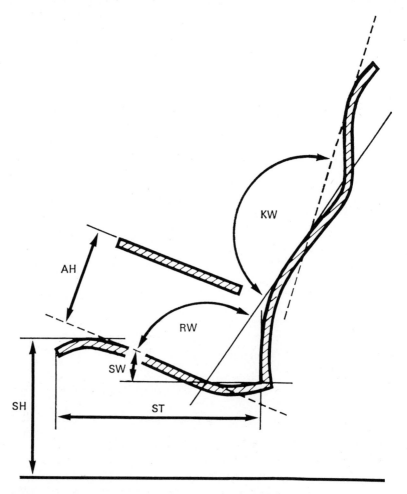

Figure 55   Definition of the angles and lengths quoted in Table 55   SH = height of seat. AH = height of arm-rest. SW = tilt of seat. RW = slope of backrest (angle between seat and backrest). KW = slope of headrest. ST = depth of seat

Basis for the compromise proposals

The compromise proposals were worked out as follows: A sharp backward tilt of the seat prevents forward sliding and causes the occupant to lean against the backrest with the lower part of his back, sacrum and lumbar spine; unfortunately, the more the seat is tilted, the more difficult it becomes to rise from it. This point needs particular consideration where old people are concerned.

The most comfortable slope of the back rest in relation to the seat shows a greater range of variation among the people with bad backs. A confidence zone of 95% lies approximately between 101° and 113°. The proposed value of 107° also takes into consideration the pressure measurements of *Yamaguchi*. The problem of the height of the main point of support afforded by the lumbar pad can be solved in such a way that the support comes within 6 cm of its most effective position. As mentioned above, the proposed range of 8–14 cm above the seat when it is sat on is in good agreement with the orthopaedic arguments of *Schoberth* (87).

Table 55 **Average values for the most comfortable settings, and a compromise proposal** Definitions of the measurements can be seen in Figure 55

| Constructional detail | Healthy persons | | Persons with back ailments | Compromise, both reading and resting |
	Reading	Resting	Resting	
Angle of seat SW (°)	23	26	20	23
Slope of backrest RW (°)	103	107	106.5	107
Seat height SH (cm)	40	39	41.5	40
Depth of seat ST (cm)	47	47	48	48
Height of main support, point of lumbar pad (cm)	14	14	9	8–14
Height of arms AH (cm)	26	26	26	26

The most difficult compromise is that for the neck and head region, and this setting shows the greatest individual scatter. The support for the head and neck given in Figure 54 is a compromise, which would certainly be criticised by many people. We therefore feel that if the easy chair is not adjustable, a cushion for the head should be provided.

An adjustable easy chair

The ideal easy chair which can be used by the great majority of people of every size and every age in the greatest possible comfort can only be achieved if it is adjustable in most dimensions. *Table 56* summarises the amounts of adjustment desirable as found in our studies.

Le Carpentier's studies

Recently *Le Carpentier* (103) analysed the most comfortable sitting posture obtained from 20 subjects in an adjustable easy chair in which many angles and dimensions could be altered at will with the help of a motorised drive. The experiments lasted three hours each, and were repeated several times. The subjects had to be either reading or watching television. The author observed that the most comfortable setting did not change during the three hour session.

Length of time seated

From the previous observations we can make the following statements about the effect of prolonged sitting:

- comfort diminishes the longer one sits (98, 99, 100)
- the *relative* order of comfort of seats does not alter significantly with time, but the *difference* between one seat and another becomes more pronounced (99)
- length of sitting does not affect individual adjustments to the preferred settings.

Le Carpentier (103) found no difference between reading and watching television. On the other hand there was a significant difference between the 10 male and the 10 female research subjects: the men preferred an outstretched posture, with the legs extended, whereas the women would rather

Table 56 **Preferred ranges of adjustment of an easy chair with multiple positions** The ranges given approximate to the 95% confidence zones for healthy persons and for those suffering from back ailments. For definitions of the lengths measured, see Figure 55

Constructional detail	Desirable range of adjustment
Slope of seat SW	16–30°
Slope of back RW	102–115°
Height of seat SH	34–50 cm
Depth of seat ST	41–55 cm
Range of adjustment of main supporting area of lumbar pad vertically above point of contact with seat	6–18 cm
Height of arms of chair AH	22–30 cm

Table 57   The most comfortable angles and lengths of a self-adjusted arm-chair, and recommendations based on these   Activities during test: reading and watching television. n = number of research subjects. s = standard deviation. After Le Carpentier (103)

Constructional detail	n	Average	s	Recommendation for a seat with only one position	for two positions	
Frontal height of seat, unloaded (cm)	20	40	± 3.8	38	38	42
Depth of seat (cm)	20	48	± 3.2	47	47	47
Angle of seat (°)	20	10.3	± 3.4	10.5	9	12
Angle between seat and backrest (°)	20	109.1	± 5.5	110	113	105
Armrests, height above seat when occupied (cm)	12	16	± 1.6	16.5	16.5	16.5
Head rest in front of back surface	12	3.8	± 5.7	6.4	6.4	6.4
Angle between headrest and backrest (°)	12	7.9	± 3.3	8	8	8

keep the lower legs vertical. Accordingly the men preferred a smaller backward slope to the seat and a greater inclination of the back rest. On this evidence, the author recommended two kinds of easy chair. The average values of the preferred settings and the recommendations of the author for a unit chair, as well as for the two positions mentioned are set out in *Table 57*.

There is general agreement with our own results (Tables 51 and 54), with two exceptions: our subjects, both fit and unfit, set the seat with a greater tilt, and preferred higher armrests. We suspect that our back rest profile with the pronounced lumbar pad is the main reason for the difference in choice, but we have no explanation for the different preferences in the height of the arm rests.

General considerations   These various findings lead to the following conclusions concerning the design of easy chairs:

— easy chairs should ensure that the spine is kept in its normal shape, with minimum forces on the intervertebral discs, and the greatest possible relaxation of the back muscles.
— the most comfortable setting and dimensions of an easy chair vary with different activities, and there is a small range of individual variation. Hence it is desirable that an easy chair should be adjustable in several dimensions. The extent of the various adjustments is shown in Table 56.
— easy chairs should have a back rest with a convex lumbar pad and a slight concavity at the level of the thoracic vertebrae. The main supporting point of the lumbar pad should be 8–14 cm vertically above the seat when occupied, at the height of the upper edge of the sacrum and the fifth lumbar vertebra.
— easy chairs should be well upholstered, to distribute the greater part of the body weight over a large area of the buttocks. A cushion which spreads the body weight over a circle of 6–10 cm diameter on the seat would be suitable.
— if a non adjustable easy chair is to be designed, the following dimensions should be used:
— height of seat   39–41 cm
— depth of seat   47–48 cm
— slope of seat   20–26°
— angle between back rest and seat   105–110°

Proposals for a compromise easy chair will be found in Table 55.

Seats for work

Since work seats also have a place in the home, they will also be considered here.

Table 58 Results of a multimoment analysis of the sitting postures of 378 office workers. The numbers and percentages are arranged according to various groups of attributes, which are separated by the horizontal lines

Event	Observations Number	%
Working on documents	2211	45
Reading	577	12
Typing	1204	24
Using calculating machine	329	7
Speaking and telephoning	599	12
	4920	100
Sitting forward on chair	748	15
Sitting upright on chair	2533	52
Sitting back on chair	1639	33
	4920	100
Leaning back on the back rest	2066	42
Arms supported on the table	1977	40
Other attitudes	877	18
	4920	100
Legs stretched forward	699	14
Legs flexed approximately 90° at knees	2207	45
Legs flexed backwards	893	18
Legs held asymmetrically	788	16
Legs crossed	333	7
	4920	100
Feet crossed	1341	27
Feet on a footstool, drawer or chair rail	1457	30

Table 59 Complaints of pain when sitting down, made by 246 office-workers Multiple answers. The percentages relate to the 246 possible statements per question. After Grandjean and Burandt (86)

Location of pain	Number	Percentage
In the head	34	14
In neck and shoulders	59	24
In the back	141	57
In the buttocks	40	16
In arms and hands	37	15
In knees and feet	71	29
In thighs	46	19
No pain	38	15

The literature gives numerous recommendations in respect of work seats. These are given an almost complete coverage in the report by *Kroemer and Robinette* (104) and in the paper by *Damon, Stoudt and McFarland* (115). However, there have been only a few experimental studies; most recommendations are based on anthropometric data and on general orthopaedic considerations.

Use of work seats

In an investigation (86) we used multimoment analysis to study* the sitting habits of 261 men and 117 women who were occupied with normal office work. A total of 4920 observations were recorded. The experiment concluded with a survey by questionnaire of 246 office workers concerning

*Multimoment analysis permits simple observation of habits. A list of characteristics is prepared beforehand, and items are ticked off as they are seen during repeated cycles of observation.

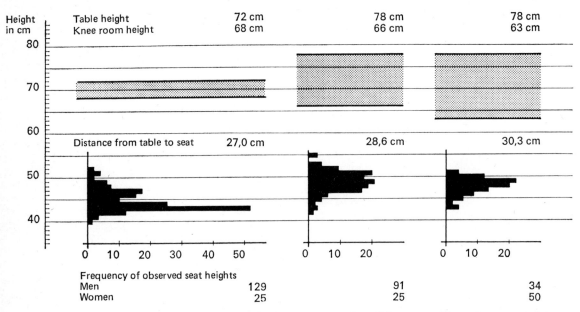

Figure 56   Chosen heights for an adjustable seat   The various seat heights are recorded in terms of the frequency with which they were chosen (black histogram). The distances table-seat are average values. After Grandjean and Burandt (86)

discomfort, together with measurements of their body size and of the dimensions of the work seat.

One section of the multimoment analysis is given in *Table 58* and the corresponding answers are given in *Table 59. Figure 56* summarises the heights of seat chosen by the office workers, divided into groups for different table heights.

To test whether there was any significant relationship between the observations made in the survey, the frequency of complaints, and the dimensions of the work places we calculated the correlation coefficient between the results (x^2 test). The results and the calculated relationships lead to the following conclusions:

— office workers prefer to have the seat at such a height that it gives them the most comfortable attitude for the upper body when working. This was achieved when the distance between desk top and seat was 27–30 cm (*Figure 56*). The preferred height of the seat was 42–47 cm.

— pain in the upper thighs was caused principally by working conditions which threw the body weight on to the upper thighs, and to a lesser extent by the height of the seat.

— a desk top height of 78 cm was acceptable to most people provided that an adjustable seat and foot-rests were at their disposal.

— 57% of those questioned complained of occasional backache. 24% noticed occasional pain in the neck and shoulders, and 15% in the arms and hands. Those who did a lot of typing were represented more often than the average in both groups. The occurrence of pain was highly dependent on the type of work being carried out.

— 42% of the subjects made use of the back rest, the adjustable back rest being used more often than the fixed one.

Forward inclined seating

Work chair seats have been the subject of many investigations and recommendations.

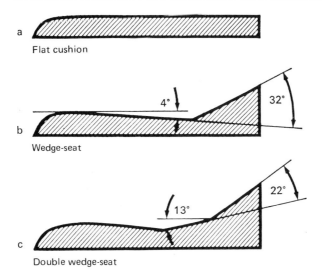

a

Flat cushion

b

4°   32°

Wedge-seat

c

13°   22°

Double wedge-seat

Figure 57   The three profiles that were studied for the seat cushion   The wedge seat *b* follows the recommendations of Schneider and Lippert (108). The double wedge *c* is a variant of this. After Burandt and Grandjean (109)

Schneider's wedge seat

On orthopaedic grounds *Schlegel* (167) required work chairs to have a seat tilting forwards, hoping thereby to produce forward rotation of the pelvis, and this to induce slight lordosis of the lumbar vertebrae. On similar grounds *Schneider and Lippert* (108) proposed a seat surface, the rear third of which was raised to form what they called a wedge-seat. The authors hoped that this would cause the pelvis to tilt forwards and thus achieve active lordosis of the lumbar region. This wedge seat was later produced commercially, as the 'Actilord seat'. We tested these theories experimentally (109) with an adjustable seat. We observed what effect tilting the posterior third of the seat had upon the posture of the back in 6 men and 6 women performing manual work for one hour. Photographs were taken of the contour of the back, as shown by markers, and the women showed no difference between a flat and a wedged seat. In contrast the men had slight lordosis of the lumbar region when sitting on the wedge seat.

Wedge seat and backache

In a further experiment we observed the reactions of 43 office-workers in three types of seat, illustrated in *Figure 57*.

Each research subject sat on one type of seat for a week at a time, taking the seats in random order, and at the end of each test week he filled up a questionnaire.

Table 60   Complaints of pain when sitting in chairs of three different profiles
Each profile was tested through the course of one week by 43 office workers. Those totals indicated by * and ** are significantly different from each other, $p < 0.01$. After Burandt and Grandjean (109)

Location of pain	Wedge seat	Double wedge seat	Flat seat
in neck and shoulders	3	4	0
in the back	13	13	5
in the buttocks	5	13	1
in thighs	13	16	6
Total	34*	46*	12**

Table 61   Distribution of body weight between different parts of the seat in different attitudes, given as a percentage of total body weight.   After Jürgens (105)

Sitting posture	Chair with seat inclined backwards: weight on			Chair with seat inclined forwards: weight on		
	Seat	Backrest	Footrest	Seat	Backrest	Footrest
Upright posture	76	–	24	64	–	36
Sitting back (fully reclining)	68	15	17	63	10	27
Sitting forward (pelvis rotated)	60	10	30	57	5	38

The first choices were divided as follows:

– for wedge seat *b*   11 subjects
– for double wedge *c*   12 subjects
– for flat seat *a*   20 subjects

Significantly, the two sloping seats were frequently thought to be uncomfortable for work. Data concerning complaints about the seats are to be found in *Table 60*.

It follows from this that backwards tilted seats produce more pain in the back, the buttocks, and the upper thighs than do flat seats. We conclude from these results that backward tilted seats may induce a certain amount of lordosis of the lumbar region, but that this attitude of the back leads to undesirable discomfort.

In a different experiment (102) using students, a seat was employed, the front of which sloped backwards up to a maximum of 15°, and in the back of which penetrated a slight upward bulge. This shape was excellent for both the upright and reclining positions because on the one hand it prevented the person from slipping forwards, and on the other hand it facilitated the straightening up of the back. We think that this result could also be considered in relation to a work chair.

Forward inclined seats and the distribution of pressures

Jürgens (105), with the aid of pressure-gauges, registered the pressure distribution between the body and the seat, the back-rest and the feet in three sitting postures. He used a seat without upholstery with a slight backwards slope, as well as a second in which the front half of the seat inclined forwards. The latter had been designed by the author as a work seat, since it should be suitable particularly for a forward stitting posture. The findings are summarised in *Table 61*.

Pressure distribution was influenced by sitting posture as well as by the shape of the seat. It was remarkable how pressure was shifted on to the feet if the seat was tilted forward, the back-rest taking only 15% of the body pressure at best. The last point has already been noted by other authors. *Branton* (101) concluded from this that the function of a back rest is not to reduce the strain on the bones of the pelvis and sacrum, but exclusively to relax the back muscles.

Forward tilted seats and attitude of the back

Burandt (106) studied 21 women switch-board operators and the effects of inclining the seat 6° forwards or backwards on the shape of the spine and the position of the pelvis. In both cases the women sat without leaning backwards. Analysis of his X-rays showed that in the majority of cases the pelvis was strongly rotated posteriorly. This means that tilting the seat forwards does *not* – as *Schlegel* (107) thought – induce a lordosis of the lumbar spine, but on the contrary the sacrum and lumbar spine are held in a straighter and flatter attitude.

In the opinion of orthopaedists such an attitude of the pelvis causes an undesirable increase in curvature in the spine, and results in a kyphosis above the lumbar region, yet there was no sign of this in *Burandt's* experiments (106).

Of the 21 women questioned, 14 gave preference to the forwards tilted seat and 5 to the rearwards tilted seat; 2 remained undecided.

It seems to us that the question of the suitability of a forwards tilted seat for a working chair is not answered by the work of *Jürgens* or of *Burandt*. The results to date are not conclusive.

The literature contains the following further suggestions concerning the seats of work chairs:

- a seat that tilts backwards by 3–5°. *Åkerblom* (90), *Keegan* (92), *Lehmann* (46).
- A seat that tilts backwards by 0–7°. *Kroemer* (110), *Stier* (111).
- tilting the front half of the seat backwards by 3–5°. *Burandt* (112) *Floyd and Roberts* (113).
- seat curved downwards both fore and aft. *Peters* (55).
- the front edge should be rounded off: all authors are agreed on this point.

Size of seat

Recommendations for depth and breadth of seats vary little: for both measurements they range between 35 and 40 cm. We hold the opinion that 35 cm is a minimum for the depth, and that 38–40 cm is advisable for a work seat to allow the subject to lean against a fixed back support.

Upholstery

As far as upholstery is concerned, *Branton* (101) indicated that on a hard surface half the body-weight pressed on 8% of the area of the sitting surface of the body. Upholstering the seat increased the proportion of the body-weight borne by the seat and spread it over a much greater area. This prevents restriction of blood flow in buttocks and thighs, and thus decreases the liability to pain or discomfort.

Kroemer (104) does not recommend a soft cushion, as the buttocks and upper thighs sink into it and the pressure areas cannot be changed when required. The author recommends that upholstery should only give under the body to the extent of a few centimetres.

We feel that work seats used for more than one hour at a time should have a light padding. This is more conducive to comfort than any sophisticated profile.

Seat covers

Seat and cushion covers should be permeable to moisture. In one experiment (114) we used blotting-paper laid on the surface to measure the absorption of sweat by 6 different seat covers.

Wool as well as Dralon showed a significantly better rate of sweat absorption than two materials made entirely of PVC. Leather and a ribbed PVC material were intermediate. Materials with small perforations must be judged unsuitable since the perforations close under the pressure of the body, and the material becomes impermeable.

Back rests

By tradition, comparatively small back rests are used for work seats. In our opinion, the future working seat should have better provision for the back to allow relaxation during periodic rest periods. *Yamaguchi* (89) suggested that work seats should have a special mechanism for inclining the seat and the back rest, and we feel that this is correct. Certainly improved back rests must be developed which will allow complete relaxation of the back muscles. Such a seat would serve as a multi-purpose seat, since it would be just as suitable for a forward sitting position as for a reclining one, and would often find a use in the home.

Recommendations

The following recommendations can be found in the literature for the design of back rests for work seats:

- a high back rest, up to the shoulders, with a lumbar pad 18–20 cm above the surface of the seat. *Åkerblom* (90), *Keegan* (92).
- lumbar supports to be as variable as possible. *Peters* (55), *Lehmann* (46) *Burandt* (112) *Grandjean* (2) and others.
- lumbar supports 20–33 cm above the seat surface, lightly convex in shape. *Floyd and Roberts* (113) *Murrell* (3) and others.
- lumbar supports 12–35 cm above seat. *Kroemer* (110).

Just above the surface of the seat, the back-rest should either be open, or at least so strongly concave that when sitting upright the ischium can be rotated backwards without hindrance (84, 85). All authors concur with this orthopaedic recommendation.

A slight spring in the lumbar pad is commonly recommended, but according to *Kroemer* (110) it should not give more than about 2 cm.

Recommended dimensions for lumbar supports:

– height   20 to 30 cm
– breadth   30 to 37 cm

Tests on students (102) showed, moreover, that they preferred a back-rest with a curvature of 80 cm radius, and a similar, or slightly lesser, curvature should be suitable for the lumbar pad.

Height of seat in relation to working surface

Our own studies on office-workers (86) have shown that a person at work adjusts the seat height in the first instance to suit the height of the working surface, as he rather tolerates pain at the back of the knees than an unsuitable posture of the upper part of the body. *The optimal height for a seat can only be decided in relation to the height of the working surface. On the basis of our survey the seat should be 27–30 cm below the working surface.*

Once a vertical distance of 27–30 cm has been obtained between the seat and the bench top, the height of the seat in relation to the height of the back of the knees above the floor can be examined. Most authors agree that the highest point of the front edge of the seat must be a little below the knee-floor height (with the feet in shoes and flat on the floor). Accordingly most recommendations for the height of the seat of a non-adjustable chair vary between 35 and 45 cm.

Height of non-adjustable seats

If an average is taken for small to medium-sized people, a compromise is reached at heights between 35 and 40 cm, but at these heights taller people are compelled to push the buttocks back and take up a position with the back more strongly curved. *For this reason we feel that foot rests should be available for shorter subjects, when seat heights of 45–48 cm are reasonable.*

Height of adjustable seats

The great majority of professional people like their work seats to adjust as far as possible, so that they can be fitted to whatever height the user wants and finds most comfortable. Desk heights between 68 and 78 cm, and a distance of 27–30 cm from desk-top to seat, mean that *the desirable range of adjustment is from 38–53 cm.*

We must emphasise at this point, however, that the question of the height of the work seat will not be solved by adjustability alone. Moreover foot-rests have to be provided for small people, because that is the only way that they can match seat height to desk height.

This leads to the conclusion that a sensible solution of the problem would be a desk 78 cm high, a seat adjustable between 48 and 53 cm, and a foot rest adjustable from zero to 18 cm

Since such a work-place would be far too expensive for home use, *a work chair with a non-adjustable seat at a height of 40 cm would be adequate.*

Final deductions

The following recommendations for the design and construction of work seats arise from the foregoing considerations:

– the work seat must have good stability. The four feet must be at least as far apart as the breadth and depth of the seat.
– the work seat must permit any movement of the arms required by the user.
– the work seat must be considered as one with the work bench or desk, so that the distance from the seat to the upper edge of the desk is 27–30 cm and the distance from the seat to the underside of the desk at least 19 cm.
– the seat should be flat or slightly concave, with the front half tilted backwards to about 3–5°, and the rear third bulging slightly upwards. The front edge of the seat should be rounded off.

- 40 cm is recommended for both the depth and the breadth of the seat.
- a high backrest, 55–60 cm vertically above the point of contact with the seat, with a slightly convex lumbar pad and slightly concave at chest height is recommended so that the back muscles can be rested periodically.
- if a traditional type of work seat with a lumbar support is preferred, then this should have as much adjustment as possible, and have light springing. The lumbar support should be 20–30 cm high and 30–37 cm broad. Back rests and lumbar supports may have a slight bulge in the horizontal plane, with a radius of between 80 and 120 cm.
- the following rules are given for the height of the seat:
  - for a non-adjustable seat without foot rests   38–40 cm
    for a non-adjustable seat with foot rests   45–48 cm
  - range of adjustment for the seats concerned   38–53 cm
- the work seat can with advantage be upholstered on both seat and back rest in such a way that the body does not sink in more than 2 to 3 cm. The upholstery should be covered with a material that has good permeability to sweat.
- the ideal work seat of the future should have a mechanism for varying the slope of the seat and back, so that it can be made comfortable for forward, upright or reclining positions.

Figure 58 illustrates the most important recommendations for the dimensions of work tables, work seats and foot rests.

Multi-purpose seats

Uses

Multi-purpose seats come into the category of furniture that may be needed for a variety of different purposes. In the home they are used at table, occasionally for working, as well as for spare chairs in living-rooms and bed-rooms. They are also to be found in restaurants, waiting-rooms and meeting rooms, so they frequently need to be stacked.

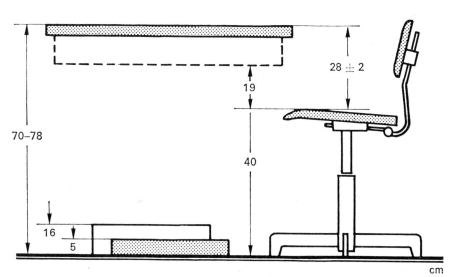

Figure 58   Recommendations for the dimensions of work tables, work seats and foot rests   Only the height is given for the footrest: its shape should be so designed that the whole foot can comfortably rest on it at heights varying from 5–16 cm above the floor. The slope of the footrest should lie between 23° and 27°

Table 62   Assessment of three constructional details of 10 multipurpose seats
After Shackel, Chidsey and Shipley (99)

Constructional detail	Opinion	A clear majority if the following measurement in cms was exceeded, or not reached, as indicated.
Seat height	too high	>45
	too low	<43
Depth of seat	too long	>41.9
	too short	<38
Radius of curvature	too flat	>42
of backrest	too curved	<24

Studies by Shackel

From a functional point of view, multi-purpose seats must basically be suitable for forward, upright or reclining positions, so that they can be used for activities at a table or desk, for any kind of entertainment, or for relaxation. *Shackel, Chidsey and Shipley* (99) investigated 10 types of multi-purpose seats with the help of 20 research subjects. 5 seats were made of wood, and 5 of synthetic materials. The people concerned had to give an opinion on particular dimensions of the seats under the experimental conditions. Their results are partly summarised in *Table 62*.

Further analysis of the results showed a majority preference for a seat breadth of 38 cm.

Studies of Wotzka and his colleagues

In one particular experiment (116) we analysed the comfort of and reactions to 12 multi-purpose seats. For this purpose, besides systematic questioning, we used the technique of paired comparisons. Six well-known firms put at our disposal 10 seats made of synthetic materials, some of the seats being prototypes and others already in production. In addition two more prototypes (pairs 5 and 6) had been made in polyester from plaster models supplied by ourselves. The seats studied are indicated by numbers in *Figures 59, 60, 61* and *62*. Seat No. 6 is broadly speaking an auditorium seat that had been developed by us after an analysis of seating comfort (102). Seat No. 5 is a somewhat simplified variant of No. 6

The 12 seats can be arranged in three groups according to the ways they support the back:

Type 1.   Seats Nos. 3, 5, 6, 9
This group is characterised by seats with the back rest built out in the lower part to give special support to the sacrum and lumbar region.
Type 2.   Seats Nos. 1, 2, 7, 12
These are seats with less lumbar support.
Type 3.   Seats Nos. 4, 8, 10, 11
These are seats without any lumbar support, or with the back-rest so steep that it encourages a sitting position with a hunched upper body.

As research subjects we used 25 male and 25 female students, with an average of 22 to 24 years. Their body-lengths were:

women   166.5 cm ± 5.2
men   177.9 cm ± 6.3

The research group were about 5 cm longer in the body than Swiss people in general, and must be taken as representative of present-day youth.

The technique of paired comparisons is like a football league championship in which each team meets each of the others, and the final order is determined by the number of wins.

The research subjects sat in turn in two of the experimental seats, without looking at them, the seats being placed behind the subject in quick succession. The seats were compared in random sequence.

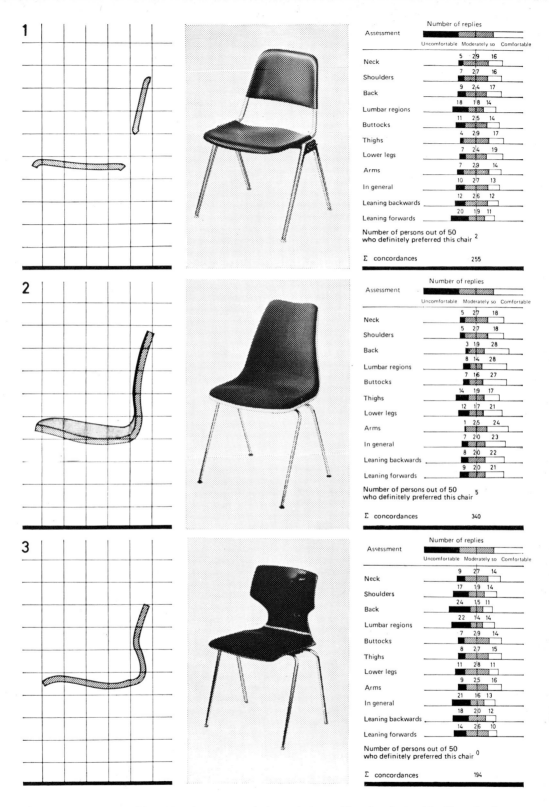

Figure 59 Multipurpose chairs Left, profiles (graticule 10×10 cm). Centre, photograph of chair. Right: results from the interrogation of 50 people

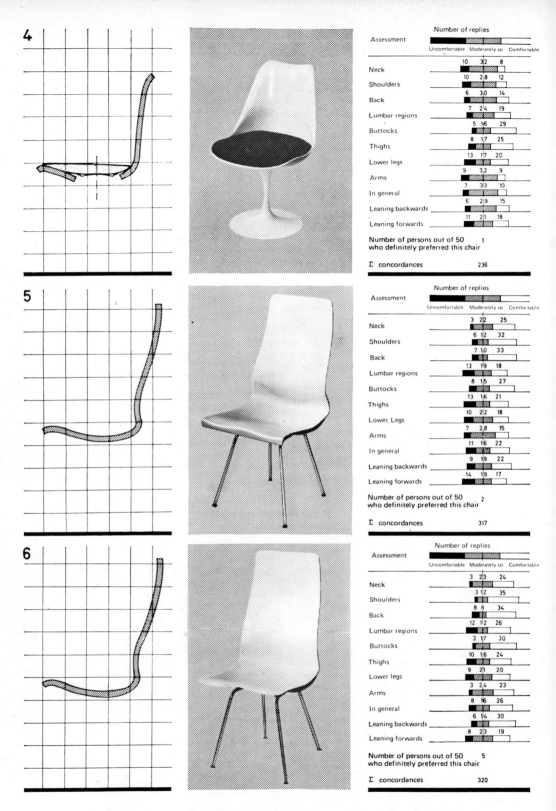

Figure 60   Multipurpose chairs   Left, profiles (graticule 10×10 cm). Centre, photograph of chair. Right: results from the interrogation of 50 people

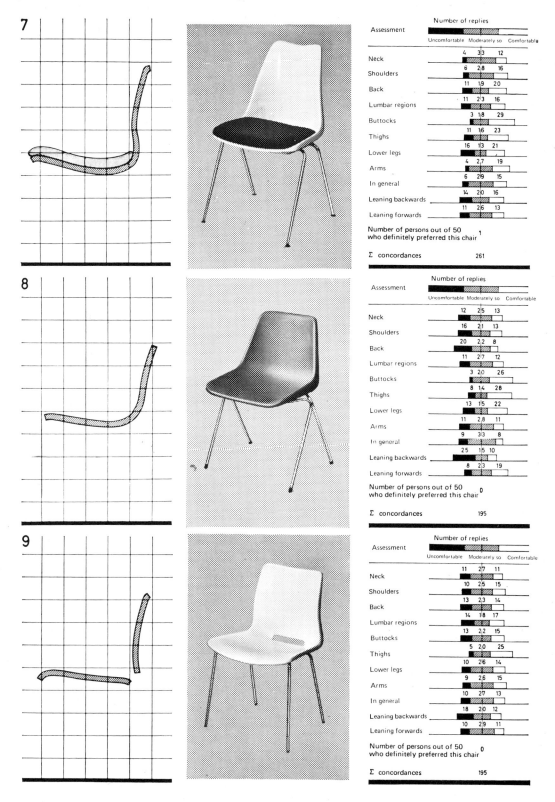

Figure 61 Multipurpose chairs Left, profiles (graticule 10×10 cm). Centre, photograph of chair. Right: results from the interrogation of 50 people

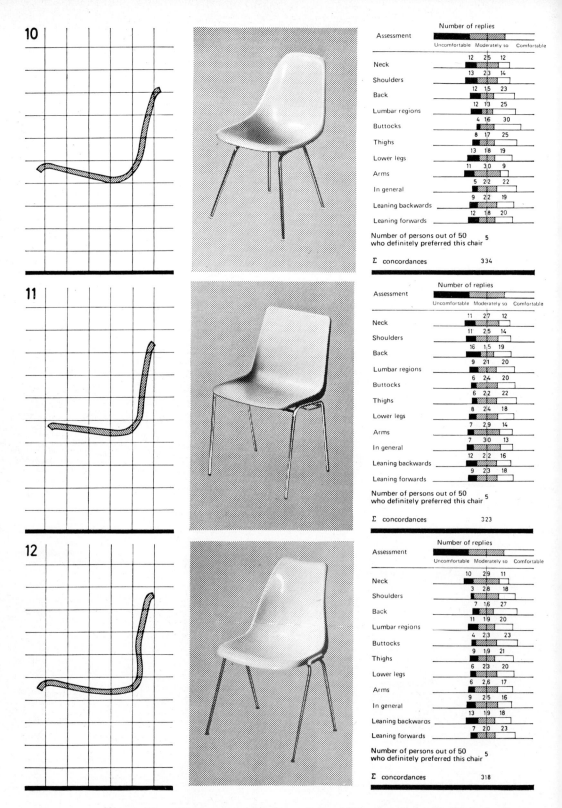

10

Number of replies		
Assessment		
Uncomfortable	Moderately so	Comfortable
Neck	12 25	12
Shoulders	13 23	14
Back	12 15	23
Lumbar regions	12 13	25
Buttocks	4 16	30
Thighs	8 17	25
Lower legs	13 18	19
Arms	11 30	9
In general	5 22	22
Leaning backwards	9 22	19
Leaning forwards	12 18	20

Number of persons out of 50 who definitely preferred this chair 5

Σ concordances 334

11

Number of replies		
Assessment		
Uncomfortable	Moderately so	Comfortable
Neck	11 27	12
Shoulders	11 25	14
Back	16 15	19
Lumbar regions	9 21	20
Buttocks	6 24	20
Thighs	6 22	22
Lower legs	8 24	18
Arms	7 29	14
In general	7 30	13
Leaning backwards	12 22	16
Leaning forwards	9 23	18

Number of persons out of 50 who definitely preferred this chair 5

Σ concordances 323

12

Number of replies		
Assessment		
Uncomfortable	Moderately so	Comfortable
Neck	10 29	11
Shoulders	3 28	18
Back	7 16	27
Lumbar regions	11 19	20
Buttocks	4 23	23
Thighs	9 19	21
Lower legs	6 23	20
Arms	6 26	17
In general	9 25	16
Leaning backwards	13 19	18
Leaning forwards	7 20	23

Number of persons out of 50 who definitely preferred this chair 5

Σ concordances 318

Figure 62 Multipurpose chairs Left, profiles (graticule 10×10 cm). Centre, photograph of chair. Right: results from the interrogation of 50 people

Table 63   Analysis of seats judged best and worst respectively, and indications of possible correlations with the characteristics of the individual seats

Criterion	Seats given a good rating, nos	Characteristics	Seats given a bad rating, nos	Characteristics
a. Neck	5, 6	Lumbar support; concave, high and inclined backrest	4, 9, 10, 12	Lumbar pad high, or wanting; slope of backrest low or steep
b. Shoulders	6	as under a.	3, 8	as under a.
c. Back	2, 5, 6	upholstered: as under a.	3, 8	low backrest
d. Loins	2, 4, 6	upholstered; no lumbar pad, or shaped as in a.	1, 3	bend or ridge on lumbar pad
e. Buttocks	6, 7, 8	hollowed out and upholstered	3, 1, 9	seat flat
f. Thighs	9, 1, 11, 8	flat support for thighs	3, 5, 2	support for thighs curved upwards
g. Seat tilted backwards	6	as under a.	3, 9, 8,	low or steep backrest
h. Seat tilted forwards	12	high lumbar pad and cavity for buttocks	3, 1	bend or ridge on lumbar pad

By means of 66 comparisons in pairs each seat was compared with each of the others, and assessed as 'comfortable' or 'uncomfortable'. Since the 50 testers each assessed all the 66 pairs, a total of 3,300 choices was given. These choices were entered directly into the formula for sequence analysis, so that the statistical results were available as soon as the experiment was over. On another day, the same persons were assembled for a second session. They sat for 5 minutes on each of the 12 chairs at a table 74 cm high. The order of presentation of the seats was at random, drawn by lot, and for each set a questionnaire was completed. Beside giving opinions about individual body positions, the following questions had to be answered: 'How does the seat feel when you lean back?' and 'How does the seat feel when you sit forward?'

Comparison in pairs gave the following groups of equal merit:

Group 1	Nos. 2, 6, 11
Group 2	Nos. 10, 12
Group 3	No. 5
Group 4	No. 1
Group 5	Nos. 4, 7
Group 6	Nos. 3, 8, 9

The results of the questionnaire are set out in *Figures 59, 60, 61* and *62*. The analysis of the completed questionnaires gave results that are summarised in *Table 63*.

The following conclusions can be drawn from this:

- the seats with a high back rest and profiles like those shown for Nos. 5 and 6, together with upholstered seats were assessed as good in respect of how they felt to the back, neck and loins, but received an unfavourable assessment for having too prominent curves and ridges in the lumbar region.
- a seat that was moulded to the shape of the buttocks was assessed better than a flat one.
- seats that were flat in the front part produced fewer complaints of discomfort in the upper thighs than seats with an upward bulge.
- seat No. 6 received favourable mention when leaning backwards and seat No. 12 when sitting forwards.

Two chairs were placed in the first three groups in each assessment, namely Nos. 2 and 6. *We conclude that chairs Nos. 2 and 6 were equally suitable for both sitting positions and that this compromise had been bought at the price of very little discomfort.*

The leading position of these two chairs is also expressed in the rating for general suitability, which agrees well with the comparison in pairs. Since seat No. 2 was upholstered, the key position of No. 6 is particularly significant.

Since multi-purpose seats are compromise furniture, and have to be suited to a forward position at table as well as a reclining position during conversation, we advocated the development of a multi-purpose profile based in the first instance on the findings on chairs Nos. 2 and 6. At the same time, we were naturally inclined to avoid all shapes that had led to frequent complaints. The shape that was evolved is illustrated in *Figure 63.*

General directions for multi-purpose seats

From the results of all the experiments, and considering the analysis set out in Table 63, recommendations for the design of multipurpose seats may be summarised as follows:

Proposal for a general purpose chair

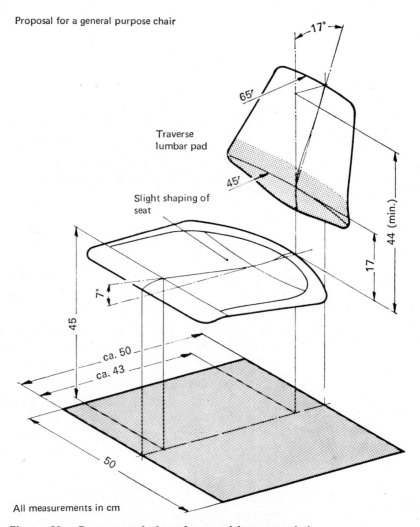

All measurements in cm

Figure 63   Recommendations for a multipurpose chair

Back rest

The profile of seat No. 6, with a gently rounded support for pelvis and sacrum, which lies between 7 and 20 cm above the deepest point of the seat, and has a gently convex back rest, is to be recommended. The height of the back rest should be at least 85 cm above the floor, provided that the highest point of the seat does not exceed 43 cm. Upholstery should be used on back rests that give lumbar support.

Seat

A seat gently moulded under the buttocks, flat in the front part beneath the upper thighs, and rising posteriorly, is recommended in view of the double function of the multi-purpose seat for leaning forward, and for reclining back. So that a back rest with lumbar support can be used for small people the depth of the seat from lumbar pad to front edge should not exceed 43 cm. Deeper seats cause the buttocks to move forward, with the result that the back is no longer supported in the region of the sacrum and pelvis. The breadth of the seat should be 40 cm.

Our recommended measurement for maximum depth of seat is about 1 cm. greater than that of *Shackel* and his colleagues (99); we consider that a moulded seat and the backrest recommended by us call for a seat-depth between 40 and 43 cm.

Height of seat

The height of the seat above the floor depends on its profile. A seat that rises in front should have a height of 43 cm at the highest point where it makes contact with the thighs, but this contact can be avoided by giving the seat a gentle curvature. A seat that is flat and in the horizontal plane may have a height of 44 to 46 cm but the front edge must be slightly rounded (as in seat no. 9).

These recommendations are approximately the same as those of *Shackel and colleagues* (99).

Upholstery and materials

A pad of 2–4 cm of foam rubber over the whole seat is recommended. Even an ergonomic seat can be made more comfortable with a cushion, a result attributable on the one hand to the wider distribution of pressure areas on the seat and on the other to the better resistance of the surface to slipping.

The covering material should be permeable to air and moisture, resistant to slip, and retentive of warmth. To avoid damp patches in the material an absorbent layer can be placed underneath it. In addition, holes in the plastic seat and back-rest may be used. Elasticity or 'give' of the unpadded shell is undesirable.

Matching of seat height to requirements

Compromises are unavoidable in multi-purpose chairs that must serve several functions and different sitting postures. Conversely, a multi-purpose chair cannot satisfy all conditions for maximum comfort in any particular situation. A particularly important item in this context is body-size, which can be catered for by providing seats of several different heights. For meeting-rooms and similar places, where requirements cannot be forecast, lower chairs are sometimes preferable to higher ones.

The Bed

Man spends round about one third of his life in a bed, which among civilised peoples is by far the most important and most universal item of 'sleeping furniture'. Moreover, when we consider how vital deep and satisfying sleep is to health, it is remarkable that science has given so little attention to bed design. The recommendations for the design of beds that are to be found in the literature are concerned, almost without exception, with what is the general practice.

Dimensions of beds

When designing a bed it is necessary to consider both the body length of the occupants, and the provision of a certain amount of room for movement. Hence not average lengths but those of the tallest people should be taken into account. Furthermore, allowance must be made for secular increases in size, which have resulted in todays young adults being about 5 cm taller than the general population of adults.

Length of beds

To provide adequately for these particular requirements *most recommendations for the length of a bed (internal measurement) lie between 190 and 210 cm. We feel that 190 cm is a minimum and that 210 cm is desirable.*

Width

The width of a single bed must allow enough room for a person lying on his side to bend the knees. For tall people this means 70 cm, and allowing 15 cm on each side for movement the total width becomes 100 cm.

The recommendations given in the literature for single beds for adults vary between 90 and 100 cm. We are of the opinion that 100 cm is desirable and that many people would find 110–120 cm very acceptable

The literature recommends widths of 140–180 cm for double beds. A width of 140 cm should be regarded as a minimum; 180 cm is satisfactory for double-beds, but not for bed-making.

Height of bed

Interior decorators have sharply reduced the heights of beds in recent years, to keep them in proportion to the heights of the rooms. *The 'victim' of this reduction is the housewife, who has to bend her back more than with previous designs. For this purpose low beds are unsatisfactory.*

For convenience in bed-making the top of the mattress should be between 70 and 90 cm from the floor: however, heights of between 50 and 60 cm are more convenient for getting in and out of bed. *Hence a compromise height of 60–70 cm is arrived at.* Unfortunately this height is completely out of favour with modern interior decorators. A change of fashion is very desirable if housework is to be made easier.

Room for bed making

The correct attitude when making beds is either to squat down or to go down on one knee on the floor, and people who suffer from backache should adopt one or other of these postures for the good of their discs. Nevertheless many people content themselves with bending at the knees and hips, and these movements may be correct if the bed is higher (50 cm or more from the floor). The following allowances for space for bed-making result from these ergonomic considerations:

| | Working space round bed | |
Type of bed	Minimum	Maximum
low beds (less than 50 cm)	95 cm	100 cm
high beds (more than 50 cm)	66 cm	80 cm

Allowances in foreign countries vary between 40 and 85 cm. The English rules (67) distinguish between room for walking about round the bed (70 cm) and the minimum that will suffice for bed-making (40 cm). Another consideration is the space necessary for cleaning the floor under the bed. According to *McCullough* and his colleagues (49) a space of 122 cm on one of the two long sides of the bed must be allowed for this purpose.

Three requirements for mattresses

According to *Belart* (117) there are three requirements that apply to mattresses on medical grounds:

- comfort when lying down
- good heat-retention
- adequate absorption of perspiration

Comfort when lying down is particularly important to sufferers from rheumatism, since a bad back and aching joints need to be relieved from muscular tension and from the weight of the body. Comfort when lying is provided by mattresses that give as nearly as possible the same support to the body whatever its position and profile.

How yielding should a mattress be?

According to Belart *(117) a mattress should be so constructed that at every change of position it should yield gently to each of the bodily projections (shoulders, hips, pelvis) while supporting the body as a whole, including the concavities such as the sides and the hollow of the back. It is equally important that the mattress should preserve its shape; it should not settle into a boat shape, nor take an impression of the body lying on it.*

These requirements are obviously logical, and they have also been formulated in similar ways by other medical men. *Figure 64* shows a correct and an incorrect attitude when lying down.

Hard or soft under-mattress?

A hard wooden support beneath the mattress has been recommended by various authors particularly for people with back ailments, but experience up to date has shown no decisive results. Many people have had good results, but many others have suffered from increased back-ache. To quote *Belart* (117) verbatim: 'The board beneath the mattress so often recommended for bad backs makes sense only if the mattress is too soft. It is usually superfluous with a good spring mattress'.

So the question whether a hard underlay is suitable either for healthy people or for those with back ailments remains completely open. It is to be hoped that medical scientists will take up this problem experimentally.

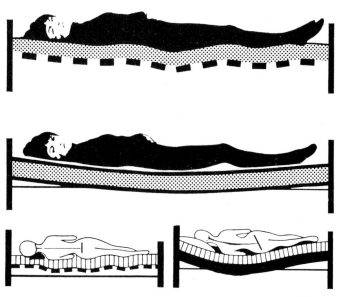

Figure 64   The top photograph and the lower left drawing show a correct posture when lying in bed. The middle photograph and the lower right drawing show a bad posture arising from a boat-shaped mattress. After Neumeyer (118)

The mattress and depth of sleep	*Kanz and Gertis* (119) studied the effect of different sets of bed-clothes on the depth of sleep of 4 research subjects. For this purpose they developed an apparatus to register all movements and changes of position of the body during sleep. The sum of all these movements was used as an index of the depth of sleep. *The combination of a spring-mattress with a feather pillow gave the best average depth of sleep.* The combination of a latex mattress with a feather pillow gave a wider scatter of results, but the authors rated it on the average as equal to the first-named combination. On the other hand, the combination of a latex mattress and a latex foam pillow caused a greater number of movements. Polyurethane mattresses with polyurethane pillows, and kapok mattresses with feather pillows were intermediate in their effects. The authors established that the pillow had more effect on the depth of sleep than the types of mattress that were tested.
	Investigation of the damping qualities of the mattress, that is how much it oscillated after a force was exerted on it, gave better results for a latex mattress on top of a rigid board than for latex on tightly stretched springs. A spring mattress gave the best damping, and polyurethane the least. Nevertheless it must be stated that the oscillation characteristics of the mattress have not so far been proved to have any effect on the depth of sleep.
Mattresses and hygiene	*Kanz and Gertis* (119) carried out an enquiry into experience with mattresses in 20 hospitals, with nearly 8,000 beds. One hospital liked mattresses of latex and polyurethane, but the others were either doubtful or rejected them. *Kanz* approved of foam mattresses on grounds of hygiene, because foam rubber has bacteriostatic properties. Moreover, this material is washable and practically dust-free, is also vermin resistant and is free from toxic substances that might set up allergies.
Heat-retention	Mattresses and underlays should be good heat-insulators, so that the body does not lose any of its warmth during sleep. The more porous a mattress is, and the more air it retains, the better it acts as a heat-insulator. Spring, latex and polyurethane mattresses were all good in this respect. A horsehair mattress is equally good, if it is of good quality, and if enough sheeps wool is mixed with it.
Body transpiration	Sufficient absorption of body transpiration (i.e. water-vapour and sweat) is an important hygienic characteristic. Mattresses and underlays must take up water vapour, but at the same time they must be sufficiently permeable for the moisture to be able to evaporate during the course of the day. Wool-clippings are very good in this respect.
General impressions	*Belart* (117) had a good all-round opinion of the spring mattress since it keeps its shape and is good in all the other respects. He had reservations about latex and polyurethane, which had low permeability to moisture, and about horse-hair mattresses, which over the years lose their elasticity and become flat or shaped to the body.
	For bed springs the author recommended the usual types, among which patent mattresses with metal braces were particularly good. He considered wooden laths to be too hard. *Neumeyer* (118) recommended 'Lattoflex' under-springing; this is built up from criss-cross wooden plates which in turn are laid on rubber bearers so that they conform to the shape of a person lying on them.

5 Layout and Dimensions of Rooms and Buildings

Summary
Kitchens

Modern kitchen areas of 7–8 square metres do not meet the requirements of the great majority of tenants, who want to take at least one meal a day in the kitchen, as well as using it for purposes such as washing and ironing. We therefore recommend that kitchens should be larger, and with a dining alcove should have a gross area of at least 12 square metres; 15 square metres should be allowed where possible.

Data are given for passage ways and service areas which will improve working efficiency and safety and make homework less arduous.

Recommendations for the arrangement of work-areas on various ground-plans are illustrated in a figure. For households with more than 2 persons the preference is for a two-sided kitchen.

Rules are given for the front-length and for a uniform height for work surfaces; for the amount of cupboard space and for the heights of partitions and shelves. In both wall and floor cupboards all divisions should have the maximum possible adjustment.

Closed internal kitchens pose special lighting & ventilation problems, and working kitchens without daylight are not recommended on psychological grounds. On the other hand, internal cooking areas in an open plan are beneficial, since they allow the cook to remain in contact with the family and their guests.

Baths and W.C.'s

Bathroom and W.C. should be separate: separation is desirable in households of more than one person, and is a hygienic necessity in households of more than three people. Direct access from the hall or corridor is necessary, and is desirable from the bedrooms. Tables give recommended measurements for fittings, space for movement, and ground-plans of bathrooms and W.C.'s. In contrast to the norms usually quoted, we recommend that a space 100 cm deep should be left clear in front of all bathroom and toilet fitments; this allows mothers enough space to tend their children.

Living rooms and dining rooms

The dimensions of living rooms are dictated by domestic behaviour, by the space needed for furniture and by irrational psychological factors. In modern life a multi-purpose living room with a dining alcove is preferred to the physical separation of living and eating areas in two rooms. Tables and a figure give recommended measurements for the space needed for furniture and circulation areas, and hence give the minimum areas for the living room. At best, current norms take account only of the opinions given by the groups of occupants who happened to be questioned, and so have limited value. It seems highly probable that most people would be happy to have a larger living room, and architects and building contractors should work towards bigger living rooms – without putting up prices.

Bedrooms and children's rooms

Bedrooms for adults are little used during the day and so, if necessary, can face north. Children's rooms are used in daylight hours and should face the sun. Bedrooms and children's rooms should be separated from communal areas, and have direct access to bathroom and W.C. if possible.

Tables and a figure set out recommendations for furniture and circulation space, and for the dimensions of these rooms. Modern children's rooms are usually too small.

Balconies

Balconies belong to living space in the narrow sense, and serve for relaxation, for work and for children to play. A width of 150 cm and an area of 3 square metres must be regarded as minimum requirements; balconies of 5–6 square metres are preferable. Plenty of sunlight, direct access to communal areas, and seclusion from neighbours and their noise are necessary. For safety's sake balconies should have a balustrade 100 cm high, not climbable by children. A safety screen 2 metres high is the only way to ensure that children cannot fall over the balustrade.

Front door and entrance hall

Climbing stairs consumes a great deal of energy. Stairs are a great handicap to old and infirm people, and for them lifts must be provided. The most efficient slope for stairs is 30°, with a tread-height of 17 cm and a depth of 29 cm. Stairs of these dimensions prevent stumbling. Hand-rails should be 85–90 cm high. Stairs and front doors should allow the passage of furniture as well as people.

Communal rooms for
washing and housework

Washing household linens is a tiring task which takes up 10–15% of the total working time in the household, and calls for suitable equipment including washing-machines, as well as space in a communal laundry. Drying space of 22–25 square metres is recommended for every 6 households in the multi-family block. Where there is a utility room in the flat, an area of 7–9 square metres is needed for this purpose. In dwellings with a total area of less than 100 square metres, some washing will be done in the bathroom, and the bathroom must be large enough to accommodate a washing machine, a drier, and a basket for dirty linen.

When dealing with the washing, a housewife needs a separate work-space of 1.6–2 square metres for her equipment and for room to operate it. In some cases this space is provided in the utility room; in other cases use is made of the multi-purpose living room, the dining alcove, or the area is included in the kitchen space.

The kitchen

Types of kitchen

Among the types of kitchen that are common nowadays, three groups can be distinguished :

— the enclosed working kitchen
— the dining kitchen
— the open working kitchen

The enclosed working kitchen is a self-contained space in which all the ordinary kitchen work can be carried on. It does not include a dining area that forms part of the general living space, and it is divided from living rooms, dining-room and dining alcoves *by a door. The dining kitchen* is an enclosed working kitchen which is enlarged by the addition of a dining area that forms part of the general living space. *The open working kitchen* is a kitchen which does not include a dining area, but which has an open link with adjoining rooms. The partition between the open working kitchen and the living room, dining room or dining alcove may consist of :

— furniture, such as a hatch or a dining counter
— masonry, but without a door
— a curtain
— or no partition at all.

Whatever partition exists, the kitchen should have a window over the working area. Enclosed working kitchens without a window, or open working kitchens that have no window over the working position are described as 'internal' kitchens.

Areas of kitchens

The research into the utilization of kitchens (34, 35, 38, 39, 40), cited in Chapter 2, show that in the great majority of contemporary households the kitchen is used for meals, and for activities such as washing, ironing and so on. *We must therefore ensure that future kitchen areas are suitable for these various uses, and provide adequate space for them.*
Nowadays, kitchens commonly have a gross area of 7—8 square metres. The more extensive the use of the kitchen, the bigger is the kitchen area that must be provided. When installing a dining kitchen, the area for a dining space given in *Table 64* must be added to the gross area of 7—8 square metres, so that the total area for a 4-person household will come to 12 square metres.
If nevertheless there are special reasons why a purely working kitchen must be planned, then this too should be not less than 8 square metres, since otherwise there will not be room for either working areas or for cupboard space. On the basis of these considerations, and taking into account current results of research into domestic ergonomics, the following rules are recommended for consideration as applying to households of 3—4 persons.

	Square metres Minimal	Desirable
— working kitchen without a dining alcove (e.g. open working kitchen)	8	10
— kitchen with dining alcove	12	15

Circulation and operating space

Unrestricted passage when carrying pots and pans is important not only for convenience, but also for safety's sake. Enough elbow-room when using

Table 64   Recommended dimensions for meal area in the kitchen (cm)
After Huser, Grandjean and Suchantke (120)

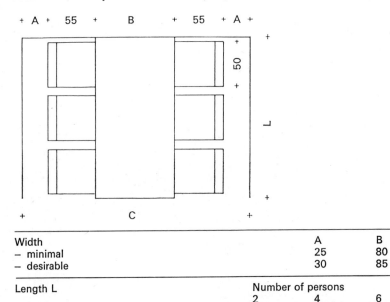

Width		A	B	C
— minimal		25	80	240
— desirable		30	85	255

Length L	Number of persons			
	2	4	6	8
— minimal	80	120	170	230
— desirable	80	120	180	240

Passage-way	60			

Area of eating surface	Number of persons			
	2	4	6	8
— minimal (square metres)	3.4	4.3	5.5	7.0
— desirable (square metres)	3.6	4.6	6.1	7.7

drawers, cupboards and other installations reduces the changes in bodily posture that are necessary, and makes a not insignificant contribution to lightening the labour involved. *Figure 65 a–f* summarises recommendations for operating space for equipment and installations in kitchens as well as circulation space. The values given there are based upon anthropometric considerations and also take account of recommendations put forward in the literature (49, 54, 67, 128).

Work areas

Arrangement

As already set out on page 86, *the work-areas should be arranged from left to right in the order: sink — main work surface — oven — somewhere to put things down.* This arrangement allows the work to flow smoothly without unnecessary movements.
The kitchen plans given in *Figure 66* conform to these principles.
The kitchen with everything along one wall is usually too long, and is suitable only for one or two roomed dwellings. A kitchen with equipment on both sides has no corners that cannot be used, although the work triangle referred to above can be interrupted by people passing through. Still, the different work areas are not far apart. This type of kitchen is often combined with a balcony. An L-shaped kitchen allows the work triangle to be maintained without interruption, and in addition the free corner is often turned into a dining

65a
Passage between wall and table,
hands free

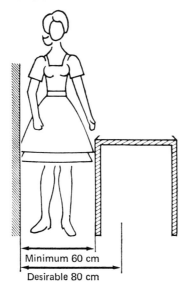

Minimum 60 cm

Desirable 80 cm

65b
Passage between wall and table
when carrying

Minimum 80 cm

Desirable 90 cm

65c
Room for movement in front of
sink, cooker or working surface

Minimum 40 cm

Desirable 80 cm

65d
Free space in front of
refrigerator

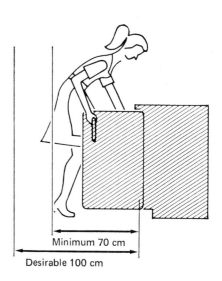

Minimum 70 cm

Desirable 100 cm

Figure 65   Recommended dimensions for passages and circulation spaces in kitchens   After Huser, Grandjean and Suchantke (120)

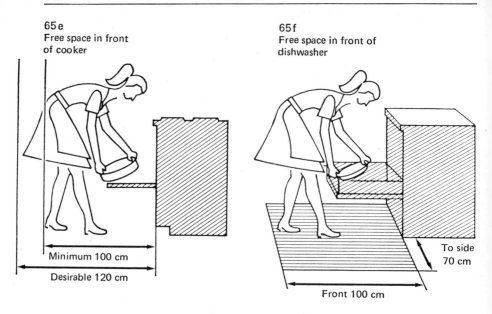

65 e
Free space in front
of cooker

65 f
Free space in front of
dishwasher

Minimum 100 cm

Desirable 120 cm

Front 100 cm

To side
70 cm

Figure 65   Recommended dimensions for passages and circulation spaces in kitchens   After Huser, Grandjean and Suchantke (120)

alcove. A disadvantage is that this corner often has cupboards that are difficult to use. This applies even more to U-shaped kitchens, though in this shape of kitchen the work triangle is not interfered with, and the work centres are close together. A U-shaped kitchen is particularly suitable for large dwellings.

On balance, the kitchen with equipment on two sides is to be preferred for households of more than two people.

Width of work areas

Our recommendations for minimal and desirable widths for work areas are summarised in *Table 65*. They include the measurements recommended by various institutions on the basis of scientific research (54, 67, 128, 129, 130, 131, 132).
The width of 60 cm prescribed in DIN 18022 (133) for the main working surface has proved insufficient in practice (134). If there is no dishwasher, there should be a double sink.
A sufficiency of places to put things down must be provided. Utensils and crockery used more than once during the preparation of a meal must be put down where they can be seen easily and reached when wanted again. *Having plenty of places to put things down avoids unnecessary walking and stooping.*

Working heights

On pages 73–85 correct working heights were dealt with. In the present section, heights for working surfaces in the kitchen are repeated in the form of recommendations.
Research has shown (53, 64) that the optimal heights of the three main working surfaces were different: the upper edge of the sink was 10–15 cm higher than the cooker and the work table standing between them was intermediate. We feel that there is more to be said for a uniform height, reducing both the amount of handling of pots and pans and the risk of hitting them against the raised edges.

We suggest a uniform height of 90 cm for all three work-surfaces

Table 65   Recommended   front-lengths   of   work-centres   After   Huser,
Grandjean and Suchantke (120)

Work-centre	Front lengths in cm	
	Minimal	Desirable
Main working surface	80	100–120
Place to put things down near cooker	40*	60
Place near refrigerator		60
Second working surface	100	120
Sink with two washbowls; each bowl length	2×35	
Sink with one bowl; bowl length	40	50
Sink with one bowl: drying surface (draining board)	60	80
Depth of surfaces for putting things down or for working	60	60

* At 40 cm the lower cupboard can be used for pans.

Kitchen lay-outs which conform to the principles of rational planning of work

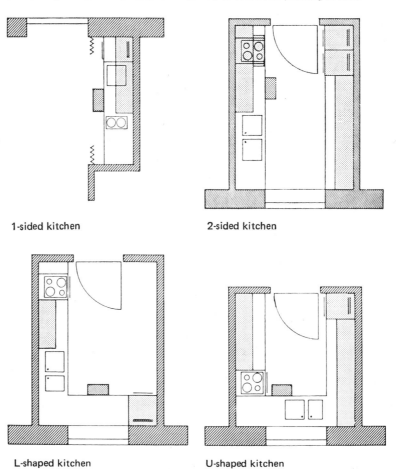

1-sided kitchen   2-sided kitchen

L-shaped kitchen   U-shaped kitchen

Figure 66   Arrangement of work centres in different kitchen lay-outs   After
Huser, Grandjean and Suchantke (120)

Figure 67   Heights of reach in the kitchen   The height of the woman is assumed to be 161 cm. After Berg, Boalt, Holm and Leander (69)

Cupboards and shelves

Height of reach

On page 85 measurements for the layout of cupboards and shelves were given, and our recommendations for kitchen fitments are summarised again in *Figure 67*.

The most convenient height of reach – which lies between 65 and 150 cm from the floor – extends only to the lowest shelf of the upper cupboard and to the front half of the top shelf of the lower cupboard.

At this point, we must repeat the recommendation that shelves should have the maximum possible adjustment in both upper and lower cupboards so that they can be altered to suit individual requirements

The housewife should be encouraged to arrange kitchen utensils and provisions according to the frequency with which they are used, keeping together those that are used in combination. Utensils that are often needed should be within easy reach, those used rarely being stored in the furthest corners.

We recommend a minimum of 40 cm and a maximum of 50 cm for the space between upper and lower cupboards. A smaller space certainly gives more useful cupboard room, while a bigger space is more convenient for handling utensils, but means a loss of much of the most useful space in the cupboards. *The upper and lower cupboards for a kitchen for 4–6 persons should take up from 5–5.9 metres of frontal length inclusive of two high cupboards.* This total includes the work surfaces, excluding that of the oven top. It does not include the broom cupboard, which for practical reasons is better outside in the corridor. *The total shelf area of all kitchen cupboards should be at least 6 square metres. The capacity of the refrigerator for a 4-person household should be at least 150 litres and preferably 200 litres.*

The required amount of cupboard space is achieved automatically if the recommended dimensions are followed for the work surfaces, the upper and lower cupboards, as well as the two high cupboards. The high cupboards can then contain the refrigerator and the eye-level grill.

Cupboard space

The dining kitchen

The dining alcove in the kitchen is mainly used on weekdays. Apart from this it is used occasionally for a few household activities, possibly for hobbies, children's play and so on.

There are basically two possibilities for dining arrangements in a dwelling:

a. One place for meals in the kitchen and one in the living room, or in some other room
b. Only one place for meals and that in the kitchen

If only one place for meals is provided then there must be enough room for at least two guests, and so solution *b* cannot be recommended on social grounds. Dimensions for a dining alcove in the kitchen are given in *Table 64*. If there are two dining areas in the dwelling, then the minimal suggestions are sufficient, but if there is only one place for meals, then the measurements given as 'desirable' must be adopted.

Internal kitchens

Internal kitchens are either completely enclosed working kitchens without windows, or open kitchens which have no window over the working area. It is still a matter of dispute whether kitchens of this type are desirable. What the occupants think of them depends on how well certain problems of hygiene have been solved, in particular those relating to ventilation and lighting. Closed internal kitchens bring into play a psychological factor: many women feel shut in if they cannot look out of a window, and they dislike such kitchens on this ground. *Closed internal kitchens seem to us to be undesirable on psychological grounds.*

It is rather different with open internal kitchens, which have no window over the work-place, but do have open access to adjoining rooms. According to a Danish study (121) such kitchens are not disliked provided that they have plenty of light and air. The contact with family and guests while working was particularly appreciated. It seems not impossible that this solution will be adopted more in future, *since it seems likely that women will look for fulfilment less in absorption in work in the kitchen and more in social contacts.*

In any event, the following points may be made about open internal kitchens:

– artificial lighting must be improved to the point that it is almost as good as natural light

- a ventilator fan with a flow of 250 cubic metres per hour should be provided
- it must be possible to cut down the flow to 50 cubic metres per hour when cooking is not going on, to avoid draughts
- a fume hood must be installed over the cooker
- the mechanical extraction of air by fan and fume hood can with advantage be supplemented by a fresh air inlet
- the flow of fresh air should be regulated by means of an adjustable air-brick in an outside wall
- the air brick must be placed in such a position that it does not cause an annoying draught
- the ventilation equipment should not produce a noise level in the adjoining room exceeding 25 dB(A) at the lowest setting, or 30 dB(A) at maximum output.

Interior fittings and balconies

Walls

The exposed walls of the kitchen should be washable up to a height of 1.4 metres. Ceramic tiled surfaces are good in this respect, and are particularly necessary behind the working surfaces.

Floor-covering

The same rules apply to floor-coverings in kitchens as in the rest of the house:

- *non-slip surface*
- *adequate thermal insulation*
- *sound damping of footsteps*
- *ease of cleaning*

Since in a kitchen hard and heavy objects as well as hot liquids may fall on the floor, the floor-covering must be resistant both to mechanical impact and to hot oils and other fluids. The same applies to the coverings of the work surfaces, and to the fronts of kitchen fitments.

Kitchen balconies

A working balcony in front of the kitchen is desirable for performing cleaning operations that should be carried out in the open air, such as working with chemical cleaning fluids or sprays. In addition to this the kitchen balcony provides an extra space where materials and utensils can be put down and dried, so long as they are not affected by the weather (mops, dust-bins, bottles etc.) Minimal dimensions for a kitchen balcony are 120 × 60 cm and desirable ones 150 × 90 cm. The parapet should be unclimbable, so that children cannot fall over it, and a height of 100–110 cm is recommended.

Bathroom and W.C.

Bathroom and W.C. are the rooms set aside for bodily care and personal hygiene, and are recognisable by having the appropriate equipment.

Separation of bathroom and W.C.

In public authority housing bathroom and W.C. are often combined for reasons of economy, but this is a very questionable measure for households with several inhabitants. Many responsible institutions and public health officials advocate the physical separation of bathroom and W.C. on account of the better use of space, the avoidance of smells, and general hygiene. The *minimal requirements* that are given in the literature can be seen in *Table 66*.

We recommend the following rules:

- *for households of up to two persons a single combined bathroom and W.C., with all the necessary equipment, is acceptable.*
- *separation of the bathroom and W.C. is desirable for dwellings intended for more than one person.*
- *for households of three or more persons separation is a necessity.*

Table 66   Minimum conditions for which a W.C. separate from the bathroom must be provided   After Huser, Grandjean and Suchantke (120)

Country	Literature	Separate provision is based on the number of persons	Rooms
Switzerland	(135)		4
Germany	(133)	5	
	(136)	5	
	(137)		4
Austria	(136)	3	
Sweden	(138)	5	
Finland	(139)		4
Norway	(139)	5	
Holland	(139)		5
Great Britain	(139)		4
Roumania	(139)		4

Location in dwelling

Bathroom and W.C. should be so located in the dwelling that they can be entered directly from the corridor or hall, and direct access between bathroom and adults' bedroom is generally appreciated. On technical grounds and for reasons of economy it is advisable for the bathroom and W.C. to share a common wall with the kitchen: they may be located on the north-facing side of the house. The question as to whether these sanitary rooms should be planned as internal rooms is, in our view, predominantly a question of ventilation. If this problem is satisfactorily solved, then there is no serious reason why they should not be internal rooms.

Sanitary arrangements

The following arrangements are necessary for a family of four:

– a bath-tub with hot and cold supply, a mixer, and a variable spray nozzle: provision for a shower is desirable
– a wash basin with hot and cold supply, provided with a mixer with swivel-arm
– a toilet cupboard with a mirror
– a shuttered socket for electrical apparatus (illegal in England)
– holders for soap, glass and hand-towel near the washbasin
– soap holder, grip handle and bath towel holder near the bath-tub
– cupboard for storing bathroom linen
– a lockable medicine cupboard, out of the reach of children.

In many households the bathroom is also used for laundry. If this use is contemplated, then the bathroom must be made bigger to allow for a washing-machine, drier and more dirty clothes storage. Other suitable equipment includes an airer and drier for hand-towels in the form of several heating tubes arranged one above the other.
A special shower cabinet close by the bathtub is strongly to be recommended, particularly for older people with bodily infirmities.
When the W.C. is separate from the bathroom, it should be fitted with a hand washbasin as well as with a lavatory pan. A low flush pan is specially recommended. It is difficult to judge whether a bidet is necessary or not. Different regional customs in bodily hygiene are involved in answering this question, but a bidet has positive value from the point of view of hygiene.
Small dwellings which have no separate W.C. and dwellings for five or more persons should have an additional lavatory pan in the bathroom.

Size of water installations

Table 67 summarises recommendations for the dimensions of sanitary fittings, providing for people of average height, 172 cm (men) and 161 cm (women).

Table 67   Proposed minimum sizes for baths and WC's After Huser, Grandjean and Suchantke (120)

| Equipment | Dimensions in cm | | |
	Breadth	Depth	Height
Bathtub	170	75	45 int
			55 ext
Water taps beside bath	–	–	70
Shower cabinet	90	90	
Shower head			190–200
Wash basin	60	50	80–90
Water taps above wash basin	–	–	100
Shelf above wash basin	–	–	115
Upper edge of mirror	–	–	190
Lower edge of mirror	–	–	130
Bidet	40	65	40
WC	40	50	40
Hand basin	40	30	80–90

It may be mentioned here that our recommendations for bath-tubs and wash-basins are above the usual norms, to make allowance for the space necessitated by physiological considerations.

On the question of the height of the lavatory seat there are two opposing factors:

– a lower seat makes defaecation easier
– old people and cripples find it difficult to rise from a low seat.

We therefore recommend a moderate height of 40 cm for the seat, and the provision of an appropriate hand-grip.

Falls in the bath

In deciding on the dimensions of the bath-tub, the first consideration is to prevent the very dangerous falls that can occur. The bottom of the bath must be flat or – better still – have a non-slip surface. A rubber mat is equally satisfactory, provided that it can be cleaned periodically, and kept in good condition. A handle to grip when getting up reduces the risk of slipping. This question of falling down in the bath seems to us to be so important that we shall mention it twice, at this point and in the section about accidents in the home. The dimensions of the bathroom and lavatory must be determined by the space needed to accommodate the equipment and to use it. The space that is advisable for people moving about, standing and sitting is dealt with on page 68.

Space required in front of sanitary equipment

Table 68 summarises the minimal spaces that are given in the literature to be provided in front of installations in the bathroom and W.C.

We are of the opinion that many of these norms, especially the depths, are too low. We advise that there should be free space 100 cm deep in front of each installation.

This is not only sufficient for an individual adult to move about freely, but also a welcome elbow-room when mothers are tending their children.

Overall size

The overall size of the room is the sum of installation space plus circulation space, and we give our recommendations for this in *Table 69*.

Cupboard space

It should be possible to store in the bathroom the necessary toilet articles, linen for the bathroom, towels and cloths, and medicines and a first-aid outfit. A cupboard with a mirror is convenient for the toilet articles, and a separate cupboard should be provided for bathroom linen, possibly beneath the washbasin. It is advisable to have a special cupboard for medicines and the first-aid outfit, that can be locked or otherwise secured against unauthorised access and is high enough to be out of the reach of small children. A separate W.C. should have a smaller cupboard for articles of personal hygiene, again possibly beneath the wash-basin.

Table 68   Recommended space in front of items of equipment in bathroom and WC   After Huser, Graendjean and Suchantke (120)

Equipment	Space to be allowed, cm		Country	Literature
	Depth	Width		
Bathtub	80	160	Switzerland	(135)
	75		Germany	(133)
	130		Sweden	(140)
	70		Holland	(54)
Shower	80	80	Switzerland	(135)
	75		Germany	(133)
	70	90	Holland	(54)
Wash stand	55	90	Switzerland	(135)
	75		Germany	(133)
	85		Sweden	(140)
	70		Holland	(54)
Hand basin	45	70	Switzerland	(135)
	75		Germany	(133)
	50–70		Sweden	(140)
Bidet	40	80	Switzerland	(135)
	75		Germany	(133)
	50		Sweden	(140)
WC	50	80	Switzerland	(135)
	75		Germany	(133)
	50–100		Sweden	(140)

Table 69   Recommended overall areas for bathrooms/WCs   The 'desirable' areas include space for a washing machine and a bathroom cupboard ; a drier would require a further 70 × 70 cm. After Huser, Grandjean and Suchantke (120)

Contents of room	Gross area, square metres	
	Minimal	Desirable
Bathroom with bath and one washbasin	3	4
Bathroom with bath, and either 1 washbasin + 1 shower, or 2 washbasins	4	5
Bathroom, with bath, shower + 2 washbasins	5	6
WC with lavatory pan + washstand	2	3
WC + lavatory, washstand + bidet or shower	4	5

Walls and floor

Bathroom and W.C. should have waterproof coverings on the walls and floor. Ceramic tiles are recommended for the walls, up to a height of at least 1.30 metres, and up to 2 metres round the shower. A good form of flooring is a small mosaic to reduce the risk of slipping, with underfloor heating.

Provision for washing small articles

Even if there is a washing machine in a communal wash-house, smalls are often washed in the bathroom. For this reason we recommend some provision for drying hand washing over the bath, and it is desirable, as we have already said, for there to be enough room for a small washing machine.

Living and dining rooms

Fundamentals

From the results set out in Chapter Two we can extract the following as relevant to the design of living and dining rooms :

— the living room and the dining room are the focus of the communal life of the family
— they are scarcely used during the daytime, but in the evening they serve almost entirely for leisure activities

- the amount of time that the living room is in use increases considerably if it includes a dining space and a television set, when it becomes a multi-purpose living room
- the living room still preserves its traditional function in many regions, although a change from its being the 'best room' is detectable
- passive activities such as resting, listening to radio, watching television, and reading do not require much space for movement in front of the furniture. More vigorous activities such as children's play, offering refreshment or looking after infants, take up a good deal of space
- the demand for space depends not only on physiological considerations but also on irrational psychological factors. These include the associations of space with security and the fuller life, and confinement with repression.

A proportion of occupants is interested in the shape of rooms, though the numbers are smaller than architects often suppose. Psychological factors are just as important as are physiological factors, in spite of their irrational nature. Unfortunately they have been very little studied up to now.

Living and dining rooms

The commonest variants in present-day arrangements are:

- separate living and dining rooms
- living room + a dining alcove
- a living room big enough to include a dining table and chairs (multi-purpose living room).

The two last arrangements approach the use of the living room as an all-purpose room. If living space is restricted it is sensible to sacrifice the dining room in favour of a bigger, multipurpose living room, and this is adequate for the modern way of life.

Nevertheless, the question of where to eat is still not clear. The greater proportion of occupants like to eat in the kitchen, and many of these would also like an additional dining area in the living room, or in a special dining alcove. For everyday use the most important consideration is to have a convenient place to eat. With more and more women going out to work inconvenient location of the dining area should be avoided.

Furniture in the living room

A multi-purpose living room usually requires two groups of furniture for different activities:

- a *dining suite* if there is no dining alcove or separate dining room
- a *'cosy corner'*, usually two armchairs and a sofa.

Table 70 sets out the furniture for which space should be provided in a living room designed for four people. These data are derived from the analysis of the literature made by *Huber* (122) and take account of the furniture that is usual in Switzerland (123)

Analysis of dwellings and of questionnaires show that the following items of furniture are occasionally required:

Table 70   Space required for items of furniture in a multipurpose room for a family of four   After Huber (122)

Furniture	Number of units	Space required per item (cm)
Sofa	1	220 × 90
Armchair	2	100 × 80
Dining table	1	110 × 80
Chairs	6	55 × 50
Chest for storage	1	210 × 60
Radio, TV, gramophone	1	60 × 50
Sewing machine table	1	120 × 60
Work-table	1	120 × 80
Bookcase	1	180 × 40

- piano
- display cabinet
- sideboard
- a table for flowers
- a low table in the 'cosy corner'
- couch.

Space for standing furniture

Data given in the literature (120, 122) for the space (standing and circulation space) needed to accommodate different groups of furniture depend on how they are set out, and vary between the following limits:

Dining-table group with 4 places	4.2–7 square metres
Dining-table group with 6 places	5.4–10.2 square metres
Settee group with 2 easy chairs	8–10 square metres
Work-table with a chair	1.1–3.2 square metres

These figures must be increased in each case by allowing space for access and for additional pieces of furniture.

Figure 68 shows the space required for furniture and for people to move around it for the usual activities that are carried on in the living room.

Space in living rooms

By adding together the space required for the different groups of furniture a quantitative estimate can be arrived at for the total space needed in living rooms. This procedure does not take into account the functional relationship between the groups concerned, nor does it make any allowance for the irrational factor of the feeling of space, or lack of it, and the impression created by the proportions of the room.

Huber (122) summarised the sizes of living rooms as they were chosen, or recommended in the literature. Depending on the location of the dining area and the overall size of the dwelling, his provision ranged from 18–27 square metres.

In the studies carried out by *Meyer-Ehlers* (40), three-quarters of those questioned declared themselves satisfied with a living room space of 20–24 square metres. Our own studies (124) confirmed these findings: 87% of the 203 persons questioned in one piece of research thought a living room, which includes a dining area, of 21 square metres to be just right, though it should be clearly understood that there was no space needed in this living room for through passage. All other rooms opened into the corridor. On the other hand, living rooms with areas of 23.5 square metres which led to the bedrooms and to the kitchen were thought big enough by only 75% of those questioned.

Table 71 summarises the minima for areas of living rooms.

There was a strong desire for bigger living rooms, but *not* at the expense of smaller bedrooms, children's rooms and particularly kitchens.

Exclusive of space within the kitchen, the following areas were calculated for a dining suite exclusive of a sideboard, a dresser or passage-room:

4 persons	6 square metres
6 persons	8 square metres
8 persons	10 square metres

Studies of the sizes of separate dining rooms or dining alcoves lead to the conclusion that 10 square metres would meet most requirements.

Table 71   Minimal areas for living rooms   After Huser, Grandjean and Suchantke (120)

Size of apartment (number of rooms)	Minimal areas in square metres	
	Living room *with* dining alcove	Living room *without* dining alcove
2–3	20	18
4	22	20
5	24	22

The norms are minima   Here again it must be asserted that the values given in *Table 71*, as well as those arrived at by following the rules given for dining suites and dining alcoves should be regarded as minima. They are derived from data about what is customary and therefore they are seen from the standpoint of occupants who have never had occasion to compare them with bigger living rooms.

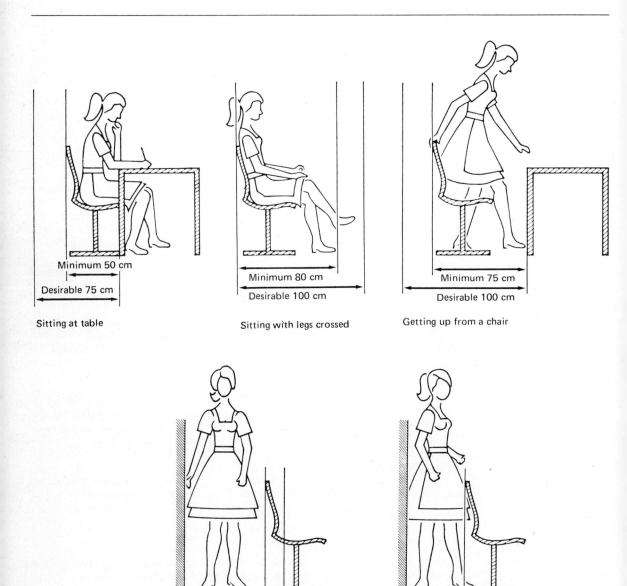

Minimum 50 cm
Desirable 75 cm
Sitting at table

Minimum 80 cm
Desirable 100 cm
Sitting with legs crossed

Minimum 75 cm
Desirable 100 cm
Getting up from a chair

Minimum 65cm
Desirable 80cm
Unrestricted passage behind a chair

Minimum 45 cm
Restricted passage behind a chair

Figure 68   Recommended minimum circulation measurements for the distances apart of furniture, and for circulation spaces in a multi-purpose living room

Figure 68 continued

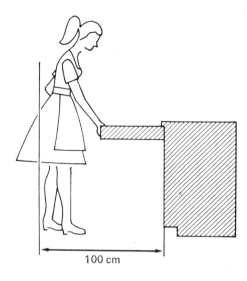

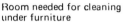

120 cm

100 cm

Room needed for cleaning
under furniture

Space for opening a drawer

We think it is likely that most people would be happier in larger living rooms. It would therefore be something to be grateful for if architects and building contractors were to include bigger living rooms in their plans – without raising their prices.

Ground plan

For a room to be practical in use, its shape and the arrangement of the doors are important as well as its total area. Long rooms are generally easier to furnish, especially when the furniture needs to be arranged in two groups. On grounds of both shape and furnishing, however, the living room should not be narrower than 3.8 metres. The width of the room must ensure free access to the balcony as well as a big enough space close to the balcony for the three-piece suite.

The arrangement of the doors must be functional: i.e. if more than one door is necessary, they must be so placed that they do not prevent parts of the room from being furnished. To avoid difficulty, there should be easy access between the kitchen and the dining area. A common complaint is the length of the walk between these points. During our own studies 25% of those questioned criticised the long distances from kitchen to dining table, and for this reason a distance of 3.5 metres should not be exceeded; a good-sized service hatch is desirable.

Open plan

'Open plan' means any ground-plan in which the living room, dining room and the corridor lead into one another, and are not separated by doors. Our own investigations (124) indicate that this solution was accepted by the majority of those questioned: 75% of the 172 questioned agreed, on condition that the living room did not thereby become a passage way. However, if the bedroom could be reached only by passing through the living room then the level of satisfaction fell to 66% of 124 questioned. Rejection was on grounds of disturbance by or to children and of insufficient privacy.

If a ground-plan with an open living room is chosen, then it should be well away from the front door of the dwelling, and as far as possible from the children's room.

Bedroom and children's room

Family structure and number of bedrooms

In principle each member of the family except the parents should have a room of their own in the dwelling. The claim for a separate sleeping place for *adults* of different sexes is self-evident. If the infants sleep in their parents' bedroom at all, they should not do so after they are two years old. (66, 81, 141) and this room should have a place for the perambulator to stand, or if possible a child's cot. This makes it easier for the mother to keep an eye on the child in special circumstances, for instance when the child is ill.

A common bedroom may be accepted for small children, but the sexes should be separated in the sixth year, or at latest by the 12th year (81, 141). In any event, a private bedroom for each child is desirable by the time they are ten years of age.

Place of bedrooms within the dwelling

On the basis of research mentioned in Chapter Two, and with special attention to the results of *Meyer-Ehlers* (40) the following rules can be formulated:

- bedrooms should be divided off from the living part of the dwelling, and should be near the bathroom and W.C.
- to make it easier to watch over small children at least one child's bedroom should be close to that of the parents.
- bathroom and W.C. should be accessible from the children's room without their having to pass through the living room
- because the parents' bedroom is used so little during the day, it may face north
- On the other hand, since children's rooms are used so much in the daytime, they should face south, south-east or south-west

Cupboard space

The importance of cupboard space cannot be overestimated, either for the parents' bedroom or the children's rooms. A shortage of cupboards makes housework much more difficult. The resulting disorder and lack of system means that things have to be looked for and complicates one's work in many different ways. For this reason many surveys on housing put 'having room for things' high on the list of good points.

From a survey of the number of cupboards and investigations into whether they were wide enough across the front (34, 54, 142) it can be said that the

Table 72   Recommended spaces for cupboards in bedrooms   After Huser, Grandjean and Suchantke (120)

Room	Minimal (cm)	Desirable (cm)	Depths (cm)
Parents' bedroom	240	300	60
Childrens' room, 2 beds	120	180	60
Childrens' room, 1 bed	120		60

Table 73   Recommended additional space for built-in cupboards   After Huser, Grandjean and Suchantke (120)

Type of cupboard	Front-lengths, (cm) Minimal	Desirable	Depths (cm)
Linen cupboard			
– 1 or 2 persons	40	60	40
– 3 or more persons	60	60	40–60
Wardrobe			
– 1 or 2 persons	60	60	60
– 3 or more persons	100	120	60

percentage of positive votes remains constant after a cupboard frontage of 140 cm per person has been reached (34, 142). By the same means it was established that the preference for hanging space or shelf space in built-in cupboards was in the ratio of 3 : 1 or 2.5 : 1.

Equivalent Danish recommendations (143) set the total cupboard area at 2–3% of the gross floor area of a dwelling.

Table 72 summarises our recommendations for cupboard space in bedrooms and children's rooms. They correspond closely with the latest recommendations of the Staatlichen Bauforschungsinstitut, Stockholm (144).

According to these a dwelling should also have the built-in cupboards given in Table 73.

Clothes closet

Nowadays clothes closets are increasingly to be found in place of wardrobes or built-in cupboards. These are often economical of space and contribute to a greater freedom in the furnishing of bedrooms. A walk-in clothes closet must have an entrance 50–60 cm wide, it must be ventilated and have artificial lighting, and it must be near the bedroom. If such a type is chosen, there should nevertheless be some provision, however little, for storing clothes as well as laundry in the bedroom.

Furniture space

Table 74 summarises the furniture specified by Huber (122) and the area that it usually occupies. The data are derived from lists of furniture given in the literature and from measurements of the furniture commonly found in Swiss homes.

Figures 69 a–g illustrate the amount of elbow-room that is needed for certain activities that are frequently carried out in bedrooms. They are based upon the ergonomic considerations set out on page 136, and on recommendations given in the literature (49, 54, 67, 126, 138, 143, 144).

On page 136, on ergonomic criteria and making allowance for the larger woman, we give the space round the bed required for bed making as 95–100 cm for low beds and 66–80 cm for high beds. In addition it was shown that a

Table 74   Space needed for furniture in bedrooms   After Huber (122)

Item of furniture	Number of items	Space required for each item (cm)
Parents' bedroom		
– bed	2	210 × 100
– night-table	2	50 × 45
– cupboard	1	240–300 × 60
– chair	2	45 × 50
– chest of drawers	1	120 × 50
– possible work-table	1	150 × 80
– possible armchair	1	60 × 65
Childrens' room with 2 beds		
– bed	2	210 × 200
– possible child's bed (cot)	1	130 × 70
– night-table	2	50 × 45
– cupboard	1	120–180 × 60
– table for homework	2	120 × 60
– shelves for books and toys	1	90 × 45
– space free for playing	–	120 × 180
Child's room with 1 bed		
– bed	1	210 × 200
– or cot	1	130 × 70
– night-table	1	50 × 45
– cupboard	1	120 × 60
– table for homework	1	120 × 60
– shelves for books and toys	1	90 × 45
– space free for playing	–	120 × 180

69a
Passage between cupboard and bed

70 cm

69b
Free space when dressing

120 × 120 cm

69c
Free space in front of a mirror

115 cm

69d
Free space in front of dressing-table

110 cm

69e
Space for making the bed

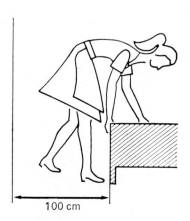

100 cm

69f
Space for cleaning under the bed

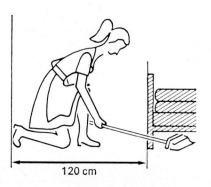

120 cm

69g
Space for opening drawers

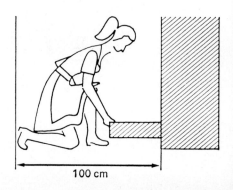

100 cm

**Figure 69
Free space needed
in bedrooms**

Table 75   Recommended areas for bedrooms After Huser, Grandjean and Suchantke (120)

Room	Areas in square metres		Breadth Minimal (cm)
	Minimal	Desirable	
Parents' bedroom	14	15–16	340
Children's bedroom 2 beds	12	14	280
Children's bedroom 1 bed	8	10	240

space of 122 cm along each side of the bed was desirable for cleaning beneath the bed. The recommendations that are given in *Figure 69* take account of these ergonomic factors.

Measurement of width Proposals for the dimensions of bedrooms that are derived from the space that is needed for items of furniture to stand together with space to use them give useful approximations, at least in principle. It is desirable, however, that they should be as flexible as possible in use, so that a bedroom may occasionally be used as a second living room, as a dining room or as a study. The parents' bedroom should always be capable of being furnished with a double bed, or with twin beds.

A children's room must certainly have a clear play space of 120×180 cm, and the double bedroom 240 cm wide that is common nowadays cannot satisfy this requirement. At most such a room should be planned as a child's room with a single bed.

Floor area The findings given in the literature for minimal and correct measurements of the area of bedrooms for parents range from 12–16 square metres, according to whether they have a free standing wardrobe, a built-in cupboard or a walk-in closet outside the bedroom. For double bedrooms the areas range from 10–13 square metres, and for a single bedroom from 6–12 square metres. Parents' bedrooms of 13 square metres and more were rated as big enough by a majority of those people questioned in Germany (40). According to our own studies (124) this held good for areas of 17 square metres in 80% of cases.

Twin bedded rooms with an area of up to 12 square metres, and a width of 240 cm were judged to be too small for children, as were single bedrooms for children if they had an area of less than 8 square metres. In a Swiss investigation (38), too, children's bedrooms of 10 square metres with widths of 240–270 cm were considered as being, at most, big enough for single bedrooms. Our own researches (124) show that children's bedrooms with an area of 11 square metres and width of 255 cm were considered big enough by only 50% of the 203 people questioned.

For parents' bedrooms we recommend a minimum area of 14 square metres, which includes standing space and a wall length of 240–300 cm for cupboards. If there is little cupboard space available outside the parents' bedroom, then an area of 15–16 square metres is recommended. Bigger areas than these seem to us to be unjustified because these rooms are so little used.

For children's bedrooms with two beds we recommend a minimum area of 12 square metres, with a minimum width of 280 cm. An area of 14 square metres is desirable, especially in small dwellings, so that sufficient play space is available. Such a size would also make it possible to refurnish the room as a parents' bedroom is necessary. If several twin bedded rooms for children are planned at least one of them should have an area of 14 square metres, and the others 12 square metres. *For single rooms for children, we recommend a mimimum area of 8 square metres, but 10 square metres is better, the minimum width being 240 cm.*

Besides the recommended area, a good arrangement of doors and windows is needed if a children's room is to be furnished properly. These doors and windows should not impair flexibility in the use of the room, and they should be so arranged that no bed has to stand against the outside wall.

Table 75 sets out the areas recommended for bedrooms.

Balconies

Usage

Table 76 summarises the results of surveys of the usage of balconies in Switzerland (38), in France (39) and in Sweden (125).
It is clear from the table that the balcony is an integral part of the living space of the dwelling. It is an additional place for recreation, for working, and as play-space for the children where it is simple to keep an eye on them. These principal functions dictate the dimensions and location of the balcony.

Dimensions

In order to cater for the activities set out in *Table 76* the furniture listed in *Table 77* must be provided.

The dimensions of the balcony should allow for two reclining chairs along with a small table. If a table with four chairs is preferred to the reclining chairs, then the depth of the balcony must be at least 150 cm.

It appears from the survey carried out by *Holm* (34) that a majority of people questioned were satisfied with their balcony only if its area exceeded 3 square metres.

The following recommendations for the area of the balcony can be found in the literature : (120)

Germany	2.8–3.75 square metres
Denmark	3–5 square metres
Sweden	2.8 square metres
England	4 square metres

Values for the minimum depth ranged between 125 and 150 cm.

In our opinion balconies of 150 × 200 cm, with an area of 3 square metres are the smallest that are advisable for 3–4 room dwellings, and that areas of 5–6 square metres are desirable

Table 76   Surveys of the uses of balconies in Switzerland (38), France (39) and Sweden (125)   * no statement made

	Switzerland	France	Sweden
Number questioned	160	1070	507
Use	%	%	%
Resting, reading, doing nothing, knitting	85	64	82
Cleaning clothes, and polishing shoes	82	17	96
Hanging out washing	68	51	96
Drinking coffee	*	*	77
Eating	36	13	31
For storage	*	*	26
Airing bedlinen	*	*	86
Doing other household jobs	10	*	*
Growing flowers	*	73	*
Keeping an eye on children playing below	*	53	*
Letting small children play	48	41	*
Chatting with neighbours	*	16	*
Balcony not used	5	15	*

Table 77   Furniture needed on the balcony, and the space required   After Huser, Grandjean and Suchantke (120)

	Number	Space needed (cm)
Table and 4 chairs	1	100 × 190 + 50 (free space)
Deckchairs	2	200 × 70
Perambulator	1	120 × 70

Orientation in relation to the sun

Plenty of sunshine is just as important in the location of the balcony as its relationship to the other rooms. It is generally desirable that a person standing in the centre of the balcony on 21 March and 23 September should have at least the upper part of the body in sunlight. On 23 July, on the other hand, it would be convenient if a person sitting in the centre of the balcony could have at least the head and shoulders in the shade, and that the floor of the balcony along the back wall should be shaded to a depth of at least 80 cm for half the length of the balcony. To fulfil these conditions, a balcony in our latitudes should be orientated towards the south as nearly as may be convenient. In this situation, the balcony is in full sunshine all day long throughout the period March—September. An orientation towards the South-West also has its advantages, since sunshine between 1700 hours and sunset is possible if there are no other buildings in the way.

The duration of sunshine in *loggias* is only slightly reduced by the side-walls, but against this the room that lies behind the loggia lies in shadow. On the other hand, a window facing south on to a balcony is penetrated by the sun least in the hot months of the year and most in the cold months. Some means of shutting out excessive sunlight from loggias and balconies is indispensable. A suitable way of doing this is with a sunshade and sunblinds at the sides.

Relation of balcony to the rest of the house

The location of the balcony in relation to the other rooms admits of various solutions, four of which are briefly described below :

— Balcony outside living room

Access to the balcony is through the living room, and the balcony is to some extent set back. In this arrangement windows, walls and parapet must be so designed as not to interfere with light passing into the living room, or with the outlook from the room. Small children playing on the balcony can be supervised from the living room. This arrangement is recommended in Denmark and in Germany.

— Balcony outside parents' bedroom

Access to the balcony is still from the living room, and the balcony is still to some extent set back. This arrangement does not cut off light from the living room, nor make it difficult to see out. Children on the balcony can be watched from either the living room or the bedroom.

— Balcony outside the dining alcove

Extending between kitchen and living room, access from dining alcove, balcony partly set back. Does not cut off light, nor make it difficult to see out of either living room or bedroom. In this arrangement the balcony can be used for more different purposes, for meals, for the housewife to carry out certain jobs, and for the children to play, but supervision of the children is possible only from the dining alcove. This is a recommended arrangement in Sweden and Denmark.

— Balcony between living room and bedroom

This is an angled balcony, with access from the living room. It does not interfere with light or vision in either of the adjacent rooms, and children can be supervised equally well from either.

Each of the four arrangements has its advantages. Since it is just as important to let sunlight into rooms as to see out of them, in doubtful cases the admission of sunlight should be the deciding factor.

Privacy

Protection of one's privacy is very important to well-being, and neighbours should certainly be prevented from overlooking the balcony. Furthermore sound-proofing must be such that at least conversation is not overheard, and it is desirable that loud speech and music should be reduced to a tolerable level. The most important factor in protecting privacy is undoubtedly to set the balcony back into the body of the building. Other devices that are occasionally recommended, such as for example transposing balconies between the storeys, or having blinds at the sides if required are much less advantageous.

Parapet of the balcony

The main considerations which affect the height of the parapet are its effects in preventing people from falling, in retaining privacy and the exclusion of draughts. Its height should be at least 100 cm with no horizontal gaps: vertical separation of rails should be not greater than 7 cm.
Security against children falling is guaranteed by having thick strong netting to a height of 2 m.

Entrance-hall and front door

Climbing stairs is the most strenuous of everyday activities. If the stairs rise at a slope of 30.5° and are climbed at a rate of 17.2 metres per minute, energy is consumed at the rate of 13.7 kcal per minute, that is at twice the rate as when shovelling, cycling or mowing a lawn. One would know about it if one had to climb stairs for 5–10 minutes without stopping. For this reason the staircase is a problem for old or infirm people, and it can be an insurmountable obstacle to the handicapped.

It is clear that buildings housing several families should have lifts for the use of this section of the populace. Conversely people who have a sedentary job can be urgently advised to take the stairs and not the lift whenever they have the choice. In this case climbing stairs is an effective (and free!) way of strengthening the heart and circulation, besides making a small contribution to the achievement of a slim figure.

On the other hand housewives, as well as all those people who find stair-climbing fatiguing, should go about it with as little effort as possible, and with the greatest care not to fall.

Energy consumption when climbing stairs

Lehmann (9) found that the lowest consumption of energy, 10 calories per kilogram-metre, occurred when the slope of the stairs lay between 25° and 30° and so he advised that whenever possible stairs should be constructed with 17 cm risers and 29 cm treads, giving a slope of 30°. Stairs like this are not only the best from the point of view of energy consumption, they are also the safest.

The stair formula is therefore:

$2r + t = 63$ cm
where r = riser and t = tread.

In our opinion the angle of slope illustrated in *Figure 70* and the relationship between treads and risers shown there can be recommended for both internal and external stairs.

In cellars and attics the stairs must sometimes be designed to save space, and since they are little used in such places a slope of 45°, with risers and treads both 20 cm, can be accepted.

Hand-rails

A suitable form of hand-rail is very important in making stair climbing both easy and safe.
The *height of the hand-rail* above the front edges of the treads should lie *between 85–90 cm*. The hand-rail should be easy to grasp and made of a

Stair formula
2 risers + 1 tread = 63 cm

Energy consumption per mkg

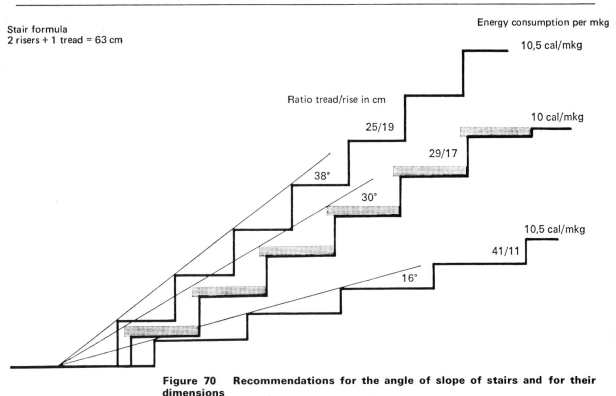

Figure 70   Recommendations for the angle of slope of stairs and for their dimensions

Spiral staircases

material that is not cold to the touch. The best thickness for a hand-rail is 6–10 cm.

Spiral staircases are unsatisfactory from a physiological point of view, since the treads are very narrow on the inside. *Neufert* (126) recommended that the treads of a spiral staircase, when measured 15 cm from the inside corner, should be not less than 10 cm deep.

On physiological grounds, it is to be recommended that there should still be a minimum depth of 20 cm at a distance of 25 cm from the inside corner.

When working out the dimensions of landings and spiral staircases, it should be borne in mind that sick people on stretchers may have to be carried up and down them. A stretcher, including handles, is 230–250 cm long and 40–50 cm wide, and the smallest dimensions of any kind of spiral staircase should pay regard to this.

Staircases must be of such a height that cupboards, beds and other pieces of furniture up to 140 cm wide can be moved easily. The British Ministry of Housing (67) recommends the following minimum dimensions for stairways:

Width	90 cm
Height vertically above front edge of a step	200 cm
Height at right angles to slope of stairs (measured from edge of a step)	155 cm.

The minimum width of 90 cm is very low, considering that two people carrying loads need 200 cm to pass. *We are of the opinion that in a multi-family house without a lift the stairway must be wide enough for people to pass each other without hindrance. We therefore recommend as widths for the stairs*

Minimal   120 cm
Desirable   180 cm

The minimum figure of 120 cm allows one person to stand sideways while another person passes carrying a load. At the desirable width of 180 cm two persons with loads can pass each other without hindrance.
The chapter headed 'accidents in the home' goes into more detail about the measurements necessary to avoid any danger of stairway accidents.

Entrance doors

In bygone days, the front door of a house, together with the façade, was a status symbol, and showed how well-off the occupants were. Today little of this function remains in modern house-building. Yet the entrance door is still rather bigger than it need be for strictly functional reasons, and it is often furnished with a porch, special lighting and perhaps other purely ornamental features.
From an ergonomic point of view, there has to be some kind of door to provide an entrance to the dwelling. When it is closed it should protect against noise. Its function in excluding sound is dealt with in the chapter on 'Noise'. In the present context we shall only make a few comments on its dimensions. Similar considerations apply both to the entrance door and the entrance hall: it must be of such a size and shape that the usual furniture can be carried through it as conveniently as possible.

The biggest items of normal furniture require an entrance door 80–100 cm wide

The usual height of 210–220 cm for the doorway should be sufficient if the articles of furniture are carried at the right angles, even for a double bed 160×210 cm, a baby grand piano 140×170 cm or a wardrobe 120×200 cm.

However, if a doorway is to admit a fat person carrying a burden then it must be 100 cm wide

It is self-evident trom these considerations that *doors into the entrance hall of dwellings should have a width of*:

Minimal   90–100 cm
Desirable   100–110 cm

Internal doors usually range from 70–90 cm in width, but in our opinion doors less than 90 cm wide make it difficult to move furniture from one room to another. We recommend a width of 90 cm, so that, for example, a table 80 cm high can be carried through on its side. Wide doors contribute to the 'mobility' and 'flexibility' that are often asked for in the design of dwellings. The door giving principal entrance to a dwelling should be correctly proportioned in relation to the others, and must match the façade and harmonize with the windows and other features of the building.

Communal laundry and utility rooms

Laundering habits

A washing-machine firm declared from unpublished statistics that in 1967 91.2% of Swiss housewives did the main washing themselves. Only 8.8% of the housewives sent the washing out. 83.5% of the households where the washing was done at home had the use of an automatic washer, and 42% of them also had access to a spin-drier.

71a
Space for sorting the
washing on a table

71b
Space at the washtub

71c
Space in front of the washing machine
or tumbler—dryer

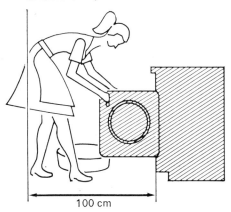

Figure 71   Recommended space to be allowed when doing the washing
After Huser, Grandjean and Suchantke (120)

Time consumed

According to investigations carried out by the Bundesforschungsanstalt für Hauswirtschaft (127), a household of four people needs from 5.8 to 9.6 hours a week for dealing with the washing. *Thus the week's washing takes up to 10–15% of the total working time.* As mentioned in the first chapter, a housewife still has to work very hard on washdays, mainly as a result of the muscular strain of carrying and hanging out the washing, and while ironing.

Laundry spaces

The operations of cleaning and caring for clothes include: storing and sorting the dirty washing, soaking, washing, rising, draining, drying, folding and ironing, and the space needed to carry out these tasks without hindrance is illustrated in *Figures 71 a–c*. These are derived from data given in the literature of Germany, Sweden and U.S.A., and cited in reference (120)

Communal Laundries

Equipment

If the individual dwellings are not equipped with their own automatic washing machines, then every multi-family block must have a communal laundry, with adequate drying facilities. The equipment that is in common use must be on such a scale that each family has a chance to do their washing once a week. We recommend that a communal laundry should have the following items of equipment for every 12 users:

- 1 automatic washing-machine, with a capacity of 6 Kg. of dry washing
- 1 automatic washing-machine for 4 Kg of dry washing (on physiological grounds, front-loading machines should stand on a base 30 cm high)
- 1 single-compartment washing trough with a cold-water supply and a minimal capacity of 40 litres.
- 1 washing trolley
- 1 table for sorting (measurements 80 × 120 cm, height of upper edge 90 cm from floor)
- 1 electric spin-drier outside the room, in an ante-room or an adjoining room that is completely accessible, and with a lid that locks automatically while the machine is in operation.

Surface areas

We recommend the following measurements for the floor space of a communal laundry, taking into account both the items of equipment themselves and the space that is needed to operate them:

	Square metres	
	Minimal	Desirable
Laundry with one set of equipment (a washing-machine, and 6 users)	6	8
Laundry with 2 sets of equipment (2 automatic washing-machines for 12 users or 1 washer and 1 drier and 6 users)	7	9
Laundry with 3 sets of equipment (2 automatic washing-machines and 1 drier for 12 users; or 3 automatic washing-machines for 18 users)	8	10

Fitting-out

From the constructional point of view, the communal laundry must be fitted out as a damp place. The floor covering must be non-slip and drain off the surplus water. The walls must be covered up to a height of 130–160 cm with a waterproof surface resistant to physical damage.

A communal laundry being used by 12 families, for which it is desirable to have two washing-machines, should have three mains sockets, so that if the users like they can also have a drier. The ante-room should have a main socket for a spin-drier. All switches and sockets must be damp-proof.

Drying room

Enquiry has shown that the presence or absence of a drying room is often the limiting factor in the capacity of a laundry. The washing machines cannot be used to their full capacity because there are not enough facilities available for drying the washing. To make it possible for the laundry to be used by two sets of people on the same day, and thus, for example, to allow all the housewives in a 12-family house to do their washing once a week, we recommend that *for every 6 users there should be a drying room with at least 60 metres of plastic-covered clothes line*. Clothes lines should be at a height of 180 cm, and 30 cm apart horizontally.

Hence a drying room for 6 families should have an area of 22–25 square metres.

Equipping the drying room

A big window is necessary both in the laundry and the drying room, to provide light and ventilation. A suitable type can either tilt or rotate, and can be converted from one to the other by changing the fittings.

The laundry door should have a grille of suitable dimensions to provide a continuous draught to speed up the drying of clothes.

The future will very probably bring large and efficient drying apparatus, either tumbler-driers or drying cabinets. Yet even then, a small drying room will still be required for small items of drip-dry washing, curtains and so on.

Equipment for washing clothes in the utility room

In certain countries – especially Germany, Sweden and the U.S.A. – there is a tendency to keep the washing of clothes even more private. This development means going over completely to domestic washing equipment and relegating communal washing facilities to occasional and transitory use. Trouble-free washing *within the home* requires well-designed and well-equipped places in suitable rooms.

The location of completely automatic washing equipment inside a dwelling allows of two possibilities:

– putting it in a room of its own.
– doing the washing in the bathroom.

Utility room

A utility room is a self-contained room in the house which enables all the various laundry phases to be carried on conveniently in one room. It must have a window and a water-supply, and must also be damp-proofed.

To plan for the future, it would be a good idea to enlarge the domestic sphere with a utility room provided that it was big enough for its purpose, and did not spoil other rooms.

The high cost of a utility room both in materials and in complicating the building, makes it possible in municipal housing only if it is justified by an increased output and more intensive use of the facility.

As for the *location* of the utility room within the dwelling, we recommend a central position and a wall in common either with the kitchen or the bathroom. To have it as close as possible to these is sound not only on technical grounds, but also because it facilitates concentration of the housewife's work.

Our recommendations for the furnishing of a utility room are as follows:

– an automatic washing machine, not bolted to the floor
– a tumbler-drier, or a drying cabinet
– possibly an automatic ironer
– wash basins with hot and cold water, as well as a mixer and places at the side and underneath for a bucket
– drying facilities over the wash basin for hanging damp-dry washing
– a work surface for standing jobs (height 90 cm).
– well ventilated storage for dirty linen
– a hanging cupboard for washing and cleaning materials as well as a pile of clean cloths
– a high cupboard for tools and accessories
– a shoe cupboard with special shoe rests and drawers for shoe brushes and polishes
– a sewing table (70 cm high) with an electric sewing machine stored underneath it, and with provision for storing sewing accessories.
– a hanging cupboard for tools and materials
– perhaps a broom cupboard
– a work stool or chair.

For the floor covering, the same requirements apply as for the kitchen, and for the overall size, we recommend:

| Minimal | 7 square metres |
| Desirable | 9 square metres |

Provision for laundry in the bathroom

In dwellings where there is less than 100 square metres of living space, there is a case for bringing the automatic washing equipment into a room which already satisfies the requirements of a place where conditions of high humidity exist – i.e. to the bathroom. This will necessitate an additional space of at least 60×60 cm for the machine to stand, and an equivalent space for some kind of drying equipment is desirable. A further requirement is room to stand a container for dirty washing.

On hygienic grounds it is undesirable to set up laundry equipment in the kitchen.

Ironing and folding washing

If the dwelling has no utility room, then some place must be set aside where the washing can be ironed and folded. This should be somewhere central, because these jobs (ironing, repairing and renovating linen and clothing) take a long time. A table 50×120 cm, and 70 cm high is needed, and an area of 1.6–2 square metres must be allowed if circulation space is included.

The multi-purpose living room, the dining alcove, or a kitchen that has been extended for this purpose, all suggest themselves as places where this sort of work can be carried on. The working place should be so arranged that an unfinished job can be left lying about for a short time.

6 The Indoor Climate

Summary

The thermal balance of the human body is controlled by a regulatory centre in the brain which, under normal conditions, maintains the internal temperature at 37 °C. The sensations of comfort or discomfort in both man and animals act as stimuli to preserve this balance. The body loses heat to its surroundings through conduction, convection, radiation and the evaporation of sweat from the skin. This heat exchange is affected by the heat-conducting properties of the material in contact with the body, the temperature of the surrounding air, the air velocity, the surface temperature of the walls, ceiling and floor of the room, and the relative humidity of the air. A comfortable indoor climate is essential for the well-being and efficient working of the occupants. The principal recommendations for a favourable microclimate in the home are as follows:

- in winter the temperature of living rooms should be within one degree of 21 °C, and should be capable of being regulated between 20° and 23 °C. In other rooms lower temperatures are suggested. Temperatures between 20–24 °C are comfortable in summer.
- the temperatures at the surface of the surrounding walls etc. should be of the same order as the air temperature. Differences from the mean temperature should not exceed 2–3 °C, and differences in surface temperatures should not exceed 3–4 °C.
- Air with a relative humidity of 40–45% is comfortable in winter: below 30% the air is too dry, and may cause discomfort from desiccation of the respiratory tract.
- Air movement past a seated person should not exceed 0.2 metres/second.

The ergonomics of modern central heating systems is considered, and the use of humidifying equipment is discussed.

Windows are important to the indoor atmosphere. They present cooling surfaces in winter and admit radiant heat from the sun in summer, which may overheat the room (greenhouse effect). The current architectural fashion of large windows makes rooms unreasonably hot. Means of excluding sunshine are discussed.

The atmosphere inside buildings is affected by pollution of the outside air, by human emissions and by smells from the kitchen, bathroom and W.C. In living rooms human odour is the determining factor in how much fresh air is needed, and as a rough rule there should be 30 cubic metres per person per hour. *Table 87* gives rules for regulating air changes in living rooms, derived from discussions concerning ventilation techniques.

Definition of terms

The indoor climate may be defined as the condition of the air within a room characterised in physical and chemical terms. The following climatic factors affect the human body:

- air temperature
- the temperature of surrounding surfaces
- air movement
- air humidity
- the quality of the air: i.e. the degree to which it is polluted by gases and solid particles.

To understand the effects of the indoor climate, the following definitions should be understood.

The absolute humidity is the amount of water vapour actually present in the air, measured in grams per kilogramme, or in grams per cubic metre, of dry air.

The relative humidity is the absolute humidity expressed as a percentage of the amount of water needed to saturate the air. The latter increases rapidly as air temperature rises.

The dew point is that temperature to which the air has to be cooled to become saturated.

Dew is formed when any part of the building is cooled to the dew point of the air and water vapour condenses as droplets.

The psychrometer is an instrument for giving an indirect measurement of the relative humidity of the air by the use of two thermometers. One thermometer has its bulb wrapped in a wick that is kept soaked in water ('wet bulb'), while the other thermometer is kept dry ('dry bulb'). As the air to be measured flows past the wet bulb it causes evaporation in proportion to the saturation deficiency – the lower the relative humidity the greater the evaporation. This cools the wet bulb, and brings about a difference in the readings of the two thermometers from which the relative humidity of the air can be deduced. In practice the humidity is read off from a table by looking up the readings of the two bulbs. *Figure 72* shows such a psychrometric table, which gives values for the absolute and relative humidities, the saturation value and the dewpoint.

The degree of comfort is the subjective feeling of well-being of people in relation to the climatic factors operating in their surroundings.

Human heat balance

Body temperature

Bodily heat derives from the conversion of energy-producing substances present in nearly all tissues of the body. This process is set out on page 18. The body temperature is not uniform in all parts of the body. Only in the brain, the heart and the abdominal organs does the temperature remain within narrow limits around 37°C (the core temperature). A constant core temperature is essential for normal functioning of the deep organs, and warm-blooded animals cannot tolerate sudden or long-continued deviations.

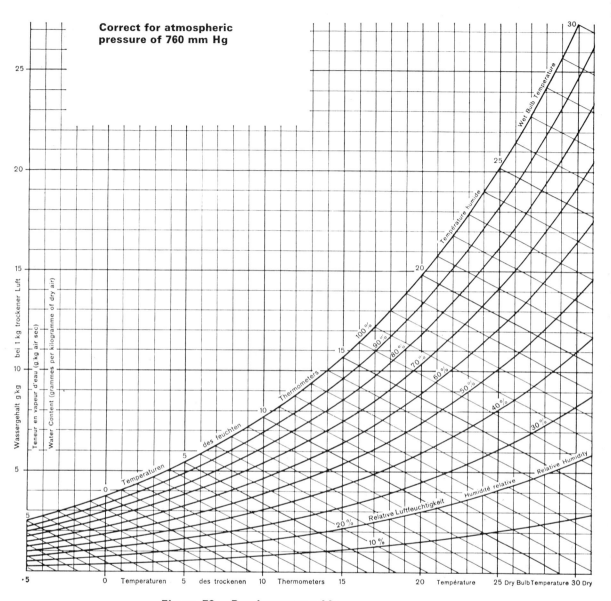

Figure 72   Psychrometer table

In contrast to the core temperature, the temperature of the muscles, the limbs, and most of all that of the skin can vary considerably (the superficial temperature). Physiological research has shown that when the surrounding air is cold, there is a steep temperature gradient in the skin from within outwards. For example in very cold conditions the temperature 2 cm below the outer surface of the skin may be as low as 35 °C whereas in warmer surroundings it may have risen to between 35 and 36° within a few millimetres of the surface. This ability to adapt to one's surroundings makes it possible for man to tolerate a heat loss which over the whole body may amount to several hundred kilocalories. Since the production of heat internally in the body varies

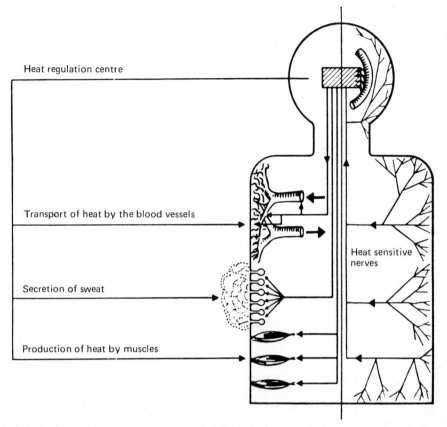

Heat regulation centre

Transport of heat by the blood vessels

Heat sensitive nerves

Secretion of sweat

Production of heat by muscles

Figure 73   How the temperature of the body is controlled   The heat regulating centre in the hypothalamus of the brain regulates the supply of blood to the skin and the secretion of sweat, and this changes the conditions to suit varying circumstances inside and outside the body

Temperature regulation

greatly and the surrounding temperature is equally variable, there are various thermo-regulators in the body which keep the internal temperature constant. *Figure 73* shows diagrammatically the thermo-regulatory control mechanism. The central feature in temperature regulation is the heat centre in the mid-brain, which supervises the heat budget of the body. It can be compared with a thermostat. The nerve-cells of the heat-centre are informed of the body temperature, in part directly from the blood, and in part through heat sensitive nerves in the skin. To maintain a constant internal temperature a balancing mechanism is operated by nervous connections from the heat centre. Primarily control is exercised by adjustment of the circulation, by the secretion of sweat, and by the production of heat, to meet the requirements of heat balance in the body.

Transport of heat by the blood

Blood plays a most important role in thermo-regulation by transporting heat from place to place in the body. The blood-vessels, especially the capillaries, act as heat exchangers, picking up heat from hot areas and giving it out again to tissues at a lower temperature. The blood transports heat from the interior of the body to the skin where it can be lost to the external environment; or, alternatively, when artificial heat is supplied to the skin, it can carry it to the internal organs. *The regulation of the blood supply of the skin is the principal factor of this control mechanism, and forms the basis of heat exchanges between man and his surroundings.*

Secretion of sweat

The second control system, that of the secretion of sweat, also originates in the heat centre in the brain.

Muscle-tremors: shivering

The third control mechanism consists of increasing heat production to prevent further cooling of the body. This is achieved by raising oxygen consumption in the musculature and other organs. 'Shivering with cold' is a particularly obvious way in which the muscles produce more heat by increasing their metabolism.

Heat exchange between the human body and its surroundings

Heat exchange

As mentioned on page 18, the internal organs transform the chemical energy of food into mechanical energy plus heat. The body maintains a constant internal temperature by releasing superfluous heat to the environment. Hence there is a continuous exchange of heat between the body and its surroundings, depending partly on a physiological regulatory mechanism and partly on the physical laws of heat exchange. This exchange may take place in four physically different ways:

– conduction of heat
– convection of heat
– evaporation of water
– radiation of heat.

Conduction

The contribution that conduction makes to the heat exchange process depends first and foremost on the thermal conductivity of the substances in immediate contact with the skin. Anyone who sits down in winter, first on a stone and then on a log, can feel this for himself: the stone feels cold, because its high conductivity draws away heat from the body; the log feels distinctly less cold because its lower conductivity draws away less heat than the stone.
The loss of heat by conduction is of practical importance in the choice of floorings, furnishings and surface materials of all kinds. The local loss of heat from the feet or other parts of the body through contact with a highly conductile material is certainly to be avoided, because it feels uncomfortable, and may result in ailments such as inflammation of the joints or rheumatism. So table surfaces, machine components, levers and tools should always be covered with heat-insulating materials such as felt, leather or wood.
The insulating properties of floor-coverings are particularly important, both for comfort and health. The later chapter on 'Floor-coverings' will discuss in detail the question of keeping the feet warm, and deal with the conductivity of various materials.
Air has a particularly low conductivity, its coefficient of thermal conductivity λ ranging from 0.02–0.05 kcal/m/h/°C. For this reason porous materials are good insulators of heat; this explains why textiles, especially wool, retain heat so well.
In conclusion, it may be noted that as a rule a clothed person does not lose any great amount of heat by conduction. The physiological significance of heat conduction is limited to the local cooling of particular parts of the body when they come in contact with cold materials that are good thermal conductors.

Convection

By convection is meant the direct transfer of the molecular vibrations of heat from the human body into the air, or more rarely from the air to the body. This form of heat exchange depends primarily on the temperature difference between the skin and the surrounding air, and upon how much the air is moving: heat loss is proportional directly to the temperature difference, and to the square of the wind velocity. Under normal conditions convection accounts for about 25–30% of the total heat exchanged.

Perspiration

The loss of heat by perspiration arises because the evaporation of sweat abstracts heat from the skin (cooling by evaporation). *The loss of heat by this means amounts to 0.58 kcal per gram of water evaporated.* Since a human being normally loses one litre of water per day in perspiration (insensible perspiration), the body loses 600 kcal or more from this source every day, amounting to about one fourth of the total heat loss.

Whenever the temperature outside the body rises above comfort level, the heated skin initiates reflexes which lead to a massive release of sweat, the resultant evaporation greatly increasing heat loss. The extent to which heat is lost by evaporation depends on the area of skin from which perspiration is taking place, and on the difference in water vapour pressure between the air in contact with the skin and the rest of the surrounding air. *Hence the relative humidity of the air is particularly important in this form of heat exchange.* Air movement is less important: it steepens the gradient of water vapour-pressure, but convective cooling of the skin checks perspiration.

When the surrounding temperature (air and walls) is above 25°C, the clothed human body cannot get rid of enough heat by either convection or radiation and the loss of heat by perspiration becomes the sole compensatory mechanism. This is why the secretion of sweat rises very rapidly if a certain critical temperature is reached outside the body.

Thermal radiation

Heated bodies send out electromagnetic waves of long wave length (infra-red radiation), which are absorbed by other bodies and turned back into heat again. This radiation is not dependent upon any material medium for its transmission, and is known for short as thermal radiation. Heat-exchange by means of radiation takes place between the human body and the walls and other objects surrounding it. In contrast to the physical factors already discussed, the temperature, humidity and movement of the air have practically no influence on the amount of heat transmitted, which depends primarily on the difference in temperature between the skin and the surfaces that surround or enclose it. In our climate, surrounding objects are generally cooler than the skin, and so the human body loses an appreciable amount of heat by radiation

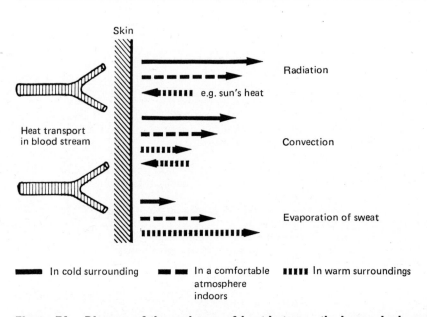

Figure 74   Diagram of the exchange of heat between the human body and its surroundings   The length of the arrows indicates the amount of heat that is gained or lost by the three ways, under different circumstances

every day. The loss of heat is not perceptible as long as the quantity is not too great. *Nevertheless an unpleasant sensation of chilling can occur, if one stands close to a cold wall or a large cold window pane, even though the air temperature may seem to be high enough. In this situation a comparatively large amount of heat is lost because it is the temperature difference between the skin and the wall that matters, and not the temperature of the air.* The daily loss of heat by radiation from a clothed person varies greatly according to his surroundings. Not counting hot summers, it can be reckoned that under our climatic conditions a person can lose 1,000–1,500 kcal daily by radiation, which amounts to 40–60% of the total heat loss.

Total heat exchange   *Figure 74* illustrates graphically the three processes of heat exchange most important for the human body.

To summarise we can say that the four following physical factors determine the exchange of heat with one's surroundings:

- the air temperature for heat exchange by convection
- air movement for heat exchange by convection
- the surface temperature of the enclosing surfaces (walls, ceiling, and floor) for heat exchange by radiation
- the relative humidity of the air for heat exchange by perspiration.

Comfort

The physiological meaning of 'comfort'.

Discomfort   As a rule one is hardly aware of conditions in a room so long as they are comfortable, but discomfort becomes noticeable as conditions depart from this optimum.

The feeling of discomfort can escalate from inconvenience to pain, depending on how severely the thermal balance of the body is upset. This sensation is a practical system of biological regulation, which allows both humans and animals to set in action the necessary measures to restore heat balance. The animal's immediate reaction is to seek out some place where it is neither over cooled nor over heated; man, on the other hand reacts by varying his clothing and his actions, and is also able to make use of artificial heating or cooling.

Other symptoms of discomfort   Disturbances of one's comfort are accompanied by functional changes which affect the whole organism. Excessive heat first of all makes one tired and sleepy, reducing one's alertness and increasing the tendency to make mistakes. This reduction in bodily activity has the effect of reducing the internal production of heat. The reduction of efficiency when overheated has been confirmed in several experiments. Bodily efficiency was sharply reduced as soon as the external temperature rose to 27–28°C. The main cause must be the increased demand for blood flow to the skin to take away excess internal heat, leaving less blood to supply the working muscles.

Other experiments have shown that an overheated room also reduces one's efficiency for intellectual work. Thus, for example, *Ryd and Wyon* (189) observed that a room-temperature of 27°C caused a significantly poorer performance in learning tests by 13 schoolchildren.

On the other hand if the organism is threatened with too much cooling, then it fidgets, lessening attention, especially the concentration necessary for intellectual work. In this case more internal heat is produced by stimulation of the entire body and particularly those parts associated with movement.

Hence a comfortable atmosphere in a room is a necessary condition if one is to stay content and fully alert

Reactions to temperature

The complex that makes up the atmosphere in a room

As has already been discussed, the exchange of heat between a person and his environment depends not only on the air temperature, but also on that of the surrounding surfaces, on the relative humidity of the air and on air movement. Hence it is clear that comfort, too, depends on these four factors. Each factor has a certain weighting and physiological research has shown that each factor is effective only within certain limits.

In view of this complex situation it is understandable that several research workers have tried to bring the various factors into a single measurement.

Initially, the degree of cooling was measured with an instrument called a katathermometer, and this reading was used as an index of comfort. This technique was not a success because in practice there was often no correlation between the anticipated degree of comfort and the actual sensations of the research subject.

Use of sensation itself as a measure

Because of this failure of correlation it is becoming more and more the practice to use sensation itself as a subjective measure of comfort rather than any physical measurement: hence the expression the 'experienced' or 'effective' temperature.

By 1923 *Houghten and Yaglou* (145) had already worked out a comparison between the temperatures and humidities of the air that induced the same effective temperatures.

Later on this research was followed by others in which relationships were traced between effective temperatures and air movement, as well as heat radiation. After the second world war this development led to the creation of indices of comfort which could be set out on a nomogram as so-called 'comfort-zones' in relation to the four climatic factors specified.

Although these ways of measuring comfort were based on subjective feelings, in their application they were not without criticism. In recent years several of the basic values have been shown to be incorrect, and in practice there are uncomfortable situations which ought to have been comfortable according to the indices.

The Frigorimeter

Calorific loading of surfaces

In Germany *Frank* (146, 147, 148) and *Lutz* (149) measured the flow of heat from a body to its surroundings. *Frank* determined the heat flow as the density of the heat stream in kilocalories per square metre per hour. With an air temperature of 20°C he obtained the following values:

- head   104 kcal/m²h
- hands   63 kcal/m²h
- feet   123 kcal/m²h
- clothed body   42 kcal/m²h

The so-called calorific loading of the surface of the body was based on these values, and *Frank* (146) designated a calorific loading of 104 kcal/m²h for the head as 'comfortable'.

The direction-sensitive frigorimeter

These authors (147, 149) developed a direction-sensitive frigorimeter, which made it possible to measure the calorific loading of an artificial head in different directions. By this means *Frank* (147) established that variations in the density of the heat stream gave rise to the following impressions in his seven research subjects:

Variations in density of heat-stream kcal/m²h	Sensation of the seven research subjects
less than 20	not detectable
20–35	distinctly noticeable
35–55	uncomfortable
greater than 55	very uncomfortable.

Research work with modern frigorimeters is still in progress, and no final opinion can yet be given on the possibilities of using them in practice. Above all we still lack physiological studies which would give us a correlation between readings of the frigorimeter and the concurrent sensations of a representative number of research subjects.

In this situation it seems sensible for the time being when recording degrees of comfort, to arrange correlations between effective temperatures in pairs as follows:

— temperature of air with temperature of surrounding surfaces
— temperature of air with relative humidity of air
— temperature of air with air movement

These three correlations will now be considered separately in regard to their effect on comfort.

Effective temperature in relation to the temperature of the air and to that of the surrounding surfaces.

Physiological research has shown that the effective temperature corresponds, as a first approximation, with the average of the temperature of the air and the temperature of the surrounding surfaces. This result can be expressed simply as follows:

$$t_E = \frac{t_L + t_U}{2}$$

where t_E = effective temperature
t_L = temperature of the air in the room
t_U = average temperature of all the surrounding surfaces.

Rule of thumb

In this respect there is an important limitation on comfort. *The effective temperature can be comfortable only if the difference between the air temperature and that of the surrounding surfaces is not very great. It should be a general rule that the average temperature of the surrounding surfaces should be not more than 2° or at most 3°C above or below that of the air.*
Moreover it must be said that up to the present we still know little about the effect of having just one wall cold or warm, nor do we know the distance at which a single wall or window can affect our comfort.

Effect of a single wall

Besides the foregoing work of *Frank* (148), in which he measured the impression created by different densities of heat-flow on the two halves of the face, a publication of *Schlüter* (150) seems to be of interest in this context. The author investigated the threshold of perception of 30 research subjects for walls that were cooled and walls that were heated. Either the face or the knee was used to detect cold. From the angle of radiation and the measured temperature difference, the loss of heat from the face or the knee could be calculated in millicalories per square centimetre per second, and then the sensation felt by the subject could be ascertained and set against the actual heat loss.
Figure 75 gives the results of these investigations.
It appeared from these that people are very sensitive to the surface temperature of a single wall. With an air temperature of 21 °C, wall temperatures could be detected if they were below 18°C or above 24°C. On the basis of these studies it is to be expected that under certain conditions the surface temperature of a single wall, or of a big area of window can be detected as uncomfortable if they differ by more than 3°C from the temperature of the air. It may therefore be asked whether this is not an indication that the rule of thumb enunciated above applies not only to the average temperature of all the surrounding walls, but also to any single big surface.

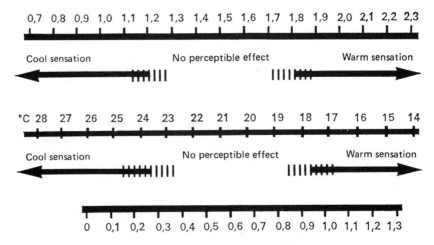

Heat given off by the face in millicalories per sq. cm per sec.

Cool sensation   No perceptible effect   Warm sensation

Cool sensation   No perceptible effect   Warm sensation

Heat given off by the knees in millicalories per sq. cm per sec.

|||||||| Zone in which the threshold of sensation
            lies with 99% certainty

Figure 75   Perception of temperature differences by the face and by the knees, in relation to the heat given off by these parts of the body on the one hand and the surface temperature of a semicircular vessel on the other   The irradiation factor of this vessel is unity. After Schlüter (150)

Effective temperature in relation to the temperature and relative humidity of the air.

The research of *Houghten and Yaglou* (166) attracted widespread attention and led to the construction of psychrometric tables showing effective temperatures.

At regular intervals the comfort zones (in relation to air temperature and relative humidity) of the American Society of Heating and Ventilating Engineers have been re-tested on long series of research subjects, and fresh values obtained. The surveys show that:

— thermal comfort levels have risen steadily over the last 30 years
— they are higher in summer than in winter
— age, sex and fashions in clothing are important factors in individual variation.

Smaller effect of relative humidity

Later on the dependence of effective temperature upon the relative humidity was seriously questioned. *Koch* and his co-workers (151) repeated the work of *Houghten and Yaglou* (166), in which first of all the research subjects were questioned about their subjective impressions after a period of 3 hours in the test room. In contradiction to earlier findings this more extended research showed that relative humidity had little effect on the effective temperature, as long as the temperature of the room remained close to the optimum. For American conditions, these authors found the same assessment of comfortable temperature to be made at all points between 30% relative humidity at 24.8°C and 85% R.H. at 24.2°C. This survey shows, therefore, that so long as it lies within the tolerable range, relative humidity has small effect on effective temperature, even after prolonged exposure.

Table 78   Effect of air movement on perceived temperature, when the air is dry and when it is moist After Yaglou (153)

Air movement metres/second	Equivalent temperatures in °C to give same impression in dry air	in moist air
0	20	20.3
0.5	21	21.3
1.0	22	22.2
1.5	22.8	23
2.0	23.5	23.8

Nevins and his co-workers (152) repeated the work of *Koch* (151) on a total of 360 men and women. They tested 72 combinations of air temperature and humidity, to each of which the research subjects were allowed 30 minutes to record their impressions. The findings confirmed those of *Koch*: the curve for the same feeling of a comfortable temperature ran from 70% R.H. at 25.1 °C to 20% R.H. at 26.2°C.

That is, to maintain the same sensation of temperature while the relative humidity fell by 50%, the air temperature had to be raised by only 1.1°C. The determination of effective temperatures by *Houghten and Yaglou* was seriously challenged by the results of *Koch and Nevins*, which showed completely that relative humidity had very little effect on effective temperature as long as the air temperature was within the comfort range. The effect is so slight that it can be ignored in practice when laying down standards of comfort.

Nonetheless, relative humidity is important for health reasons

This does not mean, however, that relative humidity has no effect on well-being and health. This effect will be treated separately on page 191. Here it will only be noted that most professional people find a relative humidity of 40–45% comfortable during the period when heating is needed. Values greater than 55–60% easily give rise to condensation, and below 30% the air is regarded as being too dry.

Dependence of effective temperature on air temperature and air currents.

The principal studies on the effects of air currents on effective temperature were carried out by *Yaglou* (153), and the relationships that he found between air-currents and sensations of heat are summarised in *Table 78*.

No conclusions concerning comfortable wind speeds can be drawn from these pairs of values for equal effective temperatures. These questions will be dealt with more fully on page 195.

Recommendations for room climate

Comfortable temperatures in rooms.

All experts agree that the air temperature inside a house or flat must be kept within comfort limits, but these limits vary from one country to another, depending on custom and clothing. In addition it should be noted that comfortable temperatures have shown a distinct upward tendency in recent years, primarily as a result of changing fashions in the amount of clothing worn. Earlier findings should therefore be treated with caution.

Individual variations

All these studies have shown that individual impressions of what is a comfortable temperature are subject to considerable variation. The most important causes of variation are differences in:

- clothing
- behaviour
- age
- sex.

Because of their lower level of metabolism, old people and invalids feel more comfortable at a higher temperature and need an appreciably warmer atmosphere within a room (154). Women are supposed to like higher temperatures than men.

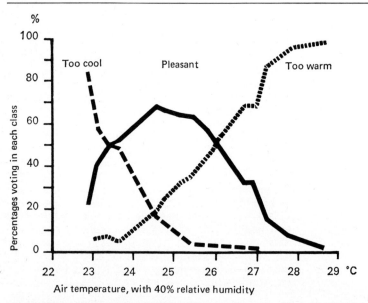

Figure 76   Percentage of 745 office-workers in New York who voted conditions 'too cool', 'pleasant' or 'too warm', as the air-temperature varied   After McConnell and Spiegelman (282)

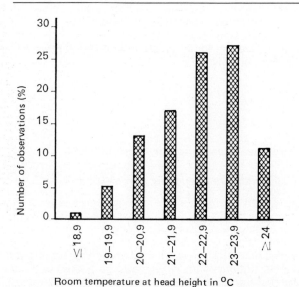

Figure 77   Room temperatures in 168 office-rooms during the period when the heating was in operation.   A survey during the winter of 1964/65

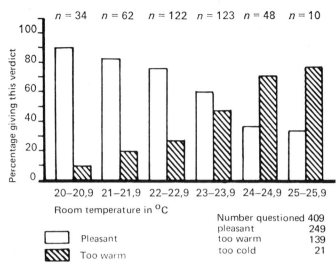

Figure 78   Survey of the impressions of temperature experienced by 409
office-workers during the winter of 1964/65 n = number of persons questioned.
They were asked the question: 'Do you find the atmosphere in this room today pleasant,
too warm, or too cold?'

Comfortable temperatures in offices

The relationship between individual comfort and room temperature has often been studied in offices. In *Figure 76* the findings of *McConnell and Spiegelman* (282) are illustrated, resulting from the questioning of 745 office workers in New York in the summer of 1940.

The outstanding result was the wide individual variation. In the best case – at 24°C – only 65% of those questioned found the temperature comfortable, the remainder finding it either too warm or too cold.

In winter

In one of our own studies (161), carried out in the winter of 1964/65 in 168 offices in Switzerland, we measured the atmospheric conditions and questioned 410 people (140 men and 270 women) who worked in them.

The air temperatures are shown graphically in *Figures 77* and *78*.

The rooms were at a high temperature and the most frequent values lie between 22 and 24°C. *The reply 'the atmosphere in this room is pleasant' came less frequently the higher the temperature, while the reply 'too warm' increased.* We suspect that those who were responsible for the heating had a tendency to provide a high air temperature indoors, because they rather tolerated complaints about rooms that were 'too hot' than about rooms that were 'too cold'.

We must conclude from the survey that *for sedentary work the Swiss are most comfortable in the range 21°–23°C*, and that this value is also correct for living rooms.

In summer

Equivalent studies (162) were carried out in the summers of 1966 and 1967 in 318 office-rooms with 1191 office-workers. The results are illustrated in *Figures 79* and *80*.

In rooms that were not air-conditioned air temperatures varied between 20 and 27°C. The majority of the employees considered temperatures above 24°C too warm. From this one can conclude that *air-temperatures of 24°C are comfortable in summer*, and this certainly ought to apply to conditions in houses and flats as well.

A similar investigation was carried out by *Franzen* (163) in Sweden, and the results of his temperature measurements were very similar to ours, both in winter and in summer. The people questioned often described the temperature as too warm, and the proportion satisfied varied between 20% and 75%.

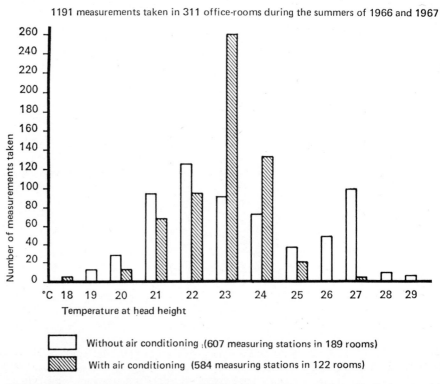

Figure 79   Room temperatures during the warm months of the year   A random survey during summers 1966 and 1967

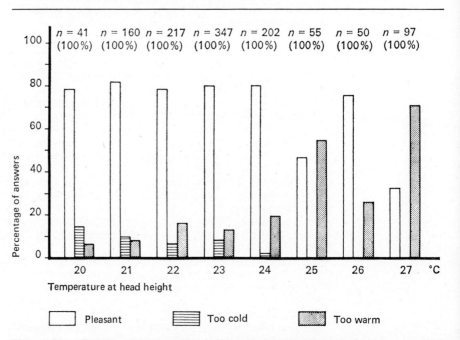

Figure 80   Survey of impressions of temperature taken during the summer n = number of persons questioned. The question put before them was: 'Do you find the atmosphere in the room to-day pleasant, too warm or too cold?'

Table 79   Guidelines for indoor air temperature during winter (°C).

Country	Literature	Year	Living room	Bedroom	Kitchen	Bathroom	WC	Corridor	Entrance hall
England	(155)	1945	15.5–20	12.8–13.9	15.5	12.8–13.9	12.8–13.9	7.2–10	–
England	(67)	1961	17.5	17.5	12.5	–	–	12.5	12.5
Germany	(156, 157, 158, 159)	1959 to 1969	20	20	20	22	15	15	10
France (degree of comfort)									
– high	(160)	1962	22	22	22	22	22	22	–
– medium	(160)	1962	18	18	–	22	–	–	–
– low	(160)	1962	18	12	–	22	–	–	–
Sweden	(138)	1967	20	20	20	20	20	20	–
Holland	(54)	1963	19–21	15–17	17–19	20–22	12–14	12–14	12–14

Table 80   Air temperatures indoors recommended in Switzerland during the cold months of the year   Air temperatures between 20 and 24°C are comfortable in summer. The air temperatures indoors apply to a relative humidity of 40–50%, with surrounding surfaces not differing from the air by more than 3°C, and with air-movement less than 0.2 metres/sec.

Room	Air temperature in the room, in °C	
	Minimal requirements	Desirable range over which the temperature can be regulated
Living-room	21	20–23
Bedroom	18	17–20
Kitchen	18	18–20
Bathroom	20	20–23
WC	16	16–19
Corridor	18	18–20
Entrance hall	14	16–18

Comfortable temperatures in the home

When comfortable temperatures in the home are being considered, it is necessary to take into account the activities and behaviour of the occupants. The following ranges of air temperature are recommended, and they depend on the amount of heat being generated by bodily activity:[*]

– mental work while seated	21–23°C
– light manual work while seated	19–20°C
– light manual work while standing	18–19°C
– heavy manual work while standing	15–17°C

Temperatures must be lower in rooms where manual work is often performed than in rooms where people are sedentary or resting.

The bedroom presents a special problem. Many doctors advise sleeping with a window open, on grounds of general hygiene, and this advice is often followed, so that many people have to cope with temperatures between 14–17°C whenever they are asleep. It should not be assumed from this, however, that a heating system is adequate so long as it provides an air temperature of 14–17°C.

When the temperature is as low as this there is a danger of condensation on the inside surfaces of exterior walls, and this should be avoided as it encourages the formation of mould. Besides, if the bedroom windows are kept closed, it should be possible to raise the temperature to at least 18°C.

[*]These values are valid for a relative humidity of 50%, air-currents of less than 0.2 metres per second, and surrounding surfaces that do not differ more than 3°C from the temperature of the air.

*Since people differ in their ideas of a comfortable temperature, it is ad-
vantageous to be able to regulate the heating in each room independently,
so that each person using a room can regulate the temperature to suit himself*

**Recommendations
for living rooms**

Table 79 summarises foreign guidelines for living room temperatures in
winter, but most of the values quoted are based on general practice. As far as
we know, surveys have not been carried out in actual dwellings.
On the evidence of surveys in offices, and taking into account the special
needs of particular rooms, we propose temperatures for winter as set out in
Table 80.
*A temperature range of 20–24°C can be considered as comfortable during
the summer months.*

Requirements for surrounding surfaces

The most important physiological requirement for surrounding surfaces
follows automatically from page 180.

Recommendation

*The internal surface temperature of the walls, the windows, ceiling and floor
should, on average, be about the same as the air temperature. In no case
should they differ from it by more than two or three degrees*

Now we must go further and state that the average temperature of any one of
these surfaces (e.g. outside wall with window, or a floor) must not be more
than three or four degrees different from that of the air.

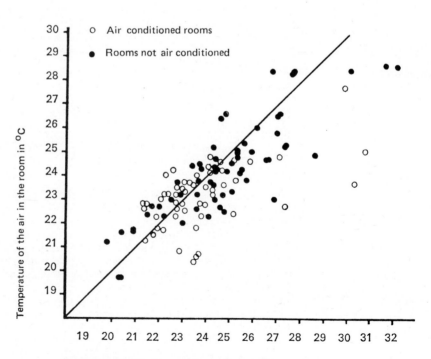

**Figure 81   Temperature of room air, and mean temperature of surrounding
surfaces in summer in 129 office rooms**   After Grandjean (162)

Studies carried out in offices	In our own studies mentioned above (162) we measured the temperatures of the surrounding surfaces in summer in 129 office-rooms, and calculated an approximate average. The result is shown in *Figure 81*. The temperature of the surrounding surfaces was an average more than 2°C higher than the air temperature. Since the interior walls, the floor and the ceiling are usually at the same temperature as the air, it follows that exterior walls and window-panes had very high surface temperatures. This was so in fact: on sunny days temperatures of 30–40°C were often measured at the windows.
Moisture on walls	Outside walls allow not only air, but also the moisture contained in it, to pass through to the exterior. This takes place whenever the temperature inside the room is higher than that outside. If the air escaping from the room reaches its dew-point, then dew, or water of condensation begins to form. If cooling is intense then the air deposits this water in the fabric of the wall. In this way moisture accumulates in the wall, and this may become visible on the internal surface. Since the material of the wall becomes a better conductor of heat as it becomes moister, this accelerates the loss of heat, and leads to heavier condensation. The danger of condensation and penetration of moisture into the wall is particularly great on north-facing walls, or on those which receive little sun. On south-facing walls the sun usually dries out the brick-work. For these reasons, wall design and its thermal insulation properties must be tested and planned with care in sites facing north or receiving little sunlight. The risk of condensation in the material of a wall is especially serious in kitchens and bathrooms where there is a high concentration of water vapour. In such rooms it is important to provide a damp-proof layer beneath the surface to prevent the penetration of damp.
Health factors	Rooms with cold exterior walls which collect moisture are not only un-comfortable, they are also hygienically undesirable. Many micro-organisms grow on damp walls – including visible moulds – and their spores float in the air of the room and cause allergic illnesses (asthma, allergic inflammation of the respiratory tract, and allergic skin diseases). Furthermore, mites thrive in damp dust, and these, too, can cause allergic diseases of the respiratory tract. Cold and damp rooms are bad for rheumatics. The chilling of particular parts of the body (knees, hip-joints, elbows) lowers resistance, and encourages acute rheumatism.
Thermal insulation of exterior walls	For reasons already mentioned, exterior walls must be of such a thickness that in winter the dewpoint comes to be as far outside them as possible. Occasional exposure to the sun, or dry weather will dry them off again. The better the insulation and the lower the permeability of a wall, the less danger is there of excessive condensation. A measure of penetration of heat into a wall that is much quoted is the *permeability number k*. This tells us how much heat in kilocalories flows through a structure of a given thickness per square metre per hour, if the temperature difference between the surface layers of air on the two sides is 1°C. (kcal/m²/h/°C). The reciprocal $1/k$ is often used, and it is then called the resistance to heat penetration. The greater the permeability (the higher the value of k), the lower the temperatures on the inner surfaces of the exterior walls, and the more unpleasant is the atmosphere of the room.
Values of k that are physiologically desirable	On medical and ergonomic grounds we may therefore propose the following guidelines for the construction of dwellings:

– minimum value for k   0.8
– desirable value for k   0.5

As far as possible, it should be arranged that living rooms and bedrooms are on the south, south-west or south-east of the building, the north side being used for staircases, corridors, W.C., bathroom, store-rooms and kitchen.
In municipal building and in rural areas, where for reasons of economy (or tradition) buildings are very spartan, there are problems of penetration of moisture and of the formation of mould, and of ice in winter, on the exterior

walls and even in the corners of rooms behind furniture with consequent damage to the structure of the building.

Here we can only give a few basic recommendations for the planning, construction and use of such buildings:

Measures against damp walls

- all rooms must have some form of heating, either as a part of the central heating system, or as an independent source. *On no account must they depend for their heat on warm air from an adjoining kitchen or living room.*
- if the kitchen is small, or if it is intensively used for other purposes, the water-vapour generated must be expelled by an efficient extractor fan.
- the external walls on the north side and the weather side must be given better heat-insulation than the others
- the external rendering of walls on the weather side must be particularly well-constructed to prevent the penetration of driving rain, while at the same time allowing moisture from inside the house to escape.
- corners of rooms that include an external wall need extra thermal insulation, because their reduced ventilation and heating may result in dampness and the formation of mould
- large items of furniture (cupboards, trunks, chests of drawers, beds) should not stand along walls that face north or west because damp and mould can easily collect behind them
- every room, particularly small kitchens and those facing north and west, must be heated continuously throughout the cold months of the year, either

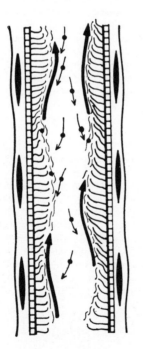
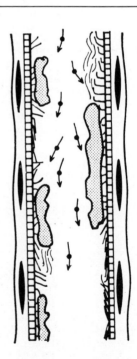

Normal bronchial tube
Ciliated epithelium
conducts mucus and dust away

Desiccated bronchial tube
Glutinous masses prevent the
self-cleaning process

Figure 82   Diagram of a respiratory passage, under normal conditions (left), and when the mucous membrane is desiccated (right)   Normally the ciliary epithelium gets rid of the mucus as it is secreted. On the right the desiccated epithelium is only partly exposed, and the dried-up mucus builds up incrustations. Dust particles and micro-organisms are no longer conducted away.

by central heating or from their own heater. If their only source of heat is warm air from adjoining rooms (as it often is in the country) then damp and even ice can collect.
— every room should be ventilated several times a day, to obviate the gradual accumulation of damp in both structure and furnishings.

Requirements of relative humidity

For reasons set out on page 183, it may be accepted that a relative humidity of 40–45% feels comfortable during the period when heating is needed, whereas in fine weather in summer 40–60% is almost universally agreeable.

From the medical standpoint
From the medical standpoint the problem of the moisture content of the air is more important for comfort than its temperature. The interior of the nose, the respiratory passages and the lungs, down to their smallest branches, the alveoli, are coated with a layer of mucus which is continually replenished. This mucous membrane consists in part of hair-like processes – the cilia – which are in continuous motion, and under the microscope look like a field of waving corn.

Nose, throat and air passages function as an air-conditioning plant, where the air that is breathed is cleaned, warmed and moistened. The swirling and centrifugal action of the air stream throws dust particles on to the mucous membrane, where the action of the ciliated epithelium mixes them with the mucus. The nose and air passages constitute a self cleaning filter. The abundant blood supply and continuous wetting of the mucous membrane raises the incoming air to the same temperature as the blood, and its humidity almost to saturation.

Drying of the mucus
If relatively dry air is inhaled for a long time the mucous membrane can become too dry. The first signs of this are unpleasant feelings of dryness in the cavities of the nose and throat, which can increase to a painful irritation. It often becomes difficult to speak, and sometimes to swallow. The dryness interferes with the action of the ciliated epithelium, the mucus accumulates, and remains in glutinous masses which cover the mucous membrane. Thus the self-cleaning system is impaired and bacteria may find a favourable medium in which to develop. They become established easily in the dried-up mucus, and produce symptoms of inflammation.

Figure 82 shows diagrammatically the ciliated epithelium as it is in a normal and in a desiccated bronchus.

Numerous specialists attribute the increase in colds during the winter months to the dryness of air in heated rooms. This explanation is confirmed by observations in which certain bacteria and viruses were found to survive longer in air at a lower relative humidity than in air of 40–60% R.H.

Frequency of illness
Studies of the effects of dry air indoors on the frequency of illness were carried out by Serati and Wuthrich (164) on postal workers and by Ritzel (165) in kindergartens. While the former authors were not able to detect any effect of atmospheric humidity on the frequency of illness, Ritzel (1965) showed a significant drop in school-absences from colds in kindergartens when the air was moister.

The results of these surveys are set out in Table 81.

Self-cleaning of the respiratory passages
Ewert (166) observed the flow of mucus produced by the ciliated epithelium. Figure 83 reproduces his results, which were obtained by the use of spots of colour.

The 174 measurements gave an average velocity of 4.2 mm per minute at 43.6% average relative humidity. When the relative humidity was lower there were more cases where the flow of mucus ceased, and a well-authenticated link was demonstrated between relative humidity and the rate of flow of mucus (in smokers $r = 0.67$). In relative humidities of the order of 40% the secretion of mucus is often no longer sufficient to moisten the mucous membrane, and so no measurement of the velocity of flow can be made.

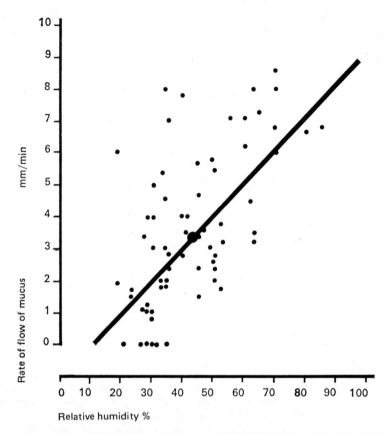

Figure 83 Effect of the relative humidity of the air on the rate of flow of mucus in the sinuses of the nose and throat in healthy people (smokers) After Ewert (166)

Table 81 Frequency of absences from colds among 230 pupils of 5 mixed infants' schools. After Ritzel (165)

Type of school	Maximum possible attendances	Days absent from colds
With air humidifiers	6306	195
Control schools	5910	338

Recommendation

Air humidity during the winter

These physiological studies confirm the clinical picture, in which a relative humidity of less than 30% leads to undesirable drying of the mucous membrane. To summarise, it may be said that *relative humidities of 40–45% are desirable in heated rooms, and produce an agreeable atmosphere, but a relative humidity of less than 30% is hygienically undesirable because it gives rise to unpleasant dryness in the mucous membranes of the nose and the respiratory passages.* In practice these hygienically desirable limits are often not attained. In our own studies (161) we recorded relative humidities below 30% (average: 28%) in more than half of the offices during the period when heating was in operation. *Figure 84* shows the frequency distribution of the values for winter and summer, and *Figure 85* how those for winter compare with the comfort of the room.

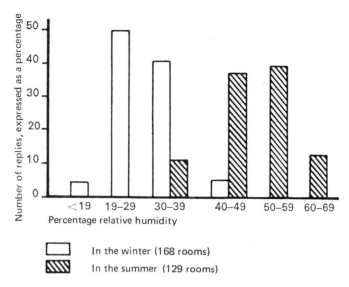

Figure 84   Relative humidity in 297 offices   Both in winter and in summer the total number of rooms surveyed is taken as 100%

The relative humidity of the air (in rooms) is significantly lower when heating is in operation than during the summer months. If the relative humidity was below 40%, the majority said that the air was too dry, yet it was remarkable how little this impression was removed as the humidity rose. Apparently the human body is poorly equipped to estimate the moisture content of air, so that this atmospheric factor is difficult to assess subjectively.

Nemeček, Wanner and Grandjean (167) investigated students in an air-conditioned auditorium, and showed that the assessment 'too dry' increased with the room temperature even if the relative humidity remained constant. This finding confirmed the opinion of *Franzen* (163) that his office-workers had only a vague idea of the atmospheric humidity and tended to express their discomfort at the high temperature by saying that it was 'too dry'.

Finally it may be mentioned that many professional people complained about the damage caused by excessive dryness to wooden furniture, to works of art (the wood of statuettes, or the colours of old pictures) and to plants. Static electricity increases as the air becomes drier.

Physiological assessment of humidity

Measures to counter excessive dryness in heated rooms, — other than air-conditioning — include humidifiers, of which there are a number of different types on the market. Natural ventilation takes away quite a lot of the moisture in a room. It is estimated that:

— *in small rooms of up to 50 cubic metres in volume, 0.3–0.5 litres of water should be evaporated per hour*
— *in bigger rooms, or interconnecting living spaces of up to 100 cubic metres, 0.6–1.0 litres per hour should be evaporated.*

It is therefore stressed that only those forms of equipment that can provide at least this rate of evaporation should be installed: anything less is a waste of money.

Inefficient ways of increasing the humidity in a room include: Opening windows (because the cold outside air in winter has a very low absolute humidity); introducing plants into the room (because at the most these will give off only 10–30 millilitres of water per hour); and the many kinds of

M

humidifiers that stand on top of the radiators, because they give off only 20–100 millilitres of water per hour, which has no measurable effect on the humidity of the room.

Among the efficient forms of humidifiers on the market three types can be distinguished:

– atomisers
– vaporisers
– evaporators.

Atomisers

An atomiser projects water into the air in the form of fine droplets (an aerosol) which vaporise in a short time. Atomisers are usually efficient, and raise the relative humidity of the air in a room in a useful space of time irrespective of what the humidity is to start with. This apparatus can also be used to spray disinfectants and deodorants. In hard water districts, it is advisable to soften the water first.

Vaporisers

These heat water and moisten the air through the escape of water vapour. Two systems fall into this category: one brings the water to boiling point, while the other only raises the water temperature to 60° to 70°C, at which level water vapour is also given off into the atmosphere. Good designs of both types can be found which will give off between 0.3 and 2 litres of water per hour.

The main advantage of the vaporiser lies in the fact that no dirt can collect in the water, and the high temperature of the water kills any microorganisms that it might contain.

Evaporators

The evaporator uses a blower to expose the air in the room to the maximum possible water surface, which is created by foam rubber or other spongy material dipping into a water bath, or sprayed with water. To increase evaporation the water may be warmed. The efficiency of this apparatus depends upon the level of humidity in the air in the room, and one can only recommend designs which can release at least one litre of water per hour into a relative humidity of 25%. This device is particularly suitable for big rooms. With good design it is silent and efficient. The water that is vaporised does not pollute the air, but the apparatus needs to be cleaned periodically – about once a month.

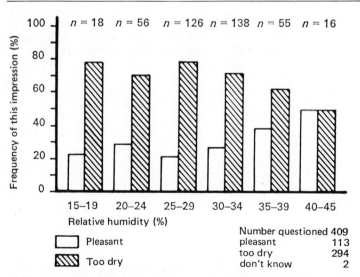

Figure 85   Percentages of those questioned answering 'pleasant' and 'too dry' respectively, arranged in groups with the same relative humidity $n =$ number in each group, which = 100%

Requirements for air movements

Recommendations

It appears from the literature that in most European countries air velocities of more than 0.2 metres per second are regarded as being unacceptable for seated persons, and hence the relationship between air currents and subjective impressions of temperature given in *Table 78* have only a theoretical interest. *In practice it is a good thing to keep below a maximum of 0.2 metres/second.* In Switzerland it has occasionally been found that air currents of 0.1 metres/second were thought excessive by people doing very delicate work. In contrast, when working standing up, and particularly when vigorously active, substantially high air flows of up to about 0.5 metres/second can be tolerated without inconvenience.

Draughts in offices

Our own investigations in conventional offices (162) and in open-plan offices (168) showed that the borderline of 0.2 metres per second was only rarely exceeded, yet in spite of this a high proportion of the office workers (about 30%) complained of draughts. No correlation could be demonstrated between the air currents as measured and the frequency of complaint. *Franzen* (163) came to very similar conclusions – although the air currents at nearly all the measuring points were less than 0.2 metres per second, 10–40% of the people questioned in each office complained of draughts. These results lead one to suppose that the air currents as measured were not the real cause of complaint, which depended on the temperature and the direction of air flow, as well as on what part of the body was exposed: e.g. the neck.

Summary of recommendations

The following guide-lines can be formulated for the design of rooms for people to sit in:

– the air temperature should be 21 °C (± 1 °) in winter and in summer 20–24 °C is comfortable
– the average temperature of the surrounding surfaces should not differ from the air temperature by more than 2–3 °C, nor that of any single surface by more than 3–4 °C
– a relative humidity of 40–45% is comfortable in winter, and less than 30% is undesirable on hygienic grounds. In summer the natural relative humidity is comfortable
– air currents at any seat should not exceed 0.2 metres per second. For very delicate work while seated (e.g. sewing, or fine mechanical work) a limit of 0.1 metres per second is recommended.

Heating

Basic requirements of a heating system

Consideration of medical ergonomics and the physiology of daily life, leads to formulation of the following requirements:

– *small temperature gradients.* This means that up to 2 metres above floor level the temperature must vary as little as possible both in the vertical and the horizontal plane. In every room where people stay for any time, temperatures must be kept within the limits of comfort.
– *large heating surfaces.* This requirement makes it possible to keep the temperature of the heating surface relatively low, so ensuring a good distribution between radiation and convection heat.

— the least possible scorching of dust-particles. Heating elements that operate at a high temperature scorch dust particles present in the atmosphere. This is regarded as particularly unhealthy by most public health doctors, because it is likely to lead to symptoms of irritation in the air passages. It must be assumed that scorched dust particles have a greater irritating effect on the mucous membranes than the usual substances with which these deal, which are mainly water and particles containing a certain amount of organic matter

— easy cleaning. Heating equipment, which tends to accumulate dust, should be easily accessible for cleaning

— easy regulation. The heating should be easily regulated, so that variations in demand for heat should not cause wide variations in the air temperature

— use as a drier. The housewife often finds heaters useful for drying linens.

Various heating systems from an ergonomic point of view

Central heating with radiators

As a rule central heating systems are easy to service. They are easy to regulate, and if the radiators are suitably distributed, give a mild and pleasant warmth everywhere. Comfort in rooms is obtained by:

— radiators arranged under the windows, to keep temperature gradients low
— radiators which are not enclosed, so that they can be cleaned periodically to avoid the production of scorched dust.

Central heating with convectors

Convectors heat a small volume of air, which then rises and cooler air takes its place. Compared with radiators, convectors take less time to heat up, and occupy less space. On the other hand they have a relatively high surface temperature, and being inconvenient to clean, are liable to produce scorched particles.

Ceiling — and other radiant heaters

These can be made to serve as a central heating system. There are two basic types, those built into the fabric and those which hang below the ceiling. The latter have the advantage of heating up more quickly than the former, and they may act as sound insulators according to the system used. Moreover, the operating temperature of heaters which hang from the ceiling is such that they can be used as additional radiators, for example in entrance halls and corridors. With ceiling heaters the greater part of the heat is projected into the room by radiation from above, and so its primary effect is to heat the floor, the furniture and the walls, whence the air receives its heat secondarily by convection.

Most important advantages: The surrounding surfaces are as hot as, and occasionally hotter than the air; up to a height of 2 metres above floor-level temperature gradients are small in all planes and all directions; there is no scorching of dust particles; no space has to be found in the room for heating units.

Most important disadvantages: sluggish to regulate; the housewife cannot use them occasionally to dry things; *objets d'art*, plants and musical instruments may suffer from the radiant heat. Other complaints include drying of the air in the room, and unpleasant effects (e.g. headaches) from radiant heat on top of the head.

In the research previously mentioned (161), carried out in 168 office-rooms, we found that the relative humidity of the air was not affected by the various heating systems used. The average value was the same in rooms with ceiling heating as with radiators. Moreover the temperature of the ceiling above the heater was more often below than above 32°C.

Although the atmosphere in offices with ceiling heating did not differ from that produced by other heating systems, 70% of the 212 persons questioned thought it was a bad system. The commonest objections were concerned with dryness of the air, unpleasant heat radiation, headaches, excessive heat and not being able to regulate it.

Stoves

In the country the stove is often a tiled stove, which is operated from the kitchen, and which has a great capacity for storing heat. Its most important advantages are its use for drying purposes and its large heating surface, which does not scorch the dust. In the country, too, it is economical to be able to use it as an incinerator. Its disadvantages are its extreme sluggishness and the inconvenient arrangement in the room, giving a steep fall of temperature towards the window.

Iron stoves are hardly used now in apartment blocks, though they are occasionally put into temporary buildings or barrack rooms. They produce very high surface temperatures which lead to scorching of dust particles. While the stove is in operation the floor gets dirty, and dust is produced. Temperature gradients are high, and the atmosphere in the room is usually uncomfortable.

Electric heaters

Electrical energy can be made to produce various forms of heating. A particularly interesting form nowadays is the electric storage heater, which stores heat during the night (e.g. in a special form of magnesite stone) and gives it out again to the room during the day.

Early versions were poorly regulated, but newer types equipped with an over-load cut-out and a temperature regulated ventilation system should be better. There are no ergonomic data about them, so that it is still difficult to appraise this system of heating. *Liese* (159) gave a cautious evaluation of the heating of houses and flats by electric storage heaters and drew attention to the need for improved thermal insulation of the structure of the building, to the high surface temperature of the storage heater (scorching of dust particles?), to the likelihood of nuisance from draughts of hot air, and to the noise of the ventilator fan.

Other electrically operated heating systems, for example infra-red radiators, or small electric stoves are not considered for regular heating of dwellings since electricity is still dear in the daytime. On the other hand there is no objection to their occasional use.

Under-floor heating

Under-floor heating can be provided by hot water from a central heating system, or from electric storage heaters in the floor. The heat is released partly by direct convection in the air, and partly by radiation to the surrounding surfaces. The most important consideration is the effect of a warm floor on the feet of the occupants. If the floor is made too warm, the feet become too hot for comfort, sweat too much, and occasionally swell. *Chrenko* (169) tested the effect of various floor-temperatures on people when sitting and when moving about. There were noticeable ill-effects if the skin temperature rose above 29°C. Half of the test subjects thought it was disagreeable if the floor-temperature was 30°C when they were moving about and 33°C when they were sitting still, from which the author concluded that a level of 24.5°C should not be exceeded.

Frank (170) studied the effects of air and floor temperatures on the temperature of people's feet and their general comfort, when they were wearing shoes. He found that a floor temperature of 25°C and an air temperature of 16°C were still considered comfortable.

Aikäs and his colleagues (171) in Finland compared the effects of under-floor heating with that from radiators. Complaints about being cold when near a window were commoner where the heating was under-floor, and none of the forms of under-floor heating had any physiological advantage over radiators. These authors, too, came to the conclusion that the floor could be heated up to 25°C without any ill-effects.

Schüle and Lutz (172), in three houses, studied the effects of electric storage heating in the floor, combined with additional wall heating. At night the floor temperature rose to 30°C, and that of the air to 24°C. During the day they reached 26°C and 19–22°C respectively, but the electric wall heating had to be switched on to reach these temperatures. The output of the wall heaters was between 13 and 39% of the total. The authors came to the conclusion that this combination of heating systems resulted in a satisfactory atmosphere in the room. In another piece of research *Schüle* (173) drew attention to the need for better thermal insulation of the outer walls when electric heating was installed.

The verdict on under-floor heating, as far as our present experience goes, is as follows:

— it can be recommended for rooms in which it is customary not to take off one's overcoat in winter: e.g. passenger terminals, waiting rooms, churches, entrance halls
— it is satisfactory as an addition to ceiling heaters or radiators in bathrooms, in rooms without an underfloor space, where the floors are particularly cold, in swimming baths, and in certain parts of hospitals
— under-floor heating with additional heating elements (e.g. in the walls) can be used without physiological drawbacks in houses and flats
— under-floor heating is said to be adequate by itself provided that the outside walls are given better thermal insulation, but objective studies on this point have still be to made.

Hot-air heating

In hot-air heating, air in the central part of the house or flat is heated to between 30° and 70°C, and led through ducts or pipes into the connected rooms. The air may be propelled by electric fans, or may circulate by natural convection. Unlike the Americans we do not use this system much in Europe, though we occasionally use heated air from a tiled stove. *Ihle* (174) recommended hot-air heating for halls, garages and workshops, but for home use it has the drawbacks of noise and smells travelling along the ducts, scorching of dust particles in the air, occasional draughts of hot air, and sharp gradients of temperature. If hot-air heating is to be freed of its hygienic objections the air must be filtered and humidified, ending up with complete air-conditioning.

Windows

Effect of windows in winter

Loss of heat

In recent years architectural fashion has increased the size of windows, and windows which take up more than 50% of the outside walls are very common nowadays.

Big windows act as cold surfaces in winter. The loss of heat from the room is governed by the conductivity factor k of the windows, and according to *Caemmerer* (175, 176) the values set out in *Table 82* must be taken into account.

It can be deduced from these figures that if 50% of the outside wall is window, this accounts for 80% of the total heat loss from the room, even if the window is double-glazed.

Table 82   Heat-conductivity factors of various types of window   After Caemmerer (176)

Type of construction	Heat conductivity factor k in kcal/m²h°C	
	Wood-framed	Steel-framed
Simple window	4.5	5.0
Double-glazed	2.8	3.4
Sealed window	2.2	3.0
Sealed window, 3 sheets	1.3	1.9
Double window	2.0	2.8

Table 83   Temperature of the inside surfaces of various types of window with moderately severe winter temperatures outside, calculated for the three German heat-insulation zones, I, II, III   After Caemmerer (175)

Type of window	Inside temperature in °C Heat-insulation zones		
	I	II	III
Simple glazing	−1	−5	−9
Double glazed	7	5	3
Triple glazed	13.2	12.0	10.9

Surface temperature of windows

From the ergonomic point of view special importance attaches to the temperature of the inner surface of the window. Caemmerer (175) reached the values set out in *Table 83* by starting from the mean minimal external temperature appropriate to German Zones I–III for heat-insulation standards (North of the Alps Swiss standards ought to be based on Zones II and III) *According to this table the surface-temperatures of windows are very low in winter, and neither single nor double-glazed windows conform to the recommendations set out on page 188, above.* It is clear that the physiological effect of cold windows increases in proportion to their size.

Effect of windows in summer

Greenhouse effect

From an ergonomic point of view big windows are even more of a problem in summer than they are in winter, since they cause overheating of the room. The short-wave radiation of sunlight passes almost unimpeded through clear glass, and after being absorbed by the furnishings and the surrounding surfaces, is converted into heat: these objects then emit long wave heat radiation which is reflected by the windows and the heat accumulates inside the room, hence the name 'greenhouse effect'. In this way the interior of a room can be heated far above the outside temperature. As windows become relatively larger the risk of unpleasant heating in the rooms increases, and it becomes more and more urgent to have some ways of shutting out the sun and some form of air conditioning.

Heat radiation

The heat radiation in the atmosphere depends on a combination of the direction of the sun's rays, the diffused radiation (the scattering of solar radiation in the atmosphere), and the reflected radiation (heat reflected from the ground, water or buildings). On a sunny day, diffused and reflected radiation makes up about 20–40% of the total external radiation, integrated over the whole day. (*Künzel and Snatzke*) (179), *Gertis* (178).

Penetration of heat through windows

The extent to which heat passes through a window is determined by:

— transmission
— absorption
— reflection.

According to *Petherbridge and Loudon* (180) these three processes contribute the following proportions of the heat-transmission through a pane of glass, given angles of incidence up to 50°.

— reflection   10%
— absorption   10%
— transmission   80%

At bigger angles of incidence more heat is reflected.
According to the same authors (180), about 30% of the heat absorbed by glass is given off to the outside air at normal wind velocities, and the rest passes through into the room by convection and radiation. With double-glazing, 15% of the heat absorbed by the outer glass and 65% of that in the inner glass gets through into the room.

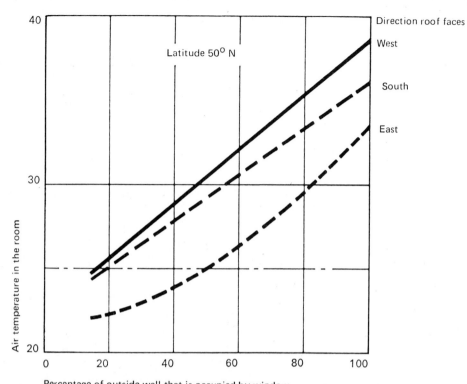

Figure 86   The heating effect of sun on the air within a room, in relation to the size of the window and the direction in which the window faces   After Caemmerer (175)

Calculation for heating a room

Effect of window area type of building and orientation

To help in understanding the heat-penetration through windows both *Gertis* (178) and *Künzel and Snatzke* (179) propose the use of the glass factor G. This quantity expresses the percentage of the solar energy that penetrates into a room through a particular pane during a radiation day, after making allowance for the continuous change in the angle of incidence of the sun. From this quantity it is possible to calculate the heating-effect inside the room, using experimental and mathematical methods for determining the heating effect from solar radiation, taking into account the most important relevant factors (type of window, direction in which it faces, type of building, size of room etc.) have also been developed by *Loudon and Petherbridge* (181), by *Caemmerer* (175) and other authors. *Figure 86* shows the room heating in relation to window area and to orientation while *Figure 87* shows the same thing in relation to the form of construction. The importance of the last should not be underrated. Lightly constructed walls have little capacity for storing heat, with the result that the air inside the room heats up more quickly than if the walls are more solidly built in traditional fashion.

Figure 88 shows the rate at which the room warms up, in relation to the thickness of aerated concrete and solid concrete respectively. *Figure 89* shows the same in relation to the time of day and the orientation of the window of a specimen house.

Window area and comfort

The results of mathematical and experimental studies of the effect of window areas on room temperature can be observed under practical conditions. During the research carried out in office-rooms in summer (162) workers in

Walls of light construction

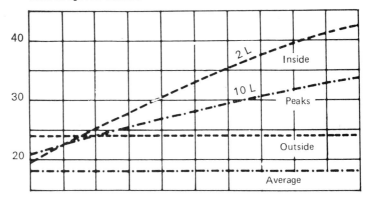

Walls of heavy construction

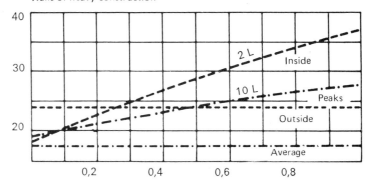

Fraction of outer wall that is occupied by window

L = number of changes of air per hour

Figure 87   The heating of the air within a room by the the sun's radiation, in relation to the relative size of the window and to the density of construction of the walls   After Loudon and Petherbridge (181)

offices without air-conditioning were asked: 'Is the air-temperature generally too high between May and September?', and were allowed to answer: 'at no time', 'rarely', 'occasionally' or 'often'. *Table 84* summarises the answers 'often too warm', divided into rooms with small windows and rooms with big windows.

This complaint came distinctly more often from offices with big windows – most of them taking up more than 50% of the outer walls – than from offices with a traditional window area of less than 30%.

Effect of window area on noise and internal atmosphere

This result was confirmed by research which was carried out, almost at the same time, by *Langdon* (186) in 2734 offices in London. The author found that in summer increased window area meant more complaints about the room being too hot, as well as of disturbance from noises outside. There was an interesting link between traffic noise and internal atmosphere: where the traffic noise was high the office workers more often complained that it was uncomfortably hot. The author suggested that the windows were closed to shut out the noise of traffic, thus increasing the risk of overheating. He concluded that modern building fashions for big windows produced offices with

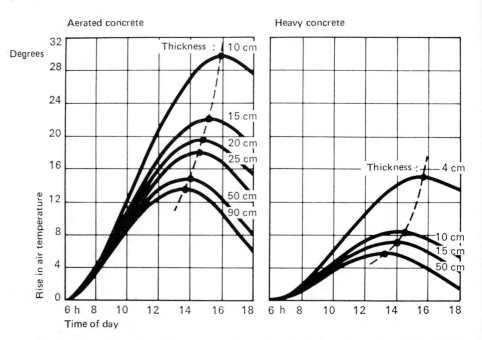

Figure 88   Extent and hourly variation of room temperature in relation to the thickness of the walls, and to the material of which they are constructed Calculations made by Gertis (185) for experimental rooms 4 × 4 × 2.5 metres with double-glazed windows of 4 square metres area facing south

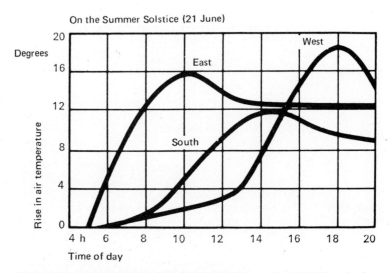

Figure 89   How the heating effect inside a room varies during the day on 21 June, according to the way in which the window faces   Experimental room: 4 × 4 × 2.5 metres. External walls built from aerated concrete, 20 cm thick. Windows are 4 square metres, double-glazed   After Gertis (178, 185)

Table 84   Effect of the proportion of window to total wall-space, assessed by the number of statements that the room was 'often too warm': offices not air-conditioned   124 persons were questioned, and the number in each group is taken as 100% for that group.

Fraction window/total external wall	Number of rooms	Number of persons questioned	Percentage of assessment 'often too warm'
Less than 30%	6	52	5.8
30% and more	18	72	59.7

big light rooms, but that this advantage had to be paid for with more disturbance from noise, and an uncomfortably warm atmosphere.

Caemmerer (187) also developed a critical view of big windows. He recommended that the following arrangements should be considered:

Proportion of window-area in external walls	*Arrangements for protection against the sun*
under 20%	no protection needed
20–50%	internal sun-blinds
over 50%	external sun-blinds.

On the basis of our own research, however, we are of the opinion that rooms without air-conditioning should have externally mounted sunblinds or shutters only.

Protection against the sun

Important measures

The most important measures to be taken against excessive heating of the air in rooms by solar radiation are:

— projecting structures (roof-overhangs, blinds, etc.)
— window-areas not too big
— window plans put back from outside wall
— shading of room by a balcony or a penthouse
— flexible sun-blinds fitted externally, made of wooden slats, fabric or synthetic materials
— internal shading (curtains, slats)
— reflective glass.

All experts are agreed that external sunshades over the windows give the most effective protection.
Projecting structures are most effective on south-facing walls, and are less satisfactory on east or west walls because the sun is lower when it is in these

Table 85   Transmission of heat through various sun blinds   The 'solar gain factor' that is used here denotes the relationship between the heat penetrating into the room and that which falls on the outside walls. After Loudon (184)

Window or sunblind	Solar gain factor
Simple window, single glazing	0.77
Double glazed window	0.67
Dark green plastic blind inside	0.64
Venetian blind inside	0.46
Curtain of white material inside	0.41
Venetian blind between panes, double glazing	0.28
'Stopray' reflective glass	0.25
Dark green plastic blind outside	0.20
Venetian blind outside, at 45° angle	0.12
Roller blind outside	0.11

Table 86   Heating effect, apparent temperature, and illumination in six experimental rooms with different settings of the venetian blinds and other anti-sun devices   The angles given are those of the slats of the blinds in relation to horizontal. NGVBO = normal double-glazed clear glass with an external venetian blind Stopray NVB = Stopray reflective glass without any venetian blind. GGNVB = double glazing with green absorptive glass outside, and no venetian blind. 3 × NGNVB = triple glazing without any venetian blind. T_A = air temperature T_S = average temperature of surrounding surfaces

Measurements	NGVBO 70°	NGVBO 45°	NGVBO 0°	STOPRAY NVB	GGNVB	3 × NGNVB
Increase of air-temperatures at head-height	1.6	2.2	5.9	5.0	8.6	11.8
Raising of window temperature	3.5	5.1	9.0	8.4	21.3	14.4
Temperatures of surrounding surfaces (mean between 12–15.30 hrs)	23.5	24.3	26.1	26.5	29.0	30.4
Apparent temperature $\frac{T_A + T_S}{2}$	24.0	24.8	27.7	26.5	29.5	31.9
Light intensity at 15.45 hrs, in lx	340	1050	2500	1900	3400	3800

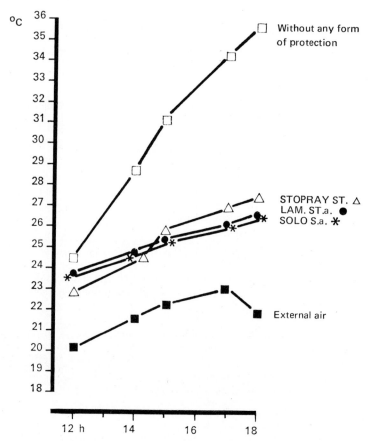

Air temperature in the room

Average for 11, 12 and 13th September 1969

Figure 90   The effect of different forms of protection against the sun on the temperature of the air in the room   Stopray St. = double glazing with STOPRAY reflective glass, with the addition of vertical plastic curtains inside. Lam. St. a = aluminium venetian blinds fitted to the outside. Solo S.a. = plastic curtains outside (a film of transparent glass fibre, covered with PVC)

directions. To assess the efficiency of various forms of protection against the sun on windows, the so-called 'sun-protection factor' is often used. This expresses the heat-transmission through the device compared with that through an equal area of clear glass. This factor is only relative, and says nothing about the absolute quantity of heat transmitted.

Loudon (184) used the 'solar gain factor' which compares the flow of heat into the room with the total heat radiation. A few values for the sun-protection factor are brought together in *Table 85*.

Protection against the sun in experimental rooms

In one of our own studies (182, 183) we investigated the effect of various types of anti-sun equipment on six experimental rooms which faced in the same direction, and were comparable in every respect. They lay along the south-west face of the building, and had the following dimensions: volume 38.2 cubic metres; floor area 13.5 square metres; outside wall 9.45 square metres; area of the two windows 4.24 square metres. Proportion of window area to that of the outside wall = 50%. The building was lightly constructed.

Table 86 gives the average results of a series of experiments, from which it appears that external slats fixed at an angle of 45° ensure that the room receives good protection from the sun, while still being well lighted.

The average air temperature, the difference between the temperatures inside and out, and the temperature of the window, all on three successive sunny days can be seen in *Figures 90, 91, 92*.

These results clearly show the greenhouse effect. Where the window had no sunshade, the room temperature rose from 24.5°C to 35°C, whereas the shade-temperature scarcely reached 23°C. The externally mounted slatted screen, the reflective glass, and the shade made from synthetic material all

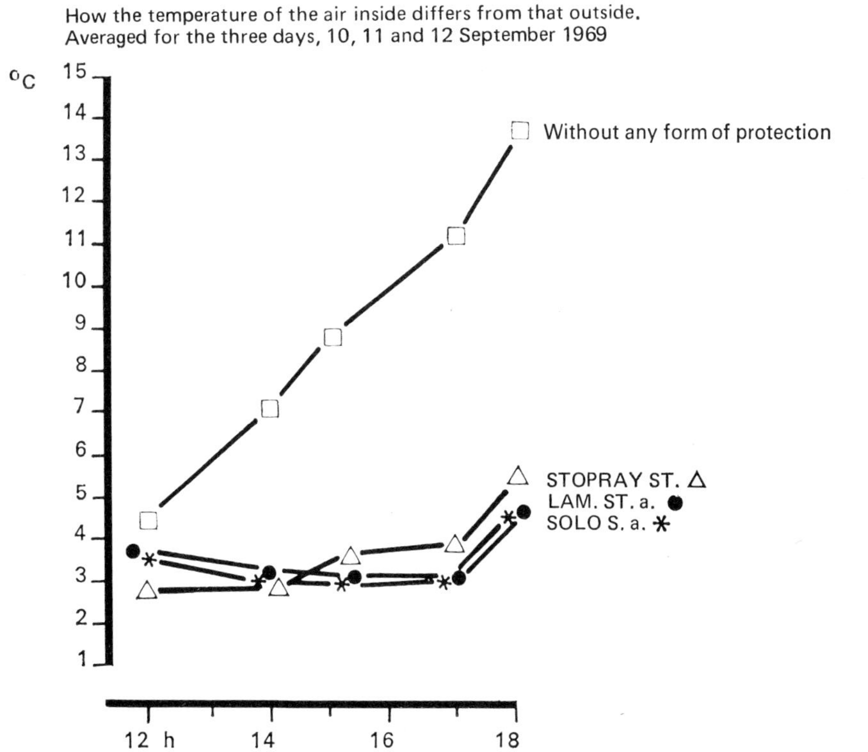

How the temperature of the air inside differs from that outside.
Averaged for the three days, 10, 11 and 12 September 1969

Figure 91   The effect of different forms of protection against the sun on the temperature difference of the internal and external air   Legend as in Fig. 90

Comparative criticisms
of sun blinds in
common use

gave good protection. The external slatted screen was superior to all the other methods in controlling the surface temperature of the window.

From the combined research results we can draw the following conclusions: In all the experiments *external slatted shutters* were effective against heat penetration from the sun. The rise in air-temperature in the room varied between 1.2 and 3.5°C, while the maximum temperature reached varied between 23.7 and 26.2°C for the air and 26.7 and 30.1°C for the window. Meanwhile the illumination within the room remained within the range of that recommended for daylight.

Some sunblinds made from synthetic materials were as efficient as the wooden slats, provided that they were fitted outside the windows. *Venetian blinds* fitted between the two windows, or *on the inside* did not give sufficient protection. When they were combined with windows of clear glass the room temperature rose to 28.2–32.5°C and that of the windows to 41.7–44°C. In the absence of air-conditioning the resulting atmosphere in the room is unbearable.

Normal windows of clear glass, without sunblinds produced room-temperatures of 29.9–35.4°C, and window-temperatures of 35.8–39.6°C.

Temperature of the inside surface of the window, averaged for the three days 10, 11, 12 September 1969.

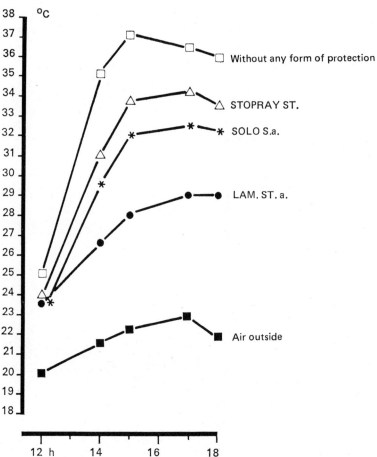

Figure 92   The effects of different forms of protection against the sun on the temperature of the inside surface of the window   Legend as in Fig. 90

Reflective glass (e.g. Stopray Glass), without the addition of slatted shutters, ensures good protection, though in comparable situations it is never as good as normal clear glass together with external slatted shutters, although light levels inside the room are better.

Absorbent glass (Green glass) gave insufficient protection unless it also had external slatted shutters. The air temperature inside the room reached 28.7–32°C, and the temperature of the window 38.3–46.2°C. This high window-temperature, caused by the absorption of solar radiation, had a particularly adverse effect on the atmosphere inside the room. Absorbent glass can be considered only if it is used in combination with external slatted shutters.

External fabric shades of a grey-green colour gave good protection. The air-temperature inside the room rose by 2.5 or 2.6°C, and reached 24.5–24.6°C, and the maximum window temperature ranged between 29.7–30.8°C. In qualification, however, it must be added that with this device the light became very poor inside the room (below 400 lx), and was mostly below the recommended limit for day-time lighting.

Opening the tilting window reduced the effect of a sun-blind by increasing the inflow of warm air from the facade of the building, the temperature of which varied from 28–34.5°C.

The angle of inclination of external slats plays a decisive part in controlling the influx of warm air. Inclinations between 70° and 45° are effective, while on the other hand, horizontal slats, which give a good field of vision towards the outside, are inadequate as a protection against hot air.

These observed effects of sunblinds agree very well with the findings of *Loudon* (184), set out in *Table 85*. He also puts the various sun-protection systems in the same order of preference as we did in our researches.

In themselves and by themselves the various reflective glasses were superior to slats as far as admitting daylight is concerned; though slatted shutters have the advantage that when the sky is cloudy they can be raised, and so admit more light. In principle it is preferable to have the more flexible system, especially considering how poor the light is in the winter months.

In this connection we may also quote a survey made by *Tonne* (188), according to which sun-protection systems in Germany were rated as follows:

— Very good	external Venetian blinds or roller blinds. external awnings
— moderately good, but often adversely assessed	blinds between double-windows, or opening casements
— mostly adverse reports	blinds or curtains inside the room heat-protective glass

Ventilation, and the quality of air

Used air

In any room that is used by people, the air is altered or contaminated in the following ways:

- dust and smells
- water-vapour
- heat given off into the air
- production of carbon dioxide and reduction of oxygen
- contamination with bacteria and viruses
- contamination from outside, or as a result of processes going on in the room.

Whereas the first four of these come from the people themselves, and so are primarily related to the capacity of the room, contamination from outside depends on the lay-out of the building and that which arises internally comes from processes carried on there. Contamination of the air with microorganisms usually arises from people, but can come in from outside.

Smells

Among the smells of human origin the most important are those caused by substances given off by the skin, since even in the lowest concentration they can give rise to feelings of disgust, discomfort, aversion and nausea. These odorificants are a mixture of organic gases and vapours which, in the concentration in which they are usually present, are not at all toxic, but they are very undesirable because of their subjective nuisance value. So far it has not been possible to identify the substances causing these odours with certainty, and so their strength has to be estimated from subjective impressions.

The build up of water vapour and of heat

Water vapour given off by the human body is made up of the evaporation of sweat and that contained in the air expelled from the lungs: while the latter is still inside the body it is saturated. The hourly output of water-vapour by man in relation to the temperature of the air, can be estimated as follows:

- at 22°C   46 g/h
- at 24°C   55 g/h
- at 26°C   67 g/h

It may therefore be accepted that 10 persons in a room give off 500–600 millilitres of water vapour per hour. The hourly output of heat of a sitting person can be estimated at 80–100 kcal. If he does manual work, this amount increases considerably.

Oxygen deficiency and accumulation of carbon dioxide

When sitting down a man uses 250 millilitres of oxygen per minute and gives out in that time about 300 millilitres of carbon dioxide in his exhaled breath. These quantities are greatly increased if he does manual work. In normally constructed living rooms and workshops, even with the windows closed the natural leakage of air through crevices in the structure is so high that the oxygen cannot fall so low, nor the carbon dioxide rise so high as to be harmful. On the other hand dangerous situations can arise in tightly closed spaces such as air-raid shelters, tanks or containers. The free atmosphere normally contains 21% of oxygen; if this is reduced to between 14 and 10% breathlessness ensues, and at 7% unconsciousness and death.

The air exhaled during respiration contains 3–4% of carbon dioxide, whereas in the free atmosphere it varies around 0.03%. If the level of carbon dioxide in a room rises to 2–4% there is difficulty in breathing and at 10% death ensues through paralysis of the respiratory nerve-centre.

Micro-organisms

The air in every room contains a certain number of floating microorganisms (bacteria, viruses, and fungus spores). The extent of the contamination is determined by the number of microbes present. In living rooms with a normal number of occupants there are between 200 and 500 microbes per cubic metre of air: the number increases steeply with the number of occupants. Most of these germs are harmless to man, and here it may be mentioned again that illnesses caused by infective agents are usually transmitted direct from one person to another by droplet infection.

Air pollution

Pollution of the air can be by solid particles or by gases, and the source of these can be either in the dwelling itself (particularly in the kitchen, bathroom or W.C.) or from outside. In houses and flats it is smells that are the commonest cause for complaint, but today the pollution of the outside atmosphere is becoming increasingly important because it naturally penetrates indoors.

Dust

Dust consists of mineral substances, organic materials and particles of soot. The last comes from the burning of coal and fuel oil. 'Clean' country air contains about 10^8 particles per cubic metre, whereas in urban communities the dust-content ranges between 10^{10} and 10^{12} particles per cubic metre. By weight 'clean' country air contains about 0.5 milligrams per cubic metre and urban air 1–5 milligrams per cubic metre. Modern ideas of hygiene set an upper limit of 10 milligrams per cubic metre as the extreme of tolerance.

| Gaseous pollution of the air | The commonest forms of gaseous pollution, and those of greatest hygienic importance are: |

- sulphur dioxide
- nitrogen peroxide
- formaldehyde
- incompletely burnt hydrocarbons
- carbon dioxide
- carbon monoxide.

These pollutants mostly come from domestic fires and from the exhausts of motor-vehicles. In industrial areas they are reinforced by emissions from factories. The effects of pollution by solid and gaseous substances are:

- ill-health
- annoyance from smell and irritation of the eyes
- damage to the fabric of buildings
- toxic effects on animals and plants.

People have an elementary right to clean air

The right to clean air	Unfortunately there is no generally accepted way of either defining or measuring what is meant by the term 'clean air', so the demand for clean air is still for the present a matter for individual discretion.
Quality of the air	In the domestic circle one tries to achieve a satisfactory level of air purity by means of ventilation. To this end we have to be content with rather imprecise recommendations, according to which the air should be free from objectionable smells, excessive numbers of germs, and too much pollution with factory emissions, or solid and gaseous substances.
Actions to be taken	It is very difficult to do anything about air-pollution that enters the home from outside. Possible actions that can be taken include: better ventilation of the entrance hall and stairs; resiting of the chimney, or building it higher; more tightly closed windows; and air-conditioning of the inner rooms. Obviously these operations can be very costly.

The gadgets that are often on sale that are supposed to neutralize, and to purify the air, cannot be recommended. They are either completely ineffective, or effective only under conditions that are dangerous to health. This is the case, for example, with all equipment which ozonises the air, as well as those which ionise it, or create an electro-magnetic field. Their effect on people in a house or flat is not yet proved: in any case any advantages are still very questionable.

The most effective and most important action to ensure that the air in a room is of good quality is to provide enough ventilation to replace the used and polluted air with fresh clean air from outside.

Ventilation terms

The following two terms are useful when determining fresh air requirements:

- *air capacity*. This means the volume of fresh air that must be fed into the room in cubic metres per hour. Occasionally the air-capacity depends on the number of people present, so then it is given as the volume of fresh air needed, measured in cubic metres, per hour, per person.
- *air-change number*. This is the number of times per hour that the entire volume of the air in the room must be changed. The air-change number is

commonly used as a way of expressing the amount of fresh air needed (so many changes per hour), even though this is a difficult quantity to measure in practice, and it is only rarely specified.

Measurement of air-changes

To measure the rate at which the air in a room is being changed, a different gas is introduced in the room which can be detected chemically. If the concentration of this introduced gas is determined by analysis at regular intervals, the rate at which the concentration declines gives a measure of the change of air within the room. Nitrous oxide (laughing gas) is a suitable gas to introduce for this purpose.

Ventilation techniques

According to *Liese* (159) the following ventilation techniques can be recognised:
- free ventilation
- forced ventilation

Free ventilation includes:
- natural ventilation (also called self-ventilation)
- ventilation by window
- ventilation by shafts
- ventilation by skylights

Forced ventilation includes:
- extractor fans (reduced pressure in room)
- blower fans (increased pressure in room)
- combined ventilation (extractor+blower).

If the incoming air in a forced ventilation system is brought to a particular temperature, humidity and purity, then we have air-conditioning.

In free ventilation the change of air is brought about by the natural forces due to temperature differences and wind pressure. In forced ventilation motor driven ventilators provide the necessary movement of air.

Natural ventilation

Natural ventilation is the change of air that takes place when all windows and doors are shut, because they are not hermetically sealed, and because the structure of the building allows air flow to occur. The extent of this depends on temperature differences, the quality of the building, and the wind-strength. Natural ventilation gives rise to air-change numbers of 0.3–0.7 in new buildings and 1–2 in old ones.

Ventilation through windows

The extent of ventilation through windows depends on what forces are in operation between the air in the room and that of the atmosphere outside. Besides the wind-pressure, temperature differences are decisive here. The pressure-distribution in a room is shown diagrammatically in *Figure 93*.

Warm air rises because it expands, and so produces a relatively higher pressure in the upper part of the room, and a relatively lower pressure below. With a high window, therefore, air from outside enters the room through the lower part of the window, and displaces air through the upper part. In summer, if the air in the room is cooler than that outside, then the pressure distribution and air flow are the reverse of this.

In this context it is self-evident that high, narrow windows are considerably more efficient ventilators than low, broad windows.

Low windows placed at the middle level of an outside wall are in the zone where pressures are equal, and so give only a little change of air.

Cross-ventilation

Cross-ventilation comes into existence if at least one window opens on to each of two different sides of the house, and if a direct air flow can take place between the two openings. The driving forces of the cross-wind are in the first place the difference in atmospheric pressure between the two sides of

a) Air in the room colder than that outside

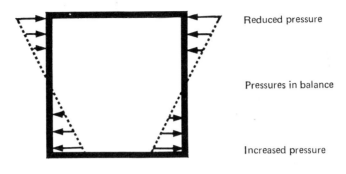

Reduced pressure

Pressures in balance

Increased pressure

b) Air in the room warmer than that outside

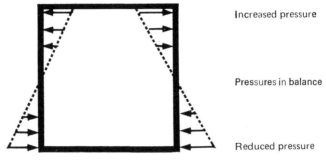

Increased pressure

Pressures in balance

Reduced pressure

Figure 93   Diagram of pressure distribution inside a room, according to the difference in air temperature between inside and outside   The arrows show the direction in which the pressure operates

the house (wind-pressure) and secondly differences of temperature. Cross-ventilation is effective and can be used successfully in schoolrooms and other rooms where the demand for air is high.

Shaft ventilation

The most important factor in shaft ventilation is the difference between the temperature in the room and the temperature over the roof, and shaft ventilation is only effective if the temperature in the room is higher than that outside. When this is so the warm air rises through the shaft, and cold fresh air comes in through the windows, doors and other openings in the lower half of the room.

Shaft ventilation is insufficient and unreliable in the warmer months of the year. It is recommended that ventilators are provided to ensure the necessary changes of air

Shaft ventilation by itself is nowadays considered only for rooms such as store-rooms, cellars, halls and corridors, where ventilation is never urgent. Shafts are only suitable for kitchens, bathrooms and W.C. if fans are fitted in the air shafts.

Roof-extension

The operation of an airshaft can be improved by fitting an extension to the opening on the roof, and providing this with a fan and a flap. Then the action of the wind will assist the action of the air-shaft. An air-shaft without a motor-driven fan is quite inadequate to ventilate enclosed spaces, besides having the drawback of having little provision for regulating its action. Finally airshafts can sometimes distribute smells, as well as noises from other rooms, or other flats.

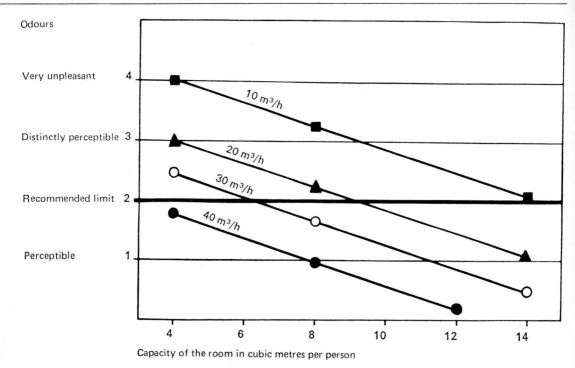

Figure 94   Guidelines for the fresh-air requirements of seated persons in relation to the volume of air per person available in the room   After Yaglou and his co-workers (190)

Volume of air needed

Rules of thumb

If people are the main cause of changes in the air in a room, then it is the olfactory substances that they give off that determine the amount of fresh air needed in the room, since it is these rather than either the carbon dioxide or the water vapour that interfere with the well-being of the occupants. A general rule that is often given for deciding what is the amount of fresh air needed by one person in a closed room is:

a rate of inflow of 30 cubic metres of fresh air per person per hour.

This figure must be taken as only a rough approximation, since the fresh air requirement in a room is closely dependent on how much air per person remains in reserve (i.e. in the total volume of air available to each person).

Figure 94 summarises the rules that were worked out by *Yaglou* and his co-workers (190) in a long series of experiments with research subjects who had been trained to detect smells.

From the results of this survey the following deductions can be made:

Smells

- the concentration of carbon dioxide in the air in the room shows a poor correlation with the strength of the smell.
- the strength of the smell – and hence also the extent of the fresh-air requirement – shows a strong correlation with bodily freshness (bathing habits) and the state of cleanliness of clothing. The fresh-air requirement is distinctly higher when there are children, or persons from low social strata.
- healthy people smell, even after a bath, and need 15 to 18 cubic metres of fresh air per person per hour. One week after a bath children's need for fresh air has risen from 18 to 29 cubic metres per hour.

- for any given room the intensity of the smell diminishes according to the logarithm of the influx of fresh air and the logarithm of the volume of space per person
- the circulating air had no effect on the amount of odour given off. The authors attributed this to the insufficient cleansing (washing, humidifying, cooling and drying) that it had undergone.

From the researches of *Yaglou* and his colleagues (190) we may derive the following recommendations:

Space per person in cubic metres	Fresh-air requirement per person in cubic metres per hour	
	Minimal	*Desirable*
5	35	50
10	20	40
15	10	30

Smoking is a special problem in air-pollution, and the following recommendation is often found in the literature:

- in rooms where smoking is forbidden	30 cubic metres/hour/person
- in rooms where smoking takes place	40 cubic metres/hour/person

Recommendations for the ventilation of homes

Guidelines

It is also true in principle for dwellings that the 'reserve of air' increases with the volume of the room, so that the demands for the air to be changed can be reduced. This factor is particularly important for kitchens, bathrooms and W.C.s.

Table 87 summarises the rules for the scale of ventilation in living quarters, based partly on data given in the literature and partly on our own considered opinions. It must be pointed out, however, that no surveys have been made in dwellings to prove the correctness of these, or any other rules.

- the ventilation of the kitchen should be controllable, so that this can be ventilated expeditiously at times when smells are being produced
- in the kitchen the windows should be supplemented by mechanical means, either a ventilation shaft extending above the roof, or an extractor fan direct to the exterior
- mechanical ventilation of kitchens should be such that it produces a reduction of pressure, so that smells are not driven out into the rest of the dwelling
- tilting sash-windows are best for kitchens since they can be used at will either as sash-windows (convenient for cleaning) or as tilting windows (convenient for continuous ventilation)
- interior kitchens need particularly efficient mechanical ventilation: while cooking is going on they require 250 cubic metres per hour, reduced to 50 cubic metres per hour at other times. Mechanical ventilation provided by a fume-hood over the cooker should be supplemented by a second shaft with natural ventilation. The fresh air inlet through an outer wall should be controllable
- if bathrooms and toilets are completely internal, they should have mechanical ventilation by means of an air-shaft with extractor fan situated in the roof-space. If separate ducts lead into a main shaft, they should open into it above the height of the ceiling
- bathrooms with outside walls should have mechanical ventilation as well as windows, to avoid the accumulation of damp in the fabric and fittings

Table 87   Guidelines for ventilation of dwellings

Room	Number of changes per hour		Type of ventilation
	Minimal	Desirable	
Living room	2	2– 3	windows
Bedroom	2	2– 3	windows
Childrens' room	2	2– 4	windows
Small kitchen, less than 20 cubic metres	10	20–30	preferably windows
Medium kitchen, 20–30 cubic metres	8	15–25	plus mechanical
Large kitchen, more than 30 cubic metres	6	10–20	ventilation
External and internal bathrooms (12–15 cubic metres)	4	5– 8	window + ventilator fan
External WC (4–6 cubic metres)	2	4– 6	window
Internal WC (4–6 cubic metres)	2	4– 6	window + ventilator fan
Corridor	1	2	doors and possibly air-shaft
Entrance hall	1	2	doors and possibly air-shaft

- when air-shafts are fitted with an extractor fan, the shaft should have a cross-sectional area that is 0.1–0.3% of the floor area of the room, and should in no circumstances be less than 200 square centimetres
- if an extractor fan is used as an additional ventilator, either in an outside wall or in the window, it should extract 5–7 cubic metres per minute
- kitchens, bathrooms and toilets should each be planned with only one mechanical ventilator.

7 Lighting

Summary   The eye can be compared to a camera, the cornea and lens constituting the optics and the retina the light-sensitive film. Its important functions include accommodation and adaptation, dazzle being an extreme disturbance of adaptation which severely impairs visual acuity.

To be able to see it is essential to have adequate light, to be free from dazzle, and to have constant levels of illumination, both from place to place within the room and at different times of day. Tables of recommended intensities for domestic lighting are given. Contrast ratios should not exceed 1 : 3 in the centre of the visual field and be below 1 : 10 at the periphery, and when repetitive activities are being performed, the eye should not have to move between dark and bright surfaces. Although fluorescent tubes are efficient as light sources. they give a flickering light that is physiologically undesirable: this effect can be avoided by using two or three tubes out of phase with each other.

A useful way of assessing the value of daylight indoors is the daylight-quotient, which expresses interior illumination as a percentage of that out of doors. The strength of daylight indoors depends on the direction of the sun, and on the amount of reflection from internal and external surfaces. The principal factor is the amount of light received from the sky, which in turn is determined by the aspect of the building, and by the height and breadth of windows. Direct light from the sky determines the level of illumination in the room as a whole, whereas areas facing away from the windows receive only reflected light; high windows are more effective than lower ones on both counts.

Based on the studies of *Barrier and Gilgen* (192), the following daylight quotients are recommended for houses and flats.

	Minimal %	Desirable %
Living room	1.5	2–3
Bedroom	1	1–2
Children's room	1.5	2–3
Kitchen	1.5	2

Sunlight in living quarters has the following effects: it dries out the walls, kills micro-organisms, helps children to grow, reduces heating expenses, and has a pleasing psychological effect. Studies by *Barrier and Gilgen* (43) lead to the following recommendations for the duration of sunlight that should be possible on the 8th February.

	MINUTES	
	Minimum	Desirable
Living-room	60–90	more than 120
Bedroom		
– in small dwellings	0	0
– in large dwellings	30	30
Children's room		
– in small dwellings	60–90	more than 120
– in large dwellings	90–150	more than 210

The last section discusses general principles concerning the psychological effects of colour and its effects on working efficiency.

Terms and definitions

Light intensity

This is a measure of the light falling upon a surface, and the unit of measurement is the *lux*.

1 lux (lx) = 1 lumen (lm) per square metre.

The human eye is sensitive to a wide range of intensities, extending from a few lux in a dark room up to 100,000 lux out of doors in the midday sun. The light intensity outdoors varies during the day from 2,000 to 100,000 lux.

Luminance (luminous intensity)

This is a measure of the brightness of a surface, the impression of brightness given by illuminated surfaces being proportional to their luminous intensity. Since luminous intensity corresponds to the amount of light radiated, that of walls, furniture and other objects in the rooms depends to a great extent on how reflective their surfaces are, whereas that of a light-source, on the other hand, depends on the amount of light that it generates.

Luminous intensity is measured in *apostilbs* (asb) or *stilbs* (sb)

1 asb = 0.32 Candela/m² or 0.3 cd per sq. metre.
1 sb = 10,000 cd/m² = 31,416 asb.

The luminous intensity of walls, furnishings and so on that do not produce light themselves is usually measured in apostilbs, whereas light-sources are normally measured in stilbs.

The following light sources are examples of high levels of luminous intensity:

the moon	0.25 sb
clear sky	0.4 sb
candle light	0.7–0.8 sb
paraffin lamp	0.6–1.5 sb
incandescent electric lamp	70–1,000 sb
fluorescent tube	0.45–0.65 sb

The units of luminous intensity and light intensity are related in the following way:

luminous intensity in asb = reflection coefficient × light-intensity in lx.

The following simple example will illustrate this relationship. If a white wall gives 80% diffuse reflection, and is exposed to a light intensity of 100 lx, then the wall will have a luminous intensity of 80 asb.

Since the impression of brightness received by the eye depends primarily on the luminous intensity within the field of view, the brightness of surfaces in a room is very important, and from a physiological point of view matters just as much as the light intensity itself.

Physiological principles

The visual apparatus

Vision entails the following sequence of events: light arising from the object under observation passes through the front aperture of the eye to be focussed on the retina, where the light energy is transformed into bioelectrical energy as nerve impulses. These pass along the optic nerve to the brain; in a first series of nerve junctions branches carry nerve impulses to a centre which

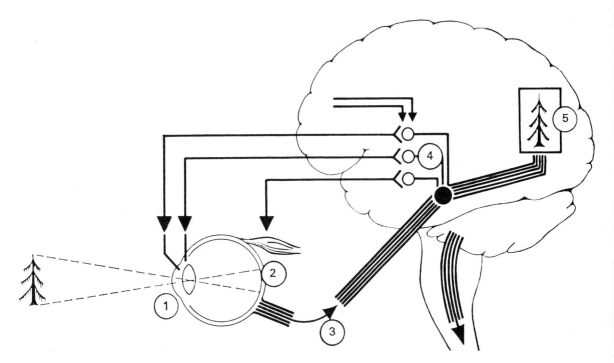

Figure 95   Diagrammatic representation of the mechanism of human vision
1 = cornea and lens. 2 = image received on the retina. 3 = transmission of nervous impulses along the optical nerve. 4 = nucleus, from which impulses are fed back to control the movement and focussing of the eye. 5 = visual perception of the outside world in the conscious zone of the brain

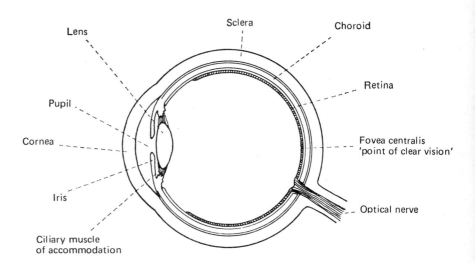

Figure 96   Diagram of the eye in longitudinal section

directs the movements of the eyes. This centre controls the size of the pupillary aperture (the front aperture of the eye), the convexity of the lens, and the movements of the eyeball. On the basis of the 'information' thus received, the optical equipment of the eyes is adjusted continuously. The regulating mechanism works automatically, without conscious control. At the same time other nerve impulses are penetrating further into the brain, and, after a certain amount of filtering, arrive at the cerebral cortex – the seat of consciousness – where a picture of the outside world is created. New impulses arise here, which are responsible for the thought, decisions, emotions and reactions that are associated with this picture; these visual processes are shown diagrammatically in *Figure 95*.

The visual apparatus comprises all the organs and nervous structures that participate in this activity, and they control at least 90% of the activities of daily life. Vision plays an essential part in virtually all forms of work, particularly in all skilled work. If we consider the large number of nervous functions that are involved in seeing, it is not surprising that the eyes are commonly an important source of fatigue.

The eye

In many ways the eye can be compared to a camera: the light sensitive film is represented by the retina, and the optical system by the cornea, the lens and the iris. Cornea and lens form a light refracting system which focusses the light on to the retina. The receptive organ is the layer of visual cells of the retina, where the 'cones' for seeing in daylight can be distinguished from the specially sensitive 'rods' for seeing in a dim light. In the visual cells light energy is changed by photochemical reaction into nervous impulses which are subsequently transmitted by the optic nerve. The human eye contains about 130 million rods and 7 million cones, each being about 1/1000 mm long with a diameter of approximately 1/1000 mm.

On the posterior surface of the eye, a few degrees from the optical axis, is the retinal pit (fovea) which can be recognised by a thinning of the retinal sheath which covers the visual cells. Because of this the light-rays penetrate directly on to the visual cells, which at this point consist entirely of cones. In the fovea the cones reach their greatest density – approximately 10,000 per square millimetre – and each cone is linked by its own fibre to the optic nerve. This endows the foveal area with the greatest possible power of resolution, about 12 seconds of arc in the visual field. Since the retinal fovea gives the clearest vision, we direct our gaze in such a way that the image of whatever we are looking at falls on this area of the retina, which is known as 'the point of clear vision'. If an object is to be seen clearly its image must fall on the fovea, which can cover an angle of view of only one degree.

Away from the fovea the cones become less dense, and several cones or rods are linked to one nerve fibre. With increasing distance from the fovea the rods increase in number and the cones diminish. The rods are more sensitive to light than the cones but less sensitive to form or colour. The rods are particularly active in night vision. As a result of this structure of the eye, stationary objects can be seen clearly only when their image falls on the fovea, and with increasing distance from this point, the visual image becomes less distinct. Generally, therefore, the eyes make quick movements to bring different parts of the visual field into the fovea, so that the brain can rapidly build up a sharp picture of the surroundings.

Visual field

The visual field, or field of view, is that area that can be seen while the head and eyes are held still. Under these conditions we can only see things sharply if they lie inside a tiny area making an angle at the eye of 1°. With increasing distance from this optical axis, objects become more indistinct and blurred. When reading, for example, we can only see a few letters clearly if we do not move our eyes; in practice we allow our glance to move in jerks, taking in about 12 letters at each step.

The visual field is divided into:

zone of sharp focus	angle of view 1°
middle field	angle of view 40°
peripheral field	angle of view 40–70°

Objects in the middle field cannot be focussed sharply, but movement or strong contrasts can be perceived there. The peripheral field includes all the extreme edges of the field of view, bounded by the head, nose and cheeks.

Accommodation

'Accommodation' is the ability of the eyes to focus sharply on objects at varying distances, from infinity to the nearest point of focus. If we look at a finger held in front of our eye we see it in sharp focus, while the background is blurred; if we then look at the background, it becomes sharp and the finger blurred. An object is thus seen clearly if it is projected as a miniature image on to the retina, by the refractive power of the cornea and lens, i.e. if the focal plane of the optical system of cornea and lens coincides with the retinal surface. The eye is focussed on to near objects by changing the convexity of the lens, and the extent of this is governed by the amount of contraction of the muscles of accommodation (ciliary processes and ciliary muscles).

When the ciliary muscles are relaxed, and the accommodation apparatus is in its resting state, then refraction is such that parallel rays of light from distant objects are focussed on the retina. If there was no power of accommodation, the image of a near object would lie behind the retina and so would be seen as a blurred impression. The ciliary muscles, however, compress the lens and bring the plane of sharpness forward on to the retina. When the eye is focussed on 'infinity', as when we allow our gaze to range over a distant view, then the ciliary muscles are relaxed, and hence the eye is being rested. Indeed it is possible that the blue and green tones that predominate in distant views help to rest the eyes. The nearer an object, the greater the strain on the ciliary muscles. The nearest point to which the eye can be sharply focussed is called the *near point*, and the furthest that can be seen clearly is called the *far point*. The near point is a measure of the power of accommodation which lessens as the eye becomes fatigued. After a lengthy period of close work with a great strain on the ciliary muscles, the diminishing power of accommodation moves the near point away from the eye.

Accommodation and age

Age has an important bearing on accommodation, because the lens loses its elasticity and hence its ability to change its shape. The effect of this is that the near point moves further and further away from the eye. On the other hand the far point usually remains the same. On average the distance of the near point at different eyes is:

At 16 years	8 cm
At 32 years	12.5 cm
At 44 years	25 cm
At 50 years	50 cm
At 60 years	100 cm

When the near point has passed beyond 25 cm the condition is known as presbyopia. The near point can be brought back by the use of suitable lenses, until a normal vision is again restored. The speed at which accommodation occurs also diminishes with age.

Accommodation and light intensity

The intensity of illumination plays a vital part in the range of accommodation of the eye. In a poor light the far point comes nearer, and the near point recedes, and at the same time the speed and precision of accommodation are reduced. The degree of contrast between an object and its immediate surroundings has a similar effect: the greater the contrast, the more quickly and accurately can the eyes accommodate.

Pupil diameter

Just as the aperture in a camera can be varied to prevent under or over exposure of the film, so in the human eye the light reflex can narrow the pupil and protect the retina against too bright a light. Adjustment of pupillary diameter takes a time which can vary between a few tenths of a second up to

Adaptation of the retina	one second. So if the light is subject to sudden, marked changes in intensity, the retina may be overexposed as the pupil closes comparatively slowly. The pupil adjusts its diameter by reflex action to a steady level of illumination, and in the daytime has an aperture of 3–5 mm, while at night it opens to 7–8 mm. At night, if we look at the headlamps of a car, we experience strong dazzle, but if we look at the same headlamps in daytime we experience no dazzle. In the daytime, if we go into a cinema in which a film is being shown, the auditorium seems very dark, but after a few minutes it becomes brighter, and objects gradually become visible. These common experiences result from the fact that the sensitivity of the retina has become adjusted to a steady level of illumination within the field of view. In darkness the sensitivity of the retina becomes many times greater than in daylight, which is why the headlamps dazzle us only at night. Conversely the sensitivity falls off in daylight, so that we can see nothing at first when we go into the cinema.

These processes of adjustment are called *adaptation*, and derive from photochemical and nervous regulation of the retina. Thanks to these processes we can see well both in moonlight and in the brightest sunshine, even though the light-intensity differs by more than 1 : 10,000,000.

Dark adaptation

Adaptation to darkness (dark adaptation) takes a comparatively long time in proportion to the extent of the change of light intensity. On going from daylight into very dark surroundings, adaptation is quick for the first five minutes, but then proceeds ever more slowly. Complete adaptation is not achieved for about an hour.

Dark adaptation should never be hurried, and 25–30 minutes must be allowed if optimal night-vision is needed. After 25 minutes about 80% of maximum sensitivity has been reached.

Light adaptation

Light adaptation is quicker, yet this, too, needs 30–60 minutes to complete. Light adaptation has a first phase (α-adaptation), lasting only 0.05 seconds, during which the sensitivity of the retina is abruptly reduced to a fifth of its initial level. This first adjustment is obviously under nervous control. The second phase (β-adaptation) proceeds slowly, and leads – like dark adaptation – to a change in the balance between decay and regeneration of the photosensitive substances in the retina.

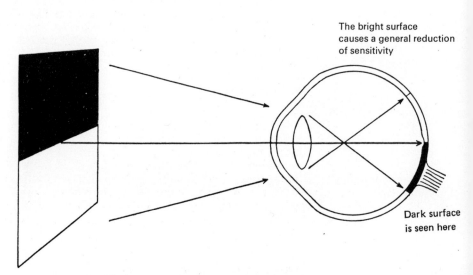

The bright surface causes a general reduction of sensitivity

Dark surface is seen here

Figure 97   The effect of bright and dark surfaces on the retina   The bright area reduces sensitivity all over. This is especially important at the fovea

The abrupt reduction in sensitivity that takes place during light adaptation affects the whole retina. If the image of a very bright surface (a window, a light-source, reflection from a table, and so on) falls on the retina next to a dark area, sensitivity not only in the area of brightness, but all over, and — of particular importance — in the retinal fovea is reduced. This process is shown diagrammatically in *Figure 97*.

Local adaptation

If the visual field has well-defined light and dark areas then the adaptation process operates over the corresponding areas of the retina, a phenomenon called 'local adaptation'. This also influences the retina as a whole, and can have adverse effects on the retinal fovea.

From all these arguments two fundamental requirements can be formulated:

- *illumination should be of the same order of brightness throughout the visual field, since otherwise reduced sensitivity will impair vision*
- *the general level of brightness should not fluctuate suddenly from time to time, because adaptation would not be quick enough to deal with it*

Dazzle

Physiologically speaking, dazzle is a gross disturbance of the state of adaptation of the retina. Three types of dazzle may occur:

- *relative dazzle* (too great a contrast within the field of view).
- *absolute dazzle* (a light source so bright that adaptation is not possible.)
- *adaptational dazzle* (abrupt change of overall light intensity.)

The following details are interesting in this context:

- the shorter the period of dazzle, the more quickly will the original state of adaptation be regained. Hence in practice single changes of brightness lasting less than one second (for example a short flash of car headlamps in a dark street) have little effect. On the other hand, repeated changes in brightness, following quickly one after another, have a very strong effect.
- in relative dazzle impairment of vision is increased the nearer the source of dazzle lies to the line of sight, and the bigger and brighter the light source.
- a source of dazzle above the line of sight does less harm than one to the side or below.
- the risk of dazzle is considerably increased if the general illumination in the field of view is low, since dazzle happens more quickly and more violently the higher the state of sensitivity of the retina. (For example: the relative dazzle from a window can be masked by increasing illumination in the room; a headlamp is not dazzling in daylight).

Physiological requirements

This section will discuss the basic physiological requirements, and will deal separately with natural daylight and artificial lighting. The following factors affect visual acuity:

- light intensity.
- freedom from dazzle.
- uniform lighting throughout the room.
- a steady level of illumination.

Table 88   Recommendations for natural and artificial lighting

Kind of work	Examples	Required intensity in lx
Rough	Stacking in a storeroom	50– 150
Moderately precise	Cooking meals	250– 500
Precise	Reading, sewing, mending	500–1000
Very fine work	Skilled manual work	1000–2000

Light intensity

First and foremost the light intensity must match the activity being performed, decisive factors being the sizes of objects to be recognised (difference between fine and coarse work), and the contrast between objects and their background. A further important factor is the age of the operative: a 60-year old requires ten times as much light as a 10-year old to see equally well.

For these reasons guidelines for light intensity can never be more than of a very general nature. *Table 88* summarises relevant recommendations.

Freedom from dazzle

It is important to avoid dazzle or glare both for comfort and for clarity of vision. The commonest and most serious errors are to place too bright lights in the field of view and to have too strong a contrast in brightness between different surfaces.

Uniformly lit surfaces

Physiological studies have shown that the best conditions for vision and for visual comfort are dependent on the distribution and contrast of the major surfaces in the field of view. Current knowledge and experience endorse the following rules:

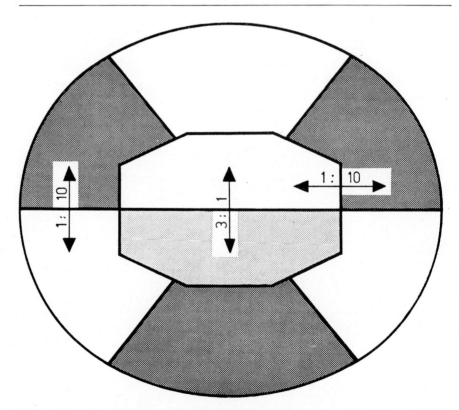

Figure 98   Permissible contrast between bright areas within the visual field
In the middle field 1:3. In the peripheral field 1:10. Between the middle field and the peripheral field 1:10

- the brightnesses of all major surfaces and objects in the field of view should be as uniform as possible.
- contrast ratio should not exceed 1 : 3 in the centre of the field of view.
- contrast ratio should not exceed 1 : 10 in the peripheral field, or between the periphery and the centre.

These recommendations are shown graphically in *Figure 98*.

- contrast between a light source and its background should not exceed 1 : 20.
- it is better both for vision and for comfort if bright areas lie in the centre of the visual field, and dark areas are in the periphery.
- contrast is more troublesome at the sides and lower half of the visual field than in the upper parts.
- the maximum permissible difference in illumination within a room is 1 : 40.

This means that in everyday practice the direction in which a person most often looks while he is working should not include:

- a bright window.
- a dazzling white wall near dark flooring.
- a black panel in a white wall.
- a reflective table-top.
- a black typewriter on a bright pad.
- highly polished machine-parts.

Since the amount of light reflected (reflectance) has a considerable effect on the brightness of surfaces, the choice of colour and materials is highly important in the design of walls, furniture and large objects for homes and offices. The following reflectances can be recommended in the design of a room:

ceiling	80–90%
walls	40–80%
furniture	25–60%
machines and apparatus	30–50%
floor	20–40%

Windows must always be provided either with a venetian blind or with light-absorbing curtains, to prevent excessive contrast from sunshine entering the room.

Uniform lighting over a period of time

A rhythmically fluctuating light-source in the field of view is more troublesome than static contrast. This is the case if an operative is required during his work to shift his gaze rhythmically between a bright and a dark surface; if light and dark surfaces pass on a production line; if polished machine-parts move in the field of view; or if a light-source flickers.

As noted above, pupil diameter and retinal sensitivity need time to adapt to changes in light intensity, and when light intensity fluctuates rapidly the eye is subjected to persistent over- and under-exposure. Hence such lighting conditions are particularly dazzling.

Physiological studies by Guth *(199) have shown that the rhythmic fluctuation of two surfaces with brightness in the ratio of 1 : 5 causes the same reduction in visual acuity as a sudden reduction in light intensity from 1,000 lx to 30 lx.*

To reduce fluctuating brightnesses to a minimum:

- surface brightness in the most frequent direction of gaze should be equalised by the use of colour and lighting.
- apparatus should be installed to stabilise lighting circuits and prevent flicker.

Artificial lighting

Lights and light-sources

Lights
    Normal lighting systems fall into the following four groups:

Direct radiants. These emit 90% or more of their light in the form of a cone of light directed on to the surface to be illuminated. This light is recognisable by its harsh shadows; and the contrast between light and shade may far exceed 1 : 10. This type of lighting is used in displays, show-cases, and entrance-halls, but at a work-place it can cause sharp contrasts between lighted areas and surrounding shadows. It can be recommended as working lighting only if the general illumination is good enough to lighten shadows and reduce contrast.

Semi direct and semi diffused radiants. By using selective shading a considerable proportion of the light (40%) shines in all directions, while the other part (60%) is directed over the ceiling and walls. This type of lighting produces moderately dense shadows with blurred edges. It finds use as general lighting in homes, factories, offices etc., but it can only be recommended for coarse or moderately fine work. Semi direct light is not suitable for the finest work. It can be recommended where uniform lighting is required within and on the walls of a room.

Free radiant lighting. Typical examples are bulbs of opal glass, which radiate light equally in all directions, and cast slight to moderate shadows. Because of their brilliance, such lights are often a source of glare, and should not be used in living rooms or work rooms: they are suitable for store-rooms, corridors, waiting-rooms, ante-rooms, toilets and similar areas.

Indirect radiant lighting. These throw 90% and more of their light on to the ceiling and walls, from which it is reflected back into the room. This system requires pale coloured ceiling and walls. The light is diffuse, and casts almost no shadows. Some architects have a predilection for this kind of lighting, since it matches their particular style of architecture and can be used for aesthetic effect. Indirect radiant lighting is only to be recommended in work rooms if additional lighting is available at the work place; in that case, indirect lighting is free of dazzle. Indirect radiant lighting is particularly suitable for exhibitions, and shops – any place, in short, where the eye of the user has to be directed on to the walls.

Light-sources
    Filament lamps and fluorescent tubes are the two principal modern sources of artificial light. The following points are important from a physiological standpoint:

Filament lamps
    Filaments emit a light that has a high red and yellow content and is therefore unsuitable for tasks requiring colour recognition or colour matching. When used at work, filaments have the further drawback that they radiate heat: lampshades may reach a surface temperature of 60°C or more, and if they are too close to the head the direct radiated heat from them may cause discomfort or headache.

On the other hand, because of its reddish-yellow colour, the light from filament lamps is warm-tinted (association with the reddish-yellow sunlight of evening) and invokes a feeling of evening leisure.

Fluorescent tubes
    In fluorescent lighting, electrical energy is changed into radiation by passing an electric current through a gas (usually argon) or a vapour (usually mercury vapour). This way of producing light is more efficient than by heating a filament, and thus the light output of a fluorescent tube is three or four times greater than that of a filament lamp for the same amount of current.

The fluorescent material with which the inner surface of the tube is coated changes the ultra-violet radiation of the discharge into visible light, the colour of which varies according to the composition of the coating. Hence fluorescent tubes can be matched with the colour of filament lamps (warm tone), of daylight under a cloudy sky (white tone) or with blue light (day-light lamps). The advantages and disadvantages of fluorescent tubes may be summarised as follows:

Advantages

High light output and long life. If frequently switched on and off their life is reduced almost to that of a filament lamp.
Low intensity of the light source: minimal glare. The light intensity at the surface of fluorescent tubes lies between 0.45–0.65 sb, that of filament lamps 70–1,000 sb.
With tubes colour-matched to daylight there is no difficulty in obtaining a smooth transition from daylight to artificial light. Colour perception at work is not impaired.

Drawbacks

Visible and invisible flicker (stroboscopic effect). Brightness of fluorescent tubes fluctuates at mains frequency, 50 Hz in Britain. This frequency lies above the level of visual persistence and is thus not visible directly; how-ever, when reflected from moving objects, such as shining machine parts or tools, movement flicker may be produced by stroboscopic effect. The de-gree of fluctuation is greater in daylight tubes than in either warm tone or white tone tubes.

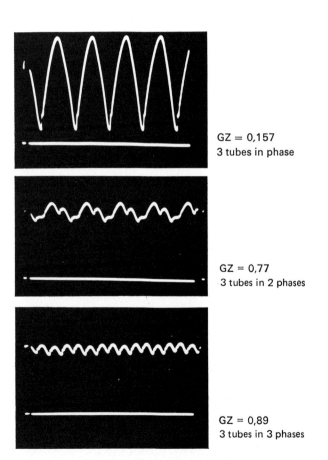

GZ = 0,157
3 tubes in phase

GZ = 0,77
3 tubes in 2 phases

GZ = 0,89
3 tubes in 3 phases

Figure 99   The effect of different phasings of multiple fluorescent tubes on the uniformity of light   G.Z. = uniformity index = minimum emission/maximum emission. The wave-forms represent the invisible flicker, that can be registered by a photoelectric cell; the horizontal lines are the axes from which the intensity is measured

When tubes are old or defective the discharge may become faulty, and create a slower flicker visible to the eye; this is particularly marked at the two ends of the tube.

Visible and invisible flicker are both undesirable in working situations. After prolonged exposure many people complain of headache and painful irritation in the eyes, accompanied by tears and redness of the conjunctiva. Our own researches (191) have shown that the invisible flicker from a fluorescent tube causes an increase in physiological fatigue as well as a measurable reduction in visual efficiency.

The invisible flicker at 50 Hz (and also the stroboscopic flicker) can be largely prevented if lighting units are used which contain two or more fluorescent tubes put out of phase with each other by suitable equipment (duo-equipment, 120° – switching, or three-phase switching). In this manner, the fluctuation of light-intensity can be significantly reduced; with three-phase switching it is almost as steady as filament lighting. *Rooms in which people remain for more than a few minutes at a time should not be illuminated by single fluorescent tubes, but always by two or three tubes out of phase with each other.*

Invisible flicker in lamps is expressed by the uniformity-index, the ratio between the minimum and maximum light intensity (trough to peak). For various fluorescent tubes this number ranges from 0.2–0.6 whereas with filament lamps the index exceeds 0.9. *Figure 99* shows the uniformity indices of various arrangements of fluorescent tubes.

Fluorescent tubes that emit a visible flicker should be replaced immediately. New tubes should be carefully tested, and rejected if faulty. It is worth while to cover the two ends of the tube, since this makes flicker less annoying, but in any case a faulty tube must be replaced as soon as flicker becomes perceptible.

Cold, pale light. Fluorescent tubes are often blamed for generating a cold and unfriendly atmosphere, and this accusation is justified if white tone or daylight tubes are used. Tubes of these types seem colder and paler with lower general levels of illumination. With a light intensity of 1,000 lx or more the overall lighting is very similar to daylight, and the impression of coldness is largely nullified. Hence if daylight or white tone tubes are to be used, the general intensity should be high: over 800 lx for business offices and shops and over 500 lx for workrooms. In living rooms, restaurants and other places where there is no need to imitate daylight, warm tone fluorescent tubes can be used to avoid a 'cold' atmosphere.

It is clear that, by suitable installation, the drawbacks of fluorescent tubes can be largely overcome, and any residual disadvantage will be outweighed by their other advantages.

Physiological design of artificial lighting

Light intensity

Comparison of today's guidelines with earlier ones shows that the recommended level of light intensity has risen, and this can be attributed to the following causes:

– increasing light intensity makes seeing more comfortable – a realisation that has only come in recent years.
– installation and running costs have become relatively cheaper.
– installation techniques have progressed, so that nowadays the output from artificial lighting to a large extent conforms with physiological requirements.

On the basis of present-day knowledge and experience, the levels of artificial lighting in dwellings given in *Table 89* can be recommended.

Placing of lights

The dazzling effect of badly placed lighting units can be avoided by using the following notes for guidance:

Table 89   Guidelines for artificial lighting in the home

Room	Lighting intensity in lx
Living-room	120–250
Bedroom	50–120
Childrens' room	120–250
Kitchen	250–500
Bathroom	100–400
Stairs and passages	120–250
Spot-lighting for reading, writing, sewing, mending and ironing	500–1000

- no light source should be in the field of view of any subject: a direct view of any light should be avoided.
- in principle no unshaded light should be used in living rooms.
- all lights should be shaded so that the average light intensity should not exceed 0.3 sb for general lighting and 0.2 sb for lighting at a work place.
- the angle between the horizontal direction of gaze and the line from eye to lamp should exceed 30° (see *Figure 100*).
- if in larger rooms an angle of less than 30° is unavoidable, then the lights must be fitted with effective lateral shades. If fluorescent lighting is used, it is best if the tubes are set at right angles to the line of sight.
- to avoid dazzle from reflections work places should be so placed in relation to the lights (or the lights in relation to the work place) that the most frequent line of sight avoids any reflection, and reflections elsewhere should be below a contrast ratio of 1 : 10 (see *Figures 101, 102*).
- in principle the use of reflective colours and materials on table-tops and other installations should be forbidden, so that reflection is completely avoided.

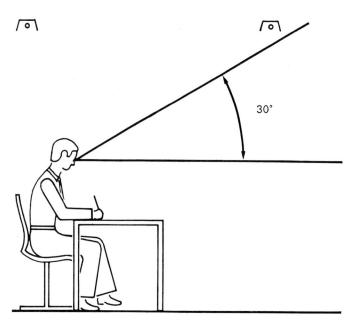

Figure 100   The angle between the horizontal line of vision and line between eye and light source should be greater than 30°

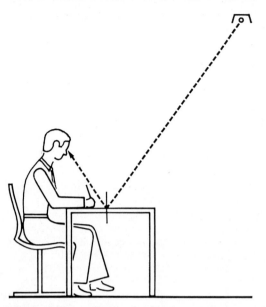

Figure 101   A bad positioning of the light   The reflected light from the table
enters the line of vision, and causes dazzle

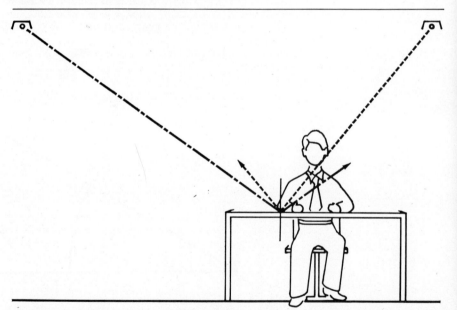

Figure 102   A good positioning of lights   When the lamps are placed to the side
dazzle from reflected light is greatly reduced

Daylight

Besides being a source of light, natural daylight in a room provides a link
with the outside world and a clear view of one's surroundings, so that one
can see what is going on, and what the weather is like. To measure daylight
indoors, we must start with light from the sky, and this is taken to be that
from an overcast sky, or in the shade. The current standard of reference for

daylight, E_a = 5,000 lx, is for a uniformly overcast sky in the open. Lighting technique is required to provide windows and skylights to give sufficient light indoors under standard conditions.

Daylight quotient

The Daylight Quotient DQ is a measure of the light intensity at any particular point inside a room. So that this figure is independent of fluctuations in daylight, every measurement inside is accompanied by a measurement of the light intensity outside with a clear view of the horizon. The daylight quotient DQ is always given as a percentage of the light-intensity in the open air;

$$DQ = \frac{\text{light-intensity at measuring point } (E_i)}{\text{light-intensity in the open } (E_a)} \times 100$$

As a rule DQ is measured 100 cm above the floor. It is a useful quantity in assessing the distribution of light inside a room, and calculating the dimensions of windows, and other values that are affected by the strength of daylight.

On physiological grounds it is desirable for DQ to be as high and as uniform as possible throughout the room. The higher the DQ, the less the need for artificial lighting; this is particularly true in winter, because under an overcast sky in December, a DQ of 10% would only give a light-intensity of 500 lx for four hours of the day, from 10 a.m. to 2 p.m.

A reservation is necessary here. Big windows give high DQ values on the one hand – which is a good thing – but on the other hand, as discussed on page 199, they produce a great deal of heat radiation in sunny weather. These two factors have contradictory physiological effects. It is up to the architect to weigh up the pros and cons of big and small windows, and try to find solutions that will satisfy the conflicting demands for brightness without discomfort.

Light-intensities within a room

In general the light intensity E_i at a particular spot in a room is made up of the following components:

E_H = direct light from sky
E_V = light reflected from surfaces outside – surrounding buildings, trees and shrubs, rising ground, etc.
E_R = light reflected from surfaces inside the room.
Therefore $E_i = E_H + E_V + E_R$.

Barrier and Gilgen (192) have calculated the quantitative effects of these different factors in a model room, and their conclusions may be summarised as follows:

direct light from the sky contributes mostly to the general level of lighting over the whole room, and particularly to the half nearer the window. In existing buildings it can be measured in a simple way be using the horizontoscope devised by *Tonne* (193). For houses at the planning stage there are graphical methods for estimating light levels, such, for example, as Waldram's diagram (see 192).

external reflection usually makes little contribution to general indoor lighting, with some exceptions, such as the presence of water or snow immediately outside the windows. These exceptions apart, a reflection coefficient of about 10% on the average can be allowed for external reflection. Externally reflected light can be measured in the same way as light from the sky, either by horizontoscope or by graphical methods.

internal reflection is not important near windows, but it helps to raise the level of illumination in the rest of the room, as long as the walls and furnishings have reflective surfaces.

Direct light from the sky depends on:

the angle subtended by adjacent buildings.
the height of the windows.
the width of the windows.

A few recommendations can be given as guidelines:

the incidence of daylight is substantially reduced if adjacent buildings subtend an angle of more than 25–30°, and so it is desirable that the nearest building should be at least twice as far away as its own height. This can be compensated for to some extent by making windows higher and wider. If the angle subtended by the nearest building goes up from 18–33°, a window 120 cm wide needs to be increased in height from 98–159 cm to offset this completely (192).

high windows are more effective than wide ones of the same area, since the light is able to penetrate further into the room. The lintel should not be deeper than 30 cm. With a window 125 cm wide an increase of height from 125–150 cm means that a light intensity that existed 490 cm into the room now exists 584 cm from the window.

every window should receive direct light from the sky, and it is desirable that some sky is visible from every work place.

the lightest possible colours should be used in inner courtyards, as well as in the interior of deep rooms, so as to reflect as much light as possible, and give high values of DQ.

Recommendations in the literature

The daylight requirements set out in the literature are in general agreement with experience. *Büning* (194) recommended a DQ of 1% in line with the window, half-way back in the room, and 80 cm above the floor.

Pleijel (195) proposed for Sweden a DQ of 2.5% in living-rooms and bedrooms, 1.5 m behind the window, and 85 cm above the floor and a DQ of 1% in kitchens and offices, 0.5 m in front of the rear wall.

Tonne (196) called for isolux curves with a DQ of 1.8% over an area of 1.5–4 square metres.

An international specification (197) recommended that in line with a window, and half-way back in the room, there should be a DQ of 3% for precision work and 0.8% for rough work.

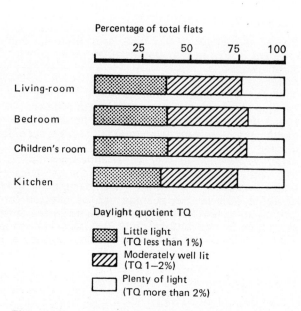

Percentage of total flats

Daylight quotient TQ

Little light (TQ less than 1%)

Moderately well lit (TQ 1–2%)

Plenty of light (TQ more than 2%)

Figure 103   Analysis of daylight quotients in various rooms of the 335 flats studied   After Barrier and Gilgen (192)

Table 90   Results of a questionnaire concerning nine housing criteria 335 people responded.   After Barrier and Gilgen (192)

People responded	Percentage Fully satisfied	Moderately so	Dissatisfied
Nearness to shops	86	11	4
Light enough	84	10	5
Gets enough sun	83	9	8
Enough greenery nearby	79	13	9
Large enough	75	16	9
Proximity to place of work	74	20	6
Level of internal noise	73	15	13
Level of external noise	39	22	39
Balcony	70	16	12

Hopkinson (198) recommended that at least 50% of the floor-area should have a DQ of 1% in the living-room, 2% in the kitchen and 0.5% in bedrooms (for 75% of the floor-area in this case).

Recommendation DIN 5034 prescribes at half the room-depth, one metre above the floor, a DQ of 1% in living-rooms, bedrooms and kitchens.

Research in houses and flats

In the town of Zürich in 1969 *Barrier and Gilgen* (192) studied 335 rented dwellings of different sizes and rent levels. They were predominantly (87%) for 2 adults and 1–5 children. DQ was measured in the middle of the room, 1 metre above the floor, with a horizontoscope, and the light from the sky and that from external reflection were measured separately.

Effective DQ in dwellings

The results are set out in *Figure 103*, and show no great differences between different types of room, and that in more than one third of the room DQ-values of less than 1% were measured.

Comparisons of DQ between dwellings of different rent levels showed significant differences only in respect of the living-room: 46% of low-priced dwellings had a DQ of less than 1%, but this was so in only 33% of the more expensive dwellings.

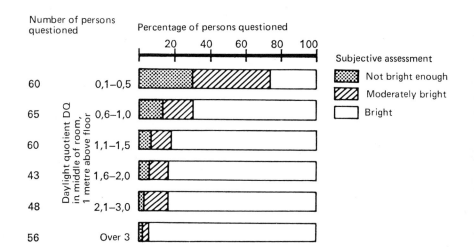

Figure 104   Subjective assessment of the amount of daylight, as compared with the measured value of the daylight quotient, in living-rooms   Total number of person questioned = 332; the total questioned in each of the groups is taken as 100% for that group.   After Barrier and Gilgen (192)

Number of persons
questioned

Percentage of persons questioned

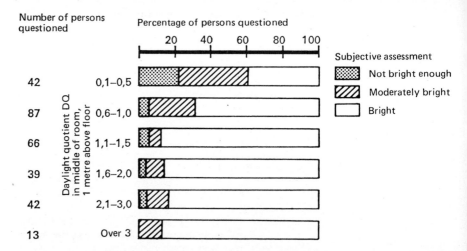

Figure 105   Subjective assessment of the amount of daylight, as compared with the daylight quotient, in bedrooms   Total number of persons questioned = 289 ; the total questioned in each of the groups is taken as 100% of the group.   After Barrier and Gilgen (192)

Number of persons
questioned

Percentage of persons questioned

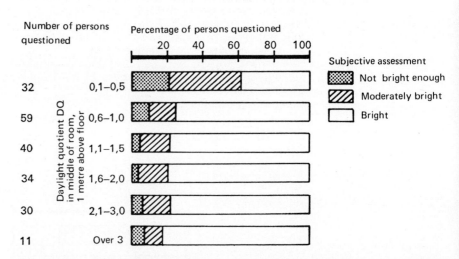

Figure 106   Subjective assessment of the amount of daylight, as compared with the daylight quotient, in children's rooms   Total number of persons questioned = 206 ; the total questioned in each of the groups is taken as 100% of that group

Brightness as a measure of desirability in a house

In a preliminary interrogation the tenants — an overwhelming majority being housewives — were presented with 9 criteria which they were asked to place in order of priority in their estimation. The answers were arranged in three groups, and the findings are set out in *Figure 19* (page 52). 50% placed the criterion 'bright enough' among the first three, and overall room brightness was placed third after 'enough sunshine' and 'space in the home'. For each of the nine criteria, those questioned were required to say whether or not they were satisfied with the existing situation in their home. *Table 90* gives the answers.

Table 91   Guidelines for natural daylight indoors   Daylight quotient DQ
measured in the centre of the room, one metre above floor-level

| Room | Daylight quotient DQ, percentage of external light | |
	Minimal	Desirable
Living-room	1.5	2–3
Bedroom	1	1–2
Childrens' room	1.5	2–3
Kitchen	1.5	2

The level of satisfaction was high for eight of the nine criteria, and was low only for the criterion 'noise from outside'. In reply to a direct question about what brightness they preferred, the great majority replied that they preferred a high level of brightness in all the rooms concerned in the investigation. The most marked preference for brightness was in the children's room (97%) and the living room (95%).

DQ and subjective impressions

Figures 104, 105 and *106* set the measured values of DQ against the impressions recorded. For this purpose the DQ values were divided into six classes, and the corresponding answers put beside them.

As the DQ values rose, the proportion saying 'bright' also rose, and the number saying 'not bright enough' declined. This shows that there is a correlation between the measured values of daylight and subjective impression.

Minimal requirements

From these results *Barrier and Gilgen* derived proposals for minimum daylight in rooms, with three requirements:

- the DQ must be so high that distinctly more than half of the people questioned assess the room as 'bright'.
- the proportion of the people questioned who say 'bright' should not rise significantly if the DQ is raised still further.
- the proportion of those questioned who rate the room as 'not bright enough' should be less than 10%.

On the basis of these figures Barrier and Gilgen (*192*) *arrived at DQ values of more than 1% for living rooms, bedrooms, children's rooms and kitchens.*
About 40% of the rooms investigated during this survey satisfied these minimal requirements.

Standard values for dwellings

On the basis of these surveys and after taking into consideration the recommendations of other authors, the standard values set out in *Table 91* can be recommended.

Sunlight

Effects of solar radiation

Life on earth is only possible thanks to solar radiation, and man has always been aware of its importance. The sun always played a great part in ancient religions and cultures. Our sense organs register the electromagnetic waves from the sun as heat or light, depending on the wavelength.
Solar radiation is commonly classified into the following three categories:

Range of wavelengths

Range of wavelengths   *Nature of radiation*
in nanometres (10^{-9} metres)
290–400   short wave and ultra-violet
400–750   visible light
750–3000   infra-red (heat)

Ultraviolet radiation effects metabolism and bodily growth by producing Vitamin D from ergosterol. This part of sunlight is indispensable for growth a lack of ultra-violet radiation being one of the causes of rickets, causing defective bone formation in children.

Visible light and long-wave infra-red radiations are absorbed by the earth and transformed into heat.

Effects of sunlight

Ergonomically speaking, sunlight has the following effects:

- drying buildings, especially their outside walls.
- disinfecting living spaces.
- warming buildings.
- psychological effects.

Continuous drying of building materials, particularly in the cold months of the year, is most important from an ergonomic point of view. A sufficiency of sunshine is indirectly beneficial to the insulating properties of outside walls, and hence to maintaining a comfortable temperature in the home.

Solar radiation has an extraordinary power to kill bacteria and other micro-organisms, which are completely killed after a comparatively short period (5 to 10 minutes) of exposure to sunshine.

In our latitudes the heating effect of sunlight is very important during the winter months, when savings of from 50–80% in the cost of heating are not unusual on sunny days. The value of sunshine in saving heating bills increases with the size of the windows (greenhouse effect). The psychological value of sunshine can scarcely be exaggerated. Dark and sunless housing is cheerless, and fosters gloom in the truest sense of the word, whereas sunny homes seem gay and happy. The craving for light and sunshine increases in higher latitudes. In the intermediate latitudes of Europe the desire for sun-shine affects nearly everybody.

It must be assumed that the emotional need for sunshine is to a large extent conditioned by an unconscious awareness of its effects, in particular in drying and warming and in killing bacteria.

Measurement of solar radiation

Thermal radiation

In our latitudes thermal radiation from the sun reaches the values set out in *Table 92*.

Heat radiation depends not only on latitude and aspect, but also on height above sea-level. The radiant heat from the sun increases with altitude, be-cause less is absorbed in passage through the atmosphere. Two methods are used for measuring solar radiation:

- intensity of radiation in kcal.
- duration of sunshine.

In discussing duration of sunshine a distinction is drawn between the maximum possible in a cloudless sky and duration in practice, as taken from meteorological averages.

The horizontoscope

The horizontoscope devised by *Tonne* (193) is well suited for measuring the incidence of sunlight into existing buildings. With this apparatus, in which the horizon is reflected, and using a standard sheet with sun-tracks drawn on it, the greatest possible duration of sunshine can be read off for every

Table 92   Intensity of solar radiation from 0500–1900 hrs, in relation to aspect

Date	Solar radiation in kcal per square metre							
	NE	E	SE	S	SW	W	NW	N
1st July	1725	2740	2670	2080	2670	2730	1675	315
8th February	–	150	650	1070	790	240	15	–

Diagrams

Key-date

twentieth day of the twelve months of the year. Using other standard sheets the solar heating effect in kilocalories per square metre can be determined, as can the daylight quotient (page 231).

Besides this simple apparatus there are other methods which, with the help of diagrams, can be used to estimate the incidence of sunlight into houses that are still at the planning stage. Among these may be mentioned the sunlight-incidence diagram of *Schatt* (200), suitable for determining the shadows that will be cast by buildings; the standard diagram of *Neumann* (201), and *Roedler's* (202) process which enables the incidence of sunlight and the amount of radiant heat to be determined for individual months.

All the specialists have agreed to take February 8th, the so-called midwinter day, as the key-date on which the necessary minimum of sunshine must be possible. In our latitudes February 8th is the central point of the dark half of the year.

Surveys of sunlight in houses and flats

Since the psychological effects of the sun are very important and to some extent must be regarded as the summation of all the other effects, special significance attaches to those two pieces of research which dealt with the incidence of sunlight in dwellings and the subjective reactions of the tenants.

TNO-studies

Need for sunshine

In Holland *Bitter and van Ierland* (203) used a horizontoscope that they had developed to determine the maximum duration of sunlight in 112 dwellings, and questioned the tenants about their impressions and wishes in this respect. Within the framework of a broader survey more than a thousand housewives were questioned about their wishes in regard to sunlight indoors. The results can be summarised as follows:

- 'sun and light' were among the advantages most often mentioned, along with 'position and view', 'heating' and 'comfort'.
- 80–90% of those questioned wished for 'plenty of sunshine' in their home, preferring midday sun in the living-room, and morning sun in the kitchens and bedrooms.
- the commonest reasons given for wanting sunshine could be summarised as 'warmth, brightness and for its tonic effects'.
- 67% of those questioned agreed in sacrificing sunshine in the bedroom in favour of the living room. About 70% gave sunshine in the living room preference to having a view from the window.
- if the possible duration of sunshine in mid-winter was compared with the answer 'satisfied with sunshine' the following correlations can be established:

less than 2 hours	57%
2–3 hours	100%
more than 3 hours	93%

- on the basis of these surveys the authors recommended a possible duration of sunlight in the living room on Midwinter Day of 2 hours, taking as a measuring point the middle of the window-ledge inside the window.

Researches of Barrier and Gilgen

Barrier and Gilgen (43), in their research mentioned already, studied 335 rented dwellings in Zürich in 1969 and determined the incidence of sunlight, using a horizontoscope like that of *Tonne* (193). All the measurements were taken in the middle of the rooms, one metre above the floor. The possible duration of sunshine on 8th February as seen from the measurement point was determined, taking all windows into account.

Figure 107 gives the results of these measurements, and it can be seen that on February 8th, 30% of living rooms, 41% of bedrooms, 50% of children's rooms and 63% of kitchens were virtually sunless.

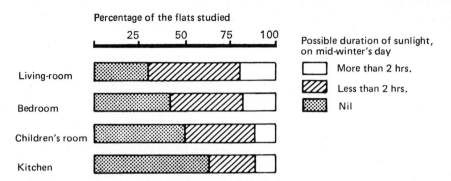

Percentage of the flats studied

Figure 107   The possible duration of sunlight, as measured on the 8th February, in 335 flats in Zürich   After Barrier and Gilgen (43)

Incidence of sunlight in relation to rent level

A comparison between rent and incidence of sunlight showed that the more expensive apartments had more sun in living rooms and bedrooms. In the low rent category, 44% of living rooms and 52% of bedrooms had zero hours of possible sunshine on 8th February as compared with only 18–35% in the higher rent group. A difference was evident when it came to children's rooms, which in general had much more sun in the cheaper apartments than they had in the dearer ones. This leads to the conclusion that architects of more expensive apartments tend to give the living room as much sunshine as possible, partly at the cost of the children's room.

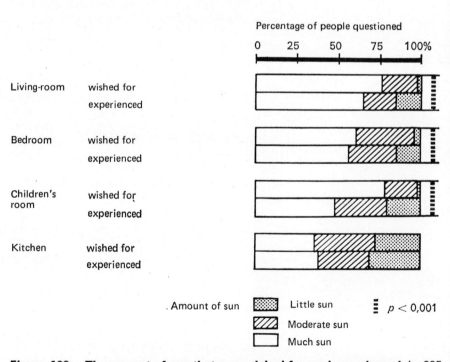

Figure 108   The amount of sun that was wished for, and experienced, by 335 people who were questioned. The differences between living-rooms, bedrooms and children's rooms are statistically significant ($p < 0.001$). After Barrier and Gilgen (43)

Criteria

Figure 19 has already given a summary of the order of importance into which 9 criteria were placed by 335 tenants, predominantly housewives. It showed that the criterion 'enough sun' along with 'space in the home' were placed in the first three by 59% of those questioned. This confirmed the findings of *Bitter and van Ierland* (203) who showed that in Holland the most important characteristic of a good home was 'sun and light'.

Satisfaction with the amount of sunshine

Table 90 showed that of the 9 criteria mentioned, the question 'enough sun?' was answered 'satisfactory' by 83% of those questioned.

Figure 108 summarises their wishes in regard to sunlight, and their assessment of the sunlight that they experienced in practice. Analysis of the answers to the relevant question showed that sunlight was desired mostly in living rooms and children's rooms.

Desire for sunlight

There was a certain amount of discrepancy between the amount of sunshine that people wanted, and what they actually experienced, and this was statistically significant for the living room, children's room and bedroom. The results showed *that in all the rooms in use in the daytime people wanted more sunlight than they actually had. This can be generalised by saying that, while people on the whole were satisfied with the amount of sunshine they were getting, they would nonetheless have liked more.*

Subjective and objective assessment of sunlight

The authors set the subjective estimates of sunshine against the measured values for the maximum possible on the 8th February. The results can be seen in *Figures 109, 110* and *111*. In addition *Table 93* gives subjective assessments in relation to a more detailed subdivision of the values for incidence of sunlight.

The following conclusions can be drawn:

— a correlation exists in all three rooms between the subjective assessment and the measured duration. This means that if the tenant questioned speaks of 'little' or 'much' sunshine in the room, she really did notice the sunshine, and also that the measured duration reflects the experienced amount of sun.

— the fact that the considerable fraction of people questioned who had zero hours of sunshine on 8th February still replied 'much sun' must lead to the conclusion that the room in question must receive a certain amount of sunlight in summer, and to a lesser extent in spring and autumn.

— in living rooms the assessment 'much sun' increased with the measured duration, up to a value of 90 minutes, while the assessment 'little sun' decreased correspondingly.

— in bedrooms the assessment 'much sun' similarly increased up to a duration of 90 minutes, but on the other hand the assessment 'little sun' reached a minimum at 30 minutes duration, and did not decrease further if the duration of sunlight were increased.

— in children's rooms the assessment 'much sun' increased up to a duration of more than 2 hours. Correspondingly the assessment 'too little sun' decreased as the duration rose from 120 to 180 minutes.

Table 93   Relationship between the possible duration of direct sunlight in a living-room in midwinter and the subjective impression of being 'sunny'

Number questioned	Duration of possible sunlight in minutes	Subjective impressions: 'too little sun' (Percentages)	'moderately sunny'	'very sunny'
100	0	25	30	45
34	30	20	15	65
30	60	13	12	75
46	90	12	8	80
46	120	14	26	60
40	180	0	25	75
28	300	0	10	89

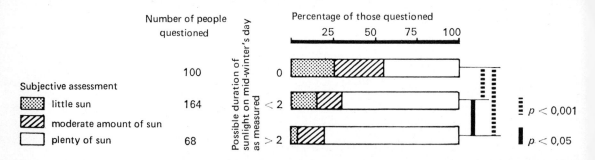

Figure 109   Subjective assessments of the amount of sunlight, as compared with the measured possible duration on mid-winter's day (8 February), in a living-room   332 persons were questioned, and the differences between groups are statistically significant. After Barrier and Gilgen (43)

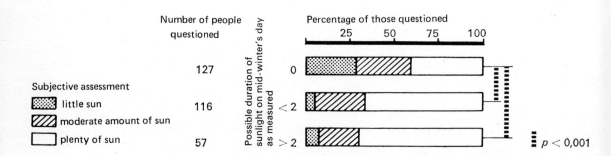

Figure 110   Subjective assessments of the amount of sunlight, as compared with the measured possible duration of sunlight on mid-winter's day (8 February), in a bedroom   300 persons were questioned. The horizontal lines indicate which differences are statistically significant ($p < 0.001$). After Barrier and Gilgen (43)

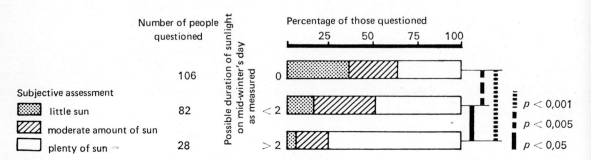

Figure 111   Subjective assessments of the amount of sunlight, as compared with the possible duration on mid-winter's day (8 February), in children's rooms.   216 persons were questioned, and the differences between the groups are statistically significant. After Barrier and Gilgen (43)

Recommendations for sunlight in dwellings

Several recommendations can be found in the literature, some of them conflicting. Here are a few of them:

Bitter and Ierland (203)
2 hours possible sunlight on 8th February (measuring point – window ledge).
Roedler (202)
A minimum of 50 hours each in the months of December, January and February in:
1 of the living rooms in 1–2-room dwellings
2 of the living rooms in 3–4-room dwellings
3 of the living rooms in 5-room dwellings
(measuring point: on window wall)
Regional planning in Canton, Zürich, Switzerland, 1957 (204)
On 8th February the possible duration of sunshine should not fall below the following values:

1-room dwellings	3 hours	no north-facing room
2-room dwellings	3 hours	1 north-facing room
3-room dwellings	5 hours	1 north-facing room
4-room dwellings	6 hours	1 north-facing room
5-room dwellings	6 hours	2 north-facing rooms

(measuring point: on window wall)
Panzhauser (136)
1 hour sunshine possible on 8th February in
1 of the living rooms in 1–2-room dwellings
2 of the living rooms in 3 or more room dwellings
(measuring point: middle of the chief window with a minimum vertical angle of 6° and lateral angle of 15° for incident sunlight)
Neumann (201)
Total radiant heat from sun on 8th February
300 kcal/square metre
(measuring point: middle of window-pane)
Lange (205)
This author calculated the minimal amount of sunshine in relation to distance away from other buildings. H = height of building; A = distance away from building.

Direction of visible sky	Optimal value	Minimal value
Double-sided ground-plan for households without children.		
NW–SE	A = 5 H	A = 3.5 H
N–S	A = 6.5 H	A = 6 H
NNW–SSE	A = 6 H	A = 5 H
NNE–SSW	A = 6 H	—
Double-sided ground-plan for households with children:		
NW–SE	A = 5 H	A = 3.5 H
WNW–ESE	A = 3.5 H	A = 2 H

Apart from the recommendations of *Bitter and van Ierland* (203) all the specifications given in the literature are derived from theoretical considerations, and advocate more or less arbitrary values which conform with previous experience and custom.
Barrier and Gilgen (43) were led by their surveys to make recommendations with which we can concur. By laying down a *minimum duration of sunlight* they arrived at the requirement that on the 8th February there must be such a duration of sunlight that a clear majority of tenants should put it in the

Recommendations based on surveys

Table 94   Minimal requirements for the amount of sunlight in dwellings measured as the duration of sunlight possible on a day in midwinter (8 February), in the centre of the room, one metre above the floor. After Barrier and Gilgen (43)

| Size of dwelling (number of rooms) | Minimal possible duration of sunlight, in minutes | | | |
	Living-room	Bedroom	Children's room	Total
1–2½	60–90	–	–	60–90
3–4½	60–90	–	30	90–120
5 and more	60–90	30	30	120–150

Table 95   Amount of sunlight desirable in dwellings in midwinter   Measured on 8th February, in the middle of a room, one metre above the floor. After Barrier and Gilgen (43)

| Number of rooms | Desirable possible duration of sunlight, in minutes | | | |
	Living-room	Bedroom	Childrens' room	Total
1–2½	more than 120	–	–	more than 120
3–4½	more than 120	–	more than 90	more than 210
5 and more	more than 120	30	more than 90	more than 240

category 'much sun'. Moreover if the duration of sunlight were to be further increased the frequency with which this assessment was given would not rise. To satisfy the requirement of *optimal duration of sunlight*, the fraction of those questioned who voted 'little sun' should have fallen below 10%.

The recommendations of *Barrier and Gilgen* (43) are summarised in *Tables 94* and *95*.

It should be noted that the authors described their research as a pilot-study, and that their recommendations should be regarded as provisional.

Colour in the home

Colour can be said to have the following functions:

– helping to locate and arrange things.
– to ease work loads.
– psychological and subjective effects.

We shall say nothing here about aesthetic or cultural significances of colour, which does not mean that these effects are unimportant. On the contrary, it is known that these aspects of colour are very real, and can have a decisive importance for people's well-being. Nevertheless the treatment of these questions is beyond the competence of the author, and would go far beyond the scope of the present book.

Locating objects and easing work loads

The use of colour to make work easier depends on the production of colour contrasts and the use of colour to attract attention. When planning colour contrasts one must distinguish between the colours of large areas (walls, furniture and so on) and smaller areas such as knobs and handles. The colours for large areas should be chosen so that they all have similar co-efficients of reflection, the eye then having distinctive colour contrasts without having to deal with big differences in brightness. This is important in avoiding eye strain. Furthermore, large areas and big objects should not be brightly coloured (no pure colours) since large brightly coloured areas fatigue the retina and produce after-images. Walls, alcoves, table tops etc. should therefore have matt surfaces and pastel colours.

No brilliant colours

Colour contrasts and work places	The location and handling of working materials is facilitated if colour contrasts are provided between the materials and their immediate surroundings (work bench or machine top). This matter should be taken into account when working areas are being designed. When providing colour contrasts, differences in brightness should be avoided. For example, when a component is made of wood, leather or similar material of an ochre or brown colour, the underlying surface should be dark ivory, or light beige. The surroundings of the machine or of the work bench might be painted in neutral, pastel, yellow-green or blue tones.
Eye-catchers	Eye-catchers work by using strongly contrasting, bright colours. Colour is used in this way in Nature: a red strawberry among green leaves, or bright flowers attract insects and other creatures by their colour contrast, which is why it is essential to conserve the environment as well as the animals in it. On the other hand, Nature also uses colours for camouflage: defenceless creatures in the wild are neutral in colour and merge into the background and escape the notice of other animals.
	Under certain circumstances, it is right to arrange for a few eye-catchers in conspicuous colours; for example some of the important controls in the kitchen, in the heating appliances, or in the bathroom may be designed to stand out. When such eye-catchers are small (not bigger than a few square centimetres), they should contrast strongly with their surroundings not only in colour but in brightness. They then become more conspicuous, it takes less time to find them, and there is less distraction while they are being located.
Too many eye-catchers are a nuisance	The greatest danger in the use of colour is excess, and this is particularly true of conspicuous colours. Too many eye-catchers, and too many different colours make a working-place restless and distracting. Designing with colour does not mean gaudy design! *The demands of ergonomics call for the greatest possible restraint in the use of colours, restricting them to three, or at most five, eye-catchers on any one piece of equipment.*
	This also applies to the use of colour in schoolrooms, restaurants, dwelling-houses etc. – in short anywhere where people work or take recreation. Less restraint is necessary in window-displays, stores, and warehouses, where the user needs to be attracted or distracted by eye-catchers.
Psychological effects	Psychological effects of colour mean the sensory stimulation and effects on the mind that colour can produce. Mostly these effects occur through the subconscious. In part they come about through subconscious association with previous experience and in part from hereditary and constitutional tendencies. These effects involve emotions and suggestibility, and hence the whole of human behaviour. Response to art is one of the aspects of reaction to colour.
	Psychological effects can to some extent result from colour in rooms, but rooms generally have a particular function, and so cannot be designed entirely from an aesthetic standpoint. *It is all the more essential that physiological and psychological requirements should be taken into account: there is still plenty of latitude for aesthetic design within this framework.*
Stimulating and misleading the senses	Individual colours have their own particular effects, which differ considerably. The most important concern illusions relating to distance, or to temperature and effects on the general mood. *Table 96* summarises the effects of particular colours.
Light colours	*It is generally true that all dark colours have a depressing effect; they also make it more difficult to keep places clean. All light colours make life easier, brighter and more friendly; they reflect more light, brighten the room, and encourage cleanliness.*
	If the activities going on in a room need a high degree of concentration, then the colours should be extremely restrained, to avoid unnecessary distraction. In this case walls, ceilings, and other structural features should be as light as possible, with faint colours. In all living rooms the colours should above all give an impression of rest and recuperation. Here again the colours

should be light without attracting attention. Yellow, red or blue walls are pleasing at first sight, but after a time they become tiring to the eyes. Hence such rooms are often disliked after a while.

Strong colours

Strong colours can be used with advantage only in rooms that mainly have a transitory use: for example entrance halls, corridors, toilets or anterooms. In such places strong colours can be used to compensate for architectural deficiencies.

The planning of colours for schools, hospitals, administrative buildings, and so on, should be along similar lines to that of dwellings.

Table 96   Psychological effects of colours

Colour	Impression of distance	Impression of warmth	Mental stimulus
Blue	further away	cold	restful
Green	further away	very cold to neutral	very restful
Red	near	warm	very stimulating, unrestful
Orange	very near	very warm	stimulating
Yellow	near	very warm	stimulating
Brown	very near, restricting	neutral	stimulating
Violet	very near	cold	aggressive, depressing

8 Noise in the Home

Summary

Noise is any disturbing sound, the unit of disturbance by noise being the decibel (A). Nowadays, to designate prolonged harmful noise, figures are used which express both the intensity and the frequency of noise, or the total amount of sound energy (Noise and Number Index, Traffic Noise Index etc.). The inner ear changes the mechanical energy of sound into bioelectrical nervous impulses, which pass along the auditory nerve into the brain, where finally they are integrated into a sensation of 'hearing'. Branches of the auditory nerve pass to the reticular activation system, where they serve to alert consciousness, and, via the sympathetic nervous system, affect the internal organs, especially those controlling the circulation of blood.

The most important effects of noise are:

— damage to the hearing mechanism (not to be expected from domestic noises).
— interference with verbal communication.
— interference with thought and concentration.
— irritability.
— disturbed sleep.
— psychological stress.
— injury to health.

Sources of sound may be divided into:

— *External noise* (from vehicles, trades people, builders, and general noises in the neighbourhood).
— *Internal noise* (from inside the buildings; neighbours, footsteps, machinery, music, etc.).

Most surveys show that street noise from vehicles is a widespread, major source of domestic disturbance. Surveys in Sweden and Austria agreed that about one quarter of people in domestic circles were disturbed by vehicular noise, if this reached a level outside the windows of 45–50 dB(A) by day or 35–40 dB(A) by night. Tables give permissible values for vehicle and aircraft noise in living quarters and other localities. Research into internal noise showed that the commonest sources of disturbance come from the entrance hall and from the neighbours above. According to Dutch and French research it is essential to have sound insulation for lower frequencies (60–120 Hz).

It is of questionable value to fix limits for permissible noise inside buildings, since in the main these deal only with disturbance caused inside the building by external noise. These permissible limits do not affect noise from neighbours or from the entrance hall.

Important factors in protection against noise are the layout of the dwelling (division into noisy and quiet areas), and the presence of adequate sound insulation in walls and ceilings. The amount of sound-proofing present in many modern homes is too little by physiological standards. A desirable level of insulation against air-borne sound should have an insulation factor R of 55 dB, or an Insulation Index I_a of 58 dB.

Finally a few effective measures against noise emanating from kitchens, bathrooms and lavatories are enumerated.

Terms, definitions, units

Noise

The simplest definition is: *'Noise is any disturbing sound'*.

Hawel (206) made this definition more precise: a sound is disturbing only if the subject finds it inappropriate for his activity at the relevant time.

A sound is produced whenever a gas, a fluid or a solid body is subjected to an unequal distribution of pressure. The resultant fluctuation of pressure spreads through the medium as a mechanical vibration in the form of a wave. As long as this change of pressure comes within a particular range of intensities and frequencies it is felt as sound by the human ear. The pressure wave is called a sound wave and the number of waves per second is termed the number of cycles per second. The magnitude of the pressure change determines the loudness, and the number of cycles per second (or Hertz = Hz) determines the pitch.

The physical unit of pressure is the *microbar* (= 10^{-6} bar). The human ear can detect sound-waves in a wide range from 2×10^{-4} microbars to about 200 microbars. All acoustic response lies within this range, from the gentle murmur of a brook to the howl of an aero-engine.

Decibels

To find a practical measure for such a wide range, a new measure called the *Decibel* (dB) was invented, which increases in logarithmic ratio to the pressure of the sound-wave. 20 decibels express a difference in pressure of 10 : 1. In other words: if the pressure of a sound is increased tenfold, then the sound is increased by 20 dB. The sound intensity in decibels (P_{dB}) is formally defined in this way:

$$P_{dB} = 20 \log \frac{P_x \text{ (microbars)}}{P_0 \text{ (microbars)}}$$

where P_{dB} = sound intensity in dB
P_x = sound pressure in microbars
P_0 = standard of sound pressure, internationally fixed at 2×10^{-4} microbars.

Subjective impression of loudness in relation to frequency of sound

The human ear registers sounds with frequencies between 16 and 20,000 Hz, covering nearly nine octaves. Frequencies below 16 Hz are felt as subsonic vibrations. The region above 20,000 Hz constitutes ultrasonic vibrations; these are used therapeutically in medicine. The subjective impression of loudness depends not only on the amplitude of the sound, but also on its frequency. The low notes seem less loud than high ones. This is shown particularly clearly by the curve of the threshold of audibility for notes of different frequency, presented in *Figure 112*. The curve shows that the maximum sensitivity of the ear lies in the frequency range 2000–5000 Hz, and that the ear is only one-tenth as sensitive as this in the range of the human voice (100–300 Hz).

The phon

Figure 112 further shows curves of equal apparent loudness, taking the impression of loudness at 1000 Hz as the standard of reference. The unit of apparent loudness is then the *phon*. In the past, the value in phons has been used as a measure of loudness, but this unit is not used much today as curves of equal apparent loudness based on a phon scale are valid only for pure tones.

The currently accepted measure of loudness is called the 'weighted noise level'. This involves measuring the total level of sound after part of the energy in the lowest and highest frequency ranges has been filtered out. In

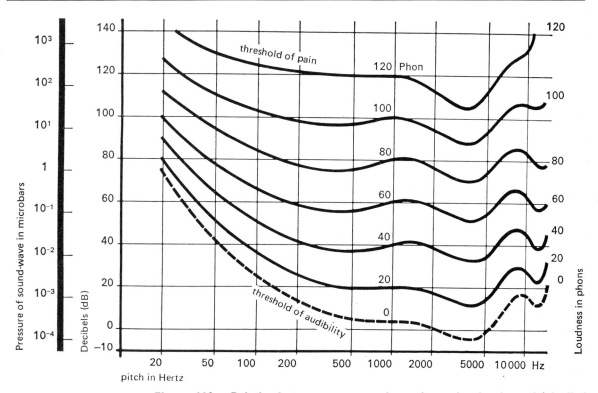

Figure 112   Relation between pressure of sound wave in microbars, the decibel scale, and curves of equal subjective loudness on the phon scale   I.S.O. Norm. 1957

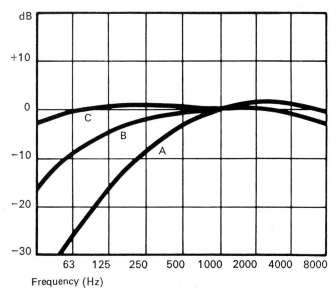

Figure 113   Three curves of noise-level based on dB(A), dB(B) and dB(C) respectively   The curves indicate how much of the sound energy is filtered out of the total in each frequency range.

this way only a small allowance is made for the lowest and highest frequencies.

dB(A)

The three curves of sound rating currently recommended are set out in *Figure 113*: dB(A), dB(B) and dB(C). *The weighted noise level in dB(A) is used most commonly.* Numerous physiological studies have shown that *the noise level measured in dB(A) is suitable for measuring the subjective disturbance arising from many sources of noise.*

Noise load

In what follows we shall use the term 'noise load' to mean the sum total of all the different sounds that operate over a considerable period, for at least a whole day or a whole night. 'Noise nuisance' will refer to the subjective disturbance that arises from the noise load.

Surveys of the extent of annoyance from aircraft and street noises have shown that noise level is not the only operative factor: how often the noise occurs, and other things are equally important. Accordingly, methods have been devised which combine the various components of the disturbance into a single quantity; the methods assume that the annoyance from noise at any particular point can be indicated by a single number.

Although such methods are not yet fully developed, the most important will be defined briefly below.

NNI

The Noise and Number Index (NNI). Psychosociological surveys in England (207) have shown that the degree of disturbance from aircraft noise is much affected by the number of aircraft movements, and therefore *the Noise and Number Index* was devised to take account of both the level of noise and the number of aircraft movements. It is obtained from the following formula:

$$NNI = L + 15 \log N - 80$$
L = average peak noise level in PNdB*
N = number of flights per day or per night.

The term $15 \log N$ is included in the equation, because English surveys have shown that *doubling the number of flight movements is equivalent to a rise in peak noise of about 4.5 PNdB.*

The subtraction term (-80) was included since surveys had shown that no noise load arises if the average peak noise is 80 PNdB ($= 67$ dB(A)) or less.

L_{eq}

In Germany, workers in acoustics started from the hypothesis that total sound energy must be an appropriate way of measuring noise load. This led to the concept of the *equivalent level of sustained noise* L_{eq}, which was designated as the level of moderate disturbance. This way of measuring made it possible to compare the disturbance from an intermittent noise with that from a persistent source. This method is based on the concept that the disturbance caused by an intermittent noise is not the arithmetic mean of the separate noise levels, but is the mean of the total noise intensity. To calculate the equivalent level of sustained noise in dB, the formula is:

$$L_{eq} = \frac{10}{\alpha} \log\left(\Sigma \frac{1}{T} \cdot 10 \frac{\alpha L_i}{10} \cdot t_i \right)$$

where

L_{eq} = equivalent level of sustained noise
α = equivalence constant
T = total time of measurement
L_i = noise level at the relevant time interval
t_i = length of the relevant time interval.

Acoustic specialists use a different equivalence constant for each different source of noise. In practice there is still considerable uncertainty over the

*PNdB = Perceived Noise Decibel is a weighted noise level, in which the different frequency ranges are given different weightings according to their physiological effect. The relation to dB(A) is approximately dB(A) = PNdB−13.

definition and use of equivalence constants (α). Two proposals can be discussed here:

If $\alpha = 1$, then the equivalent level of sustained noise is related to the frequency of occurrence of the peaks of sound by the following formula:

$$L_{eq} = \frac{S_{50} + S_{99}}{2}$$

where

S_{50} = summated frequency of occurrence for 50% of the time
S_{99} = summated frequency of occurrence for 99% of the time.

This sustained noise level with $\alpha = 1$ is occasionally designated as the equivalent level of sustained noise for purely energetic sources (L_{eq}–REM). Under these conditions *the equivalent level of sustained noise in dB is approximately equal to the mean of the 'background noise' (S_{50}) and the 'common peak level' (S_{99}).* Hence, if the duration of the noise is doubled, L_{eq} rises by 3 dB.

L_{eq} – Q

$\alpha = \frac{3}{4}$ is occasionally used to express traffic noise, this equivalent level of sustained noise also being known as the index of disturbance, Q.
Hence L_{eq}–Q increases by about 4 dB if the duration of the noise is doubled. L_{eq}–Q is about 3 dB above the background noise S_{50}.

TNI

In England *Langdon and Scholes* (232) developed the *Traffic Noise Index* to express the noise load from traffic, taking into account the summated frequencies of occurrence, S_{10} and S_{90}. TNI is calculated according to the formula:

$$TNI = 4(S_{90} - S_{10}) + S_{10} - 30$$

Where:

S_{90} = summated frequency of occurrence for 90% of the time
S_{10} = summated frequency of occurrence for 10% of the time.

This formula makes use of the summated frequencies as used in Germany and Switzerland. The authors found a good correlation (r = 0.88) between the values of TNI for 24 hours and a survey of the responses of 100 people.

Damping of airborne sound

'Damping' of airborne sound means the amount absorbed when sound passes through a wall from one room to another. To measure the damping effect a filtered sound is produced in a transmission room, and the noise level is measured in a receiving room. The difference in noise level is a measure of the insulating effect (D).

$$D = L_1 - L_2$$

Insulation index R

The insulation index R is calculated from the following formula:

$$R = D + 10 \log \frac{F}{A} \text{ (dB)}$$

where

D = difference in noise level
F = test area of the structure
A = equivalent sound absorbing area of the receiving room.

To determine sound insulation in an existing building, the insulation index R', is measured in a similar way, taking care to include passage of sound by other routes.
Nowadays new methods and new units of measurement often come into use to measure sound insulation.

I_a

In Switzerland the SIA (208) proposed the use of an Insulation Factor I_a (in dB). This method of assessment is based upon the ISO-Norm R 717 (1968), the procedure being as follows:

The measured frequency-related curve of the sound insulation factor R (or R') was evaluated by means of a curve of ISO-norms, the normal curve being displaced by an appropriately calculated tolerance in relation to the curve of measured values.

The Insulation factor I_a for air-borne sound had the number of decibels corresponding to the point of intersection of the displaced norm-curve with the ordinate of 500 Hz. Insulation against air-borne sound is better the greater the Insulation factor I_a. For details and examples see reference (210).

LSM

The German DIN 4109 (209) recommended the *Luftschallschutzmass* LSM. This method, too, sets a curve of measured values alongside a standard curve, displaced by a permitted amount. The LSM was obtained by determining the difference in decibels between the displaced standard curve and the normal standard curve. When LSM = 0 dB the standard curve lies within the permitted mean displacement of 2.0 dB.

Relationship between I_a and LSM

The Insulation factor I_a and the Luftschallschutzmass (LSM) are approximately related by the formula:

$$LSM \sim I_a - 52 \text{ (dB)}$$

Insulation against footsteps

Insulation against footsteps on the floor above is tested by hammering on the floor with a device and seeing how much of the sound-energy is absorbed by the ceiling. The effectiveness of the insulation is measured by the amount of airborne sound that penetrates into the room below. The hammering device normally consists of 5 steel hammers, each of 500 grams, with a drop of 4 cm, and a frequency of 10 strokes per second (DIN 52210). The noise level in the room below is measured for each octave of frequencies, and a correction is applied for the normal sound absorption in the test-room.

I_i

In Switzerland the *Trittschallisolationsindex* I_i in dB is measured in accordance with proposals set out in SIA (208). The method is analogous to that for the determination of the *Insulation factor I_a* and is similarly based on comparison with an ISO-norm curve (ISO-Norm R 717, 1968). In the range of the measured frequency-related noise level, the norm curve is displaced by a specified tolerance. *The index I_i then has a value in dB corresponding to*

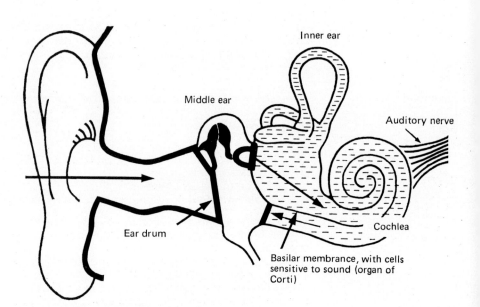

Figure 114   Mechanism of the ear

the intersection between the displaced norm curve and the ordinate at the frequency of 500 Hz. The lower the index the better the insulation.
For details and examples of these methods see reference (210).

TSM

In Germany the effectiveness of sound insulation against footsteps is expressed quantitatively by the *Trittschallschutzmass* TSM. According to DIN 4109 (209) a standard curve is displaced over the range of the measured noise levels, and the difference between this displaced curve and the normal standard curve in dB gives the *Trittschallschutzmass* TSM.

Comparison between I_i and TSM

This can be expressed approximately by the following formula:

$$TSM \sim 68 - I_i \text{ (dB)}$$

Anatomical and physiological principles

The hearing organs

A sensation of hearing arises when sound waves pass through the external auditory passages into the inner ear: there the sound energy is transformed into nervous impulses, which reach a particular centre in the brain and are recognised as sound.
Figure 114 is a diagram of the principal parts of the ear. Sound waves set the tympanic membrane in vibration and are passed to the inner ear by the auditory ossicles which reduce the amplitude but increase the energy level. The fluid of the inner ear transmits the vibrations to the beginning of the

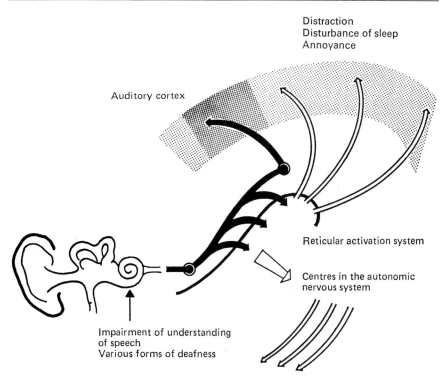

Figure 115   Diagram of the auditory tract, and its connections with different sections of the brain, where the most important effects of noise are localised

cochlea, and then onwards in the endolymph through the foramen rotundum. The cochlea is divided into two chambers by the basilar membrane, which supports sound-sensitive cells transforming the mechanical impulses of sound into nervous impulses. Each cell is sensitive to a particular range of frequencies, and is stimulated by vibrations that fall within that range; it transmits this excitation to a particular nerve-fibre. Sound is analysed by the inner ear into separate ranges of frequency and this information is transmitted to the brain by thousands of nerve fibres. The auditory nerve passes through the medulla to the brain and connects with two auditory centres in the cortex. Here all the incoming impulses are integrated and perceived as sound or, if appropriate, as understandable communications.

Hearing is thus located in the conscious sphere of the cerebral cortex: the ears and other intermediate structures are nothing more than a transmission system.

Other connections

The path by which sound is transmitted to the brain is illustrated in *Figure 115*. The diagram also shows that nerve fibres branch out from the auditory path to the activation centres of the *reticular formation*. From here nerves pass to the whole of the conscious sphere of the cerebral cortex. Nervous impulses which arrive in the *reticular formation* thus produce an alerting effect on conscious activity. In this way noise distracts attention, disturbs sleep and has other disturbing effects.

Autonomic effects

Nerves from the reticular activation centres join others from the neighbouring hypothalamus to pass to autonomic nerve centres, which in turn operate through autonomic nerves to control the activities of the internal organs of the body, particularly those concerned with the circulatory system. Through these pathways the alerting effect of noise influences the internal organs, the heart and the blood vessels. Hence shock produced by the impact of a loud noise is accompanied by rapid pulsing of the heart, and other sensations, difficult to define, which affect the body as a whole.

The hypothalamus is also very closely linked with the hypophysis (pituitary gland), a gland of internal secretion. Repeated stimulation of this gland causes far-reaching changes in many organs (the stress reaction), which among other effects can cause a lasting increase in blood pressure. Effects of this kind have been demonstrated in animals exposed to noise, though possibly they arise in man only under exceptional circumstances.

It appears from this review that noise not only has acoustic effects on the human body, it also affects several nerve centres which can influence all regions of the body.

Depending on its intensity and direction, noise may have the following effects:

— damage to the inner ear (partial deafness)
— making speech inaudible
— physiological effects (distraction, reduced concentration, psychomotor damage, disturbed sleep, and excitement of the autonomic nervous system)
— psychological effects (tenseness and fatigue)

These effects will be described briefly in the next section.

The effects of noise

Noise deafness

Damage to hearing

Strong and repeated stimulation by noise leads to impairment of hearing, which at first is only temporary. If such 'deafening' noise continues, it can lead gradually to irreparable damage, known as 'noise deafness'. This is produced by slow degeneration of the sound sensitive cells of the inner ear, which are overtaxed by the noise. The greater the intensity and duration of the noise, the more common and more serious is the damage.

Noise deafness occurs in people exposed all the year round to sources of very loud noise in industry, in some trades and in the armed forces (noise of firing): in the home noise is unlikely to be severe enough to cause noise deafness.

Understanding conversation

It is common experience that our ears become less sensitive to particular sounds such as conversation as the noise level rises. The ability to pick out a particular sound from others depends on its threshold of audibility, and this increases almost linearly with noise level up to a background noise level of 80 dB.

When listening to another person, however, it is not enough to hear only the pitch; much more important is the ability of the ear to discriminate between sounds, particularly consonants, because these create significantly lower air-pressures than do vowels.

Syllable comprehension

Since the understanding of either words or whole sentences is affected both by individual intelligence, and by familiarity with the language, studies of the disturbing effects of noise make use of syllable comprehension. In this method a speaker utters a large number of syllables which are meaningless in themselves, and the number of syllables correctly understood is compared with the total. It has been shown that the sense of sentences can be made out even though not all syllables are understood. *Figure 116* compares the comprehension of syllables with that of sentences. A sentence comprehension of 80% is possible when syllable comprehension is as low as 20%, and if half the syllables can be understood (S = 0.5) then about 95% of sentences are comprehensible.

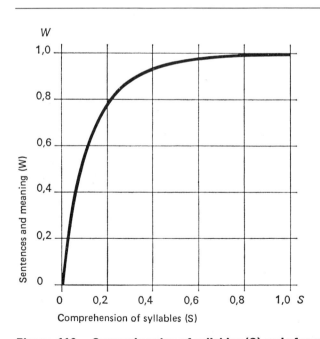

Figure 116   Comprehension of syllables (S) and of sentences and meaning (W)
Both scales show comprehension as a fraction of the total number of syllables or sentences that were presented to the test persons

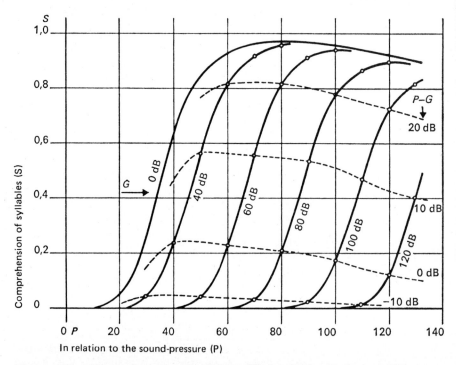

Figure 117   Comprehension of syllables (S), in relation to the sound-pressure (P) of the speech and to the level of background noise (G) in the room   The dotted lines join all the points which are characterised by differences of 20, 10, zero and −10 decibels between the level of sound of the speech and the background noise (i.e. P–G)

Noise level and comprehension of speech

Speech comprehension is considerably affected by the level of background noise and by the sound level of the speaking voice. This relationship is shown in *Figure 117*.

The figure shows that, a syllable comprehension of 40–56% is obtained if the voice is 10 dB above the background noise level. As shown in *Figure 116*, this will produce a comprehension of sentences of 93–97%.

Experience shows that this degree of comprehension of sentences is adequate in homes, factories and offices. Speech comprehension is unimpaired if its intensity is 10 dB above the average level of background noise.

When unfamiliar words and phrases have to be transmitted, higher levels of syllable comprehension are necessary. It has been shown that in such cases syllable comprehension of 80% must be aimed for, requiring a difference between the voice and the background noise of about 20 dB.

Sound levels in general conversation

The average intensity of human speech in a room at normal voice levels at a distance of one metre lies within the following ranges:

quiet conversation	60–65 dB
dictation	65–70 dB
speaker at a conference	65–75 dB
lecture in an auditorium	70–80 dB
calling out	80–85 dB

If the voice is to be used at work to give information, or for dictation, it should not exceed 65–70 dB at a distance of 1 metre. For this voice level to be heard undistorted and without fatigue, the general level of background noise should be at least 10 dB below this, setting an upper limit to background noises in offices of 55–60 dB. If higher demands are made on speech comprehension (e.g. many strange words, or unfamiliar names) then the general level of background noise should not exceed 45–50 dB.

Speech comprehension in the home

When talking about the home, we can start from the level of quiet conversation (60–65 dB), and say that *in the home understanding of speech will be unimpaired if the average noise level lies below 55 dB.*

When dwellings stand on a street with moderate to high traffic density, the noise level can only be kept below 55 dB by shutting the windows. In the summer, when windows have to be open for much or all of the time, noise levels in the building may reach 70 dB, with peaks of 75 dB.

Concentration and intellectual pursuits

General experience shows that mental concentration during intellectual activities, and the vigilance required for skilled jobs are both disturbed by noise. Since in the home such activities are carried out during leisure time as much as in normal working hours, these effects of noise must be considered. This class of activity includes children's homework and studying in general, adults bringing work home, and leisure pursuits such as reading, playing music, playing chess, etc.

Vigilance

Laird (211), *Sanders* (212), *Broadbent* (213), *Grimaldi* (214), *Jansen and Hoffman* (223) and many other research workers observed during the laboratory experiments that psychological tests showed that exposure to noise leads to loss of efficiency. Other authors came to different, and partly contradictory results. Thus, for example, *Tarriere and Wisner* (215) noted that vigilance lasted for a shorter time in a quiet situation than in a noisy one.

Broadbent (216, 217, 218) later succeeded in classifying the psychological effects of noise on concentration. He was able to demonstrate that concentration was hardly impaired by noise, if the research subject knew at what moments it was necessary to concentrate on a problem. On the other hand, noise caused considerable disruption of test performances if the person being tested did not know when it was necessary to concentrate, and so had to remain in a state of vigilance for long periods. Modern psychology teaches that people cannot maintain their alertness without pause: after concentrating for a time, breaks occur in both alertness and observation, somewhat comparable with the blinking of the eyes. Broadbent (*216*) *found that a noisy situation made breaks in concentration more frequent, and thereby impaired performance in psychological tests which called for continuous attention.*

Distraction

Besides these direct effects on concentration, unexpected and unfamiliar stimulation from noise is also generally distracting, removing attention from what one is doing and directing it towards the source of the noise. These effects are traceable to the activation centres in the reticular formation, which react to noise stimuli by alerting the whole of consciousness. This alarm signal acts as a diversion, and it is easy to see that this must distract a person who is concentrating on a particular activity.

Investigations both in factories and in laboratory situations have shown that people think noise is disturbing and unpleasant, and that to perform difficult tasks in noisy conditions is always associated with a feeling of great stress and requires a great effort of will.

We are well able to perform tasks that call for a high level of thought, concentration and skill in noisy surroundings, but this necessitates unnecessary expenditure of nervous energy and mental strain to isolate ourselves from the noise and to prevent it reaching consciousness.

The following factors determine the effects of noise on intellectual activities:

- an unexpected or interrupted noise is worse than continuous noise.
- noises with a predominance of high frequencies are more disturbing than lower ones.

– activities requiring prolonged vigilance are more susceptible to noise than others.
– activities which include elements of learning are considerably more susceptible to noise than routine work.

The foregoing research does not permit us to draw precise conclusions about noise limits as far as they refer to concentration, or intellectual work. *Nemecek and Grandjean* (168) measured noise levels in 15 open-plan offices, and simultaneously questioned 519 of the occupants about disturbance from noise. The background noise (S_{50}) varied on average between 47–52 dB(A), while the frequent peaks (S_{99}) reached 57–65 dB(A). Although more than half of those questioned said that they were disturbed by noise, there was no correlation between the frequency of this complaint and measured noise levels. It must be assumed that the distracting effect of noise is not necessarily expressed by its value in decibels.

Effects on the autonomic nervous system

Lehmann and his colleagues, *Tamm, Meyer-Delius* and *Jansen* (219, 220, 221, 222) studied the effects of noise on autonomic functions in the body, in particular on the cardio-vascular control systems. These, and other studies, show that both in man and other animals exposure to noise has the following effects:

– raising the blood-pressure
– speeding up the pulse-rate
– contracting blood-vessels in the skin and increasing metabolism
– reducing the activity of the digestive organs
– increasing muscular tension

These reactions correspond to the spreading of the alarm reaction to all parts of the body from an increased level of autonomic stimulation. This alarm reaction constitutes a protective mechanism against danger, readying all the organs for fight, flight or defence. It must not be forgotten that throughout the animal kingdom hearing is primarily an alarm system which alerts the animal against danger. This primitive function of hearing is still preserved in man.

Disturbance of sleep

Restorative function of sleep

The alternation of exercise by day and recuperation during the night is presumably necessary for the maintenance of life. During sleep the activities of the muscles, the brain and numerous other organs are reduced to a minimum, while the only organs to continue to function without rest are those concerned with assimilation of food and restoration of strength (digestive and metabolic organs). If sleep is cut short, or is disturbed, the recuperative functions are impaired, and if this happens frequently, it has an adverse effect on performance as well as on health.

Waking up

Of all the senses, hearing is the one that wakes people up most easily. Whereas during sleep optical stimulation can largely be avoided by closing the eyes, hearing is only slightly diminished: *its function as an alarm-system continues during sleep.* Experience certainly shows that familiar noises are less likely to waken one than strange noises. People who live close to a railway are not awakened by the noise of passing trains; in contrast, dutiful mothers waken at even slight sounds from their children. Obviously people can 'adapt' themselves to particular sounds, so that they wake to some and not to others, but there is little protection against unfamiliar or unexpected sounds. Hence unaccustomed and unexpected noise has a considerable waking effect.

Depth of sleep

Deep sleep is to be distinguished from light sleep : the latter is medically known as 'twilight sleep'. Noise either wakes a person completely, or changes deep sleep into light sleep. These phenomena cause changes in the electrical activity of the brain, and can be studied by the electroencephalogram. From studies of *Lehmann* and his colleagues (224), *Jansen* (225), *Richter* (226, 227) and other authors it emerges that noises do not often wake the sleeper immediately, but usually lead him into a less deep sleep.

Richter (226, 227) designated this reaction 'internal waking', the sleeper moving from a deep sleep into a state of superficial sleep, from which he is easily aroused. This reaction lasts for between five and twenty seconds, after which deep sleep is resumed unless the sleeper is wakened by further noise. Even very faint sounds lasting for only a few seconds can reduce the depth of sleep by about one stage. The louder and longer the noise the shallower becomes sleep, until finally the sleeper wakes. This shows that the effect of noise on sleep cannot be assessed by considering only the depth of sleep and whether the sleeper wakes up. *Frequent noises of relatively low intensity decrease the depth of sleep and lessen its recuperative effect.*

Steinicke (228) studied 350 persons of all ages in an experimental investigation of the waking effect of artificial noise. The research took place in the bedrooms of the test personnel between 0200 and 0700 hrs. The noise lasted for three minutes, and increased in steps of 5 DIN-phons, from 30 DIN-phons until the subject woke up. The effective frequencies lay between 60 and 5000 Hz (these DIN-phon values are of the same order of magnitude as the values of dB(A) in current use). It was found that at a level of 35 DIN-phons 23% of the subjects woke up, a relatively high percentage of them being young persons up to the age of 30 years. At 45 DIN-phons 52% of all

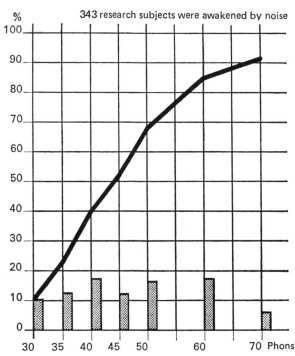

Figure 118   Threshold values of an experimental noise (60–5000Hz) which wakened research subjects   The phons are DIN-phons, and are comparable with dB(A) values. The graph is a summation curve, and the vertical columns indicate the percentage of people who were awakened by each level of noise. After Steinicke (228)

subjects were awake. The author came to the conclusion that the noise level in bedrooms ought not to exceed 35 DIN-phons. The results of this investigation are illustrated in *Figure 118*.

Since the experimental situation in this work cannot be interpreted without knowing more about conditions in the bedrooms, we cannot base any recommendations upon it at the moment. On the other hand *Steinicke* (228) established the interesting fact that individual response to noise varies widely, 90% of his subjects being wakened by noises ranging from 10 to 70 DIN-phons.

Psychological effects: annoyance

Annoyance from noise

Everyday experience shows that many kinds of noise have emotive effects on people. They evoke subjective feelings depending on how much the person is used to noise. *Hawel's* definition (206) that noise is sound that does not fit in with a given activity, is central to the present context. Take music as an example: one person feels an urgent need for music, while another person who wants to rest may regard it as a great nuisance. Thus the question of whether music is welcome or not, depends on the circumstances of the moment.

The domestic activities most liable to be disturbed by noise are undoubtedly resting, conversation, intellectual activities such as reading, and some other leisure pursuits.

Need for rest

People need a certain amount of rest, during which they can recover from the physical and mental stresses of their daily work. This is a platitude, along with the statement that noise disturbs rest and recuperation. This effect of noise is particularly important at home because the home is a person's private sphere, to which he retreats for protection. Here he builds up his own private world, where he can spend his leisure time as he likes, satisfying his own needs, and where he can relax, shut off from the outside world. *External noise is an invasion of privacy, and robs the home of its most important asset, that of being a place for rest and recuperation.*

Research subjects in many investigations have said that noise in the home was 'annoying', usually without defining this any more closely. It can be confidently assumed that the subjective impressions of disturbance and annoyance arise from the cumulative effects of noise.

Factors involved in annoyance

The following factors determine the disturbance and annoyance caused by noise:

- noise intensity.
- its nature: unexpected, or irregular noises are more disturbing than regular ones.
- the overall frequency: high frequency sounds are more disturbing than low notes.
- what the subject is doing. Noise is most disturbing during leisure, when resting or asleep, or during intellectual activities.
- one's psychological attitude to the source of the noise: disapproval (for example neighbours one dislikes) makes the noise more disturbing, whereas approval of the source (for example one's own car, power equipment, radio, etc.) often minimises the disturbance.
- previous experience of the particular noise: for example, a noise that has often disturbed one's sleep before, has often interfered with one's activities, or caused distress, will seem particularly unpleasant.

Section 'Noise indoors' will deal with the frequency and extent of subjective disturbance and annoyance from noise in the home. The feelings of annoyance engendered by noise are the most important of all its effects, not only because they are the most universal, but because of the accumulation of conscious and subconscious reactions to them. Annoyance, therefore assumes the

Table 97   Comparison of the disturbance from noise recorded in surveys in England in 1948 and again in 1961   Noise Final Report (207)

| Reaction noted | Percentage of those questioned affected by: | | | |
| | External noise | | Internal noise | |
	1948	1961	1948	1961
Disturbed by noise	23	50	19	14
Noise noticed, but not disturbing	19	41	21	14

greatest importance as a way of assessing noise, and we need to develop techniques for measuring annoyance and a scale of auditory values by which to express it.

Acclimatisation to noise

The extent to which people become accustomed to noise is still not clearly understood. Experience shows that under certain circumstances a degree of adaptation takes place, but that in other cases there may either be no adaptation or reaction to the noise may increase. This process depends upon so many external circumstances and psychological factors that it is impossible at the present time to generalise about it. We can only deduce from the steady increase in the number of complaints about noise that, in general, adaptation is not keeping pace with rising noise levels, and that the limit of acclimatisation is being more and more often exceeded. The results of a survey carried out in London in 1948 and again in 1961 (207) give support to this. They are presented in *Table 97*.

This survey showed that the percentage of people disturbed by external noise had risen between 1948 and 1961, and led to the conclusion that the external noise level had doubled in that period. This supports the view that people cannot acclimatise to noise once it has reached a certain level.

Effects of noise on health

Definition of health

According to the definition of the World Health Organisation, health is a state of physical and mental well-being. If we accept this definition we must include among the injuries caused by noise, *not just loss of hearing, but frequent disturbance of sleep, delayed recuperation, and extensive intrusion into one's private life.*

Isolated 'alerts' in the brain caused by noise, which cause single incidents of either waking, or disturbance of rest, certainly count as physiological phenomena. The alarm reaction is itself a physiological process, the end-product of a self-preservative defence mechanism.

Effect of alarm reactions on health

If 'alerts' become so frequent that they interfere with the recuperative processes of the body, they upset the physiological balance and a gradual onset of chronic fatigue can be anticipated. This condition can be recognised by frequent complaints of tiredness, nervousness, and irritability, as well as by a general lowering of vitality, together with a variety of feelings of dislike. If the noise is of such a sort that it retains its disturbing effect over a long period, then signs of strain must be expected; these show themselves in a highly nervous state, with a tendency to ill-health, digestive disorders, high blood-pressure, and various circulatory irregularities.

It is still a matter of dispute as to whether, in practice, noise does actually lead to such chronic fatigue. From a study of 1005 foundry-workers, *Jansen* (222) found that those workers who were exposed to a loud noise-level (90–120 phons) more often showed signs of functional disturbance (circulatory symptoms, irregular heart-beat, nervous troubles) as well as a higher percentage of cases of inter-personal tensions. It would be unwise, however, to generalise, from these findings, because firstly the noise level of 90–120 phons to which these workers were exposed is extraordinarily high, and secondly the comparability of those heavily exposed to noise with the rest does not seem to have been entirely free from criticism.

Admissions to
psychiatric clinics

An interesting observation was recently published in England by *Abey-Wickrama* and his colleagues (229). In a retrospective study he was able to demonstrate that the number of admissions to a psychiatric clinic over the previous two years had been significantly higher among people living in a neighbourhood exposed to heavy aircraft noise than it was among people of comparable age, sex, social and economic circumstances from outside this area. A rise in the number of such admissions can be seen particularly among old women living alone, arising mainly from neurotic disturbances and psychosomatic ailments. The authors do *not* conclude from their results that the aircraft noise causes mental disorders, but they think that they have proved that intense noise can be a factor which might affect the practice of a clinic in regard to its admissions.

Medical observations

Many doctors are of the opinion that excessive noise levels can lead to unhealthy conditions in the sense of an excessively nervous state, as well as various functional disorders (headaches, loss of sleep, digestive and circulatory troubles, higher blood-pressure and so on). These are observations of general practitioners, however, and up to now have not been demonstrated scientifically. Thus, for example, the English *Noise Report* (207), after a comparison of such observations, came to the conclusion that the existing information is not sufficient to say that the ailments in question are a direct consequence of exposure to noise.

Effects on health

Effects on health can be summarised as follows: Whether noise is or is not injurious to health is primarily a question of the definition of the term 'health'. If we assume that health includes mental well-being, then it can be said without question that excessive exposure to noise causes damage. If we use the term 'health' in a limited sense, and if we look for evidence of definite bodily or mental damage that is medically and statistically certain, then – short of actual deafness – existing observations have failed to show much damage. On the other hand, they have not proved that much damage does not occur, and it must be said that the many observations concerning injury to health lead one to suppose that excessive noise can cause ill-health in the strict medical sense of the term.

Noise indoors

Classification of sources of noise

The following different kinds and sources of noise may be listed:

- *External noises*
  Street noises
  Tradesmen and builders
  Children shouting, dogs' barking, footsteps, lawnmowers
- *Internal noises*
  Doors slamming
  Walking, stamping
  Talking
  Children playing and shouting
  Radio, television, gramophone, musical instruments
  Water running (w.c., bath, kitchen)
  Vacuum cleaner, sewing machine, boiler, washing machine.

Internal noises can be further classified according to origin:

- noise from people on the same floor
- noise from flats above or below
- noise from the entrance hall
- noise from inside one's own home

External noises and their effects in the home

Street noises predominate in this group, and a few of the most important observations on this subject will be briefly reviewed. In 1960 the British Home Office established a committee to study the nature, origin and effects of noise and where appropriate to make proposals. The work of this Committee was published in 1963 as the 'Noise Report'. (207)

In 1961 and 1962, noise was measured at 540 points in London, and 1400 people were asked for their opinion about it. Street noise predominated at 84% of the measuring points, whereas industry, railways and building operations combined provided only 15% of the sources of noise. During 80% of the time (S_{80}) the following noise-levels were recorded:

S_{80} in the street

	dB(A) In daytime	dB(A) At night
On main arterial roads	68–80	50–70
On main roads in residential areas	60–70	44–55
On residential roads with local traffic	56–65	45–53
In parks, far away from the street	50–55	41–46

Tables 98 and *99* give partial summaries of the replies of the 1400 people questioned.

It appears from this that in 1961–62 noise had already become a factor of major importance compared with other sources of annoyance, and that street noises were questionably the biggest single source. People questioned considered noise to be disturbing significantly more often at home than out of doors, or at work.

French surveys

In France *Auzou and Lamure* (230) and *Lamure and Bacelon* (231) concerned themselves with traffic noise and its effects in the vicinity of motorways. There was good agreement between the frequency of reports of annoyance and the level of traffic noise, if this was expressed as a summated frequency of 50%; that is in noise values that exceeded the specified level for 50% of the time. 420 persons were questioned, all of whom lived within 10–150 metres of the motorway. The noise level (50% of the time) ranged between 53 and 81 dB(A). On the basis of 15 particular questions an index of noise disturbance was calculated, which ran from 1 (minimum disturbance) to 10 (maximum disturbance). There was good correlation between these values and the 50% noise levels (r = 0.62) for buildings alongside the motorway. The authors came to the conclusion that *noise levels at the front of the buildings of between 60–65 dB(A) for 50% of the time constituted a critical level*, and any increase of noise above this level brought a very rapid increase in personal disturbance.

Surveys in Vienna

In 1964 *Bruckmayer and Lang* (232) studied the amount of disturbance caused by traffic noise in the urban area of Vienna, using sound measurements combined with the questioning of 400 people (265 in homes, 100 in offices, and 35 school-teachers). With the windows open 49% of those

Table 98   Ranking of causes of annoyance   From surveys carried out in London in 1961 and 1962. Noise Final Report (207)

Chief cause of dissatisfaction	Percentage of those questioned
Public transport and services	14
Noise	11
The kind of people round about	11
The amount of traffic	11
Slums, dirt, smoke	10
Facilities for shopping and entertainment	7
Different reasons, or no reply	6
Not dissatisfied	30

Table 99   Disturbance from noise in relation to its source, and to where it is heard   London surveys of 1961, 1962, from Noise Final Report (207)

Source of noise	Percentage of persons questioned who were disturbed		
	When home	When outdoors	When at place of work
Street traffic	36	20	7
Aircraft	9	4	1
Railway	5	1	–
Industry and building	4	–	4
Internal noises at home	4	–	4
Noise from neighbours	6	–	–
Children	9	3	–
Adults (talking)	10	2	2
Radio and television	7	1	1
Bells and sirens	3	1	1

Table 100   Equivalent level of sustained noise Q, and frequency of reports of 'very disturbing' and 'unbearably disturbing'   Surveys in Vienna in 1964. After Bruckmayer and Lang (232)

Q in dB(A)	Percentage of persons who were 'very disturbed' and 'unbearably disturbed'			
	Windows open		Windows shut	
	Day	Night	Day	Night
20–25	–		–	0
25–30	–		0	24
30–35	–	0	9	42
35–40	0	36	9	52
40–45	14	56	15	53
45–50	30	70	40	–
50–55	47	76	–	–
55–60	60	76	–	–
60–65	68	–	–	–
65–70	70	–	–	–

questioned were 'disturbed' or 'unbearably disturbed' by the noise of cars by day, and 50% by night. With the windows shut the numbers fell to 16% and 30% respectively. The noise level in dB(A) was registered for 10 seconds in every minute, and from this were calculated the summated frequency and the equivalent level of sustained noise Q (see page 251). The difference between noise levels in the open and indoors with open windows averaged 5–7 dB. The sound insulating effect of a simple window with double glazing mostly came between 15 and 20 dB, and with sealed windows the average noise level indoors was 5 dB lower.

Disturbance in the home

The authors related the disturbance to the level of sustained noise, their most important results being set out in *Table 100*.

About one third of those questioned recorded a high level of disturbance when the level of sustained noise Q reached the following values:

With the window open:
by day   50 dB(A)
by night   35–40 dB(A)

With the window closed:
by day   45–50 dB(A)
by night   30–35 dB(A)

Thus traffic noise caused more disturbance with the window open than with it shut, and considerably more by night than by day.

Table 101 summarises noise values and extent of disturbance, divided into different types of street.

On residential roads (Q-values between 24–44 dB(A)) the proportion of people who were greatly disturbed was directly lower than on arterial roads (Q-values between 37–69 dB(A)).

Furthermore the authors were able to establish that on arterial roads the internal noises in dwellings were masked by the noise of traffic penetrating from outside, if the windows were open in the daytime. On residential roads, however, the mean level of internal noise was higher than the traffic noise, being about Q = 50 dB(A).

English research

In England *Langdon and Scholes* (233), and *Griffiths and Langdon* (234) concerned themselves with the disturbance produced by traffic noise. Questioning 100 people, they established a good correlation between the disturbance and the traffic noise, if they used the Traffic Noise Index TNI (see page 251). The authors came to the conclusion that the TNI should not exceed 74 dB(A) in a quiet house or flat.

Swedish research

In 1966–67 in Sweden, *Fog* and his colleagues (235) studied the disturbing effects of traffic noise by questioning 722 people. They obtained a good correlation (r = 0.91) between an index of disturbance and the equivalent sustained level of noise (by pure energetics) L_{eq}–REM. *More than 20% of those questioned recorded a high level of disturbance if L_{eq}–REM for 24 hours exceeded 55 dB(A) immediately outside the window. Inside the room this gave a L_{eq}–REM (24 hr.) of 45–50 dB(A) with the window open and 30–35 dB(A) with the window closed.*

In *Table 102* we have attempted to correlate the effects of traffic noise with the various studies described above, but unfortunately different units of measurement have been used in each case, so that comparison is hardly possible. We can merely say that the French results plainly differ from the rest, the values obtained in Sweden and in Austria showing a certain degree of agreement.

Standard limiting values for external noise

Many countries nowadays have recommended limits for bearable noises, mostly established from a pragmatic point of view. They are intended to be used as a basis by planning authorities.

Gilgen (236) gathered together recommendations from various countries. He rightly criticised these for lumping together noises of all kinds: this is not very sensible, if we consider how diverse are the sources of noise (aircraft, building operations, traffic, firing-ranges, etc.). *Gilgen* (236) proposed to segregate the different kinds of noise and to set out separate norms and standard values for them.

Table 103 summarises the provisional standard limiting values that were worked out by a commission of experts in Switzerland (237). It may also be

Table 101   **Equivalent level of sustained noise in various types of road, and the frequency with which they were judged 'very disturbing' to 'unbearably disturbing'**   After Bruckmayer and Lang (232)

Type of road	Windows open				Windows shut			
	Day		Evening and night		Day		Evening and night	
	Q dB (A)	Percent disturbed	Q dB (A)	Percent Disturbed	Q dB (A)	Percent disturbed	Q dB (A)	Percent disturbed
Residential	41–44	14	33–38	36	26–32	9	24–28	24
Side road	48–51	30	41–45	56	39–29	9	23–31	24
Main road	59–63	68	53–56	76	40–49	40	37–40	52
Side street in town centre	54–59	60	–	–	36–41	9	–	–
Main road in town centre	58–69	70	–	–	41–47	40	–	–

Aircraft noise

mentioned here that the background noise is comparable with a summated frequency of S_{50} and the most frequent peaks with S_{99}.

In the vicinity of airports the sound of aircraft is the loudest external noise. The disturbance they create for residents in these areas is so bad in many places that ultimately political action ensues. As a result the authorities in several countries have initiated large-scale scientific research on aircraft noise and its effects. An account of this research is outside the scope of this book, and the reader is referred to the work of *Gilgen* (236) and the critical review by *Grandjean, Gilgen and Bättig* (238). *Table 104* merely gives limiting values for aircraft noise extracted from the research results of English (207) and French (239) authors.

Table 102   Effects of traffic noise, from four studies

Country and source	Level of disturbance		Summated frequency	Percentage of people affected
France (231)	S_{50}	= 60–65 dB (A)	S_{50}	sharp rise
Austria (232)	$L_{eq}Q$ (day)	= 35–40 dB (A)	$S_{50}+3$	30
Austria (232)	$L_{eq}Q$ (night)	= 35–40 dB (A)	$S_{50}+3$	36
Sweden (235)	L_{eq}–REM (24 h)	= 55 dB (A)	$\dfrac{S_{50}+S_{99}}{2}$	20
England (233)	TNI	= 74 dB (A)	$4 \times (S_{90}-S_{10})+S_{10}-30$	rise (about 40)

Table 103   Provisional Swiss limiting values for noise-emission   Measured at an open window. The desirable level is 10 dB below this, but not less than 30 dB (A). Background noise is the average level; frequent peaks are those which occur from 7–60 times per hour, and rare peaks occur 1–6 times per hour. All in db (A)

Background noise		Frequent peaks		Rare peaks		Classification of noise
Night	Day	Night	Day	Night	Day	zone
35	45	45	50	55	55	quiet area, convalescence
45	55	55	65	65	70	quiet residential area
45	60	55	70	65	75	mixed zone
50	60	60	70	65	75	commercial area
55	65	60	75	70	80	industrial area
60	70	70	80	80	90	main traffic artery

Table 104   Limiting values for regional planning around airports   NNI values from 0600–2200 hrs. After Grandjean, Gilgen and Bättig (238)

Above 50 NNI	Industrial building, with special attention to noise insulation and air conditioning in offices and administration buildings Warehousing Areas for military or agricultural use
41–50 NNI	Business premises with special sound insulation Industrial building and factories
36–40 NNI	Mixed zone (Industry, factories and some dwellings)
25–35 NNI	Residential areas with a reasonable amount of aircraft noise Schools Hospitals if they have special sound insulation
below 25 NNI	Quiet areas, for convalescence Hospitals without special sound insulation

Internal noise in the home, and its effects

In 1947 in England *Chapman* (240) questioned 2000 people about disturbance from the noise of neighbours. In the lower and middle income brackets, living in small houses, four-fifths of those questioned were aware that noise was produced in their houses. Only about one quarter found this noise disturbing, and fewer than a fifth found that it disturbed their sleep. The commonest noises were doors shutting and water running. Depending on the age and quality of the building, 41–57% were disturbed by the sound of neighbours and 34–52% were disturbed when they were asleep. Occupants of single family houses in a street were disturbed more by traffic noise than by neighbours, but in houses with more than one family the two sources of noise were about equally disturbing.

Ceilings

In 1952–53 *Gray, Cartwright and Parkin* (241) studied three groups of flats with regard to noise insulation and complaints of disturbance. Group I had the ceilings insulated against airborne sound to about 50 dB, Group II 45 dB and Group III 40 dB. Insulation against footsteps was of a similar order of magnitude for middle and low frequency sounds, the three groups differing from each other by 5–8 dB. On the other hand the sound-insulation between flats on the same floor was about the same for the three groups, usually 50 dB. Group I comprised 377 flats, Group II 545, and Group III 569. 61% of those questioned in Group I said that too much noise came through the ceiling, 76% of Group II and 78% of Group III, but other replies were less consistent with the differences in ceiling-insulation between the three groups. Direct questions as to the kind of sounds from other flats that were disturbing gave very interesting answers, and the frequency of complaint showed the expected correlation with ceiling insulation. A few results are set out in *Table 105.*

Dutch surveys

In Holland *Bitter and van Weeren* (242) carried out large-scale systematic research into disturbance from internal noises in blocks of flats, questioning a total of 1200 persons (one per flat) in Rotterdam and the Hague. The flats had ceilings of six different kinds, but all had more or less the same sound insulation between flats on the same floor. *Table 106* summarises the replies of the complaints about the source of the disturbing noise.

Sources of noise inside the house

Astonishingly, those questioned were more often disturbed by internal sounds than by traffic noise from outside. It is of further interest that the entrance-hall was given as the commonest source.

Table 105   Penetration of noise from flats above and below   The decibel values indicate the average sound insulation of the ceilings and floors. After Gray, Cartwright Parkin (241).

Comments made	Percentages making these comments		
	Group I 50 dB	Group II 45 dB	Group III 40 dB
Too much noise through ceiling	61	76	78
Too much noise from below	38	57	66
Conversation audible through ceiling	53	72	87
Conversation audible through floor	48	59	86
Talking is heard from flats on same level	21	30	11
Radio or television, above	70	80	90
Radio or television, below	64	59	91
Radio or television from flats on same level	37	39	34
Radio or television above is disturbingly loud	21	29	20
Radio or television below is disturbingly loud	15	21	18
WC flushing heard	80	87	84
WC flushing disturbingly loud	13	28	8

Table 106   Sources of disturbing noises within multifamily houses
Multiple replies recorded. 100%=960 persons who were disturbed by internal noises.
After Bitter and van Weeren (242)

Source of noise	Percentage disturbed by it
Entrance hall	66%
Neighbours above and/or below	58%
Noises from outside	39%
Next-door neighbours	28%
Other neighbours	15%

The open question 'which noise is most often disturbing?' produced the following spontaneous replies:

doors slamming	218 times
radio	138
walking about	66
talking	59
hammering	52
children playing	46
traffic noise	46
stamping	38
playing the piano	35
dogs' barking	32

Comparison of the replies, taking account both of what sounds were noticed, and which of them were disturbing, produced an order of precedence which was applicable to the types of floor that were present in these particular blocks of flats. This list showed a good and significant correlation which was equally valid whether it was applied only to airborne sounds (radio and speech) or to a mixture of airborne sounds and footsteps (radio+speech+ walking about+stamping). Brick floors showed better results than wooden constructions both with air-borne sounds and with footsteps.

Sound insulation and frequency ranges

The authors calculated the correlation between sound insulation for different frequency ranges and the frequency of reports of sounds being heard and being disturbing. *In the frequency range 60–120 Hz these showed a high and significant correlation both for airborne sounds and for footsteps. On the other hand sound insulation against frequencies above 500 Hz had only a slight effect.*
For example *Table 107* brings together the insulation against airborne sounds of 120 Hz and the corresponding complaints about 'hearing the radio upstairs'.
Disturbance from noise in the entrance hall was particularly significant: 65% of those questioned said they were annoyed by at least one sort of noise from it, 30% rated this noise as very annoying, and 13% were disturbed

Table 107   Sound-insulation of ceilings against airborne sound with a frequency of 120 Hz   After Bitter and van Weeren (242)

Sound-insulation in dB, 120 Hz	Percentage of those questioned who heard radio from flat above
20–25	81–72
25–30	71
30–35	66–51

Table 108   Extent of penetration by, and disturbance from, footsteps in the flat above 822 persons questioned. After Bitter and Horch (243)

Density of floor kg/sq m	Footsteps heard	Footsteps disturbing	Number questioned
500	14	3	399
400	33	8	423

Table 109   Assessment of flats with regard to sound insulation and noise from footsteps above After Bitter and Horch (243)

| Density of floor kg/sq m | Percentages of those questioned: | | | Number of people questioned |
	Satisfied with flat as a whole	Satisfied with its sound insulation	Flat can be noisy	
500	21	10	12	399
400	32	42	51	423

by it when asleep. Doors slamming were the commonest cause, with children playing in the entrance hall coming second.

People were much more ready to pay a higher rent for improvements to the bathroom, or to the heating system, than for better sound insulation, but the people affected by noise were prepared to pay more for their improvements than the others were for their bathroom or heating.

Disturbance from air borne sounds compared with that from footsteps

In 1958 *Bitter and Horch* (243) studied 1000 flats to find out the effect of floor densities of 500 or 400 kg/square metre on the disturbance caused by footsteps, and some of their results are summarised in *Tables 108, 109*.

In addition 423 people were questioned about disturbance from airborne sounds. Music and talks on the radio were noticed more often as disturbing noises than were footsteps. The authors are of the opinion that the impression that a flat is 'noisy' arises quite as much from airborne sound as from footsteps. From the investigation as a whole they concluded that a floor density of 500 kg/square metre provided an acceptable amount of sound insulation whereas a floor density of only 400 kg/square metre should be rated as inadequate.

Surveys in Sweden

In Sweden *Boalt* (244) concerned himself with internal noise in 2593 flats. Of 12 criteria, on which the people questioned were required to give their opinion in relation to their own flat, 'sound insulation' received by far the worst verdict. More than 50% of those questioned named sources outside their flat as sources of disturbance, and in general the noise from neighbours was 'more irritating' than traffic noise. The commonest complaints concerned children shouting, doors slamming and the sound of water flushing. For this reason flats with the bedroom next to the bathroom/wc were condemned.

Surveys in France

In France *Coblentz and Josse* (245) carried out surveys of disturbance from footsteps in 408 flats, the results being compared with the extent to which the floors were insulated against the sound of footsteps. The authors came to the conclusion that the usual method of estimating floor insulation by hammering on the floor of the flat above did not agree with the opinions of the occupants in reply to questions. In corroboration of the results of the Dutch research, the French workers also found that sound insulation in the higher ranges of frequency had little effect on disturbing noises. The authors therefore preferred a method which measured and allowed for insulation against sounds in the lower and middle ranges of frequency.

Ergonomic recommendations for sound insulation in the home

Limiting values

Values for the upper limit of noise that is still tolerable indoors in houses and flats have been proposed by several institutions and authorities. All the recommendations are based as far as possible on general experience, and so have a certain pragmatic character. Few actual measurements have yet been made of the noisiness of neighbours, or of noises originating in the entrance hall, and what is more, we know nothing about the relationship between the amount of noise arising inside a building and the level of annoyance that it causes. The studies in open-plan offices that were quoted above (168) give cause to think *that disturbance by noisy neighbours is caused mostly by the feeling that one's privacy is being invaded, by the consequent distraction, and by disturbance of rest.* This leads to the requirement that *under 'normal operating conditions' in any given flat, the normal noise of neighbours above, below, or alongside should be unnoticeable.*

By 'normal operating conditions' we mean that an ordinary background noise of 40–45 dB(A) by day or 25–30 dB(A) by night can also be heard in the flat in question. Assuming this, it can be expected that a fresh noise of less than 30 dB(A) or 20 dB(A) by night would pass unnoticed. Since the level of background noise inside a flat is mainly determined by external noise, any proposals for limiting values indoors are still tacitly based on the assumption that these are essentially outside noises penetrating indoors.

In England (207) the following limiting values were proposed for the interior of rooms, with the proviso that they should not be exceeded for more than 10% of the time (S_{90}).

	db(A)	
Location	by day	by night
in the country	40	30
suburbs	45	35
business quarter	50	35

The German Arbeitsring für Lärmbekämpfung (246) recommended the following mean levels of background noise:

in bedrooms with the window open   25–30 dB(A)
in living rooms by day   45 dB(A)

Table 110 summarises limiting noise levels for the interior of rooms, which we have extracted from the recommendations of the *Eidgenössischen Kommission für Lärmbekämpfung*. In this table we are starting from the assumption that it should be possible to have the window open in any of the living rooms without excessive annoyance from noise.

We cannot attach too much significance to these limiting values as far as they relate to the interior of rooms because – as already mentioned – they reflect almost entirely the amount of outside noise penetrating into the room, and almost completely ignore any disturbance from neighbouring flats, or from the entrance hall.

Effect of the layout of a flat

The basic layout of a flat is of the highest importance in keeping out noise. Most experts agree that the bedroom is the room most sensitive to noise. Hence *Furrer* (247) insisted that the layout of a dwelling for several families should distinguish between a 'noise zone' and a 'quiet zone', and that the latter should contain the bedrooms and living rooms. The 'noise zone' would include kitchen, bathroom, w.c. and entrance hall. Two adjacent

Table 110   Minimal requirements for sound insulation in flats   Desirable levels are 10 dB lower than these. S_{50} and S_{99} mean that this is the level of sound not exceeded for 50% and 99% of the time respectively

Rooms, all with window open	Background level S_{50}		Frequent peaks S_{99}	
	Day	Night	Day	Night
Living-room	48	–	58	–
Bedroom	–	38	–	48
Childrens' room	48	38	58	48

flats should have their quiet zones next to each other, with either two bedrooms, or two living rooms together. The boundary between a rest zone and a quiet zone should fall entirely within one and the same flat.

DIN 4109 (209) give the following directions for basic design: living rooms and bedrooms, along with other rooms serving for rest and relaxation, should be so arranged that they receive as little noise as possible from the street, from garages, or from any other external source. As far as possible they should be cut off from staircases by other rooms such as bathrooms, kitchens, vestibules etc. Rooms from which a lot of noise arises (bathrooms, kitchens, w.c.'s) should not adjoin the living room or one of the bedrooms of the next door flat, but should adjoin similar rooms, alongside or above or below. Places where household noises originate, and any part along which noise spreads (such as conduit pipes, rubbish-shafts, lifts) should not be fitted against the walls of 'quiet' rooms, especially if the wall is thin, and lightly built. They should lie along party walls between flats only if the adjacent rooms are rooms such as kitchens, w.c., bathrooms, storerooms and vestibules, where noise does not matter very much. *Figure 119* shows examples of good and bad layouts with regard to noise.

Table 111 gives a few prescriptions for noise insulation between flats.

In 1961 *Furrer* (247) proposed the following *guidelines for sound insulation of party-walls between flats, and between flats and entrance hall.*

Sound insulation of walls

Minimum sound insulation R	52 dB
Desirable sound insulation R	57 dB

The Swiss Ingenieur- und Architektenverein SIA (208) published the recommendations set out in *Table 112*.

If we start from the assumption that a loud voice or a 'forte' from a musical performance in a room reaches peak-levels of 75 dB(A), with the further requirement that at night these peak noises fall below 20 dB(A) in the next room, then *an intervening wall with a sound insulation R of 55 dB or an Insulation Index I_a of 58 dB is required.*

We are of the opinion that some of the recommendations set out here are very inadequate. Many examples could be extracted from the literature to show that it is technically possible to attain the level of sound insulation that is desirable on physiological grounds. The problem of sound insulation during the building of flats is less a technological problem than a matter of economics.

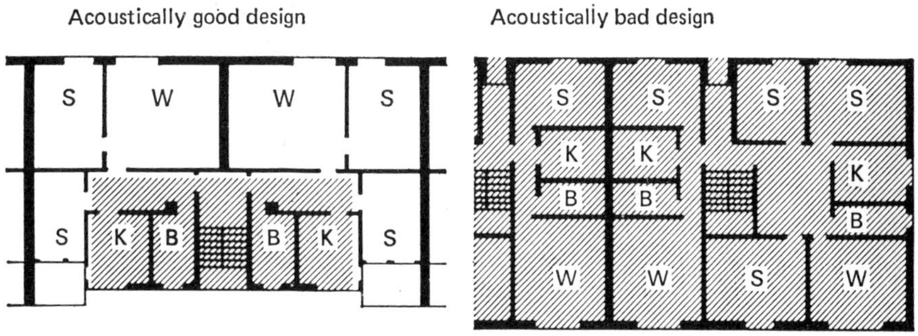

Acoustically good design   Acoustically bad design

Figure 119 Acoustically good and bad designs for a multifamily apartment
On the left: consistent separation of quiet and noisy parts of the house; interruption of the floorboards (grey shading) prevents noises from bathroom and WC from spreading elsewhere. *On the right:* no separation between quiet and noisy parts of the house, many walls are not thick enough. K = kitchen, B = bathroom, W = living room, S = bedroom. After Amrein and Martinelli (210)

Table 111   Specifications for sound insulation of party walls

Country	Insulation-number R (dB)	Necessary density for a single wall (kg/m²)	Thickness of brickwork, including plaster (cm)
Germany[1]	51	600	42
England[2]	48	350	24
Sweden[3]	48	350	24
Austria[4]			
– internal	40	100	6–8
– between two flats	48	350	24
– between two houses	53	800	56
Holland[5]	48–52	–	–

[1] DIN 4109, Jan. 1959
[2] Building Research Station
[3] Anvisningar till Byggnadsstadgan, Dec. 1945
[4] Oenorm B 8125, Oct 1949
[5] Gezondheitsorganisatie T.N.O., Oct 1952

Table 112   Limiting values of SIA (208) for insulation against airborne sound

	SIA I_a in dB minimal requirement	Enhanced requirement
Party walls; walls of entrance lobby	50	55
Ceilings between flats	50	55
Party walls and ceilings between flats and business premises, restaurants, workshops, etc.	60	65
Doors separating flat from entrance lobby	20	25
Doors separating flat from outdoors	–	25
Window or glazed door	20	30

The problems of deadening the sound of footsteps, which are just as important as insulated walls and ceilings against airborne sounds, will be dealt with in Chapter Nine, along with the physiological and hygienic requirements that apply to floor coverings.

Sound insulation of kitchens, bathrooms and toilets

Noise from water

The most important sources of noise in kitchens, bathrooms, and toilets are the noises associated with water installations, and the highest of these is the sound of water flushing.
Kurtze (248) following DIN Instruction 5045 measured these values:

water running into the bath	75 dB(A)
W.C. – flushing	78 dB(A)
W.C. – cistern re-filling	70 dB(A)

Kamber (249) measured the noise of running water in adjoining living rooms and obtained the following values:

water running into the bath	35–44 dB(A)
water running into the wash basin	26–42 dB(A)
water flushing w.c.	33–40 dB(A)
water running out of bath or wash basin	32–40 dB(A)

Recommendations

The most important forms of protection against the causes and spread of noise in and from kitchens, bathrooms and toilets can be summarised as follows:

- the water supply of all three to be on the same wall.
- use of quiet ball-cocks, designed to give a smooth flow of water.
- aerating nozzles on taps and ball-cocks can reduce the noise by about 6–12 dB.
- use of low-flush cisterns instead of high pressure heads (this can reduce noise by 20–30 dB).
- pipes should have as big a cross-section as possible, to reduce the velocity of flow.
- reduction of the water-pressure inside the house as far as is technically permissible.
- reduction of emptying noises by designing waste-pipes so that air mixes with the water smoothly and continuously.
- water-pipes should never be fixed directly on to the structure of the building, but should always be packed or wrapped with sound-deadening material.
- pipes should always be led through ceilings and walls by means of a collet made from fibrous insulating material, bituminous felt, felt, shredded cork, etc.
- sound deadening material should always be used in apparatus or fittings which generate noise, or which make loud noises when filling or emptying (e.g. washing machines, spin-dryers, baths, lavatory-pans, cisterns), especially on all the places where they are attached to the building. The outflow from a bath must not be firmly attached to the waste-pipe, and free-standing baths should have rubber mats under their feet.

9 Floorings

Summary

There are four ergonomic requirements for floorings:

– thermal insulation
– sound insulation
– anti-slip properties
– ease of cleaning

Proper flooring is important both for comfort and for health. Flooring should be 'warm to the feet' by having good thermal insulation properties. These can be measured by using either the rate of absorption of heat by the floor material, or the rate of heat loss from artificial feet. A well insulated floor absorbs heat at a rate of less than 5 kcal per square metre per minute, and causes a loss of heat from the feet of less than 9 kcal per square metre after one minute and 45 kcal per square metre after 45 minutes. As warm floor coverings, wall-to-wall carpeting, cork parquet, and wood parquet are excellent.

SIA recommendations for sound insulation are reproduced. Sprung floorings (a slightly resilient layer between the floor boards and the walking surface) are necessary to reach the required level of damping for houses and flats. The non-slip properties of a floor depend on the coefficient of friction between the sole of the shoe and the walking surface, and a sufficient degree of protection is reached if the coefficient of friction is more than 0.4. Floorings in common use have enough friction when dry, particularly wooden and cork surfaces which also have good thermal properties.

On hygienic grounds, floors should be easy to clean, and jointless or sealed floors are particularly good in this respect.

Thermal properties

Cold feet

We have frequent and sustained contact with the floor through our feet, and the greater the thermal conductivity of the flooring the more heat will our feet lose. Other factors that have a big effect on the rate of heat loss include the conductivity of the soles of our shoes, and the temperature difference between our feet and the floor surface.

If the rate of heat loss is too great, the foot temperature drops and the feet feel cold. Historically, cold feet have been considered unhealthy, leading to chills and rheumatic pains. Certainly, cold feet feel decidedly unpleasant. For these reasons architects have been searching for a long time for floor coverings with a low thermal conductivity which will keep the feet warm. *Table 113* gives the conductivities of a few floor coverings in common use. Various methods of rating the warmth-retaining properties of floorings have been put forward. One such in common use is the *heat-penetration value b*, which is proportional to the square root of the thermal-conductivity index λ, times the specific heat c, times the specific gravity γ. (b = $\sqrt{\lambda \cdot c \cdot \gamma}$). The smaller the value of b, the less is heat conducted away. According to *Eichler* (250), *Amrein* (251), *Bobran* (252) and others, heat-retaining properties can be rated as follows:

Rating	Heat penetration value b
good heat retention	less than 5
warm to the feet	5–10
moderately warm to cold	10–20
cold to the feet	more than 20

The artificial foot

Table 114 gives heat penetration values for a few types of flooring. *Schüle* (259), *Bobran* (252) and other authors consider *heat loss* as being important in assessing heat retaining properties. According to *Schüle* (253, 259) this heat loss – which of course is linked with the heat penetration value – can be measured by using an artificial foot. This method determines the rate at which the temperature of the artificial foot falls at the point where it is in contact with the test flooring. Curves can be drawn to show the rate of heat loss, and if the flooring is warm to the feet the whole of this curve should lie above the contact temperature of 26°C. Since the normal

Table 113   Heat conductivity of some common flooring materials

Flooring or floor covering	Density in kg/m³	Heat conductivity number λ kcal/m h grd
Cork parquet	200	0.05
Linoleum	1200	0.16
Oak parquet	700	0.14
Xylolite, and similar materials	830	0.22
Plaster	1600	0.60
Concrete	2000	0.65
Anhydrite (gypsum)	2150	0.68
Bituminous rendering	2200	0.76
Ceramic tiles	2000	0.90
Marble, granite, basalt	2800–3100	3.0

Table 114   Heat penetration values for floorings   Values are rounded off

Material	Heat penetration value b kcal/m²h 0.5°
Cork tiles	2
Pine wood	4
Oak wood	8
Rubber	8
Xylolite	8
Linoleum	9
Anydrite (gypsum)	18
Bituminous rendering	19
Plaster	16–21
Ceramic tiles	20
Cement rendering	17–23
Concreted stone slabs	30
Synthetic stone	34
Marble	43

Thermal conductivity

temperature of the human foot is 31 °C, this means that its temperature should not fall more than 5 °C in contact with the floor.
Figure 120 illustrates a few conductivity curves, for which the standard was a simple wooden floor with deal boards on joists. *It is clear that wooden and cork floor coverings are warm for the feet, and have a lower conductivity than other floorings.*

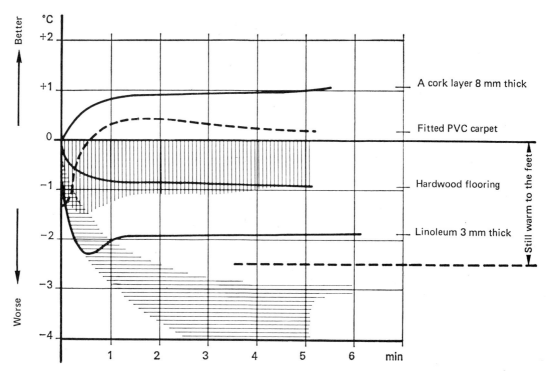

Figure 120   Curves of heat conductivity of various floorings   Standard of reference (zero line) is a wooden floor, with pine floorboards on wooden joists. The linoleum flooring lies on hard fibreboard 3 mm thick, and wooden fibreboard 20 mm thick. After Bobran (252)

Table 115 Thermal conductivity of various floorings after one minute of measuring time, with a surface temperature of 18°C After Schüle and colleagues (253), quoted by Dobran (252)

Floorings	Heat conductivity kcal/m²	Assessment
Carpeting	3.8	particularly warm to the feet
Wooden floors (pine fillets on underflooring)	6.8	particularly warm to the feet
PVC overlay (0.8 mm) on felt (5 mm)	6.9	particularly warm to the feet
Cork lino (7 mm) on concrete	7.7	particularly warm to the feet
Linoleum (2 mm) on compressed felt (1 mm)	10.9	adequate
PVC (2 mm) on concrete	10.5	adequate
Linoleum (2 mm) on heavy concrete	13.2	insufficient
Ceramic tiles on 5 mm pressed cork	16.5	cold to the feet
Exposed surface heavy flooring (e.g. cement rendering)	17.6	cold to the feet

Table 115 presents a few values for heat-conductivity and how they are rated, and it appears from these that both the surface layer and the underlays are important in this respect.

Bobran (252) gives the following ratings to the conductivity values measured by *Schüle* (253, 259):

Heat loss in kcal per square metre after one minute	after 10 minutes	rating
up to 9	up to 45	very warm to the feet
9–12	45–70	sufficiently warm
12–15	70–95	not warm enough
above 15	above 95	cold to the feet

Haller developed a similar method using an 'artificial foot' made of copper, which he warmed to 50°C and measured its loss of heat when in contact with the test floorings. A few of the results of this investigation are given in *Table 116* and *Figure 121*.

By this method floor-coverings can be rated as warm to the feet if the loss of heat amounts to:

0.8 kcal in the first two minutes
3.0 kcal in the first thirty minutes

On this basis *Haller* (254) classified floor coverings laid on a concrete surface as follows:

Coverings warm to the feet

coverings particularly warm to the feet:
fitted carpets, cork parquet, parquet.

coverings warm to the feet:
cork lino, small parquet, wood strips, wood fibre, cork.

all other types of floor covering were rated as cold to the feet.
Carpets are particularly effective, as shown in *Table 116*.
The 'warming-up time' of floorings is also important for foot warmth. According to *Bobran* (252) the surface temperature of floorings showed the following rises one hour after the air temperature had been raised from +5°C to +20°C.

cement strip (not covered)	+ 7°C
wooden floor	+12°C
cork parquet	+16°C

Table 116   Heat conductivity of various floor coverings, measured with an artificial foot   All coverings laid on concrete 12 cm thick. After Haller (254)

Floor covering	Conductivity after 2 min (kcal)	Conductivity after 30 min (kcal)
Wall to wall carpeting	0.23	1.46
Wood parquet	0.56	2.17
Wood parquet with coconut underlay	0.26	1.25
Small parquet	0.66	2.71
Wood-wire	0.78	2.08
Wood pulp	0.80	2.30
Cork parquet	0.49	2.32
Cork lino	0.63	2.95
Wood cement, with cork underlay	1.14	3.45
Linoleum	1.06	4.56
Asphalt	1.87	7.58
Stone	1.72	7.15
Mosaic floorings	1.74	6.10
Mosaic floorings with coconut underlay	0.30	1.84

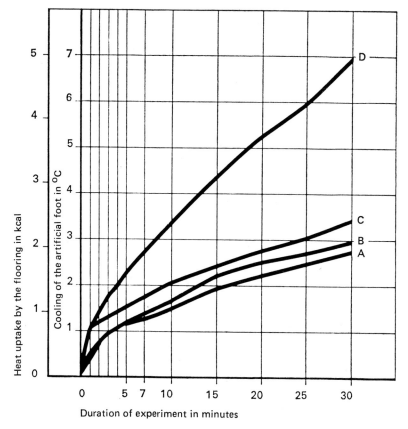

Figure 121   Fall in temperature of an artificial foot, and uptake of heat by flooring   A = wood parquet on wooden joists with cross-members. B = wood parquet on concrete. C = linoleum on wooden joists. D = linoleum on concrete. After Haller (254)

Children and floorings

It appears from all these statements that wood is particularly warm to the feet, and has good heat insulating properties.
This is a special aspect of warm floorings. Children play on the floor a great deal, often crawling, or lying down with a large part of their body in contact with the flooring. There is no doubt that it is important for the children's health and well-being that the flooring should be warm, and as clean and free from dust as possible. Wooden floors can be recommended in these respects, too.

Deadening the sound of footsteps

It was explained in the chapter on 'Noise in the Home' that noise from the flat above, and particularly footsteps were the commonest cause of complaints. There is a noise of footsteps whenever anyone walks about above the ceiling, and part of this noise is transmitted to the room below as airborne sound. The insulation of the ceiling against this noise is tested by operating the usual mechanical hammer on the floor above and measuring the level of sound reaching the test-room below.
The recommendations set out in *Table 117* apply to Switzerland.
Solid concrete floors, which protect against airborne sound, thanks to their density, are not usually effective against footsteps. In a critique of double ceilings, *Amrein* (210) came to the conclusion that in a block of flats every floor should be provided with a sound deadening covering and that this could best take the form of a resilient layer between the walking surface and the supporting floor. Wood is comparatively inflexible, and for this reason has no special advantage as a sound-deadening material, so that the details of construction are all the more important. According to *Gösele* (255), *Amrein* (210), *Wiedefeld* (260) and other authors, wood offers several useful possibilities as a constructive material for sound-deadening.

Sprung floors

The most commonly used form of construction for deadening the sound of footsteps is the so-called sprung floor, which uses an insulating layer of coconut matting, expanded polystyrene sheeting, shredded cork or glass-fibre, in thickness from 0.5–3 cm. Wooden parquet can also be laid over a sprung floor, and when laid 'floating' in this way it is not inferior to the other good floating floors, which similarly need to be laid as a double floor, with the wooden blocks separated from the supporting floor by a slightly resilient layer.
For the sake of completeness we might as well mention that sound-absorption can be further improved by a layer of carpet or other soft material.

Table 117   Recommended limits for insulation against the sound of footsteps
This is measured by the effect produced in an experimental room by using a normal hammering apparatus on the floor above. The footstep isolation index I_i is arrived at by comparing the measured curve with the ISO normal curve; the smaller the index, the better the insulation. After SIA (208), as well as Amrein and Martinelli (210).

| | Isolation index I_i in dB | |
	Minimal requirement	Enhanced requirement
Ceiling between flats	65	55
Party walls and ceilings between flats and business premises	50	45

Non-slip properties

Walking habits

Falls in the flat and in the entrance hall are the commonest cause of home accidents, and Swedish and French statistics (256) show that 2–3 accidents per 1000 people per year must be expected as a result of slipping. *Harper* (257) as well as *Harper, Warlow and Clarke* (258) made an analysis of human walking and running, and studied the conditions under which falls occurred. *Figure 122* shows the path followed by the heel of the foot during a pace. After the foot leaves the ground the heel rises steeply upwards, it then moves forwards at a lower height, and then drops down as the foot returns to ground. According to *Harper* (257), during a pace the sole of the shoe makes an angle with the floor that averages 23° in men and 19° in women. Film taken through a glass floor from below (258) shows that the sole of the shoe makes contact with the floor from behind forwards, during which action little more than half of the sole touches the floor.

Forces during walking

Harper and his colleagues (258) have measured the force exerted while walking on metal plates, by using electrical measuring strips. The horizontal (H) and vertical components (V) of force were measured and the quotient $\frac{H}{V}$ was calculated. The average values of $\frac{H}{V}$ while walking in a straight line lay between 0.16 and 0.22, and larger forces were measured while turning. The authors came to the conclusion that when walking round a corner traction forces of 150 kgcm were attained. The investigation showed that slipping occurred when either the horizontal force or the torsional force of the turn exceeded certain critical threshold values. It may be further mentioned here that the risk of slipping depends a great deal on individual gait. Old people or cripples slip more easily, because their reflexes are slower. On the other hand the gait can be suited to the construction of the floor. In practice we automatically shorten our steps on slippery floors, lifting the feet less high, and putting them down more carefully.

As well as the forces acting on the feet during walking, two other factors are critical in regard to slipping: *the construction of the floor and that of the soles of the shoes.*

Coefficient of friction

According to *Harper* (257, 258) if one is not to slip the horizontal component of force H must be smaller than the frictional resistance between the sole and the floor. *Hence the coefficient of friction f should exceed 0.4, which* Harper *considers safe against slipping.*

The coefficient of friction between shoe and floor has received much attention. Several authors distinguish between a static coefficient of friction and a kinetic coefficient. The first designates the frictional resistance against the start of a slip, the second the frictional resistance when the foot is already sliding. The coefficient of friction depends on complex interrelationships between different physical and physico-chemical processes. Important among these are the adhesive and deformatory forces of the materials being studied, which in turn depend on how these materials have been treated, waxed, washed, polished and so on. Furthermore the coefficient of friction

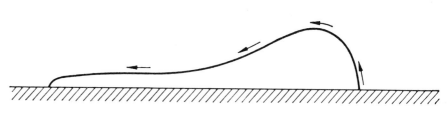

Figure 122   Path traversed by the heel during a step   Taken from a film record made by Harper (257)

depends on the slip velocity : the frictional resistance falls off with increasing velocity, but on a dry floor it remains approximately constant over a velocity-range of 0.2–0.4 metres per second.

Methods of measurement

Various methods for measuring coefficients of friction have been proposed in the literature.

The pendulum impact method of *Sigler, Geib and Boone* (261) is often used. In this method a pendulum falls from a predetermined height and strikes an object placed on the floor, the length of its further swing being measured. Its loss of potential energy is proportional to the frictional resistance of the test-object on the floor.

Another method is the drag test, in which the force needed to set a block with a flat surface in motion along the floor is measured. The ratio between this force and the weight of the test block gives the coefficient of friction, f. *Haller* (262) used this method to determine both static and kinetic co-efficients of friction.

The 'inclined leg' method measures the force necessary to initiate sliding movement in an object on the test surface. In this method the object is attached to a lever-arm, so that the movement of a leg and foot can be simulated.

Coefficients of friction floors

Sigler (263) studied many floors using the pendulum method, and some of his results are reproduced in *Table 118*.

Sigler and his co-workers (261) confirmed the findings of *Harper* (257) that floors with a coefficient of friction of more than 0.4 can be regarded as non-slip. According to *Sigler* (263) the non-slip properties of a floor can be assessed from the scales shown in *Table 119*.

If the values given in *Table 118* are compared with these guidelines it will be seen *that the usual floorings have good non-slip properties if they are in a*

Table 118   Frictional coefficients of various floor coverings   The measurements are derived by the pendulum impact method. The lower the frictional coefficient, the greater the risk of slipping. After Sigler (263)

Floorings	Frictional coefficient Leather soles	Rubber soles
Granite, dry	0.42	0.78
Granite, wet	0.41	0.6
Marble, dry	0.38	0.8
Marble, wet	0.22	0.15
Concrete, dry	0.38	0.78
Concrete, wet	0.1	0.2
Ceramic tiles, dry	0.48	0.82
Ceramic tiles, wet	0.45	0.58
Cork, dry	0.48	0.72
Cork, wet	0.21	0.38
Linoleum, dry	0.42	0.8
Linoleum, wet	0.2	0.2
Wooden flooring, dry	0.4	0.82
Wooden flooring, wet	0.21	0.4

Table 119   Guidelines for assessing the non-slip properties of floorings After Sigler (263)

Non-slip properties	Frictional coefficient Leather soles	Rubber soles
Insufficient	< 0.15	< 0.25
Moderate	0.15–0.30	0.25–0.40
Good	> 0.3	> 0.4

Table 120   Static and dynamic frictional coefficients of different floorings and shoe soles Loading 0.7 kg/cm². Surface in contact 6 × 9.5 cm. Sliding at rate of 6 cm/sec. R = coefficient of friction. After Haller (262). Values of R

Shoe material	Cork linoleum		Rubber flooring		Linoleum	
	Static	Dynamic	Static	Dynamic	Static	Dynamic
Leather	0.60	0.40	0.49	0.77	0.47	0.29
Rubber latex	1.08	1.13	0.75	1.03	0.99	1.13
Vulcanised rubber, new	0.52	0.51	0.59	0.85	0.30	0.35
Vulcanised rubber, worn	0.90	0.90	0.67	0.99	0.63	0.71
Iron plates	0.30	0.40	0.63	1.12	0.23	0.30

dry condition. This also applies to dry floors made of cork or wood, which have good thermal properties. Ceramic tiles and stone floors have good non-slip properties when wet.

Haller (262) used a grinding method, and tested three kinds of flooring, and several kinds of shoe soles, loading a test block with 40 kg and using a slip velocity of 0.06 metres per second. His results are summarised in *Table 120* The effects of treating floors with different substances — water, wax, etc. — have been repeatedly studied, and the results have endorsed current experience that floors have considerably less frictional resistance when wet, or newly polished, than when they are dry. According to *Bring* (256) the coefficient of friction was reduced if there was a film of liquid between the floor and the shoe, since this reduced the areas of the two materials which were directly in contact. For the same reason oil, milk, butter and similar substances increased the danger of slipping to a great extent. Several authors (256) feel that coefficients of friction are in poor agreement with the practical experience of everyday life, and that the gripping power should be interpreted only with extreme caution. Nevertheless during the development of new flooring, coefficients of friction should be a practical way of making them sufficiently non-slip.

Ease of cleaning

Another ergonomic requirement for floors is that they should be easy to clean. Rough or porous floors, or those with joins in them, gather dirt and microorganisms, and are thus unhygienic and may give rise to ill health. This is important in children's rooms, or in rooms where hygiene is very important (e.g. in hospitals, or in particular rooms in the pharmaceutical or food-industries). Continuous floorings are essential in such places. Floor-coverings that are easy to clean also make an important contribution to lightening the housewife's work, and for this reason sealed porous floorings, among which may be included wood-parquet, are much to be recommended. Sealing prolongs the life of the material, and does not affect anti-slip properties (262).

General assessment of floorings

The following summaries can be given for floorings in common use:

Wooden surfaces

Parquet, small parquet made of hardwood, and wood fibre sheets are warm to the feet and non-slip. They are also sound deadening if suitably mounted over a resilient floor. As a rule they wear well. The German Pavilion at the World's Fair in Brussels in 1958 had a wooden floor that gave a striking demonstration of mechanical strength. In spite of the stress of millions of visitors, and the effects of weather, this wooden floor showed no sign of wear, whereas other floors and other building materials developed serious defects. The advantages of wood as a building material have been known to man, consciously or subconsciously, for a very long time. For this reason there is a rich tradition of carpentry and wooden building construction which can be clearly seen by looking at centuries-old roofs, in country cottages and agricultural buildings.

Cork tiles

Cork flooring is second only to carpets in thermal properties, and deadens sound if suitably constructed. Cork floorings are also non-slip, but are not very suitable for rooms with heavy traffic as they wear quickly. Heavy loads in one place leave lasting impressions. They can be made easy to clean by sealing.

Cork-cement floors, with 10–20% by volume of cork granules give unsatisfactory heat insulation, but a cork-inlay 6 mm thick may be considered as a warm floor covering.

Linoleum

Linoleum is only warm enough to the feet if it is laid on a wooden floor, both thermal and sound insulation being insufficient if it is laid directly on cement or plaster. Since linoleum is impermeable to water there is a danger of rot if the underlay is of organic material. Linoleum floors are sufficiently non-slip when dry, are easy to clean, and durable.

10 Accidents in the Home

Contents of Chapter 10

Summary   Accidental death takes third place today in mortality statistics, and occupies
first place among people below 40 years of age. More children and young
adults die from accidents than from any other cause. About a third of all
accidental deaths arise from accidents in the home, and among women
death from an accident at home is more common than from an accident in
the street or at work. Similarly injury is much commoner from domestic
accidents than from accidents either in the street or at work.
Fatal accidents at home are especially common in the first four years of life
and after 65. The commonest causes of death are falls (about half of all
accidents), which occur particularly on the stairs, in the kitchen and in the
bathroom. The other common causes of death at home are poisoning, burns
and scalds, choking and electric shock.
A special section will analyse the most frequent causes of accidents to
children and to adults, and will suggest guidelines for building and technical precautions for the effective prevention of accidents.

The scale of accidents at home, and their consequences

Frequency of accidental death

In technologically advanced countries recent years have seen a change in the causes of death: infectious disease has steadily declined while chronic illness and accidental death have increased sharply, both in absolute and in relative terms. In developed countries accidents take third place, after defects of the heart and circulation, and cancer. In Switzerland accidental death already comes first for persons up to 40 years old: more children and young people below 19 years are killed in accidents than die from any other cause.

To be able to measure the relative importance of accidents compared with other forms of illness, *Bickel* (264) calculated the average age at death from this more important of causes, as well as the average years of life lost from it. The results are summarised in *Table 121*.

This shows clearly the serious loss to humanity, as well as the unnaturalness of accidental death. Besides causing a great deal of human and social misery, it has considerable political and economic consequences when it cuts down the active member of a family. The loss of so many years of life that comes with premature death underlines the situation and shows that accidents to men take pride of place in this respect, even though in actual number of killed they only come third. The situation is slightly different for females, since cancer is relatively common among young women.

Frequency of accidents in the home

While in every country attention is focussed on traffic accidents, and more and more consideration is given to accidents at work, the frequency of domestic accidents is generally underestimated. One's own home seems safe, but work carried out in the U.S.A., in England and in other countries (120) shows that this is a serious error. *The surveys sponsored by the World Health Organisation in 13 western countries in 1961 shows that on average accidents in the home accounted for one third of all accidental deaths, and that in many highly developed industrial countries the home was the most frequent location of accidents of all kinds to women.*

According to evidence provided by the Confederate Office of Statistics, domestic accidents caused 13.3% accidental deaths of males in 1966, and this proportion rose to 53.0% for females.

According to the society 'Das sichere Haus' accidents in the German Bundesrepublik are distributed as shown in *Table 122*.

It is more difficult to establish the frequency of non-fatal accidents and injuries. A survey of accidental injuries in the U.S.A. is reproduced in *Figure 123*, from which it appears that accidents at home cause considerably more injuries than accidents either in the street or at work.

Table 121   Average age of death, and number of years of expected life lost, from the commonest causes of death in Switzerland from 1960–1962   After Bickel (264)

Cause of death	Number of deaths		Average age		Collective number of years of life lost	
	Men	Women	Men	Women	Men	Women
General arteriosclerosis	3486	4139	75.9	76.2	4,890	6,190
Coronary, sclerosis and thrombosis	1990	992	65.7	72.3	14,431	5,180
Cancer	4636	4903	68.0	60.8	26,496	37,400
Accidents	2180	959	48.9	60.6	58,454	24,348

Table 122   Deaths through accidents in Germany, classified into traffic accidents, those at home, and those at work   From 'Das Sichere Haus' (266)

Year	Traffic accidents	Accidents at home	Accidents at work
1963	14,500	9,800	6,680
1964	16,500	9,400	4,968
1965	15,712	9,800	4,787
1966	16,864	11,150	4,868

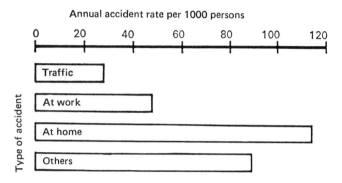

Figure 123   Analysis of frequencies of various types of accident, requiring medical treatment, or loss of work of at least one day.   After the U.S. Department of Health, Education and Welfare (267)

In general it is estimated that 150–200 serious injuries occur for every one accident that is fatal. Hence little Switzerland, for example, must count on about 150,000–200,000 injuries per year from domestic accidents. According to the statistics of the World Health Organisation (265) 5–10% of the populace suffer injury in the home, and if this percentage is applied to Switzerland 300,000–600,000 accidents per year are to be expected. If one considers the extent to which the services of doctors and nurses are needed to treat these injuries, and how much work this entails, the economic and social importance of accidents in the home will be apparent.

Age and sex
The frequency of domestic accidents varies for different age groups, and between the two sexes. On the one hand very small children, particularly boys, seem to be specially exposed to danger and on the other hand, there is a very sharp increase in accidents among old people, especially old women. *Figure 124* illustrates a typical distribution of mortality from fatal accidents, and shows greater predominance in the first four years of life, and after the age of 65.

An analysis of numerous statistics shows that children – and boys especially – suffer a high proportion of home accidents, but fortunately these carry a comparatively low fatality rate, whereas old people suffer fewer accidents than would be imagined from the mortality figures, but many more of these prove fatal. This phenomenon becomes particularly evident if the mortality rate per 100,000 is calculated.

Figure 125 shows an example of this from the U.S.A.

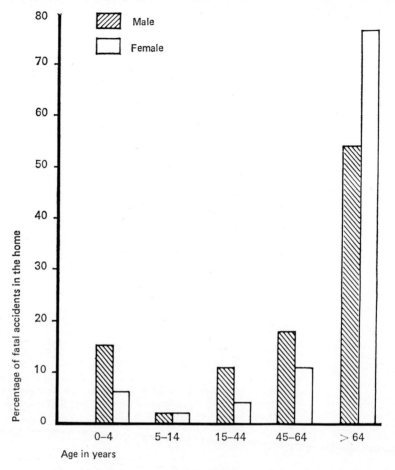

Figure 124   Distribution of fatal accidents in the home in England and Wales in 1960, according to age and sex   After (268)

Causes of accidents

The commonest kinds of accidents that arise in the home are:

— falls
— poisoning
— accidental choking
— burns, scalds, corrosive fluids
— drowning
— electric shock
— wounds
— accidents with explosives.

Table 123 summarises a few data from the World Health Organisation (269) on the distribution of accidents from different causes. It emerges from this that *falls are the commonest cause of fatalities, and account for about one half of all accidents.* Poisons and fire occupy second place, each of them making up about one fifth of the total.

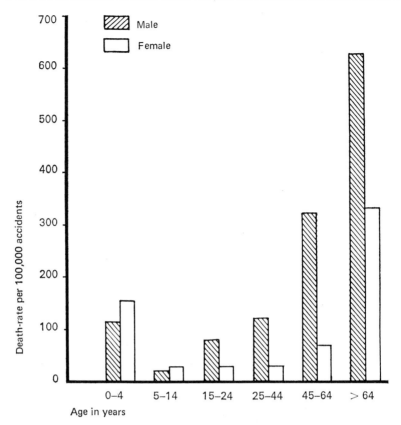

Figure 125   Death-rate from accidents in the home per 100,000 accidents
After Backett (265)

A common cause of death, which is not revealed in *Table 123* owing to lack of sufficient evidence, is choking, *whether caused by an external obstruction or by inhaling something swallowed. In the U.S.A. and England choking accounts for 11% and 7% of accidental deaths respectively.*
Statistics of causes of death at different ages can be summarised as follows:

Table 123   Analysis of the most important causes of fatal accidents in the home   Extracted from the statistics of the World Health Organisation (269)

Cause of accident	Sex	Analysis of deaths in percentages from each cause				
		USA	England	Holland	Canada	Finland
Falls	M	35.4	45.2	68.6	29.7	36.5
	F	51.3	61.9	82.4	49.2	72.1
Poisoning	M	8.5	25.1	17.7	10.9	27.0
	F	5.7	19.1	9.7	6.4	6.1
Fire	M	25.9	8.1	11.5	22.8	9.5
	F	26.6	10.1	4.8	20.9	9.2
Scalding	M	1.3	1.3	1.8	1.2	4.2
	F	1.3	0.9	2.8	1.8	1.5
Drowning	M	2.3	1.6	7.1	1.9	5.8
	F	1.7	0.8	2.1	1.3	2.7
Firearms	M	7.3	0.7	2.7	4.1	3.2
	F	1.9	0.1	2.1	0.9	0.8

- children less than a year old are most liable to death by choking
- children between the first and the fourth year most often die from burns
- men from 45–64 years old are chiefly killed by falls from a height, and both men and women over 65 from falls on the same level.

On the basis of surveys made by the Society 'Das sichere Haus' (266) in Bavaria, Hesse and Baden-Württemberg the following can be said to be characteristic of domestic accidents in Germany:

- falls are the main cause of accidental death, accounting for 77–88% of fatalities, falls on the same level mainly involving people over 60, whereas falls from a height play a larger part in accidental death of younger people, 20–60 years of age. Babies and infants are particularly at risk from choking in bed as a result of strangulation, and for somewhat older children burns take precedence.

Accidents to children

Habits of children

The first year of life is the most accident-prone, and practically all accidents at this age take place at home. The child has not yet acquired any powers of discrimination, it is unable to move without assistance, and hence is completely dependent on its mother or nurse, who must protect it from all hazards. When the child is 12–15 months old it begins to familiarise itself with its surroundings, wanting to touch everything within reach, and to put it in its mouth. Hence during this second year, during which the child develops the powers of walking and talking, it is particularly important that the child should have its own room in which it can pursue its physical and mental development free from danger. In the third year the child is in much better control of its movements, and begins to run around though a little clumsily at first. Curiosity leads it to investigate its surroundings, and the restlessness of that small child finds expression in copying other people. The child becomes steadily more active and more self-sufficient up to school-age; imitation is the motive force of all games in this age-group. The child now wants to be independent, and so easily gets itself into dangerous situations, the seriousness of which it does not yet appreciate, and from which it cannot extricate itself.

Asphyxiation of children

The commonest cause of death of babies in their first year is choking. This may happen in bed or in a cot if the pillows or bedclothes are too soft, when the baby's uncoordinated movements can end up with the bed clothes over its face. Babies at the nursling state are not yet able to get out of such a situation by themselves.

In recent years a new danger has appeared in the shape of plastic curtains and plastic accessories. As a result of static electricity such thin sheets can cover the face of a baby and choke it in a short time. Otherwise a piece of string or braid, or decorative cords on the bed with dangling toys, charm bracelets or teething rings can strangle the baby. A further cause of choking in this age-group is aspirating fragments of food.

Crying children often choke by sucking into the trachea small foreign objects such as marbles, small stones, nuts, sweets, buttons, lumps of sugar, rings, corks and so on (139). Many older children die from covering their heads with plastic bags lacking safety holes. An electric charge causes the bag to stick so closely to the head that mouth and nose are completely obstructed and the child is unable to release itself.

Many children are asphyxiated in refrigerators and deep-freeze cabinets, which they may enter experimentally or when playing hide-and-seek, and find that the door or lid cannot be opened from inside. Fortunately modern refrigerators and freezers are made only with magnetic catches, which can be opened from inside as well as outside. Models of obsolete design, many of which stand empty in cellars or store rooms, constitute a continuing danger, and their locks should be dismantled.

Falls in childhood

Falls cause nearly 40% of all accidents to children, but according to *Haggerty* (270) they result in only 5% of the deaths. They are still associated with relatively high fatality rates in babies, however, principally by falls from the nursing table. Whereas older children can put out an arm or a leg to break their fall, babies cannot do this. Their falls often cause head injuries, and these may be particularly serious because the bones of the skull are fragile for the first few months. The crawling stage is also a dangerous one for falls, because when infants begin to clamber about, their sense of distance has hardly developed.

Between the ages of 2 and 4, from the moment when children can stand up by themselves, there are more and more places where there is a risk of falling. Falls on a level become more frequent as the child jumps up and down, and there is a special risk of banging the head on a hard edge (radiator, table, chair).

Even more dangerous than falls on a level floor are those from a height. Children cannot fall out of the window if it is protected adequately by a grille. Falls from heights of more than a metre take place from bunks, while climbing on to cupboards and chests of drawers, and when jumping off window sills or beds on to the floor. Shortcomings of the building itself are occasionally the causes of falls, such for example as unsuitable spacing of rails on balconies or bannisters, which may be so far apart that they allow small children to fall through, or encourage children to climb on them.

Injuries to older children are often more serious than they are to 2–3 year olds. Fractures are more common. Moreover the location of the accident shifts: accidents to young children occur mostly at home, but among older children they occur mainly in the garden or the playground. Boys are more exposed to accidents than girls because they are more impulsive.

Burns and scalds

Burns and scalds constitute a serious risk of fatalities during childhood. In the U.S.A. they are given as the main cause of death between the ages of 1 and 14 years. In England 70% of accidents involving burns and scalds happen to children.

According to *Biener* (271) scalds mostly result from hot steam, from hot water from a tap lacking thermostatic control, from a leaking hot-water bottle in a baby's cot, from hot fluids or cooking-fat, and occasionally from laundry effluent.

Two year olds often pull at the tablecloth or grasp the handle of a hot-water jug and scald themselves in this way. Toddlers are especially prone to scald themselves with hot water or other liquids, and the highly developed curiosity and imitative habits of 3–5 year olds leads to many scalding accidents in the kitchen with pots and pans full of boiling liquids. According to *Backett* (265) and *McFarland* (272, 273) the number of fatal scalding accidents is particularly high among little girls.

Burns in childhood cause more than half of the total fatalities from burning clothing. Modern, synthetic fabrics are particularly dangerous in this context. The smallest spark is often enough to ignite such fibres. In England many accidents are caused by unprotected gas fires (*Colebrook* and his co-workers, 274). Such fires to clothing are rare in countries where central heating predominates, but open fires are a constant risk, especially if they have no fire guard.

It can be deduced from *Biener* (271) that children risk burns by:

- playing with matches.
- playing with burning cigarettes
- clumsiness with Christmas trees

- handling electric fires, which are particularly dangerous if the heating element is not fully enclosed
- playing near a fire with explosive liquids which are not in a secure container

A factor common to all burns and scalds is that they are not only extremely painful but – if not fatal – usually require nursing for 1–3 months.

Poisoning

Poisoning has increased in recent years among children and young people. In contrast with other forms of domestic accident, the incidence of poisoning rises with the standard of living, and is highest in childhood.

According to *Hauri* (275) and *Borbély* (276) this period of maximum risk starts at about the age of one year, when the infant becomes active, and ends between the fifth and sixth years before the child reaches school-age, with a peak between the second and third years.

Poisoning from decomposed food was comparatively common until recently, but nowadays, according to *Pasi* (277) the most common causes are:

– pharmaceutical products	41.9% of all cases
– household products (polishes, cosmetics, etc.)	26.6%
– insecticides	11.8%
– various chemical products, including garage and workshop chemicals	10.2%

Poisoning by so-called 'non-poisonous' substances, including many present in every household (cleaning fluids, disinfectants, pesticides, cosmetics, etc.) is a more serious risk to children than is generally realised. Among these, pesticides and cleaning fluids cause more frequent poisoning than any other. The most important pharmaceuticals are barbituric acid and its derivatives, aspirin, and other pain-killers. Cases of poisoning, including through tranquillisers, have increased in recent years.

Occasional cases of poisoning from licking or eating toxic paints may also be mentioned.

Dangerous habits of children

Many cases of poisoning are the direct result of childish curiosity. The two year old is at special risk because his instincts to grasp things and to drink are highly developed, and when exploring the surroundings he tends to put anything that he finds into his mouth. Children are imitative, and in an unguarded moment may take liquids or tablets just as they have seen grown-ups do. Often, too, they are lured by a sweet tooth, and are attracted by brightly coloured tablets and pills which may be coated with sugar or chocolate.

Adult carelessness

Adults too often forget that their immediate surroundings are also the outside world of a small child, who is both inexperienced and eager to learn. They carelessly leave dangerous substances lying about, instead of putting them out of reach of the children. As well as medicines, this applies just as much to household products and other toxic materials.

Detergents, for example, are often kept at the bottom of a cupboard, or on a low shelf, or even on the floor. There is no excuse for storing toxic fluids in bottles that have previously held beer or soft drinks, and it is useless to stick warning labels on these bottles because the children at risk are usually not old enough to read.

Drowning

Children are accidentally drowned, even in homes considered 'safe'. Small children are at risk in smooth-sided baths without a non-slip mat at the bottom, in water-butts, in paddling pools and outdoor swimming pools. The most vulnerable period is from 18 months to 3 years. Children of this age easily escape from the sight of their parents, and active little boys are particularly likely to get into trouble. They easily lose their balance and fall head-first, and find it difficult to get up again because of the weight of the head, and because their muscles are not yet coordinated. In these circumstances a very small depth of water (even 30 cm) may prove fatal.

Accidents with electricity	Children may receive an electric shock from playing with electric toys operating on a high voltage, or from poking knitting-needles, nails, paper-clips, wires, etc. into electric sockets. Electrical appliances can be dangerous if their safety devices are inadequate, or defective. It sometimes happens, too, that children bite into electric flex.
Cuts and bruises	The commonest cause of cuts in children is broken glass, from windows or door-panels, bottles, etc. Cuts caused by breaking a window have occasionally caused death by bleeding. Another frequent cause is knives, used as playthings, or occasionally, as a weapon. Other objects that can cause injury are household gadgets such as scissors and wire, or sharp metal or wooden edges.

Toys can also be dangerous if they have sharp edges or are easily broken, or form wooden splinters. Electrical toys using high voltages, and objects that are easily swallowed, or are made from flammable material have already been listed as dangerous to children, and the 3–6 year old age group is at greatest hazard from these.

Accidents to adults and old people

Falls

As *Table 123* has already made clear, falls are the most frequent cause of fatal accidents in the home. 80–90% of fatal falls involve old people, and $\frac{2}{3}$ of these cases are women over 65 years old. In this age-group deaths from falls outnumber those in traffic accidents.

Falls on a level surface may be caused by:

– slippery floors (unsuitable floor-covering, freshly waxed floors, wet patches, slippery glaze on bath or shower cabinet)
– carpet, rug or doormat slipping away
– irregularity in the surface (unexpected variation in height because of an isolated step or threshold, or the edge of the carpet turned up, or a projecting nail, or some object left lying about)
– inadequate lighting, or none at all
– unsuitable footwear
– illness or infirmity

Falls from a height are mostly caused by:

– the use of an unsuitable or defective object as a ladder (e.g., an unsafe chair, table, or window-sill).
– carelessness (stumbling on steps, or carrying an excessive load)
– badly built stairs (tread missing, stair too steep, risers unequal in height, slippery staircoverings, inadequate lighting)
– lack of maintenance (worn treads, threadbare staircarpet, burnt-out light bulbs not replaced)

Falls are particularly common in bedrooms, kitchens, bathrooms and on the stairs.

Burns and scalds

In Great Britain *Colebrook* (274, 278) investigated more than five thousand casualties in hospital because of burning accidents. It was apparent that half of the admissions to hospital and about 80% of the deaths were caused by some part of the clothing catching fire. *Colebrook* estimated a mortality of 25%. According to *Wheatley* (279) and various other authors the following factors often lead to domestic accidents from burns:

- open fires not protected and not kept under observation
- overloaded or defective electric switches
- use of petrol, benzene or other highly flammable liquid for household cleaning
- unguarded electrical equipment (overturning of electric fires; irons and toasters left switched on while standing on a surface that is not fireproof; electric blankets)
- careless storage of flammable materials (for example wood near the stove, flammable cleaning fluids near an open flame, etc.)
- smoking in bed or leaving lighted cigarettes lying about
- playing with matches
- fireworks

Burns not involving clothing can be caused by hotplates, heating-equipment, while cooking and baking with hot fat, or while soldering or welding in pursuit of a hobby.

Caustic acids and alkalis have the same effects as burns.

Scalds can arise from collisions in awkward passages in the home when carrying hot liquids; from spluttering of hot fat; from opening pressure-cookers too soon, or if the safety-valve is blocked; or from a hot-water tap if the thermostat has failed.

Poisons

Besides the common causes of poisoning that may affect children mentioned on page 296 *adults are often accidentally overcome by gas.* The fact that poisoning from the use of gas is primarily a liability of old people can in the main be attributed to two factors: for one thing old people become more forgetful (the gas is turned on and not lit, or not turned off after use), for another they begin to lose their sense of smell. The latter can mean that the presence of gas is first noticed when it has already reached a lethal concentration.

In the German Bundesrepublik it is about to be made obligatory for all gas-equipment to be made completely safe. Safety in equipment of this sort is ensured by built-in automatic lighting which prevents unused gas from escaping. Expert circles in Switzerland consider that built-in safety devices of this kind are superfluous, because in recent years Switzerland set up anti-gas-poisoning plants, by which gas free from carbon monoxide, that is, non-toxic natural gas, is supplied.

Nevertheless, if non-toxic gas is incompletely burnt, having insufficient oxygen, a secondary build-up of carbon monoxide can occur, and this may lead to cases of carbon monoxide poisoning. Moreover even non-poisonous gas has its dangers if it escapes unused into a room. This can happen, for example, if a gas-supply is interrupted and the flame goes out, or if a gas-tap is turned on by children playing, or by mistake. In such cases the gas can displace so much oxygen from the room that a person may be asphyxiated, or the mixture of gas and air may reach an explosive concentration. A number of such fatal accidents occur every year in Switzerland, even with natural gas. More details of these dangers can be obtained from the official publications (280). Bottled liquid gas, widely distributed in Europe, can be equally dangerous because it has only a slight smell, and so is often not noticed until too late. Liquid gas is not poisonous in itself, but it can mix with air to form an explosive mixture, which may be ignited by any naked flame. This gas, too, can cause asphyxiation by displacing all the oxygen in a room. In Europe liquid gas is responsible for an alarming increase in the number of fatal accidents with gas in caravans.

Carbon monoxide poisoning from stoves may also be considered in this context. In principle every incomplete combustion can produce CO. Not infrequently fatal accidents occur because stoves have been incorrectly installed, or carelessly operated, so that too little oxygen is admitted for complete combustion. Outside the home petrol engines are highly dangerous if they are allowed to run in a closed garage, and under these circumstances a

Accidents with electricity

lethal concentration of carbon monoxide can accumulate in a few minutes. 86% of the people injured by electricity belong to the 15–65 years age-group, and men – particularly do-it-yourself enthusiasts – are more often involved than women.

In the opinion of the World Health Organisation, the standard voltage of 220 V used in most European countries is unnecessarily and dangerously high. *Backett* (265), who was entrusted by W.H.O. with a study of domestic accidents from electricity, was in favour of a reduction of voltage in view of the sharp increase in the amount of domestic electrical equipment.

Even 60 volts can become dangerous if a person allows it to pass through part of his body and one of his limbs makes contact with earth. The human body becomes a good conductor of electricity if the resistance of the skin is reduced by moisture. If a person touches a wire, or any piece of equipment that is carrying a voltage, and has a good contact with earth (via a wet floor, or a water or gas-pipe, or from being in a full bath) the current flows through the body to earth and the person receives an electric shock. The effect of this shock can vary between a slight tingling feeling in the tips of the fingers to an intense muscular contraction which may make it impossible for the victim to let go which may impair the action of the heart and paralyse the respiratory centre in the brain.

The main cause of these accidents from electricity is undoubtedly lack of insulation. Defects in insulation may arise from use, alteration, wear and damage, and may allow the current to be diverted from the wire or the motor to the metallic parts of the apparatus. If the equipment is earthed, this current flows harmlessly to earth, but if not, then it may lead to electric shock.

It is obvious from what has been said that damp places such as bathrooms, kitchens, cellars and wash-houses present particular hazards.

In practice many fatalities occur in the bathroom, because the victim was using a defective hair-dryer, shaver, mains radio, or electric heater while sitting in a full bath, or standing bare-footed on the wet floor, or touching a water-pipe.

In the living room or bedroom, a defective lamp can be dangerous if, for example, the person touching it has his damp feet resting on a radiator at the time.

Explosions

The commonest risk of explosion in the home comes from leaky gas-pipes. Unburnt gas can escape if the flame goes out because the supply is interrupted, or if it is blown out by a draught or if the gas tap is opened by mistake. If the presence of gas is not noticed quickly an explosive mixture of gas and oxygen is created, which can be ignited by the smallest spark (for example, from a light-switch or the door-bell) and an explosion can occur.

Accidental explosions, often with fatal consequences, also happen from heaters using propane, butane, primagas or butagas. The danger from these is even greater than it is from natural gas, because they have so little smell.

Vapour from flammable cleaning liquids can also cause explosions. Since they are often heavier than air (e.g. benzene vapour), they can persist for a long time in a closed room and creep along until they reach a naked flame. All flammable liquids are dangerous in this respect. Even at room temperatures most of them are volatile, and mix with air to form a flammable or explosive mixture.

Aerosols can cause an explosion if they are shaken up repeatedly, regardless of whether the container is full or supposedly empty. The risk of explosion rises steeply if the surrounding temperature is much above 50 °C. These containers are highly explosive.

Guidelines for efficient safeguards against accidents in the home

The causes of accidents at home can be divided into three groups:

- human error
- defective equipment and accessories
- obstructions

Although many authors quote human error as the primary cause, it should not be forgotten that human error — whether it is physiological (fatigue, hunger, the influence of alcohol or drugs, etc.) or emotional (anger, worry, excitement, aggressiveness, carelessness, etc.) — is often associated with faulty design of equipment.

For this reason everything possible should be done, both technologically and architecturally, to reduce the risk of accidents in the home.

The recommendations of *Huser, Grandjean and Suchantke* (120) are recapitulated below in the form of aphorisms; some of them repeat what has been already said, and the reader is asked to excuse this.

Entrance to the house	— steps are better than slopes (but not isolated, single steps)
	— isolated steps should be clearly marked
	— if there are more than five steps there should be a bannister with a hand-rail
	— avoid anything that people may trip over
	— provide adequate headroom
	— protect open stair-wells, cellar-entrances, lighting-shafts etc. with a railing, or floor them over with safe materials
	— doormats and scrapers should be inset into the floor
	— the approach and entrance to house should be lit adequately
Stairs	— all steps in a flight of stairs should be of the same height
	— stairs without a vertical back wall are dangerous to children
	— stairs open on both sides should have secure bannisters on both sides
	— all stairs should have a hand-rail on both sides, especially if they have a turning, or if they lead down to the cellar or up to the loft
	— stairs behind a door need a landing at least 50 cm long
	— stairs behind a door should be clearly indicated by a distinctive notice
	— the stair covering should be non-slip and easy to clean
	— carpet-grips and edging-strips are recommended
	— bannisters: the maximum distance apart of the rails should not exceed 7 cm and there should be no projections that can be climbed
	— stairway lighting: minimum intensity 60 lux, and it should not cast confusing shadows
	— time-switches should be set so that they allow sufficient time for the old and infirm to get to the topmost storey without having to hurry
	— light-switches should be illuminated, either with luminous paint or a pilot-lamp

Further recommendations for the design of staircases are given in the next chapter.

Doors	— the arcs of swing of two doors should not overlap
	— swing-doors should allow one to see what is beyond
	— glass doors should be made from non-splinter safety-glass
	— glass doors should be made clearly visible (for example, by means of a conspicuous handle or knob, or by patches of colour or etching at eyelevel for both children and adults)
Windows	— casement windows should open inwards
	— if there is no balcony outside the window, then all the panes must be accessible for cleaning from inside the room
	— some way of securing the window when it is open is advisable
	— movable fanlights must be operated from below

	— windows which extend down to the floor must have a protective grille or mesh
	— as far as possible windows in children's room must be secure against being opened by children (for example by a window-catch that children cannot operate, or by only opening to a safe amount or by being protected by a narrow-mesh grille)
Floors	— the flooring material should be hard-wearing, heat-insulating, not slippery when wet, and electrically non-conducting
	— isolated steps and small differences of level should be avoided
	— it is better to adjust small differences by a gentle slope
	— threshold rising above floor-level should be avoided
Built-in cupboards	— edges and corners should be rounded off if possible and no sharp edges should project into the main passage-ways
	— hanging cupboards should have sliding doors if possible
	— there should be cupboards for poisonous household products and medicines which can be locked and made inaccessible to children
	— doors of larders and large cupboards should be provided with a handle inside as well as out
Built-in household equipment	— do not put the oven immediately beside the door or the window. A working-surface or somewhere to put things down is advisable on each side of the oven
	— an electric oven should have an indicator lamp
	— the oven door should have rounded corners and a transparent panel
	— big refrigerators should be capable of being opened from inside
	— washing-machines and spin-dryers should have a locking lid
Bathrooms and W.C.	— floorings should not become slippery when wet, and should be electrically non-conducting
	— bath and shower should have grip-handles at suitable places
	— the floors of bath and shower should be flat, and made non-slip either by having a ridged surface, or by the use of a rubber or plastic mat
	— *no electric sockets should be nearer than 80 cm to a bath or shower
	— a shaving point should be fitted close to the mirror over the washbasin and should be of the type approved for bathrooms
	— use only heaters that are permanently fixed
	— *use only electric sockets of the shuttered types in bathrooms. Normal 'open' sockets should only be used outside the bathroom, close to the door
	— mixer units for bath, shower and bidet should be thermostatically controlled
	— the door-catches of bathroom and lavatories should be of a type that can be opened from outside as well as inside
Lighting	— cellars, attics, anterooms and outside staircases should be adequately lighted
	— light switches should be near the entrance and level with the door-knob
	— passages should have two-way switches, operating from either end
Electrical installations	— electrical installations and equipment must satisfy the regulations as far as these are known. In every country these are laid down by specialists and should not be disregarded
	— each wall of a living room or workshop should have at least one multiple socket
	— the electric cooker, dishwasher, washing machine and refrigerator should each have a separate socket
	— on each landing of the stairway there should be a general purpose socket for vacuuming the stairs and for using power-tools
	— only shuttered sockets should be used in kitchens, bathrooms, cellars, sculleries and terraces, and they are also recommended for living rooms if there is central heating

*Illegal in Britain.

- for safety a ring-main is advisable in each living room and work-room. This should run 30 cm above floor level, and every 120–150 cm there should be a junction-box for future extensions, as well as spare sockets
- electric cables should always run either horizontally or vertically, and horizontal cables should be 30 cm above the floor or below the ceiling
- ring-mains in the kitchen can with advantage be laid at a height of 100–110 cm above the floor
- each room should have its own circuits for light and power, but corridor, bathroom and lavatory may have a common circuit
- separate cables should be provided for dishwasher, electric cooker, and washing machine, and extra circuits should be available
- the use of child-proof sockets is advised for households with children

Gas installations
- gas appliances, whether fixed or portable, should be installed only by a qualified fitter
- the official instructions must be observed
- gas cookers must have safety-ignition, to avoid risk of explosion or asphyxiation (even if 'non-toxic' gas is supplied)

Fire precautions
- the local fire regulations must be observed in the positioning and installation of the inlet, casing, and dimensions of the central heating flue
- a free-standing stove on a flammable floor must always stand on an underlay that is fireproof and adequately heat-insulating
- a fireplace in the living room should always have a movable fire guard
- there should be a fireproof underlay 40–60 cm wide in front of the fire place
- any heating in the garage should avoid the risk of an explosion from petrol vapour
- it is recommended that every house or flat should have a fire-extinguisher, kept in an easily accessible place

Openings in floors and walls
- any openings in floors (trap-doors, stair-heads, chutes etc.) should be secured aganst any person or any object falling into them (for example by railings combined with a threshold)
- the guard round a trap-door in the floor should not give children any chance to climb it or fall through
- drains and garbage-chutes, water-butts and the like should be securely covered
- old wells should be concreted over
- covers for all places that are dangerous to children should be fastened in such a way that children under 15 cannot unfasten them

Balconies
- it is advisable to have a small balcony in front of the kitchen where all dangerous cleaning materials and polishes can be kept
- every lock on a balcony door or window should also be operable from outside
- the balustrade shall be so constructed that children can neither slip through it (maximum vertical separation of rails 6–7 cm) nor climb over it. If possible one place should be provided where a child can see through the balustrade
- the height of the balustrade must be at least 100 cm, and secured against small children falling through by a wire-mesh up to a height of 2 metres
- a shuttered electric socket on the balcony may be useful

11 Flats for Old or Handicapped People

Summary

About 11% of the total population is aged 65 or more. In Switzerland it is estimated that there are 10,000–15,000 cripples, who are either confined to a wheel-chair, or can walk only with the aid of crutches, or a stick, or an artificial leg. In other countries it has been estimated that 4–6% of the populace is handicapped.

Old age is characterised by curtailment of mobility, reduced ability to react, and diminished mental ability. A consequence of these is a varying amount of arthritis (the typical effect of age on the limbs) and also, unfortunately, occasional changes on the psychological plane, with a tendency to depression, a common result of loneliness.

The reach of elderly people shrinks to a height of 40–160 cm above floor level, and the height at which things can be grasped by a person in a wheel-chair lies between 40–125 cm.

The following accommodation is particularly important for old people:

- space within the flat should be generous, because old people spend a great part of their time indoors, which has become their 'world' (20–24 square metres for a bed-sitting-room and 16–20 square metres for the living room of a two-roomed flat)
- kitchen shelves should have as much adjustment as possible in the range 30–160 cm above the floor
- all controls (switches, knobs, handles) should be made clearly visible, with automatic cut-outs for anything such as a gas-cooker or an electric hotplate, which could be dangerous to life
- a communal garbage-chute should be available
- doors should have neither a threshold nor a step
- floorings must be non-slip and warm to the feet
- window-sills must be low (at most 90 cm, preferably 60 cm)
- the bathroom should have an area of at least 4 square metres, if possible 6 square metres; taps with handles; a bathroom stool; an efficient non-slip mat in the bath; vertical and horizontal hand-grips on the bath; edge of the bath 50 cm from floor.

Many cripples can live a full life so long as they can get in and out of the flat in their wheelchair, but steps, or other obstacles can be very restricting to them. Hence a flat for a person in a wheelchair must be designed as follows:

- the entrance to the flat, and the passage to the entrance on the ground-floor or to the lift must be without steps. If need be ramps may be provided, with a slope of 5° (maximum 6°)
- a garage with a minimum breadth of 330 cm or at least a parking-place of the same size will provide for the cripple to get in and out of his motorised invalid-carriage
- the minimum parking space for wheelchairs is 135×135 cm
- minimum dimensions for a lift = 100×110 cm; preferably 135×135 cm
- breadth of all doors, including that to lift: 90 cm
- all doors to be free from thresholds or steps
- clearance height underneath a table 76 cm, under a working surface 78 cm
- working surfaces in the kitchen not to be higher than 120 cm, not lower than 40 cm
- a parking-place for the wheelchair should be provided in the W.C., close to the lavatory-pan (which should be 55 cm high): it should be 90 cm broad and be provided with hand-grips

- in the bathroom a bath with a low place for case of access, and some-where to sit on the edge close to the head-end, as well as several hand-grips
- the doors of bathroom and W.C. should open outwards, and should be unlockable both from inside and out

In the same way, all the obvious buildings — concert-halls, theatres, cinemas, museums, shopping-centres and waiting-rooms should be made accessible for wheel-chairs.

Statistical evidence

Superannuation

Table 124 shows the increase in the average expectation of life in Switzerland between 1881 and 1963 (283).

This rise is accentuated by the fact that the death-rate among children fell sharply around the turn of the century, and as a result there is a higher proportion of older people alive at present. This shift in the population is often referred to as 'superannuation'. *Table 125* gives the fraction of the population aged 60 or more as a percentage of the under 20-years, and shows that this fraction has doubled in the last 40 years.

Age distribution today and tomorrow

Table 126 sets out the age composition of the general population in Switzerland, and shows that about 11% of people are in the pensionable age-group at the present time.

Table 124   Increase in average expectation of life in Switzerland from 1881–1963   After (283)

	Expectation of life in years at various periods					Increase
	1881– 1888	1920– 1921	1933– 1937	1948– 1953	1958– 1963	1881– 1963
Men						
– at birth	43.3	54.5	60.7	66.4	68.7	25.4
– in 40th year	65.1	67.5	69.4	71.9	72.8	7.7
Women						
– at birth	45.7	57.7	64.6	70.8	74.1	28.4
– in 40th year	66.7	69.7	72.2	75.0	77.0	10.3

Table 125   Increase in number of persons over 60 years old, compared with those under 20, between the years 1910 and 1960

Year	Over sixties as a percentage of under twenties
1910	21.8
1920	24.5
1930	32.1
1940	43.6
1950	46.0
1960	48.2

Table 126   Distribution of the most important age groups in Switzerland (including foreigners) on 1st January 1967   (After 283)

Age group	Years	Percentage of total population
Infants	0–4	8.4
School-children, inc. kindergarten	5–14	15.0
Later schooldays	15–19	7.9
Adults	20–64	57.7
Pensionable years	65+	11.0

The active section of
the populace

The fraction aged 20–65, which constitutes about 58% of the population, is
not identical with the working population, since students and some women
are not gainfully employed. The O.E.C.E. (294) published brief but interesting
statistics about the earning quotient (the number of people gainfully employed as a fraction of the whole population). According to this report the
earning quotient amounted to:

– Northern Europe (Scandinavian countries)	45%
– France	40%
– Holland	35%
– Belgium	38%
– West German Republic	43%
– Switzerland	44%
– Italy	35%
– Spain	37%
– Europe as a whole	40%

The same report gives details of the increase in total population and in active
population between 1958 and 1969. If the 1958 value is taken as 100, then
1969 values amount to:

	Total population	Active population
– Northern Europe	108	111
– France	112	106
– Holland	115	115
– Belgium	107	106
– West German Republic	112	104
– Switzerland	120	114
– Italy	109	93
– Spain	111	105
– Europe as a whole	112	105

The sharp increase in total population in Switzerland is principally attributable
to the influx of foreign workers, but why the active population has not increased correspondingly is not apparent without further information. In any
case the increase in the over 65s during this period is directly linked with the
unequal rise in the two groups (total population and working population).
It may be further mentioned here that the occupations in which the working
population are engaged have changed in various ways. Taking the 1958
numbers as 100, the 1969 numbers have changed as follows:

	Agriculture	Industry	Service occupations
– Northern Europe	65	113	136
– West German Republic	64	107	117
– France	68	110	126
– Italy	58	114	111
– Switzerland	67	121	121
– Europe as a whole	82	120	123

Table 127 sets out the anticipated change in the age distribution from 1967–
87, as given by the Statistischen Amt of Switzerland. According to this the
'superannuation' of the population is not expected to proceed very much
further in the next 10–15 years: however, this is only a prognosis, extrapolated from the present-day situation.

More women, more
people living alone

Two changes affect the over 60s: the relative increase in the number of
women, and in the number of people living alone. *Table 128* gives details of
the relative increase in the number of women, showing that there are 10
women to 8 men between the ages of 60 and 70, and 10 women to 7 men
between 70 and 80.

Table 127   Estimated distribution of population by age groups now, and up to 1987   Includes Swiss citizens and those foreigners who are settled here. After (283)

Age group	Starting population on 1 January 1967 %	Predicted populations 1 January 1977 %	1 January 1987 %
0–14	23.3	24.6	24.2
15–19	8.0	7.1	7.8
20–64	57.7	56.0	55.8
65+	11.0	12.3	12.2
Total population	5,953,100	6,436,700	6,846,500

Table 128   Sex-ratio among old people over 60 including foreigners, in Switzerland on 1 January 1967   After (283)

Age group	Proportion of total population Women %	Men %	Both %
60–64	27	23	50
65–69	24	18	42
70–74	18	13	31
75–79	12	8	20
80+	11	6	17

According to an estimate made by *Schmidt-Relenberg* (286), more than half of all old people live alone.

Handicapped people

Handicapped people are those who are seriously restricted in their physical activities as a consequence of illness or accident. According to *Blohmke* (284) they may be classified as follows:

- those who are permanently dependent on a hand-operated invalid chair
- those who must always use an artificial leg, brace, crutches or stick
- those who are partially or completely blind
- those who are partially or completely deaf
- those with brain or nerve injuries
- those who are handicapped merely by old age

Blohmke (284) reported that in West Germany in 1961 3.2 million people, or about 6% of the population were physically handicapped, and that these made up of 2.6 million men and only 650,000 women. Nearly one household in six had one person physically handicapped. In Switzerland there were estimated to be 10,000–15,000 handicapped people who used a wheel-chair or other aid to walking.

Physiology, psychology and pathology: changes with age

Loss of faculties

Age is characterised by the following changes:

- reduced elasticity in almost all tissues of the body, which leads, among other things, to an increasing restriction of movement in the legs
- reduced ability of the brain to react to situations, slowing-down of all the directive functions, and loss of alertness
- reduction in mental activity, which shows itself mainly in loss of memory and reduced awareness of what is going on

These normal effects of age are accomplished with varying frequency and to a varying extent by characteristic illnesses and infirmities.

Infirmities of old age
In the forefront of these stand the rheumatic disorders that are associated with the wearing out of the skeletal mechanisms: arthritic symptoms (chronic progressive degenerative ailments of the joints) in the hands and feet, cut down strength and dexterity in all kinds of manual activities; arthritis of the spine restricts movement of the back; arthritis in the joints of hips and knees becomes all too easily a very serious handicap when walking.

For these reasons many old people are also numbered among the bodily handicapped, and this justifies us in dealing with the problems of old people and cripples in the same chapter.

Mental difficulties
Age also bring pathological changes on the mental level. Not infrequently depression sets in, commonly aggravated, if not caused, by loneliness. The lives of old people are commonly made more difficult by problems of mental adjustment, by obstinacy, and by emotional disturbances.

Schmidt-Relenberg (286) is of the opinion that old people often suffer a 'defunctionalisation and disintegration' which is associated with retirement from their occupation and the death of the marriage partner. This means in other words that it is difficult for old people to retain a sense of purpose in their lives, and this leads to a general decline in their mental powers.

A healthy old age
The preceding discussion might give one the impression that old age is a very sad time in life, but this would certainly be an unjustified generalisation. In reality many old people enjoy the last period of their lives and see a purpose in their old age. Intelligence, combined with the ability to learn from past experience, lead to that mixture of qualities that is known in short as wisdom. Wisdom, the power to weigh things up sensibly, or what is called serenity (a clear, detached attitude) are qualities which from time immemorial have been attributed to the old. This is borne out by the work of Michelangelo, Titian, Goethe, Sherrington, Sigmund Freud and many others who still remained creative in their old age.

Space needs of old people

Bodily measurements
The Swedish Institute for Building Research (287), and *Ward and Kirk* in England (288), determined the bodily measurements of representative groups of old people. *Table 129* compiles a few measurements of old women, according to the specifications laid down by the British Standards Institution (289), which are heavily dependent on the surveys carried out by *Ward and Kirk* (288).

Table 129   Bodily measurements of old women   After the British Standards Institution (289)

Measurement	Average	95% confidence zone	
		big women	small women
	(cm)	(cm)	(cm)
Height of eyes, standing	145	157	133
Elbow height, standing	97	105	88
Height of eyes above seat, sitting	69	75	61
Heel-knee hollow (seat height)	41	46	37
Elbow height above seat, sitting	21	27	15
Shoulder height above seat, sitting	54	60	48
Sacrum – fore edge of knee, sitting	57	63	51
Sacrum – knee hollow, sitting	47	53	41

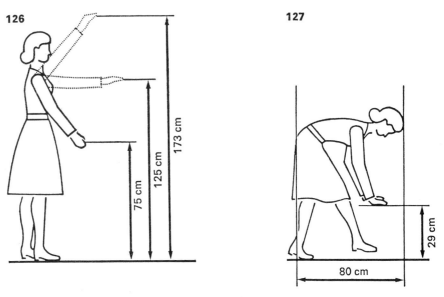

Figure 126   Average heights that an older woman can reach when standing
After the British Standards Institution (289)

Figure 127   Average amount of space that an older woman needs for movement when stooping.   After the British Standards Institution (289)

If these figures are compared with those of a normal population, it will be seen that on average the measurements of the old women are shorter by the following amounts:

standing height	−6 cm
elbow height when standing	−3 cm
eye-level when seated	−4 cm
elbow-height over surface of seat	−1 cm
heel to hollow of the knee	−2 cm

Elbow-room

The corresponding differences for old men are of the same order of size. Since elbow-room for women is primarily that needed for doing housework, this alone will be taken into account in the following discussion.
Figures 126 and 127 illustrate graphically the average elbow-room needed by old women, to conform with the *British Standards Institution.*

Dimensions of fitments in flats for old people

In discussing the dimensions of fitments we must usually start, not from the average but from what is needed by either small or large persons. *Table 130* contains a few suggestions for the dimensions of fitments, using those recommendations in the literature that are suited to the bodily-measurements of Continental Europeans.
Comparison of these proposals with the recommendations for normal people shows that working heights while standing up, and the top shelves

Table 130   Proposals for the dimensions of fittings in flats for old people
The literature cited also allows for values close to those proposed here.

Fittings	Measurement (cm)	Literature
Working heights for standing in kitchen		
– working surfaces	80–85	(289), (290)
– sink (upper edge)	80–85	(289), (290)
– cooker	80–85	(289), (290)
Working heights for seated jobs	65–70	(289), (290)
Highest kitchen shelf, without undercupboard	160	(290)
Highest kitchen shelf, with undercupboard	140	(289), (290)
Lowest kitchen shelf	30	(287), (289), (290)
Upper margin of bath	50	(287), (290)
Upper margin of WC	45	(290)
Height of washbasin from floor	85	(287), (290)

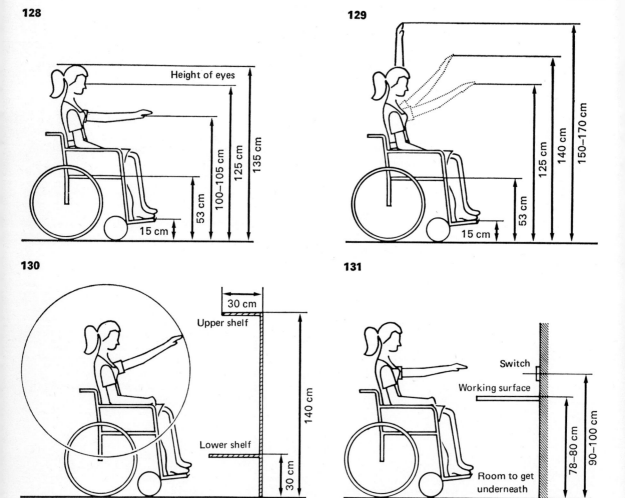

128

Height of eyes

135 cm
125 cm
100–105 cm
53 cm
15 cm

129

150–170 cm
140 cm
125 cm
53 cm
15 cm

130

30 cm
Upper shelf
140 cm
Lower shelf
30 cm

131

Switch
Working surface
Room to get underneath
78–80 cm
90–100 cm

Figure 128   Bodily dimensions when sitting in a wheelchair   From data given by the Schweizerischen Invalidenverbandes (291)

Figure 129   Space needed when sitting in a wheelchair

Figure 130   Length of reach when sitting in a wheelchair   From data given by the Schweizerischen Invalidenverbandes (291). If it is necessary to reach right to the back of the shelves, then they must lie between 40 and 130 cm from the ground (292)

Figure 131   Suitable heights for handles, switches, plugs and work-surfaces

in the kitchen need to be from 5–25 cm lower for old people. The rest of the proposals, however, are only slightly below the measurements that were put forward as being desirable in the relevant chapters.

Dimensions of fitments for physically handicapped people

Room for the wheel-chair

Whereas handicapped people who use crutches, sticks or other aids need fitments as provided for old people, the needs of anyone using a wheel-chair are quite different.
Figures 128, 129, 130 and *131* illustrate graphically the specifications of the Schweizerischen Invalidenverbandes (291) for operating space and a few dimensions of fitments needed by the user of a wheelchair. Closely similar proposals had already been worked out in 1959 by *Leschly and Exner* (292) in Denmark.

Operating space for a wheelchair

Figure 132 gives particulars of the space needed for the usual types of wheelchair.

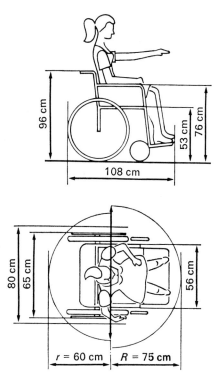

Figure 132   Dimensions of, and space required by, the usual types of wheelchair   From data given by the Schweizerischen Zentralstelle für Baurationalisierung (285)

Wheelchairs have a width of 65 cm and a length of 110 cm, and so they need the following room to operate:

— width of doorways	90 cm
— room to turn the wheelchair round	135×135 cm
— lift: minimum dimensions	100×110 cm
— lift: desirable size	135×135 cm
— lift: width of lift doorway	90 cm
— passage: minimum width	100 cm
— passage: desirable width (possible to turn round)	135 cm

Flats for old people

Requirements

Out of a comprehensive literature on the needs of old people we may start by drawing attention to an English survey made in 1962 by *Haynes and Raven* (295), of 67 flats for old people. These results are not essentially different from those of similar surveys in other countries, and so they can be taken to indicate the general trend.

Mobility

The group of people studied comprised 95 persons, 39 of whom lived alone. The following figures give details of their mobility:

— could go out without difficulty	53%
— could go out with a certain amount of difficulty	39%
— could go out only with help	8%

Loneliness

Those who lived alone often felt lonely. Of the whole group, *32% expressed the view, directly or indirectly, that living alone led to isolation and loneliness.* The relevant data are assembled in *Table 131*.

Activities

On average, the people questioned rose at about 8 a.m. and went to bed about 11 p.m., and in between these times their main occupations, besides housework, were knitting, needlework, reading and watching television. About half of the households questioned prepared two cooked meals a day, and the other half only one. Very often the reason given for only one cooked meal a day was shortage of money.

Cleaning was mostly done in the mornings. The majority of people did their housework without help, even those who were seriously handicapped.

The 67 people concerned were chosen by the investigators as follows:

— no affliction of any significance	35 persons
— slightly handicapped physically	18 persons
— badly handicapped physically	14 persons

Contentment

Visits by relatives and friends are of decisive importance in the level of contentment attained. Thus statistics show that a person who suffers from loneliness is also more than likely to be one who has few visitors, or none at all.

Table 131   Loneliness in old people's homes   95 persons between 60 and more than 80 years old. After Haynes and Raven (295)

	Number of persons	Percentage suffering loneliness	Percentage giving no sign of loneliness
Living alone	39	54	46
Household of two persons	56	16	84

When planning flats or homes for the aged it should be taken into account how far away they will be for the visits of relatives, friends or previous neighbours.

It appeared from conversation that a block of flats with some flats for old people has a certain need for a common room in which they can make social contacts. On the other hand, the authors noticed that such common rooms were often not used. A careful study of this question would therefore seem to be needed.

Other factors of great importance in making old people feel contented include the independence of the household and one's own independence in one's flat. Nearly all those questioned wanted to go on living in an old person's flat as long as possible. The authors pointed out that the length of stay in an old person's flat depended on the availability of certain services, such as laundry, household help, or the provision of adequate meals.

Schmidt-Relenberg (286) summarised the current state of sociological knowledge of the needs of old people by giving his opinion that *independence was the most important requirement for contentment in old people. This meant above all a home of their own, and to be able to look after themselves.* Furthermore, independence meant retaining familiar surroundings, that is not only social environment, but also the family house and familiar furniture.

Various ways of housing the old

A distinction can be drawn between flats for the old, settlements for the old and old people's homes: there are the following variations:

— apartments for old people as a self-contained flat in the family home, in private houses or in large blocks of flats
— flats for old people in housing estates, either in different multi-family houses or collected together into a multi-apartment house for old people
— old people's communities with flats and a central nursing-aid centre
— old people's homes for those who need care and attention

The last are provided for old people who because of their infirmities can no longer run their own household. It is estimated that about 10% of people over 65 need to go either into an old people's home or into hospital. The Eidgenössische Forschungskommission Wohnungsbau (290) sees certain advantages in the combination of old people's homes and old people's communities, of which the following may be mentioned:

— when tenants living in the community need nursing attention this can be supplied from the old-people's home
— a series of communal rooms for social contacts and entertainment, as well as bathrooms, wash-houses etc. can be used jointly by both institutions
— the step from a home of one's own to living in the old people's home is made easier

Ergonomic recommendations for flats for old people, including the handicapped with their appliances.

Old people often have infirmities that interfere with walking and other forms of bodily activity, and are comparable with that section of the populace that needs to use sticks or other walking aids. It will also be appreciated that the recommendations given apply to one- or two-roomed flats, either scattered about in normal blocks of rented flats, or gathered together in a separate community for old people.

Areas of flats

All experts on flats for old people recommend a liberal approach, and give preference to two-roomed flats, because old people spend much more time

Table 132   Recommended living space for old people's homes

Room	Living space in square metres	
	Desirable	Minimal
In 1-roomed flats		
– Living room cum bedroom (bedsitter)	24	20
– Bathroom/WC	6	4
– Kitchen	10	6
In 2-roomed flats		
– Living-room	20	16
– Bedroom	16	14
– Bathroom	6	4
– WC	3	2
– Kitchen	10	6

at home than those who are still working. Hence particularly generous living-space should be planned for them, and the recommendations summarised in *Table 132* are devised with this in mind.

Kitchens

As has already been explained on page 311, and in *Table 130*, the first requirement in the kitchen is that the height of shelves should be suitable for old people, being not less than 30 cm, nor more than 160 cm in height. *Furthermore, the shelves in all cupboards – upper, lower and full-length – should have the maximum possible adjustment. It is even more important for old people than for the young that the shelves can be adjusted to suit the individual's height and reach.*

It is less important for the sink, working-surface and cooker to be at the ideal height of 80 cm, and a compromise between this and the height recommended for normal kitchens (90 cm) is acceptable : i.e. 85 cm.

Control-knobs on cookers and other fixed appliances should be clearly marked and simple to operate, and should indicate clearly whether the appliance is turned on or not. Automatic cut-outs are strongly recommended, as old people may easily forget to switch the appliance off.

It is important for old people's flats to have a communal rubbish-chute, and each flat should have its disposal-slot, easy to get to and 50–60 cm above floor-level.

Living-rooms and bedrooms

No special fitments are needed in the living room or the bedroom. Electric switches should be simple tumbler-switches, easy to operate, and it should be possible to switch lights on and off from two, or even three points. This avoids the need to walk about in the dark.

Old people like to spend a lot of time at the window, watching what is happening in the street outside, so that the window-sill needs to be comparatively low.

Floorings

The recommendation given in Chapter 9 is particularly important where old people are concerned : *floorings that are as warm to the feet, and as non-slip as possible are essential.* Carpets must invariably be nailed to the floor.

Thresholds

Thresholds are likely to trip people up, and make it difficult for handicapped people to walk about. Flush door-closures are indicated, and passage from one room to another should be eased by the gentlest possible slope.

Store-rooms and balconies

According to the Eidgenössische Forschungskommission Wohnungsbau (290), both one-room and two-room flats for old people should be provided with two wall-cupboards, each with 3 square metres of storage-space, a balcony of 130×140 cm, and a store-room of 1.5–2 square metres, as well as a cellar.

Bathroom and W.C.

In one-roomed flats the bath and W.C. may be installed in the same room, but a separate W.C. is desirable in two-roomed flats. The controls must call for a minimum of effort, and lever-type taps are a good feature. Here too, as in the kitchen, the hot and cold taps should be clearly marked in contrasting colours. Besides the wash-basin and bath, the bathroom should have somewhere to sit while dressing and undressing; hence the need for a relatively large floor area (*Table 132*).

Bath

The bath is a common 'hazard', with the risk of heavy falls, and for this reason the recommendations made on page 301 must be observed closely. *Special emphasis must be laid on the need for a flat bottom, with an effective anti-slip device (either a ridged bottom or a non-slip mat of rubber or plastic).* The kind of hand-grips shown in *Figure 133* are recommended, both as a safeguard against falls, and to make it easier to get in and out, sit up, and so on.

Thiberg (287, 296) reported on experiments with a group of old people, to find out the best height for the side of the bath. He showed that a majority of people with restricted movement preferred a height of 50 cm, whereas only one quarter of them wanted it to be as low as 40 cm.

Hence the recommended height of baths in flats, both for old people and for handicapped persons, is 50 cm.

According to recommendations (290) the bath should be 150 cm long and 60–70 cm wide. These dimensions are less than those for young adults.

Wash-basin

Swedish research showed that old people expressed preference for *a wash-basin 85 cm high*, and this agrees to a certain extent with the recommendation of the Eidgenössische Forschungskommission Wohnungsbau (290). This is the same height that is common practice for washbasins for young people (85–90 cm).

Showers

Showers are not much used by old people at the present time, but it is quite conceivable that the next generation will be 'shower-conscious', and this will greatly ease the problem of taking a bath and of avoiding falls. It is recommended that a shower should have a (tiled) bench to sit on, and a hand-grip on the wall, and should be thermostatically controlled so that the temperature does not exceed 39 °C. A convenient size is 90×120 cm.

W.C.

The Eidgenössische Forschungskommission Wohnungsbau (290) recommend the dimensions and arrangements shown in *Figure 134*. Special consideration should be given to the hand-grips on both sides, and to the height of the seat, which are more important for old than for young adults.

Doors

Doors of the bathroom and W.C. should open outwards, and it should be possible to open the catch from outside in case of emergency.

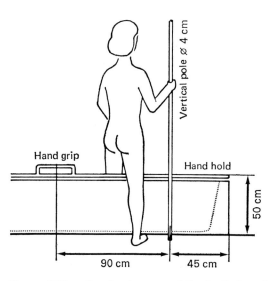

Figure 133   Hand grips round the bath for old or handicapped people   After (290)

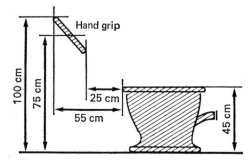

Hand grip

100 cm
75 cm
25 cm
55 cm
45 cm

Figure 134   Recommendations for the dimensions of the WC for old and handicapped people

Flats for handicapped people in wheelchairs

Architectural
obstacles

Nüscheler (297), *Oppikofer* (298), *Droin* (299) and many others point out with reason that many handicapped people could still follow a trade, take part in social activities, and generally go on as before, *if only their flat and its approaches were accessible by wheelchair.* Steps in front of the building, steps up to the lift, narrow lift-doors, and other built-in obstacles of this kind are 'life-shrinkers' to the handicapped. Both in Switzerland and abroad, authoritative norms or recommendations have been established for the design and construction of flats for handicapped people. The relevant literature differs only in unimportant details. The recommendations given below are based on the norms of the Schweizerische Zentralstelle für Baurationalisierung (285) ; on Danish guidelines (292, 293) ; on the Swiss authors quoted

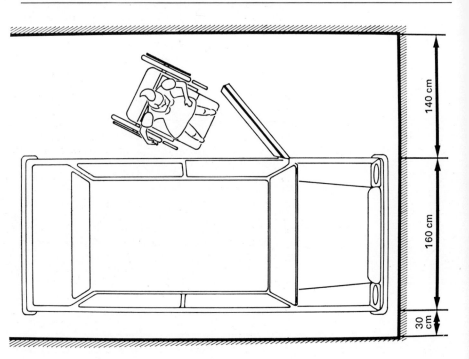

140 cm
160 cm
30 cm

Figure 135   Minimum size of garage for those who use an invalid-chair to get to the car   After (285)

above (291, 297, 298); and on information about Dutch recommendations (300, 301).

Entrances to buildings Entrances must be negotiable without steps, using ramps with a slope of 5° (or 6° at the most), and the kerb in front of the entrance must be replaced with a slope.

When it is not possible to house handicapped people on the ground-floor, a lift capable of accommodating a wheelchair is essential (see page 314).

Garage Since crippled people can now have a motorised invalid carriage, it is only fair that suitable garages should be provided. Such garages must have a width of at least 330 cm – if possible, 380 cm – and an electrically controlled door. From here to the flat itself there must be a covered passage-way without steps. *Figure 135* illustrates a ground-plan for a garage for the driver of a motorised invalid carriage.

Inside the flat All doors and passage-ways inside the flat must be wide enough for the wheelchair, and the dimensions must be as given on page 314. Obviously the doors should not have thresholds.

The window-sills must be so low that it is possible to see the street outside while still sitting in the wheelchair; they must not be higher than 90 cm, and preferably no more than 60 cm.

Working-surfaces For the wheelchair operator to get his knees under the table there must be a clear distance of 76 cm between the floor and the lowest edge of the underside of the table. If the table is used for working it is desirable that the arms of the wheelchair should fit underneath it, and so a clearance of 78 cm is necessary.

All controls (window-catches, door-handles, light-switches) should be at a height of 90–100 cm from the floor (see *Figure 131*).

Kitchen If a person using a wheelchair needs to work in the kitchen, then the following arrangements are necessary:
- plenty of room for knees beneath the three work-centres, hence a clearance of 76 cm
- in place of a big cooker, a small table-cooker
- the oven should stand close to the table-cooker
- the depth of the work-table should not exceed 45 cm
- the grasping reach on a wall above the work-table is of 30 cm
- a minimal space of 150 cm is to be kept free in front of the work-table

W.C. The arrangement of the lavatory is particularly difficult. A separate W.C. for a person in a wheelchair requires an area at least 150 cm wide and 210 cm long. The height of the lavatory-seat should be matched to the height of the wheelchair, 55 cm would be suitable. There must be a space 90 cm wide beside the lavatory seat for the wheelchair to stand, and a horizontal hand-rail fixed on the wall on each side of the lavatory-pan, 76 cm from the floor. Other forms of support can be provided according to circumstances, for example rings hanging down from the ceiling.

The required fitments for a lavatory include a wash-basin at a height of 80–85 cm from the floor.

Bathroom All authors recommend a bath specially designed for ease of access, with a fixed or folding seat attached to the head end. Two long, horizontal hand-grips should be fixed to the wall, one above the other, 75 and 90 cm above the floor, respectively. Here, too, grip-rings suspended from the ceiling may be necessary.

All along the free edge of the bath there should be a rim or handrail that is easy to grasp. In plan the bath should measure 150 × 60 cm and the recommended height is 50–60 cm. The recommendations of the Schweizerische Zentralstelle für Baurationalisierung (285) are illustrated in *Figure 136*.

Several authors recommend a hand-operated spray in the bath, but a crippled person may perform his toilet more easily in a shower cabinet than in a bath.

Doors and overall size Here, as in flats for old people, the doors of bathrooms and lavatories should open outwards and be capable of being unlocked from outside as well as from inside.

Outside the flat

A bathroom for wheelchair users should have an area of at least 200×260 cm. The foregoing sections have dealt only with requirements inside flats for elderly and handicapped people, but it is equally necessary for many other buildings to be designed to suit them. Thus, for example, the entrances of such obvious places as churches, hospitals, post-offices, and administrative buildings should be provided with ramps for wheelchairs, and the same is desirable for theatres, concert-halls, cinemas, museums, shopping-centres and many transport terminals.

It was certainly very praiseworthy that on 12th November, 1970 the Swiss Eidgenössische Department des Innern published a list of the measures to provide for the needs of handicapped people that must be taken in all buildings erected or subsidised by the state.

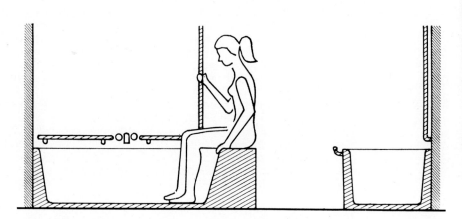

Figure 136   Recommendations for the design and installation of the bath for wheelchair users   From data supplied by the Schweizerische Zentralstelle für Baurationalisierung (285). In addition to the fitments shown there might also be a second horizontal pole for grasping, 90 cm high, a folding seat over the head-end of the bath, and grip-rings hanging from the ceiling

References
and Index

1 *Hettinger Th.:* Die Muskelkraft bei Frauen und Männern. Zbl. Arb. Wiss. *14,* 79–84, 1960.
2 *Grandjean E.:* Physiologische Arbeitsgestaltung. Leitfaden der Ergonomie. 2. Auflage. Thun/München; H. Ott 1967.
3 *Murrell K. F. H.:* Ergonomics; man in his working environment. London: Chapman & Hall 1965.
4 *Human Engineering Guide to Equipment Design.* Edited by C. T. Morgan, J. S. Cook, A. Chapanis and M. W. Lund. New York: McGraw Hill 1963.
5 *Rohmert W.:* Maximalkräfte von Männern im Bewegungsraum der Arme und Beine. Forschungsbericht des Landes Nordrhein-Westfalen Nr. 1616. Köln/Opladen: Westdeutscher Verlag 1966.
6 *Scherrer J.:* Physiologie du travail (Ergonomie). Paris: Masson 1967.
7 *Monod H.:* Contributions à l'étude du travail statique. Thèse, Faculté de Médecine, Université de Paris 1956.
8 *Rohmert W.:* Statische Haltearbeit des Menschen. Sonderheft der REFA-Nachrichten. Berlin: Beuth-Vertrieb 1960.
9 *Lehmann G.:* Praktische Arbeitsphysiologie. 2. Auflage. Stuttgart: Thieme 1962.
10 *Müller E. A.* und *Spitzer H :* Arbeit recht verstanden. München: Oldenbourg 1952.
11 *Müller E. A.:* Die physische Ermüdung. In: Handbuch der gesamten Arbeitsmedizin, Band 1, 405–441. Berlin: Urban & Schwarzenberg 1961.
12 *Karrasch K.* und *Müller E A.:* Das Verhalten der Pulsfrequenz in der Erholungsperiode nach körperlicher Arbeit. Arbeitsphysiologie *14,* 369–382, 1951.
13 *Åstrand I:* Kartläggning av husmodersarbete i hemmet. Svenska LäkT. *63,* 3671–3680, 1966.
14 *Kilbom A.* und *Åstrand I.:* Kökstudier. Fysisk ansträngning vid hushallsårbete. Konsument-institutet meddelar n: r 23. Stockholm: Statens Institut för Konsumentfrågor 1969.
15 *Kraut H., Schneiderhöhn R.* und *Wildemann L.:* Die Arbeitsbelastung der Hausfrau. Int. Z. ang. Physiol. einschl. Arbeitsphysiol. *16,* 175–302, 1956.
16 *Bratton E. C.:* Concepts of energy and work in home management. J. Home Economics *51,* 102–104, 1959.
17 *Passmore R.* and *Durnin J. V. G. A.:* Human energy expenditure. Physiol. Rev. *35,* 801–840, 1955.
18 *Steidl R. E.* and *Bratton E. C.:* Work in the home. New York/London/Sydney: John Wiley 1968.
19 *Wiggert K.:* Untersuchung der trockenen Fußbodenreinigung. Hauswirtschaft und Wissenschaft *14,* 188–204 und 220–226, 1966.
20 *Stübler E.:* Ist die körperliche Belastung noch ein Maß für die Beurteilung hauswirtschaftlicher Arbeit? Das Reich der Landfrau, Mitt.Deutsche Landwirtschafts-Ges. Heft 1, 1–3, und Heft 2, 9–10, 1970.
21 *Grandjean E., Kretzschmar H.* und *Wotzka G.:* Arbeitsanalysen beim Verkaufspersonal eines Warenhauses. Z. Präventivmed. *13,* 1–9, 1968.
22 *Knowles E.:* Some effects of the height of ironing surface on the worker Cornell University Agricultural Experiment Station Bulletin 833, Ithaca (New York) 1946.
23 *Bratton E. C.:* Some factors of cost to the body in standing to work and sitting to work under different postural conditions. Cornell University Agricultural Experiment Station Memoir 365, Ithaca (New York) 1959.
24 *Grandjean E., Kahlcke H.* und *Wotzka G.:* Ergonomische Untersuchung von Schulzeichentischen. Werk *57,* 53–56, 1970.
25 *Lundervold A. J. S.:* Electromyographic investigations of position and manner of working in typewriting. Acta physiol. scand. *24,* 57–65, 1951.
26 *Floyd W. F.* and *Ward J. S.:* Anthropometric and physiological considerations in school, office and factory seating. In: Sitting Posture, edited by E. Grandjean, p. 18–25. London: Taylor & Francis 1969.
27 *Münchinger R.:* Gewichtheben und Bandscheibenbelastung. Schweiz. Z. Sportmed. *8,* 65–78, 1960.
28 *Graf O.:* Studium über Arbeitspausen in Betrieben bei freier und zeitgebundener Arbeit (Fließarbeit) und ihre Auswirkungen auf die Leistungsfähigkeit. Forschungsbericht des Landes Nordrhein-Westfalen Nr. 115. Köln/Opladen: Westdeutscher Verlag 1955.
29 Zitiert nach *R. Bächtold:* Praktische Soziologie der Haushaltküchen. Küche *1,* 171–178, 1966.
30 *Hole W. V.* and *Attenburrow J. J.:* Houses and people. London: H. M. Stationery Office 1966.

31 *Zander E.:* Arbeitszeitaufwand in städtischen Haushalten. Hauswirtschaft und Wissenschaft *15,* 71–81, 1967.

32 *Walker K. E.:* Home making still takes time. J. Home Economics *61,* 621–624, 1969.

33 *Ellis D. S.:* Speed of manipulative performance as a function of work-surface height. J. appl. Psychol. *35,* 289–296, 1951.

34 *Holm L.:* Familj och bostad. Hemmens Forskningsinstitut. Stockholm: Svenska Tryckeriaktiebolaget 1956.

35 *Boalt C.:* Bo och bedoma: Hyreslägenheter i Stockholm. 1. Hushåll och bostad. Stockholm: Statens Institut för Byggnadsforskning Nr. 19, 1965.

36 *Boalt C.:* Bo och bedöma: Hyreslägenheter i Stockholm. 4. Skolbarn och bostad. Stockholm: Statens Institut för Byggnadsforskning Nr. 24, 1965.

37 *Krantz B.:* Bo och bedöma: Experimentlägenheter i Örebro. Stockholm: Statens Institut för Byggnadsforskning Nr. 1, 1965.

38 *Bächtold R.:* Der moderne Wohnungs- und Siedlungsbau als soziologisches Problem. Diss. Univ. Fribourg (Schweiz) 1964.

39 *Cornuau C.* et *Rétel J. O.:* Logement et vie familiale. Paris: Cahiers du Centre Scientifique et Technique du bâtiment N° 82, 1966.

40 *Meyer-Ehlers G.:* Wohnung und Familie. Stuttgart: Deutsche Verlagsanstalt 1968.

41 *Silbermann A.:* Vom Wohnen der Deutschen. Köln/Opladen: Westdeutscher Verlag 1963

42 *Henz A.* und *Vogt. W.:* Wohnung und Wunschwohnung. Planungsgrundlagen. Brugg, Schweiz: Metron 1967.

43 *Barrier A.* und *Gilgen A.:* Besonnung von Wohnungen. Forschungsausschuß für Planungsfragen, Institut für Orts-, Regional- und Landesplanung der ETH Zürich, 1970.

44 *Thiberg S.:* Anatomy for planners. Parts I–IV. Stockholm: Statens Institut för Byggnadsforskning 1965–1970.

45 *Grandjean E.* und *Burandt U.:* Körpermaße der Belegschaft eines schweizerischen Industriebetriebes. Industr. Organisation *31,* 239–242, 1962.

46 *Lehmann G.* und *Stier F.:* Mensch und Gerät. In: Handbuch der gesamten Arbeitsmedizin, Band 1, 718–788. Berlin: Urban & Schwarzenberg 1961.

47 *Kroemer K. H. E..* Heute zutreffende Körpermaße. Arbeitswissenschaft *3,* 42–45, 1964.

48 *O'Brien R.* and *Shelton W. C.:* Women's measurements for garment and pattern construction. Wright Air Development Center (USA) Tech. Rep. 56–BO, 1958.

49 *McCullough H. E., Philson K., Smith R. H., Wood A. L.* and *Woolrich A.:* Space standards for household activities. Urbana, Illinois: Illinois Agricultural Experiment Station Bull. 686, 1962.

50 *Centre d'études et de recherches psychotechniques:* Mensuration fonctionnelle pour l'adaptation de la machine à l'homme. Etude du Travail *113,* 29–45, 1960.

51 *Wisner A.* et *Monod H.:* Quelques données anthropométriques concernant un groupe de 100 femmes françaises. Biotypologie *24,* 165–176, 1963.

52 *De Félice S.:* Recherches sur l'anthropologie des Françaises. Paris: Masson 1958.

53 *Ward J. S.* and *Kirk N. S.:* The relation between some anthropometric dimensions and preferred working surface heights in the kitchen. Ergonomics *11,* 410–411, 1968.

54 *Woningbouw Houses.* Funktionelle Grundlagen der Wohnung. Rotterdam: Bouwcentrum 1963.

55 *Peters Th.:* Anthropometrische und physiologische Grundlagen zur Gestaltung von Büroarbeitssitzen. In: Sitzhaltung, hrsg. von E. Grandjean, S. 48–56. London: Taylor & Francis 1969.

56 *Barkla D.:* The estimation of body measurements of British population in relation to seat design. Ergonomics *4,* 123–132, 1961.

57 *Ebauches S. A.:* Ergonomie. Collection Travail N° 2. Neuchâtel: Ebauches S. A. 1959.

58 *Hertzberg H. T. E. Daniels G. S.* and *Churchill E.:* Anthropometry of flying personnel – 1950. Wright Air Development Center (USA) Tech Rep. 52–321, 1954.

59 *McFarland R. A.* et al.: Human body size and capabilities in the design and operation of vehicular equipment. Boston, Mass.: Harvard School of Public Health 1953.

60 *Wisner A.* et *Rebiffé R.:* L'utilisation des données anthropométriques dans la conception du poste de travail. Travail humain *26,* 193–217, 1963.

61 Zitiert nach *E. F. Le Carpentier:* Easy chair dimensions for comfort – a subjective approach. In: Sitting Posture, ed. by E. Grandjean, p. 214–223. London: Taylor & Francis 1969.

62 *Bouisset S.* et *Monod H.:* Un essai de détermination de caractéristiques anthropométriques en vue de l'aménagement de postes de travail. Etude de 110 cadres de la région parisienne. Travail humain *24,* 35–50, 1961.

63 *Bouisset S., Pineau H.* et *Vassal P.:* Recherches anthropométriques sur le jeune adulte français. Biotypologie *20,* 176–182, 1959.

64 *Bloch W.* und *Gfeller H.:* Grundlagen rationeller Küchengestaltung. Industr. Organisation *20,* 107–116, 1951.

65 *Bloch W.* und *Müller H. P.:* Untersuchungen über die arbeitstechnisch richtige Höhe von Bügeltischen. Industr. Organisation *23,* 208–210, 1954.

66 *Wenke H.:* Küchenplanung. Darmstadt: Die Planung 1964.

67 *Ministry of Housing and Local Government:* Space in the home. Design Bull. No. 6. London: H. M. Stationery Office 1968.

68 *Hemelrijk J.* and *Sittig J.:* Optimal heights for shelves in a cupboard. C.I.B Bull. *1–2*, 53–56, 1966.

69 *Berg. I. M., Boalt C., Holm L.* und *Leander U.:* Kök, planering, inredning. 6. Auflage. Stockholm: Statens Institut för Konsumentfrågor 1966.

70 *Robins W. J.:* Minimum standards for circulation spaces between walls, tables and chairs established by photography of body movements. Thesis Faculty of Technology, University of Manchester, 1968.

71 *Steidl R. E.:* Trips between centers in kitchens for 100 meals. Cornell University Agricultural Experiment Station Bull. 971, Ithaca (New York) 1962.

72 *Stübler E.:* Einführung in das Arbeitsstudium in der Hauswirtschaft. REFA-Fachausschuß Hauswirtschaft. Berlin/Köln/Frankfurt am Main: Beuth-Vertrieb 1962.

73 *Uhland G., Deist H.* und *Stübler E.:* Untersuchungen über die Einrichtung von Küchen für den sozialen Wohnungsbau. Stuttgart: Forschungsgemeinschaft Bauen und Wohnen FBW 1958.

74 *Berglund E.:* Bord för måltider och arbete i hemmet. Stockholm: Svenska Slöjdföreningen 1957.

75 *Acking C. A.* und *Küller R.:* Volymupplevelse av rum (Volumerlebnis des Raumes). Arbetsrapport 1. Lund: Technische Hochschule, Abteilung für Architektur, 1966.

76 *Acking C. A.* und *Küller R.:* Färgens betydelse vid perception av en interiör (Die Bedeutung der Farbe bei der Wahrnehmung des Innenraumes). Arbetsrapport 1. Lund: Technische Hochschule, Abteilung für Architektur, 1969.

77 *Coblentz A.* et *Jeanpierre C.:* Recherches sur les exigences dimensionnelles de l'habitat. C.I.B. Bull *1–2*, 23–25, 1966.

78 *Jeanpierre C.:* Recherches sur les problèmes spatiaux dans l'habitat. Paris: Cahiers du Centre scientifique et technique du bâtiment N° 90, 1968.

79 *Jeanpierre C.:* Approches expérimentales des exigences spatiales dans l'habitat humain. Thèse, Faculté de Médecine, Paris 1968.

80 *Chombart de Lauwe P.:* Famille et habitation. Tome 2. Paris: Centre National de la Recherche Scientifique 1960.

81 *Pfeiffer H., Kirschenmann J. C., Knorr S., Kraus V.* und *Kramer K.:* Planungsgrundlagen für den Kinderbereich in der Wohnung. Bauen und Wohnen 2, 43–51, 1969.

82 *Wespi H.:* Haltungsstörung, Scheuermannsche Krankheit und Schularzt. Z. Präventivmed. *14*, 26–35, 1969.

83 *Scheier H. J. G.:* Behandlung des Morbus Scheuermann. Z. Präventivmed. *14*, 36–45, 1969.

84 *Gschwend N.:* Schulgestühl und Haltungsschäden. Z. Präventivmed. *14*, 8–14, 1969.

85 *Schoberth H.:* Sitzhaltung, Sitzschaden, Sitzmöbel. Berlin: Springer 1962.

86 *Grandjean E.* und *Burandt U.:* Das Sitzverhalten von Büroangestellten. Industr. Organisation *31*, 243–250, 1962.

87 *Schoberth H.:* Die Wirbelsäule von Schulkindern. In: Sitting Posture, ed. by E. Grandjean, p. 98–111. London: Taylor & Francis 1969.

88 *Åkerblom B.:* Anatomische und physiologische Grundlagen zur Gestaltung von Sitzen. In: Sitting Posture, ed. by E. Grandjean, p. 6–17. London: Taylor & Francis 1969.

89 *Yamaguchi Y.* and *Umezawa F.:* Development of a chair to minimize disc distortion in the sitting posture. Paper presented at the 4th International Congress on Ergonomics, Strasbourg, July 1970, unpublished.

90 *Åkerblom B.:* Standing and sitting posture. Stockholm: Nordiska Bokhandeln 1948.

91 *Keegan J. J.:* Alterations of the lumbar curve related to posture and seating. J. Bone Joint Surg. *35*, 567–589, 1953.

92 *Keegan J. J.:* Evaluation and improvement of seats. Industr. Med. Surg. *31*, 137–148, 1962.

93 *Grandjean E.* und *Burandt U.:* Die physiologische Gestaltung von Ruhesesseln. Bauen und Wohnen, *6*, 233–236, 1964.

94 *Grandjean E., Böni A.* und *Kretszchmar H.:* Entwicklung eines Ruhesesselprofils für gesunde und rückenkranke Menschen. Wohnungsmedizin *5*, 51–56, 1967.

95 *Rieck A.:* Über die Messung des Sitzkomfortes von Autositzen. In: Sitting Posture, ed. by E. Grandjean, p. 92–97. London: Taylor & Francis 1969.

96 *Keegan J. J.:* The medical problem of lumbar spine flattening in automobile seats. Soc. automotive Eng. J., 57–65, 1964. Paper 838A presented March 1964 at the SAE Automobile Week.

97 *Wachsler R. A.* and *Learner D. B.:* An analysis of some factors influencing seat comfort. Ergonomics *3*, 315–320, 1960.

98 *Jones J. C.:* Methods and results of seating research. In: Sitting Posture, ed. by E. Grandjean, p. 57–67. London: Taylor & Francis 1969.

99   *Shackel B., Chidsey K. D.* and *Shipley P.:* The assessment of chair comfort. In : Sitting Posture, ed by E. Grandjean, p. 155–192. London : Taylor & Francis 1969.

100   *Oshima M.:* Optimum conditions of chair. Paper presented at the 4th International Congress on Ergonomics, Strasbourg, July 1970, unpublished.

101   *Branton P.:* Behaviour, body mechanics and discomfort. In : Sitting Posture, ed. by E. Grandjean, p. 202–213. London : Taylor & Francis 1969.

102   *Wotzka G., Grandjean E., Burandt U., Kretzschmar H.* and *Leonhard T.:* Investigations for the development of an auditorium seat. In : Sitting Posture, ed. by E. Grandjean, p. 68–83. London : Taylor & Francis 1969

103   *Le Carpentier E. F.:* Easy chair dimensions for comfort – a subjective approach. In : Sitting Posture, ed. by E. Grandjean, p. 214–223. London : Taylor & Francis 1969.

104   *Kroemer K. H. E.* and *Robinette J. C.:* Ergonomics in the design of office furniture. Wright-Patterson AFB (Ohio) : Aerospace Medical Research Laboratories Report AMRL-TR-68-80, 1968.

105   *Jürgens H. W.:* Die Verteilung des Körperdruckes auf Sitzfläche und Rückenlehne als Problem der Industrieanthropologie. In : Sitting Posture, ed. by E. Grandjean, p. 84–91. London : Taylor & Francis 1969.

106   *Burandt U.:* Röntgenuntersuchung über die Stellung von Becken und Wirbelsäule beim Sitzen auf vorgeneigten Sitzflächen. In : Sitting Posture, ed. by E. Grandjean, p. 242-250. London : Taylor & Francis 1969.

107   *Schlegel K. F.:* Sitzschäden und deren Vermeidung durch eine neuartige Sitzkonstruktion. Med. Klin. *51,* 1940–1942, 1956.

108   *Schneider H.* und *Lippert H.:* Das Sitzproblem in funktionell-anatomischer Sicht. Med. Klin. *56,* 1164–1168, 1961.

109   *Burandt U.* und *Grandjean E.:* Über die Wirkung verschiedenartig profilierter Sitzflächen auf die Sitzhaltung. Int. Z. ang. Physiol. einschl. Arbeitsphysiol. *20,* 441–452, 1964.

110   *Kroemer K. H. E.:* Maße und Form von Arbeitsstühlen. Dtsch. med. Wschr. *87,* 2500–2508, 1962.

111   *Stier F.:* Zweckmäßige Arbeitssitze. Rationalisierung *10,* 220–226, 1959.

112   *Burandt U.:* Schreibtische und Arbeitsstühle im Büro. Neue Zürcher Zeitung Nr. 798, 1964.

113   *Floyd W. F.* and *Roberts D. F.:* Anatomical and physiological principles in chair and table design. Ergonomics *2,* 1–16, 1958.

114   *Burandt U.* und *Grandjean E.:* Arbeitsphysiologische Untersuchungen von Bezugsmaterialien für flach gepolsterte Arbeitsstühle. Int. Z. ang. Physiol. einschl. Arbeitsphysiol. *22,* 167–180, 1966.

115   *Damon A., Stoudt H. W.* and *McFarland R. A.:* The human body in equipment design. Cambridge, Mass. : Harvard University Press 1966.

116   *Wotzka G., Hünting W., Schärer R.* und *Grandjean E.:* Ergonomische Untersuchung von 12 Objektstühlen. Z. Präventivmed. *17/2,* 1972.

117   *Belart W.:* Matratzen. Merkblatt zur Rheuma-Prophylaxe Nr. 11. Zürich : Schweiz. Rheumaliga 1970.

118   *Neumeyer G.:* Die Kolumnosen. Praxis-Kurier Nr. 5, 1–11, 1968.

119   *Kanz E.* und *Gertis W.:* Schlaftiefemessungen an verschiedenen Polsterwaren. Bekleidungsmedizin *4,* 6–14, 1964.

120   *Huser S., Grandjean E.* und *Suchantke M.:* Physiologische Grundlagen des Wohnungsbaues. Heutiger Stand der Kenntnisse und Empfehlungen. Schriftenreihe Wohnungsbau Nr. 14 des Eidg. Büros für Wohnungsbau. Bern : Eidg. Drucksachen- und Materialzentrale 1970.

121   *Gehl I.* et al. : Indeliggende køkkener-brug og ventilation. Kopenhagen : Statens Byggeforskningsinstitut, Saertryk 184, 1969.

122   *Huber V.:* Innenraum der Wohnung. Schriftenreihe Wohnungsbau Nr. 05 des Eidg. Büros für Wohnungsbau. Bern : Eidg. Drucksachen- und Materialzentrale 1969/70.

123   Eidg. Forschungskommission zur Erhöhung der Produktivität im Wohungsbau F.K.W. : Möbelstellflächen. Schriftenreihe Wohnungsbau Nr. 02. Bern : Eidg. Drucksachen- und Materialzentrale 1967/68.

124   *Huser S., Grandjean E., Gilgen A., Ries H.* und *Suchantke M.:* Erhebungen über Nutzung und Urteile von Wohnungen mittlerer Mietzinslage. Im Druck.

125   *Bark E.:* Balkonger. Stockholm : Statens Institut för Byggnadsforskning, Informationsblatt Nr. 2, 1963.

126   *Neufert G.:* Bauentwurfslehre. Frankfurt am Main : Ullstein 1962.

127   *Haushaltsberatung, Landesgewerbeamt Stuttgart:* Wäschebehandlung im Haushalt – Technisierung, Rationalisierung, Arbeitsgestaltung. Moderne Küche *3,* 9–15, 1968.

128   *Kapple W. H.:* Kitchen planning standards. Urbana, Illinois : University of Illinois Small Homes Council C 5.32, 1965.

129 *Vedel-Petersen F.:* Plan i køkkenet. Kopenhagen: Statens Byggeforskningsinstitut, Anvisning Nr. 46, 1966.

130 *Thiberg A.:* Planutformning av kök. Stockholm: Byggforskningen, Rapport 54, 1968.

131 *Die Küche – ihre Planung und Einrichtung.* Stuttgart: Gerd Hatje 1954.

132 *Kökstudier.* Funktionsstudier, grundprinciper. Stockholm: Statens Institut för Konsumentfrågor, Meddelande Nr. 24 1969.

133 *DIN 18022:* Küche, Bad, WC, Hausarbeitsraum. 1967.

134 *Scherrinsky S.:* Erprobung der Arbeitsküche auf ihre praktische Anwendbarkeit und zweckmäßige Möbelstellung. Fortschr. Forsch. Bauwesen D, Heft 21, 1955.

135 *Schweiz. Zentralstelle für Baurationalisierung CRB:* Sanitärräume im Wohnbau. Zürich: CRB 1966.

136 *Panzhauser E.:* Die Klassifizierung des Nutzwertes von Wohnungen. Aufbau (Wien) *23,* Heft 1–3, 1968.

137 *Forschungsgemeinschaft Bauen und Wohnen:* Hygienische Mindestanforderungen im Wohnungsbau. Stuttgart: FBW 1952.

138 *Die gute Wohnung.* Schwedische Richtlinien zum Wohnungsbau. Zürich: Schweiz. Zentralstelle für Baurationalisierung CRB 1967.

139 *Quality of dwelling and housing areas.* Edited by the National Swedish Institute for Building Research, in agreement with the United Nations. Report 27. Stockholm 1967.

140 *Statens planverk:* Svensk Byggnorm. Stockholm 1967.

141 *Harmsen H.:* Die familiengerechte Wohnung. In: Medizin und Städtebau, Band 2, 216–221. München: Urban & Schwarzenberg 1957.

142 *Meyer-Ehlers G.:* Einbauschränke in der Wohnung. Forschungsarbeit im Auftrag des Bundesministeriums für Wohnungswesen und Städtebau.

143 *Rasmussen A. D.:* Nyere etageboligplaner. Kopenhagen: Statens Byggeforskningsinstitut, anvisning Nr. 31, 1958.

144 *Thiberg S.* et al.: Bostadsmått. Stockholm: Statens Institut för Byggnadsforskning, Arbetshandling 1, 1968.

145 *Houghten F. C.* and *Yaglou C. P.:* Determining lines of equal comfort. ASHVE Transactions *29,* 163–171, 1923.

146 *Frank W.:* Kalorische Oberflächenbelastung, Gesamterwärmung und thermisches Behaglichkeitsempfinden. Gesundheits-Ing. *83,* 29–56, 1962.

147 *Frank W.:* Die Erfassung des Raumklimas mit Hilfe richtungsempfindlicher Frigorimeter. Gesundheits-Ing. *89,* 301–308, 1968.

148 *Frank W.:* Zum gegenwärtigen Stand der raumklimatischen Forschung. Gesundheits-Ing. *90,* 40–46, 1969.

149 *Lutz H.:* Thermische Behaglichkeit in Wohn- und Arbeitsräumen. Definition und richtungsbezogene Messung. Gesundheits-Ing. *91,* 338–350, 1970.

150 *Schlüter G.:* Die Wahrnehmungsschwelle des Menschen beim Strahlungsaustausch mit unterschiedlich temperierten Wandflächen. Gesundheits-Ing. *90,* 165–196, 1969.

151 *Koch K. W., Jennings B. H.* and *Humphreys C. H.:* Is humidity important in the temperature comfort range? ASHRAE Transactions *66,* 63–68, 1960.

152 *Nevins R. G., Rohles F. H., Springer W.* and *Feyerherm A. M.:* A temperature-humidity chart of thermal comfort of seated persons. ASHRAE J. *8,* 55–61, 1966.

153 *Yaglou C. P.:* In «Physiology of heat regulation and the science of clothing», ed. by L. H. Newburgh. Philadelphia: Saunders 1949.

154 *Committee on the Hygiene of Housing:* Construction and equipment of the home. Chicago: American Public Health Association 1951.

155 *British Standards Code of Practice,* zitiert nach Angus T. C.: The control of indoor climate. Oxford: Pergamon Press 1968.

156 *DIN 4701:* Regeln für die Berechnung des Wärmebedarfs von Gebäuden. 1959.

157 *Rietschel H.* und *Raiss W.:* Lehrbuch der Heiz- und Lüftungstechnik, 14. Auflage. Berlin: Springer 1960.

158 *Sprenger E.:* Taschenbuch für Heizung, Lüftung und Klimatechnik. München: Oldenbourg 1968.

159 *Liese W.:* Gesundheitstechnisches Taschenbuch, 2. Auflage. München: Oldenbourg 1969.

160 *Blachère G.:* How to determine and satisfy user requirements: Methods and consequences in innovation in building. CIB Congress, Cambridge 1962. Amsterdam: Elsevier 1962.

161 *Grandjean E.:* Raumklimatische Wirkungen verschiedener Heizsysteme in Büros. Schweiz. Bl. Heizung Lüftung, 3–6, 1966.

162 *Grandjean E.:* Raumklimatische Untersuchungen in Büros während der warmen Jahreszeit. Heizung, Lüftung, Haustechnik *19,* 118–123, 1968.

163 *Franzen B.:* Offices 2. A study of climate in nine office blocks. Stockholm: National Swedish Institute for Building Research, Summaries 1969.

164 *Serati A.* und *Wüthrich M.:* Luftfeuchtigkeit und Saisonkrankheiten. Schweiz. med. Wschr. *99,* 48–50, 1969.

165 *Ritzel G.:* Sozialmedizinische Erhebungen zur Pathogenese und Prophylaxe von Erkältungs-krankheiten. Z. Präventivmed. *11,* 9–16, 1966.

166 *Ewert G.:* On the mucus flow rate in the human nose. Acta oto-laryng., Suppl. 200, Stockholm 1965.

167 *Nemecek J., Wanner H. U.* und *Grandjean E.:* Psychophysiologische Untersuchungen im Versuchsauditorium der ETH Zürich. Gesundheits-Ing. *92,* 232–237, 1971.

168 *Nemecek J.* und *Grandjean E.:* Das Großraumbüro in arbeitsphysiologischer Sicht. Ergebnisse arbeitsphysiologischer Untersuchungen in schweizerischen Großraumbüros. Industr. Organisation *40,* 233–243, 1971.

169 *Chrenko F. A.:* The effects of the temperatures of the floor surface and of the air on thermal sensations and the skin temperature of the feet. Brit. J. industr. Med. *14,* 13–21, 1957.

170 *Frank W.:* Fußwärmeuntersuchungen am bekleideten Fuß. Gesundheits-Ing. *80,* 193–201, 1959.

171 *Äikäs E., Karvinen E., Noro L.* and *Tuomola T.:* Thermal comfort with floor heating and radiator heating. Helsinki: Report from the Institute of Occupational Health *1,* 35, 1962.

172 *Schüle W.* und *Lutz H.:* Untersuchungen in Wohnhäusern mit kombinierter elektrischer Fußboden- und Wandheizung. Heizung, Lüftung, Haustechnik *20,* 81–122, 1969.

173 *Schüle W.:* Der Wärmeschutz von Wohnbauten bei elektrischer Heizung. Stuttgart: Veröffentlichungen aus dem Institut für Technische Physik, Heft 60, 1969.

174 *Ihle C. L.:* Luftheizung, Lüftung, Klimatechnik. Öl- und Gasfeuerung *13,* 977–981, 1968.

175 *Caemmerer W.:* Das Fenster als wärmeschutztechnisches Bauelement. Heizung, Lüftung Haustechnik *17,* 140–148, 1966.

176 *Caemmerer W.:* Vortrag am Seminar «Raumklima» an der Technischen Hochschule Stuttgart, 14./15. November 1969. Nicht publiziert.

177 *DIN 4108:* Wärmeschutz im Hochbau. 1960.

178 *Gertis K.:* Die Temperaturverhältnisse in Räumen bei Sonneneinstrahlung durch Fenster. Deutsche Bauzeitung, Sonderduck, Stuttgart: Deutsche Verlags-Anstalt 1969.

179 *Künzel H.* und *Snatzke Ch.:* Zur Wirkung von Sonnenschutzgläsern auf die sommerlichen Temperatur in Räumen. Gesundheits-Ing. *90,* 2–10, 1969.

180 *Petherbridge P.* and *Loudon A. G.:* Principles of sun control. Architect's J. *143,* 143–149, 1966.

181 *Loudon A. G.* and *Petherbridge P.:* Heating effect of sunshine. Architect's J. *143,* 138–143, 1966.

182 *Grandjean E.:* Fenster und Raumklima. Schweiz. Bauzeitung *87,* 1–8, 1969.

183 *Grandjean E.* und *Rhiner A.:* Raumklimatische Untersuchungen über die Wirksamkeit von Sonnenschutzvorhängen aus Kunststoff, von Aluminium-Lamellenstoren und von Fenstern mit Reflexionsgläsern. Schweiz. Bl. Heizung Lüftung *38,* 74–79, 1971.

184 *Loudon A. G.:* Summertime temperatures in buildings. Garston, Watford, Herts.: Building Research Station Current Paper 47/68, 1968.

185 *Gertis K.:* Die Erwärmung von Räumen infolge Sonneneinstrahlung durch Fenster. Diss. TU Stuttgart 1969. Berichte aus der Bauforschung, Heft 66. Berlin: Wilhelm Ernst 1969.

186 *Langdon F. J.:* Modern offices: a user survey. National Building Studies Research Paper Nr. 41. London: H. M. Stationery Office 1966.

187 *Caemmerer W.:* Die Problematik des Sonnenschutzes von Gebäuden. Gesundheits-Ing. *88,* 79–86, 1967.

188 *Tonne F., Szepan W.* und *Roth K.:* Sonnenschutz an Gebäuden. Stuttgart: Institut für Tageslichttechnik, Mitteilung Nr. 11, 1966.

189 *Ryd H.* and *Wyon D.:* Methods of evaluating human stress due to climate. Stockholm: National Swedish Building Research, Summaries D 6, 1970.

190 *Yaglou C. P., Riley E. C.* and *Coggins D. I.:* Ventilation requirements. ASHVE Transactions *42,* 133–158, 1936.

191 *Grandjean E., Horisberger B., Havas L.* und *Abt K.:* Arbeitsphysiologische Untersuchungen mit verschiedenen Beleuchtungssystemen an einer Feinarbeit. Industr. Organisation *28,* 231–239, 1959.

192 *Barrier A.* und *Gilgen A.:* Natürliche Belichtung von Wohnungen. Zürich: Forschungsausschuß für Planungsfragen des Institutes für Orts-, Regional- und Landesplanung der ETH Zürich, 1970.

193 *Tonne F.:* Besser bauen mit Besonnungs- und Tageslichtplanung. Schorndorf/Stuttgart: K. Hofmann 1954.

194 *Büning W.:* Neue Bauanatomie und Hygienisches Memorandum. Stuttgart: Fortschritte und Forschungen im Bauwesen, Francksche Verlagsbuchhandlung 1947.

195 *Pleijel G.:* Daylight investigations. Stockholm: Statens Råd för Byggnadsforskning, 1947.

196 *Tonne F.:* Licht und Sonne im Wohnungsbau. Stuttgart: Forschungsgesellschaft Bauen und Wohnen FBW 1953.

197 Internationale Vorschriften und Standards des Bauwesens: Innenraumbeleuchtung mit Tageslicht, Berlin: Verlag für Bauwesen 1965.

198 *Hopkinson R. G., Petherbridge R.* and *Langmore A.:* Daylighting. London: Heinemann 1964.

199 *Guth S. K.:* Light and comfort. Industr. Med. Surg. *27,* 570–574, 1958.

200 *Schatt P.:* Besonnung von Wohnungen, Schattenwurf. Zürich: Institut für Orts-, Regional- und Landesplanung der ETH Zürich, 1966.

201 *Neumann E.:* Die städtische Siedlungsplanung unter besonderer Berücksichtigung der Besonnung. Stuttgart: K. Wittwer 1954.

202 *Roedler F.:* Die wahre Sonneneinstrahlung auf Gebäude, Berücksichtigung der Beschattung und Bewölkung. Gesundheits-Ing. *74,* 337–350, 1953.

203 *Bitter C.* and *van Ierland J. F.:* Appreciation of sunlight in the house. The Hague: Research Institute for Public Health Engineering T.N.O., 1960.

204 *Amt für Regionalplanung im Kanton Zürich:* Besonnung, Bemessung der Gebäudeabstände, Nr. 5. Zürich: City-Druck, Juli 1967.

205 *Lange B.:* Wohnhausabstände und Besonnung. Bauwelt, Heft 40, 789–796, 1954.

206 *Hawel W.:* Untersuchungen eines Bezugssystems für die psychologische Schallbewertung. Arbeitswissenschaft *6,* 123–127, 1967.

207 *Committee on the Problem of Noise:* Noise, final report. London: H. M. Stationery Office 1963

208 *Schweiz. Ingenieur- und Architekten-Verein:* Empfehlung für Schallschutz im Wohnungs- bau. Zürich: SIA, Mai 1968.

209 *DIN 4109:* Schallschutz im Hochbau. 1962.

210 *Amrein E.* und *Martinelli R.:* Schallschutz im Wohnungsbau. In: Element Nr. 17. Zürich: Verband Schweiz. Ziegel- und Steinfabrikanten 1969.

211 *Laird, D. A.:* The influence of noise on production and fatigue. J. appl Psychol. *17,* 320–330, 1933.

212 *Sander A. F.:* The influence of noise on two discrimination tasks. Ergonomics *4,* 253–258, 1961.

213 *Broadbent D. E.:* Effect of noise on an intellectual task. J. acoust. Soc. Amer. *30,* 824–827, 1958.

214 *Grimaldi J. V.:* Sensori-motor performance under varying noise conditions. Ergonomics *2,* 34–43, 1958.

215 *Tarrière C.* et *Wisner A.:* Effets des bruits significatifs et non significatifs au cours d'une épreuve de vigilance. Travail humain *25,* 1–28, 1962.

216 *Broadbent D. E.:* Effects of noise on behavior. In: Handbook of noise control, ed. by C. M. Harris. New York: McGraw Hill 1957.

217 *Broadbent D. E.:* The 20 dials and 20 lights test under noise conditions. Cambridge, England: MRC Applied Psychology Research Unit Report 160/51, 1951.

218 *Broadbent D. E.:* Noise, paced performance and vigilance tasks. Brit. J. Psychol. *44,* 295–303, 1953.

219 *Lehmann G.* und *Tamm J.:* Die Beeinflussung vegetativer Funktionen des Menschen durch Geräusche. Forschungsbericht Nr. 257 des Wirtschafts- und Verkehrs ministeriums Nord- rhein-Westfalen. Köln/Opladen: Westdeutscher Verlag 1956.

220 *Lehmann G.* und *Tamm J.:* Über Veränderungen der Kreislaufdynamik des ruhenden Men- schen unter Einwirkung von Geräuschen. Internat. Z. ang. Physiol. einschl. Arbeitsphysiol. *16,* 217–227, 1956.

221 *Lehmann G.* und *Meyer-Delius J.:* Gefäßreaktionen der Körperperipherie bei Schalleinwir- kung. Forschungsbericht Nr. 517 des Wirtschafts- und Verkehrsministeriums Nordrhein- Westfalen. Köln/Opladen: Westdeutscher Verlag 1958.

222 *Jansen G.:* Zur Entstehung vegetativer Funktionsstörungen durch Lärmeinwirkungen. Arch. Gewerbepath. Gewerbehyg. *17,* 238–261, 1959.

223 *Jansen G.* und *Hoffmann H.:* Lärmbedingte Änderungen der Feinmotorik und Lästigkeits- empfindungen in Abhängigkeit von bestimmten Persönlichkeitsdimensionen. Z. exp. ang. Psychol. *12,* 594–613, 1965.

224 *Lehmann G.:* Schlaf und Lärm. Wohnungsmedizin *2,* 21–28, 1963.

225 *Jansen G.:* Zur nervösen Belastung durch Lärm. Zbl. Arb. med. Arb. schutz, Beiheft 9. Darmstadt: Dietrich Steinkopff 1967.

226 *Richter H. R.:* Le sommeil morcelé. Dérangement du sommeil nocturne par le bruit: aspects électroencéphalographiques d'un problème de médecine préventive. Rev. Neurol. (Paris) *115,* 592–595, 1966.

227 *Richter H. R.:* Der Lärm und die Lärmbekämpfung in der heutigen Zivilisation. Universitas *26,* 403–410, 1971.

228 *Steinicke G.:* Die Wirkung von Lärm auf den Schlaf des Menschen. Forschungsbericht Nr. 416 des Wirtschafts- und Verkehrsministeriums des Landes Nordrhein-Westfalen. Köln/Opladen: Westdeutscher Verlag 1957.

229 *Abey-Wickrama I., A'Brook M. F., Gattoni F. E. G.* and *Herridge C. F.:* Mental hospital admissions and aircraft noise. Lancet *13,* 1969.

230 *Auzou S.* et *Lamure C.:* Le bruit aux abords des autoroutes. Paris: Cahiers du Centre scientifique et technique du bâtiment N° 78, 1966.

231 *Lamure C.* et *Bacelon M.:* La gêne due au bruit de la circulation automobile. Paris: Cahiers du Centre scientifique et technique du bâtiment N° 88, 1967.

232 *Bruckmayer F.* und *Lang. J.:* Störung der Bevölkerung durch Verkehrslärm. Österr. Ing. Z. *112,* 302–385, 1967.

233 *Langdon F. J.* and *Scholes W. E.:* The traffic noise index: a method of controlling noise nuisance. Garston, Watford, Herts.: Building Research Station, Current Paper 38/68, 1968.

234 *Griffiths I. D.* and *Langdon F. J.:* Subjective response to road traffic noise. Garston, Watford, Herts.: Building Research Station, Current Paper 37/68, 1968.

235 *Fog H., Jonsson E., Kajland A., Nilsson A.* und *Sörensen S.:* Trafikbuller i bostadsområden. Stockholm: Build International *1,* 55–57, 1968.

236 *Gilgen A.:* Lärm. Zürich: Forschungsausschuß für Planungsfragen, Institut für Orts-, Regional- und Landesplanung der ETH Zürich, 1970.

237 *Lärmbekämpfung in der Schweiz.* Bericht der Eidgenössischen Expertenkommission an den Bundesrat. Bern: Eidg. Drucksachen- und Materialzentrale 1963.

238 *Grandjean E., Gilgen A.* und *Bättig K.:* Die Fluglärmbelastung. Städtehygiene *20,* 73–82. 1969.

239 *Coblentz A., Alexandre A.* et *Xydias N.:* Enquête sur le bruit autour des aéroports. Paris: Centre d'études et de recherches d'anthropologie appliquée, Doc. A. A. 16/67, 1967.

240 *Chapman D.:* A survey of noise in British homes. National Building Studies, Technical Paper Nr. 2. London: H. M. Stationery Office 1948.

241 *Gray P. G., Cartwright A.* and *Parkin P. H.:* Noise in three groups of flats with different floor insulations. National Building Studies, Research Paper No. 27. London: H. M. Stationery Office 1958.

242 *Bitter C.* and *van Weeren P.:* Sound nuisance and sound insulation in blocks of dwellings. The Hague: Research Institute for Public Health Engineering T. N. O., Report Nr. 24, 1955.

243 *Bitter C.* und *Horch C.:* Geluidhinder en geluidisolatie in de woningbouw. Den Haag: T.N.O. Report Nr. 25, 1958.

244 *Boalt C.:* Bostad och buller. Stockholm: Statens Institut för Byggnadsforskning Nr. 21, 1965.

245 *Coblentz A.* et *Josse R.:* A propos des bruits d'impact. Paris: Cahiers du Centre scientifique et technique du bâtiment N° 92, 1968.

246 *Deutscher Arbeitsring für Lärmbekämpfung:* Medizinische Leitsätze zur Lärmbekämpfung. Zitiert nach H. Wiethaup: Lärmbekämpfung in der Bundesrepublik Deutschland, 33–35. Köln: Carl Heymans 1961.

247 *Furrer W.:* Raum- und Bauakustik, Lärmabwehr. Basel: Birkhäuser 1961.

248 *Kurtze G.:* Physik und Technik der Lärmbekämpfung. Karlsruhe: G. Braun 1964.

249 *Kamber F.:* Schallschutzmaßnahmen bei Sanitär- und Heizungsinstallationen. Gesundheitstechnik *7,* 15–22, 1968.

250 *Eichler F.:* Bauphysikalische Entwurfslehre. Band 1. Berlin: Verlag für das Bauwesen 1962.

251 *Amrein E.:* Der neuzeitliche Wohnungsbau und seine physikalischen Grundlagen. In: Element Nr. 12. Zürich: Verband Schweiz. Ziegel- und Steinfabrikanten 1967.

252 *Bobran H. W.:* Handbuch der Bauphysik. Berlin: Ullstein 1967.

253 *Schüle W., Cammerer J. S., Roedler F.* und *Schlüter G.:* Fußwärme, Wärmeschutz, Sonnenwärmeeinstrahlung und Raumklima. Bericht aus der Bauforschung, Heft 40. Berlin: Wilhelm Ernst 1964.

254 *Haller P.:* Das Wärmeisoliervermögen von Bodenbelägen. Zürich: Eidg. Materialprüfungs- und Versuchsanstalt, 1949.

255 *Gösele K.:* Zum Schallschutz von Holzbauteilen. Architekt, Heft 9, 1969.

256 *Bring Ch.:* Friktion och halkning. Byggforskningen, Rapport 112. Stockholm: Statens Råd för Byggnadsforskning, 1964.

257 *Harper F. C.:* Floor finishes. J. roy. Inst. brit. Arch. *58,* 182–186, 1951.

258 *Harper F. C., Warlow W. J.* and *Clarke B. L.:* The forces applied to the foot in walking. I. Walking on a level surface. National Building Studies, Research Paper Nr. 32. London: H. M. Stationery Office 1961.

259 *Schüle W.:* Wärmeschutz und Fußwärme von Holzfußböden. Deutscher Baumarkt *54,* 884–886, 1955.

260 *Wiedefeld J.:* Fußböden aus Holz und Holzwerkstoffen. Handbuch über schall- und wärmedämmende Fußbodenaufbauten aus Holz und Holzwerkstoffen. Düsseldorf: Rheinisch-Bergische Druckerei 1960.

261 *Sigler P. A., Geib M. N.* and *Boone T. H.:* Measurement of the slipperiness of walkway surfaces. National Bureau of Standards J. Res. *40,* 339–346, 1948.

262 *Haller P.:* Die technischen Eigenschaften der Bodenbeläge im Hochbau. Textil-Rundschau *7,* 159–165, 1952.

263 *Sigler P. A.:* Relative slipperiness of floor and deck surfaces. Washington D. C.: National Bureau of Standards, Report BMS 100, 1943.

264 *Bickel J.:* Wandlung und gegenwärtiger Stand der Unfallmortalität in der Schweiz. Z. Präventivmed. *12,* 76–84, 1967.
265 *Backett E. M.:* Domestic accidents. Public Health Paper No. 26. Geneva: World Health Organisation 1965.
266 *«Das sichere Haus»,* Jahrgänge 1958–1968. München: Richard Pflaum.
267 *United States Department of Health, Education, and Welfare:* Health statistics; persons injured by class of accident. Washington D.C.: Public Health Service Publ. 584, 1957.
268 *England and Wales Registrar General:* Statistical review of England and Wales for the year 1960. I. Medical tables. London: H.M. Stationery Office 1962.
269 *World Health Organisation:* Epidemiological vital statistics. Report Nr. 16. Geneva: W.H.O. 1963.
270 *Haggerty R. J.:* Home accidents in childhood. New England J. Med. *260,* 1322–1331, 1959.
271 *Biener K.:* Jugend und Unfallwissen. Z. Präventivmed. *12,* 122–129, 1967.
272 *McFarland R. A.:* Epidemiologic principles applicable to the study and prevention of child accidents. Amer. J. publ. Hlth. *45,* 1302–1308, 1955.
273 *McFarland R. A.:* The study and control of home accidents. Boston, Mass.: Harvard University, School of Public Health.
274 *Colebrook L., Colebrook V., Bull J. P.* and *Jackson D. M.:* The prevention of burning accidents; a survey of the present position. Brit. med. J. *100,* 1379–1391, 1956.
275 *Hauri D.:* Vergiftungen im Kindesalter. Z. Präventivmed. *12,* 110–124, 1967.
276 *Borbély F.:* Tätigkeitsbericht des Toxikologischen Informationszentrums des Schweiz. Apothekervereins. 1. Bericht. Zürich 1966.
277 *Pasi A.:* Toxische Gefährdung des Kindes im Haushalt. Z. Präventivmed. *12,* 102–109, 1967.
278 *Colebrook L.* and *Colebrook V.:* A suggested national plan to reduce burning accidents. Lancet *261,* 579, 1951.
279 *Wheatley G. M.:* Relationship of home environment to accidents. Arch. env. Hlth. *13,* 489–495, 1966.
280 *Cooking and Illuminating Gas.* Safety Education Data Sheet No. 20. Chicago: National Safety Council.
281 *Lundervold A.:* Electromyographic investigations during sedentary work, especially typewriting. Brit. J. phys. Med., 32–36, 1951.
282 *McConnell W. J.* and *Spiegelman M.:* Reactions of 745 clerks to summer air-conditioning. Heating, Piping, Air Conditioning *12,* 317–322, 1940.
283 *Statistisches Jahrbuch der Schweiz 1967.* Bern: Eidg. Statisches Amt 1967.
284 *Blohmke F.:* Anforderungen an Wohnungen für Behinderte. Wohnungsmedizin 3, 2–6, 1965.
285 *Schweiz. Zentralstelle für Baurationalisierung:* Wohnungen für Gehbehinderte. Norm SNV 521 500, 1967.
286 *Schmidt-Relenberg N.:* Soziologische Grundlagen zur Planung von Wohnanlagen für Betagte. Bauen und Wohnen. Heft 5, 1970.
287 *National Swedish Institute for Building Research:* Study of dimensions reequipment in housing for old persons. Report No. 19, Stockholm 1965.
288 *Ward J. S.* and *Kirk N. S.:* Anthropometry of elderly persons. Ergonomics *10,* 17–23, 1967.
289 *British Standards Institution:* Anthropometric and ergonomic recommendations for dimensions in designing for the elderly. BS 4467, London 1969.
290 *Eidgenössische Forschungskommission Wohnungsbau (FKW):* Richtlien und Empfehlungen für die Erstellung von Alterswohnungen. Schriftenreihe Wohnungsbau 03. Bern.: Eidg. Drucksachen- und Materialzentrale 1968.
291 *Schweizerischer Invalidenverband:* Richtiges Planen hilft architektonische Hindernisse vermeiden. Olten: Schweiz. Invalidenverband 1970.
292 *Leschly V., Exner I.* and *J.:* General lines in designs of dwellings for handicapped confined to wheelchairs. Part 1. Hellerup, Denmark: Communications from the Testing and Observation Institute of the Danish National Association for Infantile Paralysis, No. 3, 1959.
293 *Leschly V., Kjaer A.* and *B.:* General lines in designs of dwellings for handicapped confined to wheelchairs. Part 2. Hellerup, Denmark: Communications from the Testing and Observation Institute of the Danish National Association for Infantile Paralysis, No. 6, 1960.
294 *OECD:* Labour force statistics 1958–1965. Zitiert nach Tages-Anzeiger der Stadt Zürich vom 20. August 1971.
295 *Haynes K. J.* and *Raven J.:* The living pattern of some old people. Garston, Watford, Herts.: Building Research Station, Miscellaneous Paper No. 4, 1962.
296 *Thiberg S.:* Dimensionering för åldringar. Stockholm: Statens Institut för Byggnadsforskning, Blad 22, 1966.
297 *Nüscheler F.:* Bautechnische Forderungen behinderter Menschen. Neue Zürcher Zeitung, Beilage Technik Nr. 77, 5. Februar 1969
298 *Oppikofer K.:* Behindertenprobleme bei Bauten und Einrichtungen in Spitälern. Praxis *58,* 1225–1230, 1969.

299   *Droin D.:* Ville ouverte à tous. La libre circulation des fauteuils roulants à l'intérieur et à l'extérieur des bâtiments. Méd. et Hyg. (Genève) *27,* 1532–1534, 1969.

300   *Härting F.:* Wohnungen für Körperbehinderte (Rollstuhlfahrer). 1. Teil. Wohnungsmedizin *1,* 3–7. 1963.

301   *Härting F.:* Wohnungen für Körperbehinderte (Rollstuhlfahrer). 2. Teil. Wohnungsmedizin *2,* 1–4, 1964.